PIRE
KNIGHT

Story & Art by
**Matsuri
Hino**

Vol. 12

The Story of VAMPIRE KNIGHT

1 Cross Academy, a private boarding school, is where the Day Class and the Night Class coexist. The Night Class—a group of beautiful students—are all vampires!

2 Four years ago, after turning his twin brother Ichiru against him, the pureblood Shizuka Hio bit Zero and turned him into a vampire. Kaname kills Shizuka, but the source may still exist. Meanwhile, Yuki suffers from lost memories. When Kaname sinks his fangs into her neck, her memories return!

3 Yuki is the princess of the Kuran family—and a pureblood vampire!! Ten years ago, her mother exchanged her life to seal away Yuki's vampire nature. Yuki's Uncle Rido killed her father. Rido takes over Shiki's body and arrives at the Academy. He targets Yuki for her blood, so Kaname gives his own blood to resurrect Rido. Kaname confesses that he is the progenitor of the Kurans, and that Rido is the master who awakened him!

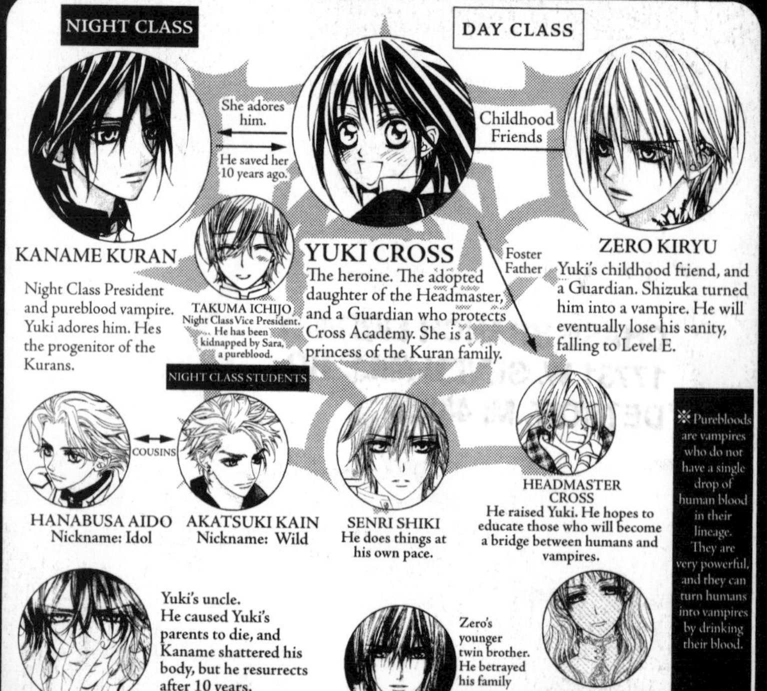

NIGHT CLASS
DAY CLASS
She adores him.
He saved her 10 years ago.
Childhood Friends
KANAME KURAN
Night Class President and pureblood vampire. Yuki adores him. Hes the progenitor of the Kurans.
TAKUMA ICHIJO
Night Class Vice President. ... He has been kidnapped by Sara, a pureblood.
YUKI CROSS
The heroine. The adopted daughter of the Headmaster, and a Guardian who protects Cross Academy. She is a princess of the Kuran family.
Foster Father
ZERO KIRYU
Yuki's childhood friend, and a Guardian. Shizuka turned him into a vampire. He will eventually lose his sanity, falling to Level E.
NIGHT CLASS STUDENTS
COUSINS
HANABUSA AIDO
Nickname: Idol
AKATSUKI KAIN
Nickname: Wild
SENRI SHIKI
He does things at his own pace.
HEADMASTER CROSS
He raised Yuki. He hopes to educate those who will become a bridge between humans and vampires.
※Purebloods are vampires who do not have a single drop of human blood in their lineage. They are very powerful, and they can turn humans into vampires by drinking their blood.
RIDO KURAN
Yuki's uncle.
He caused Yuki's parents to die, and Kaname shattered his body, but he resurrects after 10 years.
He tried to obtain Yuki, but Yuki and Zero killed him.
ICHIRU
Zero's younger twin brother. He betrayed his family to serve Shizuka.
SARA SHIRABUKI
A pureblood princess of the Shirabuki family. She is holding Ichijo captive. What is her motive?!

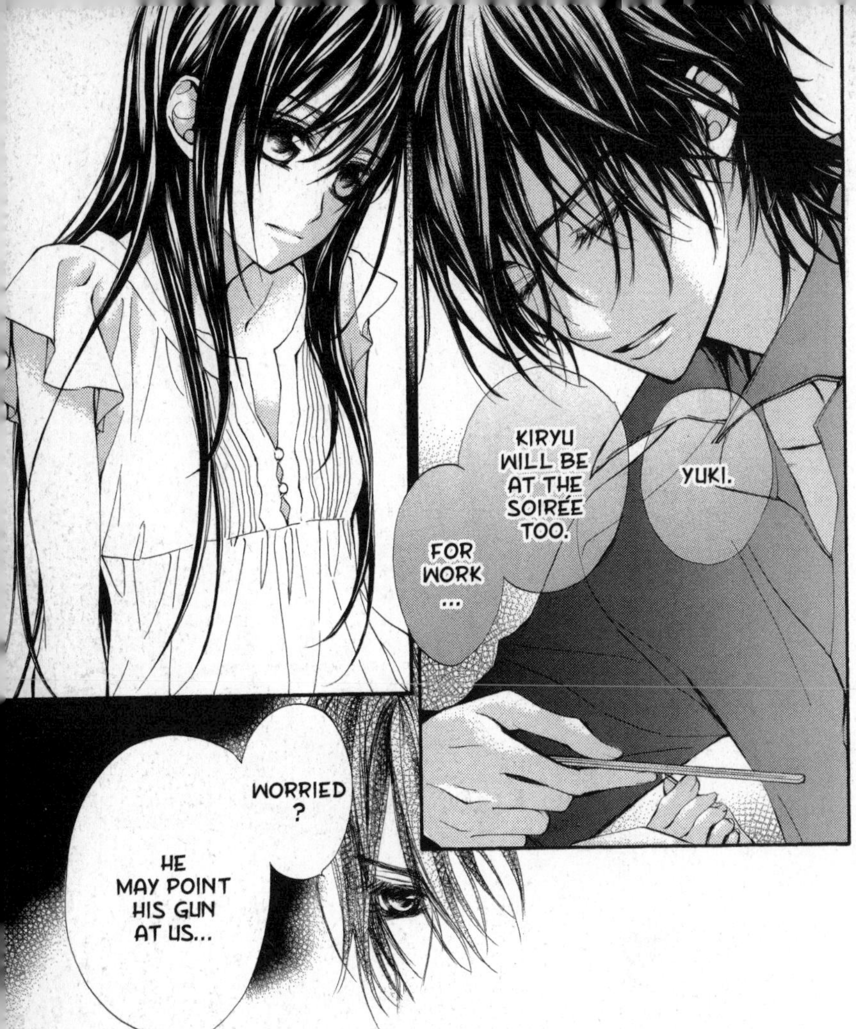
YUKI.
KIRYU WILL BE AT THE SOIRÉE TOO.
FOR WORK...
WORRIED?
HE MAY POINT HIS GUN AT US...

VAMPIRE KNIGHT

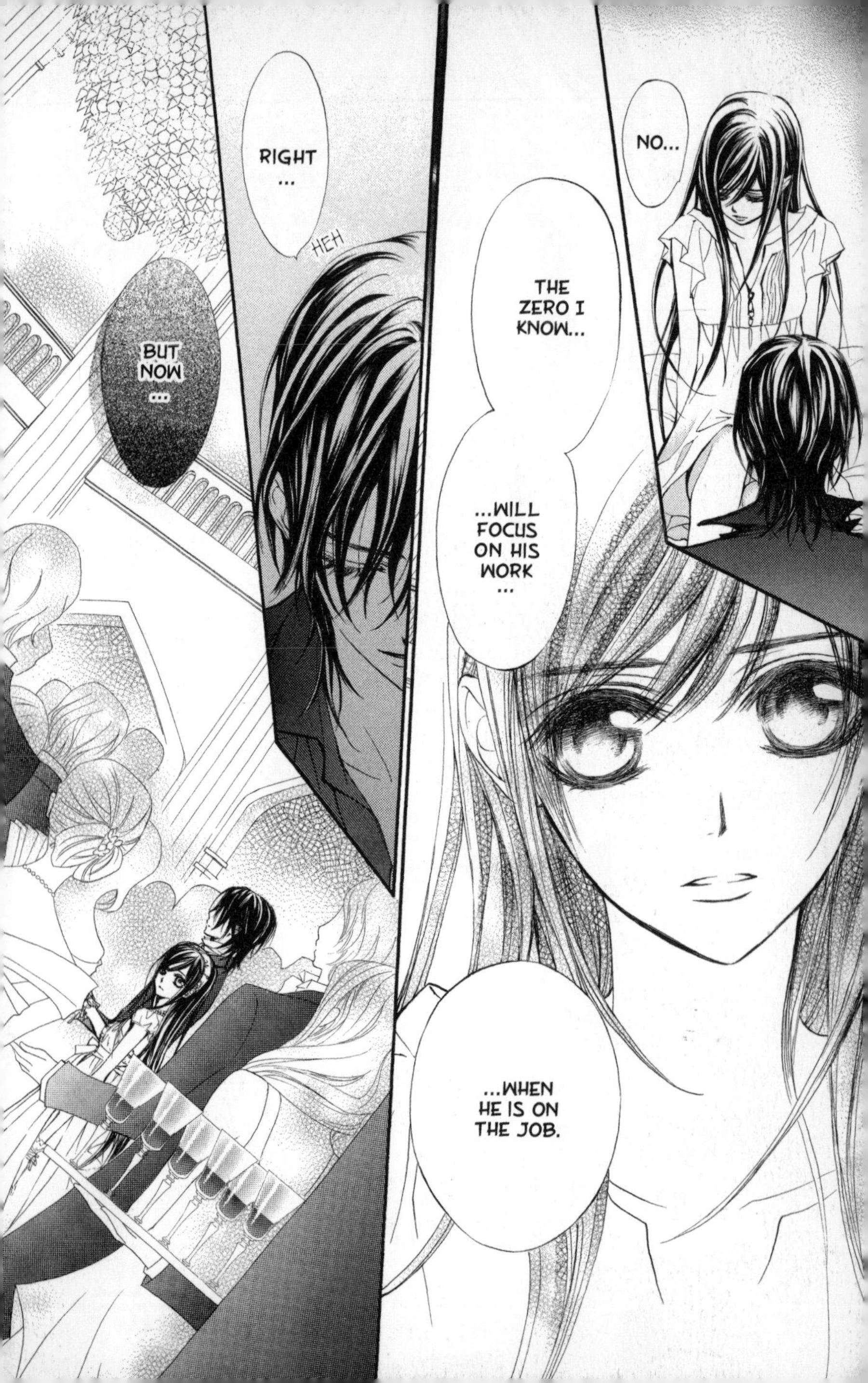
NO...
THE ZERO I KNOW...
...WILL FOCUS ON HIS WORK ...
...WHEN HE IS ON THE JOB.
RIGHT ...
HEH
BUT NOW ...

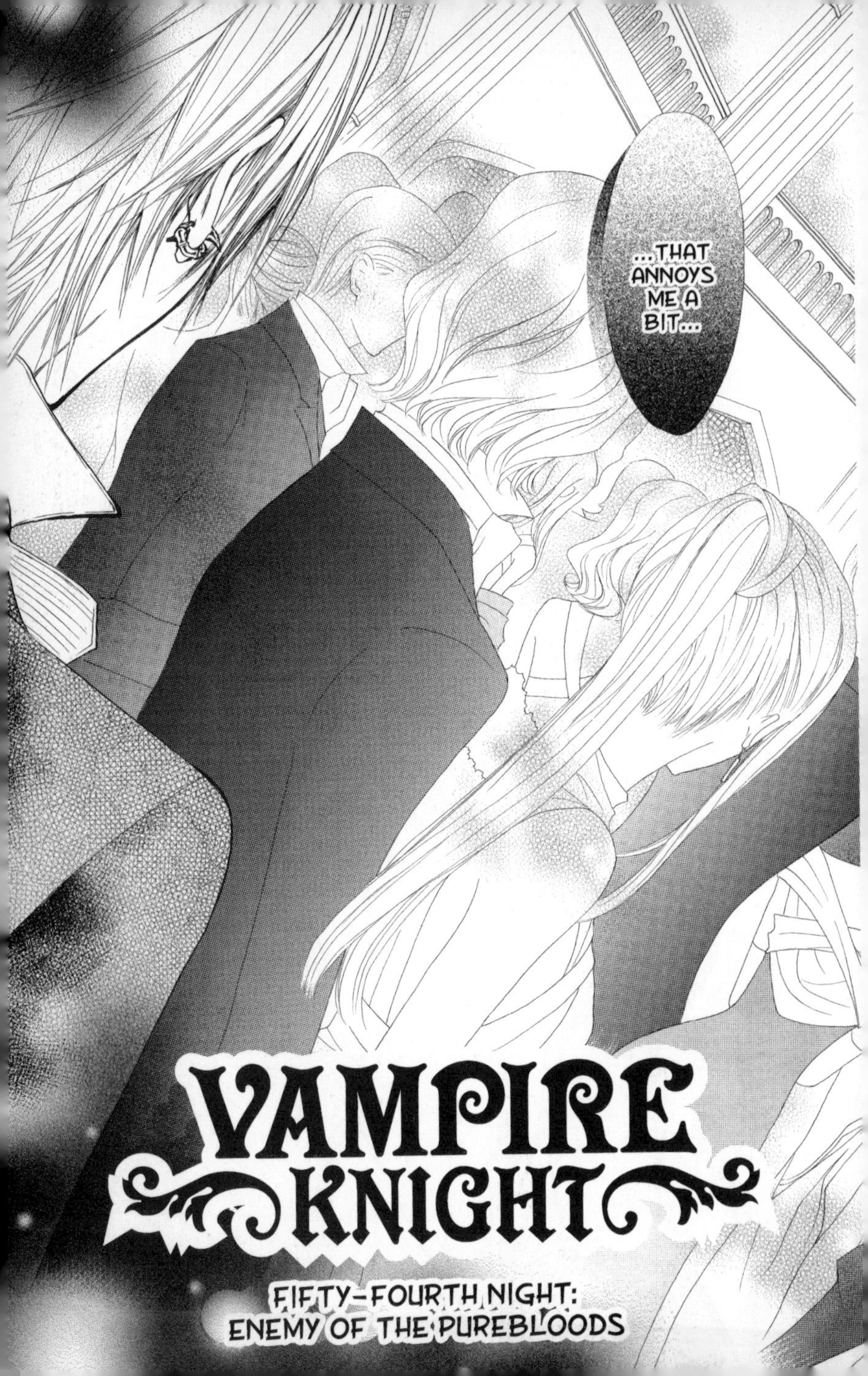
...THAT ANNOYS ME A BIT...
VAMPIRE KNIGHT
FIFTY-FOURTH NIGHT: ENEMY OF THE PUREBLOODS

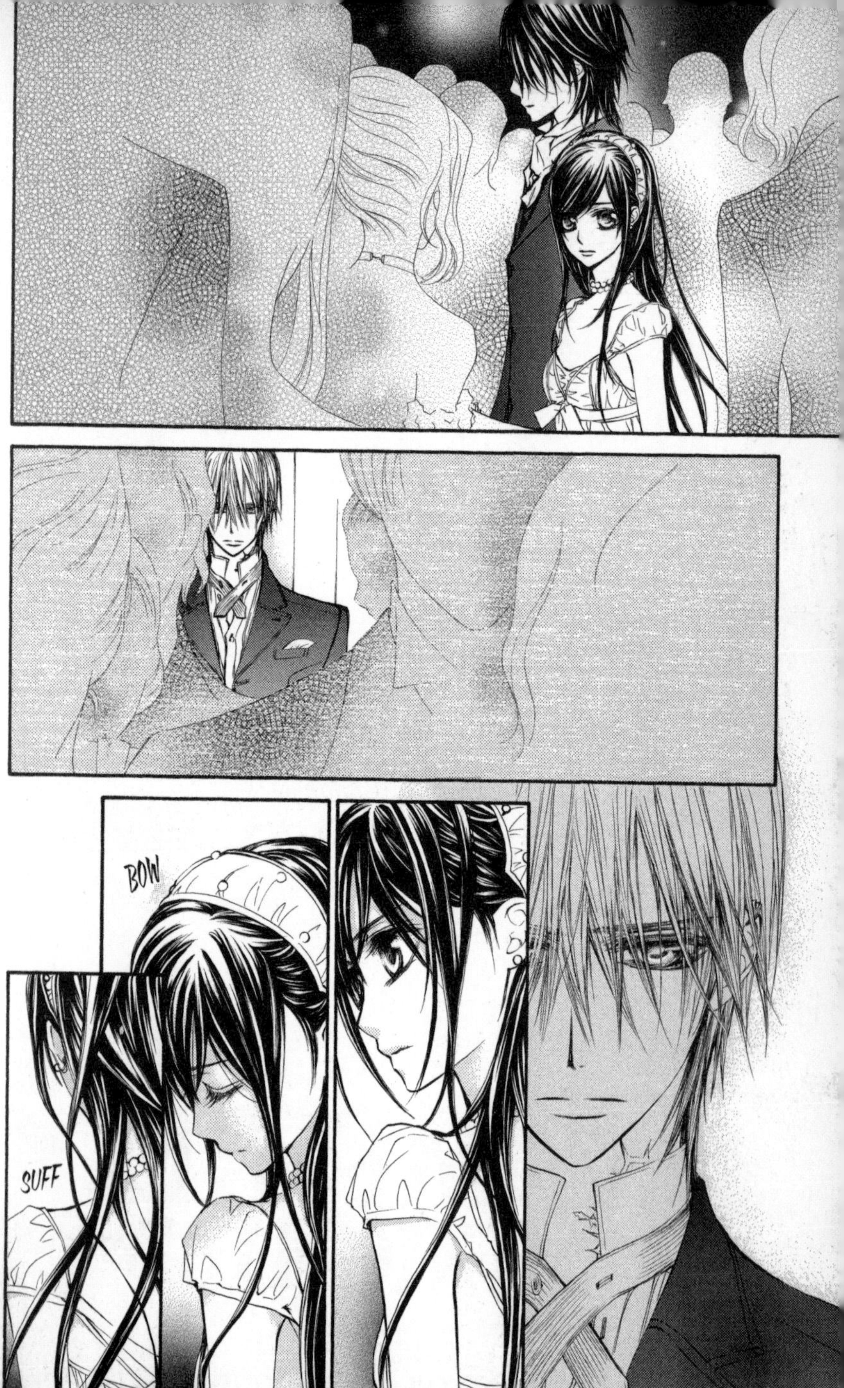
BOW
SUFF

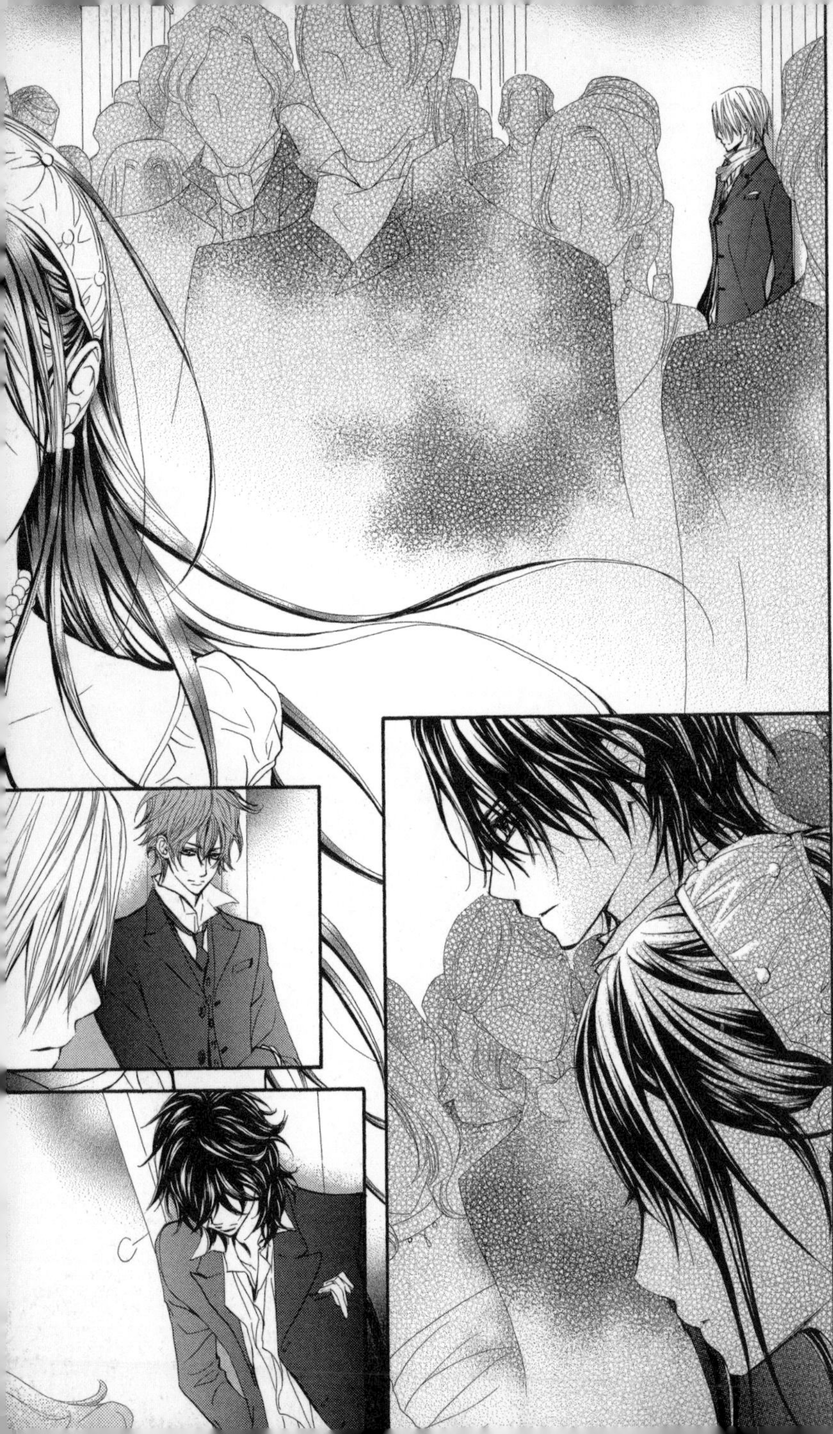

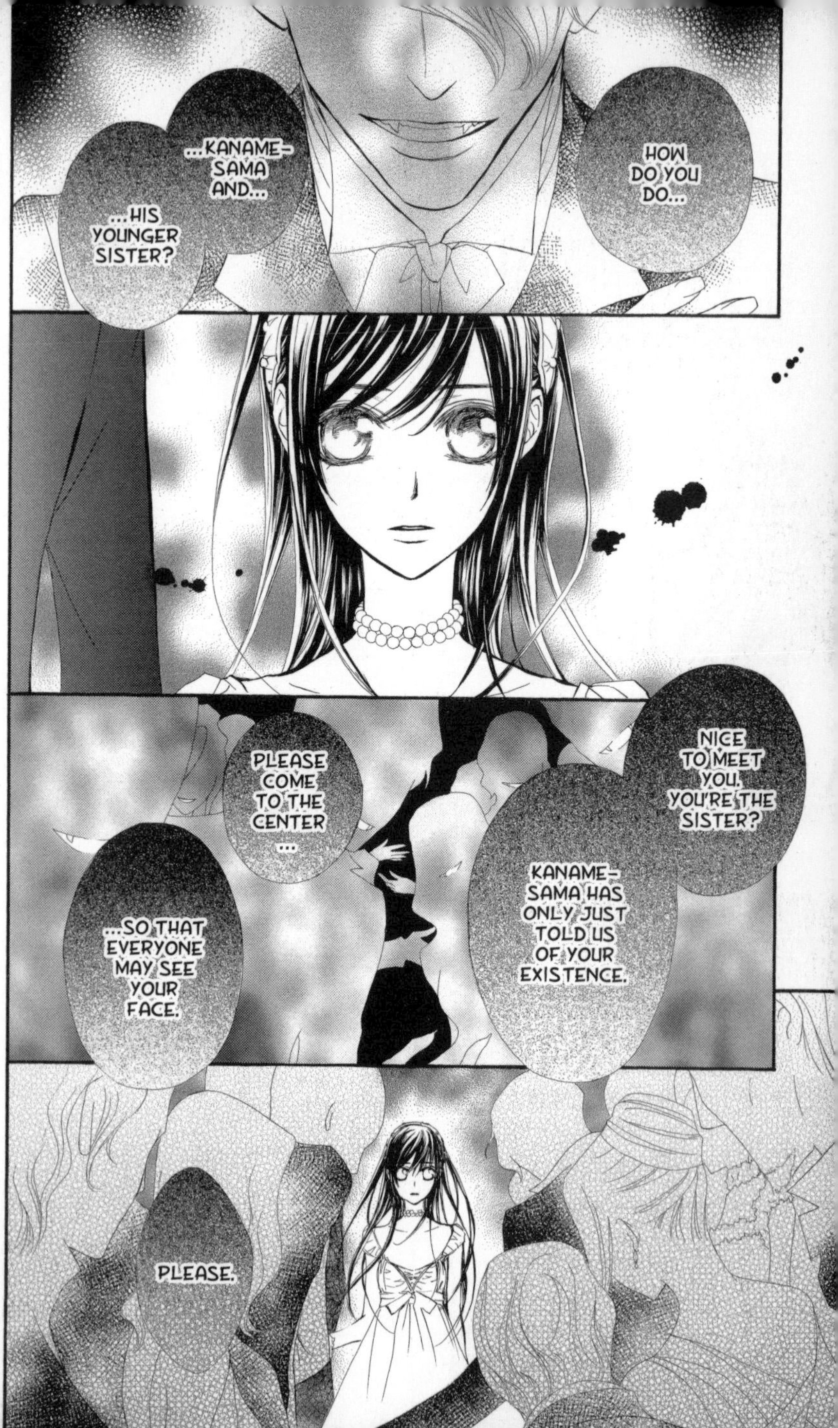
HOW DO YOU DO...
...KANAME-SAMA AND...
...HIS YOUNGER SISTER?
NICE TO MEET YOU. YOU'RE THE SISTER?
KANAME-SAMA HAS ONLY JUST TOLD US OF YOUR EXISTENCE.
PLEASE COME TO THE CENTER...
...SO THAT EVERYONE MAY SEE YOUR FACE.
PLEASE.

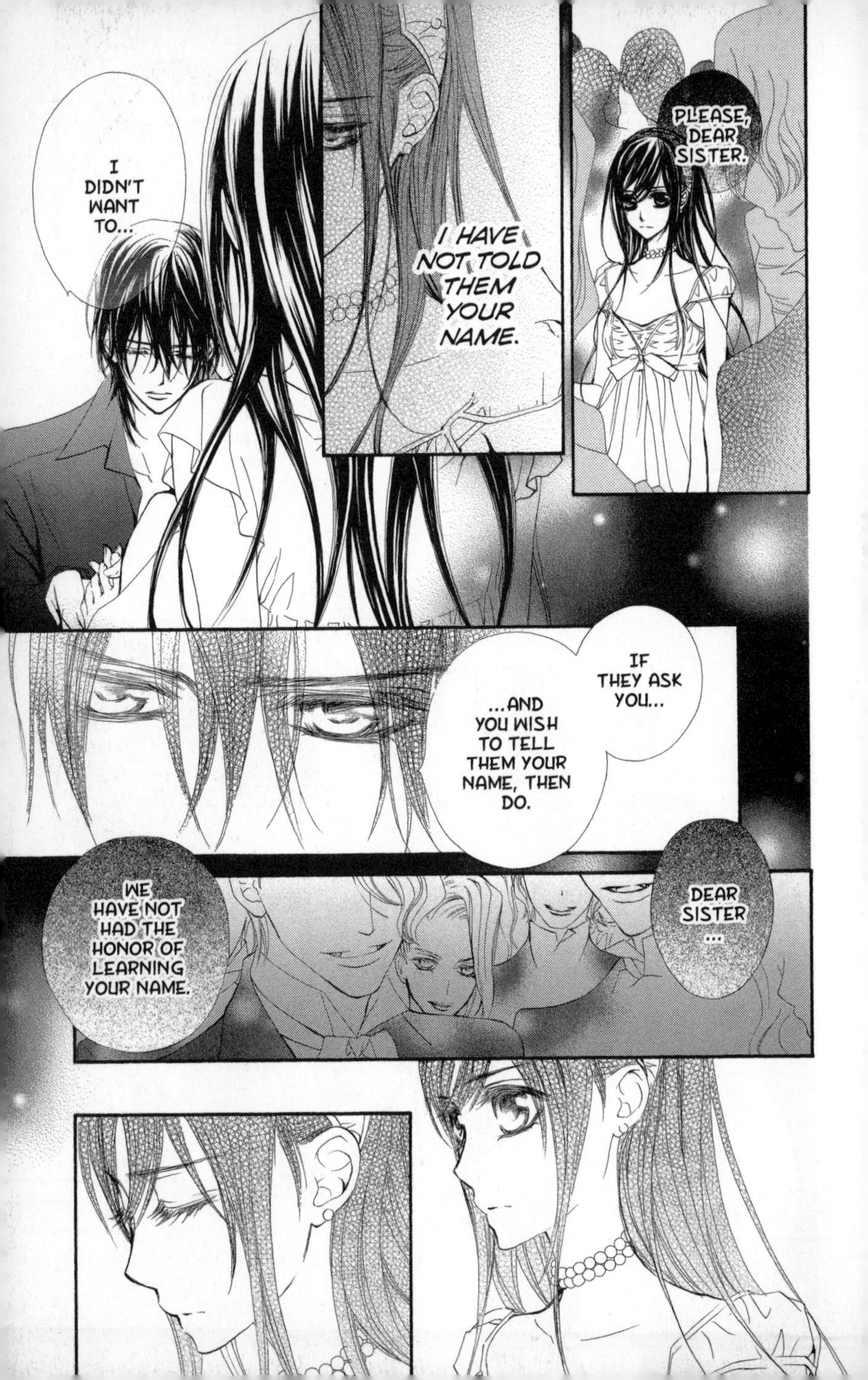
PLEASE, DEAR SISTER.
I HAVE NOT TOLD THEM YOUR NAME.
I DIDN'T WANT TO...
IF THEY ASK YOU...
...AND YOU WISH TO TELL THEM YOUR NAME, THEN DO.
DEAR SISTER...
WE HAVE NOT HAD THE HONOR OF LEARNING YOUR NAME.

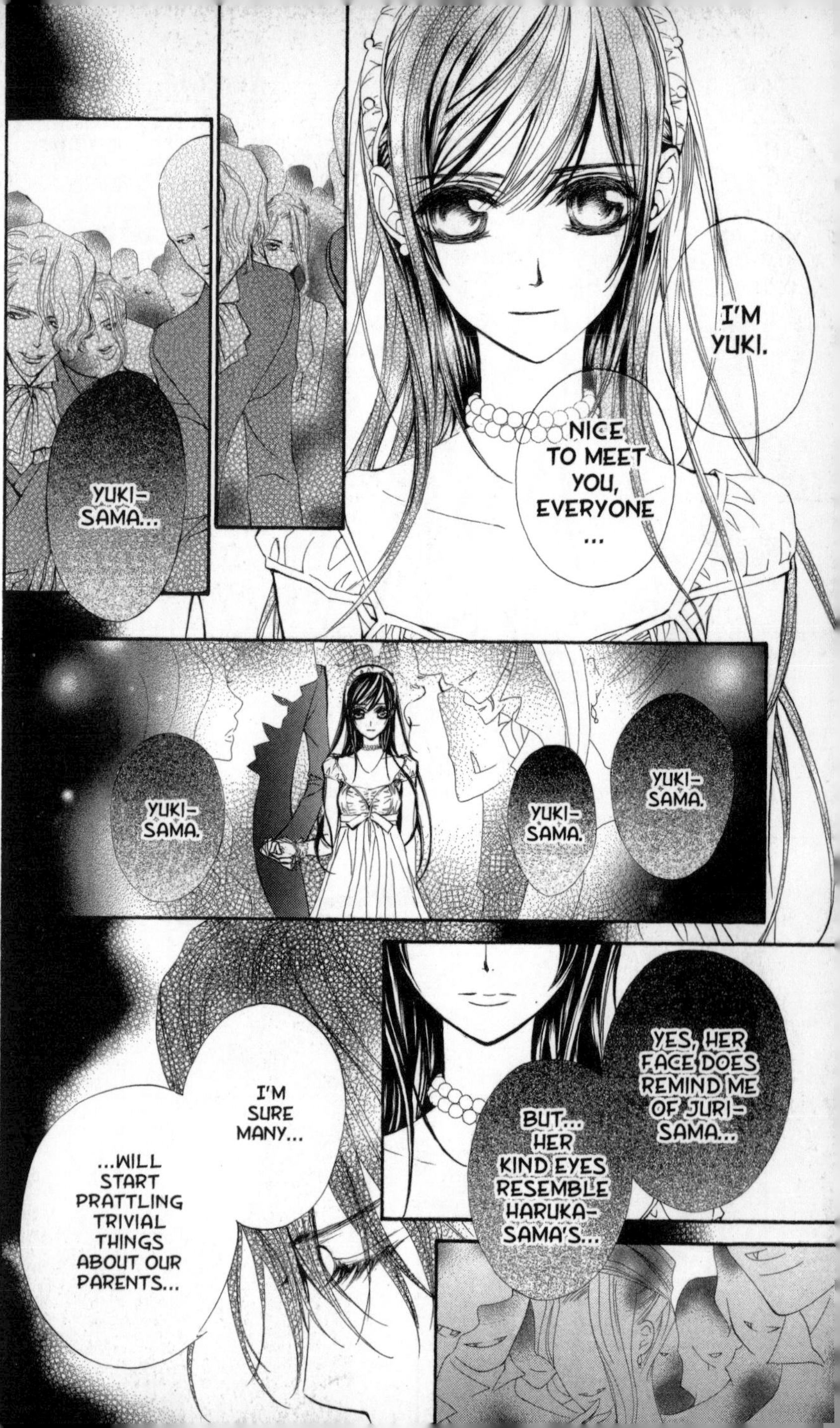
I'M YUKI.
NICE TO MEET YOU, EVERYONE ...
YUKI-SAMA...
YUKI-SAMA.
YUKI-SAMA.
YUKI-SAMA.
YES, HER FACE DOES REMIND ME OF JURI-SAMA...
BUT... HER KIND EYES RESEMBLE HARUKA-SAMA'S...
I'M SURE MANY...
...WILL START PRATTLING TRIVIAL THINGS ABOUT OUR PARENTS...

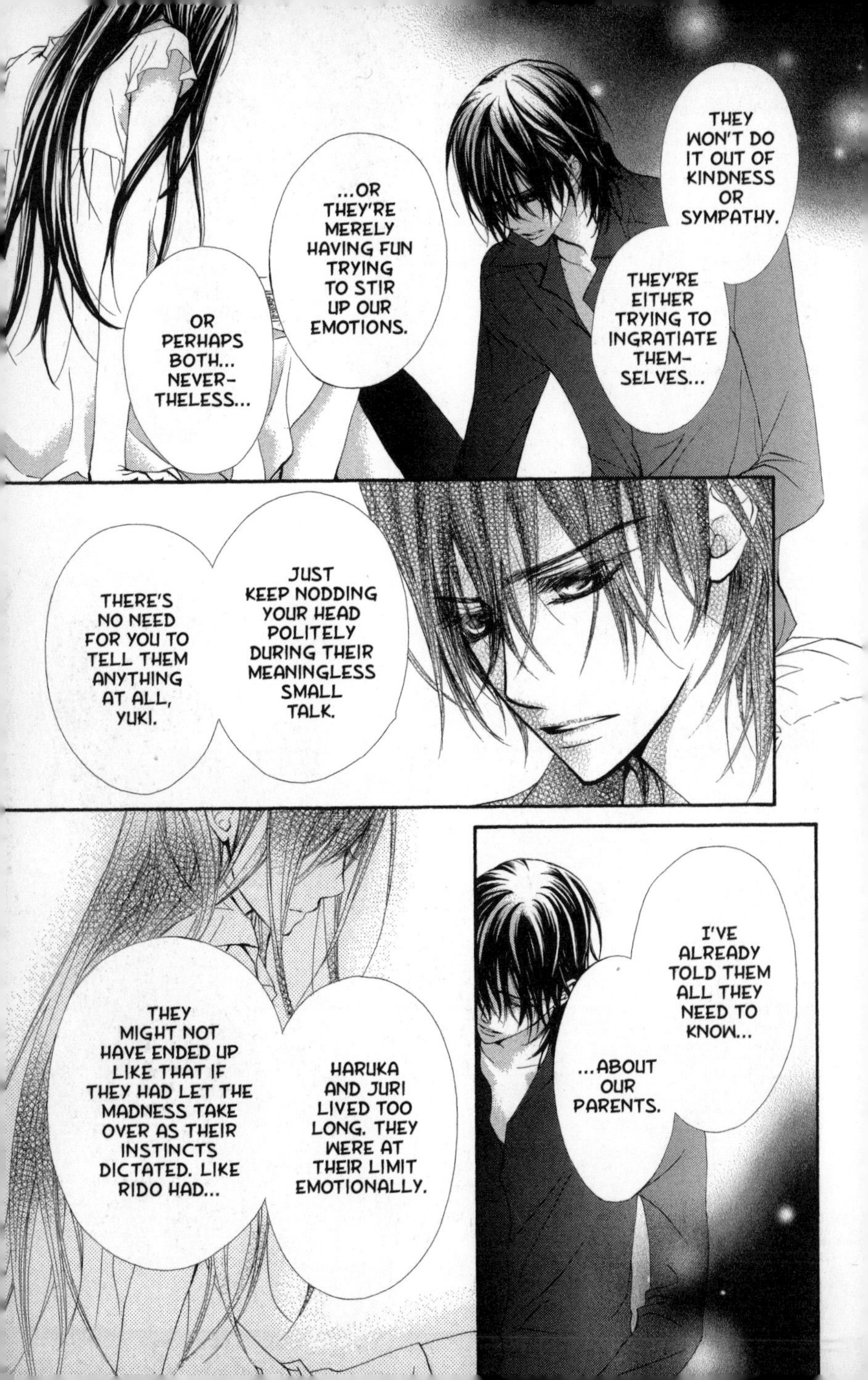
THEY WON'T DO IT OUT OF KINDNESS OR SYMPATHY.
THEY'RE EITHER TRYING TO INGRATIATE THEMSELVES...
...OR THEY'RE MERELY HAVING FUN TRYING TO STIR UP OUR EMOTIONS.
OR PERHAPS BOTH... NEVERTHELESS...
JUST KEEP NODDING YOUR HEAD POLITELY DURING THEIR MEANINGLESS SMALL TALK.
THERE'S NO NEED FOR YOU TO TELL THEM ANYTHING AT ALL, YUKI.
I'VE ALREADY TOLD THEM ALL THEY NEED TO KNOW...
...ABOUT OUR PARENTS.
HARUKA AND JURI LIVED TOO LONG. THEY WERE AT THEIR LIMIT EMOTIONALLY.
THEY MIGHT NOT HAVE ENDED UP LIKE THAT IF THEY HAD LET THE MADNESS TAKE OVER AS THEIR INSTINCTS DICTATED. LIKE RIDO HAD...

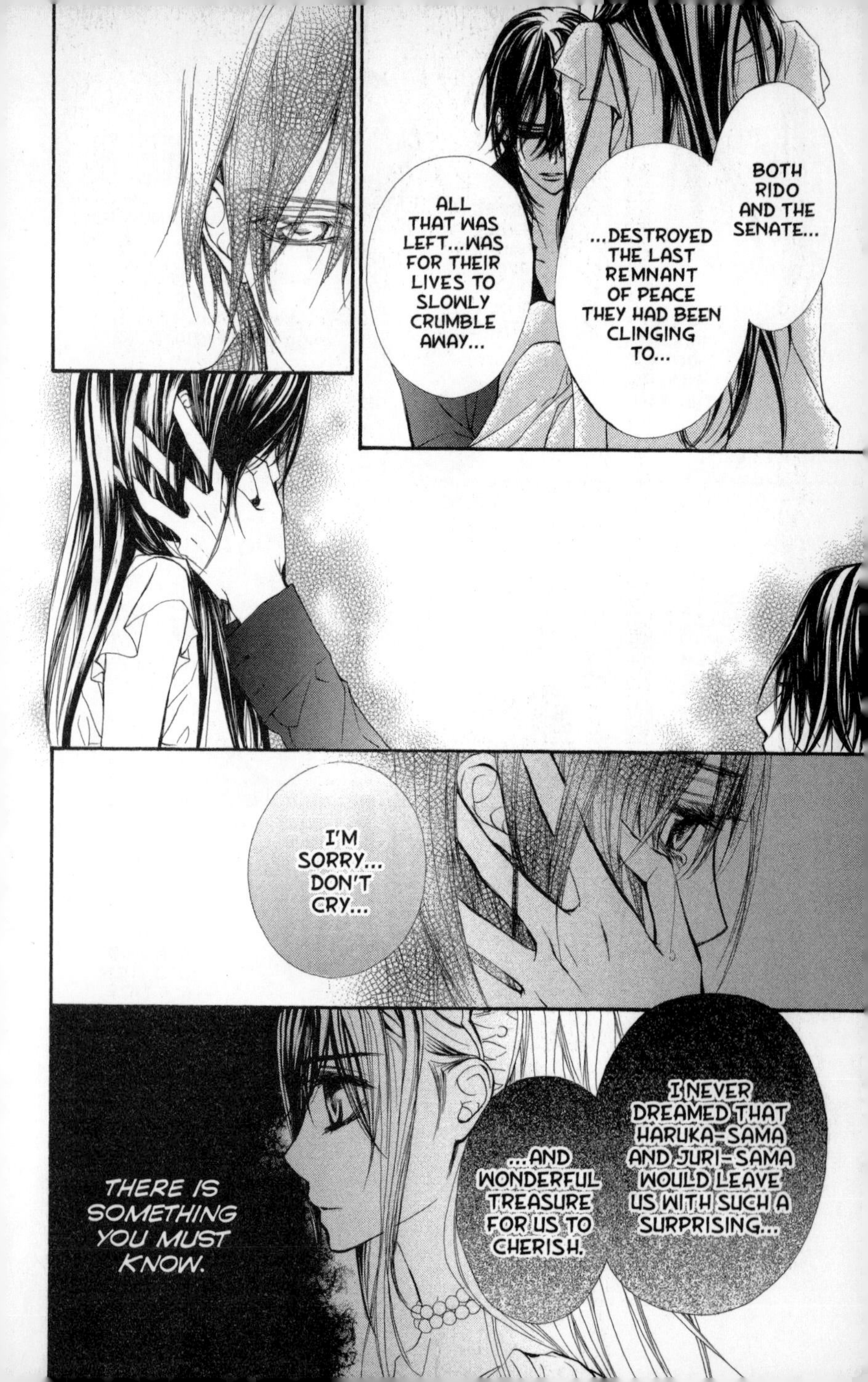
BOTH RIDO AND THE SENATE...
...DESTROYED THE LAST REMNANT OF PEACE THEY HAD BEEN CLINGING TO...
ALL THAT WAS LEFT...WAS FOR THEIR LIVES TO SLOWLY CRUMBLE AWAY...
I'M SORRY... DON'T CRY...
I NEVER DREAMED THAT HARUKA-SAMA AND JURI-SAMA WOULD LEAVE US WITH SUCH A SURPRISING...
...AND WONDERFUL TREASURE FOR US TO CHERISH.
THERE IS SOMETHING YOU MUST KNOW.

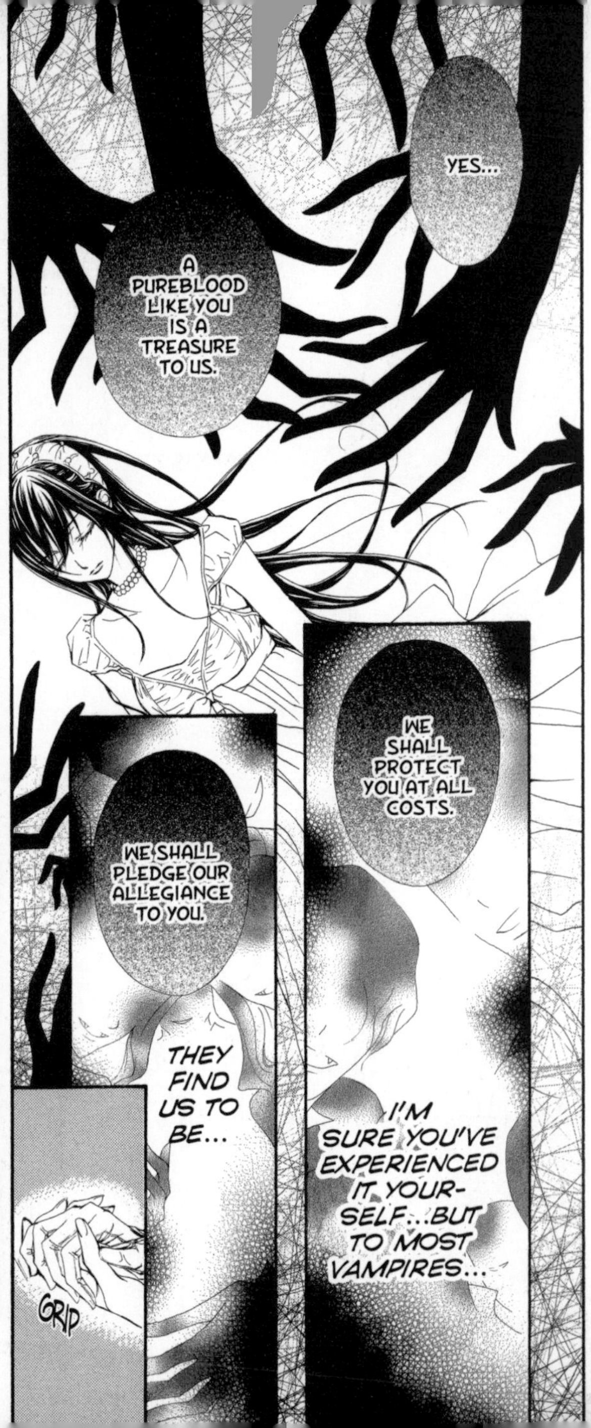
YES...
A PUREBLOOD LIKE YOU IS A TREASURE TO US.
WE SHALL PROTECT YOU AT ALL COSTS.
I'M SURE YOU'VE EXPERIENCED IT YOUR-SELF...BUT TO MOST VAMPIRES...
WE SHALL PLEDGE OUR ALLEGIANCE TO YOU.
THEY FIND US TO BE...
GRIP

Hello.

Volume 12!

Thank you very much!

As the creator, volume 11 and 12... (and probably volume 13 too...) were very difficult. I am trying hard to get over this hill, but I am able to gather my strength each time I remember all the readers who are supporting this series! I want to create some-thing you will like!!!! I will put all my effort into doing so. See you again... I'll be very happy if I'm able to see you again in volume 13.

Matsuri Hino

O. Mio-sama
K. Midori-sama
I. Asami-sama
A. Ichiya-sama

My family, friends, editor, and all the readers: Thank you very much for supporting me all the time!

(And to every-body involved, I apologize for all the trouble I've caused you...)

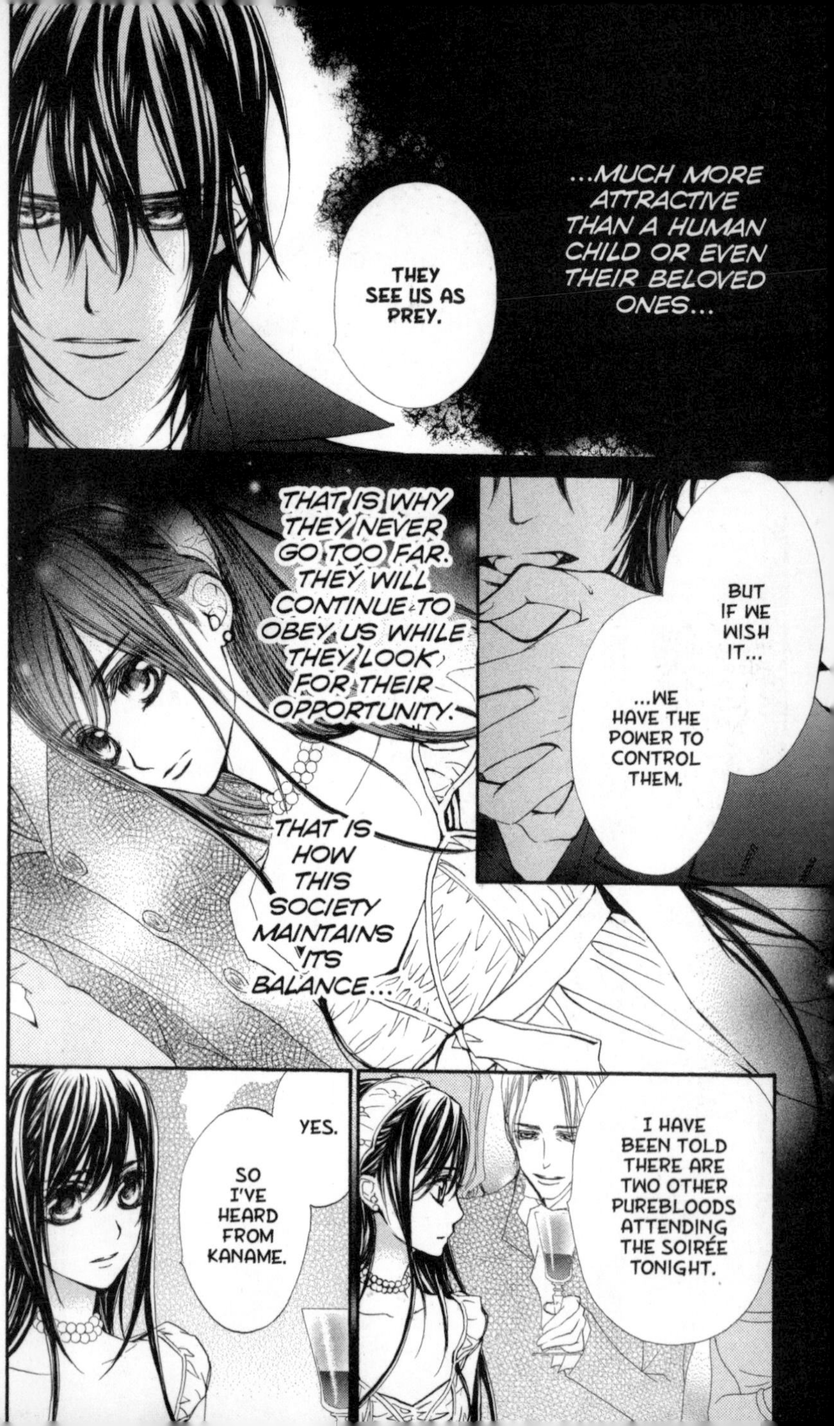
...MUCH MORE ATTRACTIVE THAN A HUMAN CHILD OR EVEN THEIR BELOVED ONES...
THEY SEE US AS PREY.
BUT IF WE WISH IT...
...WE HAVE THE POWER TO CONTROL THEM.
THAT IS WHY THEY NEVER GO TOO FAR. THEY WILL CONTINUE TO OBEY US WHILE THEY LOOK FOR THEIR OPPORTUNITY.
THAT IS HOW THIS SOCIETY MAINTAINS ITS BALANCE...
I HAVE BEEN TOLD THERE ARE TWO OTHER PUREBLOODS ATTENDING THE SOIRÉE TONIGHT.
YES.
SO I'VE HEARD FROM KANAME.

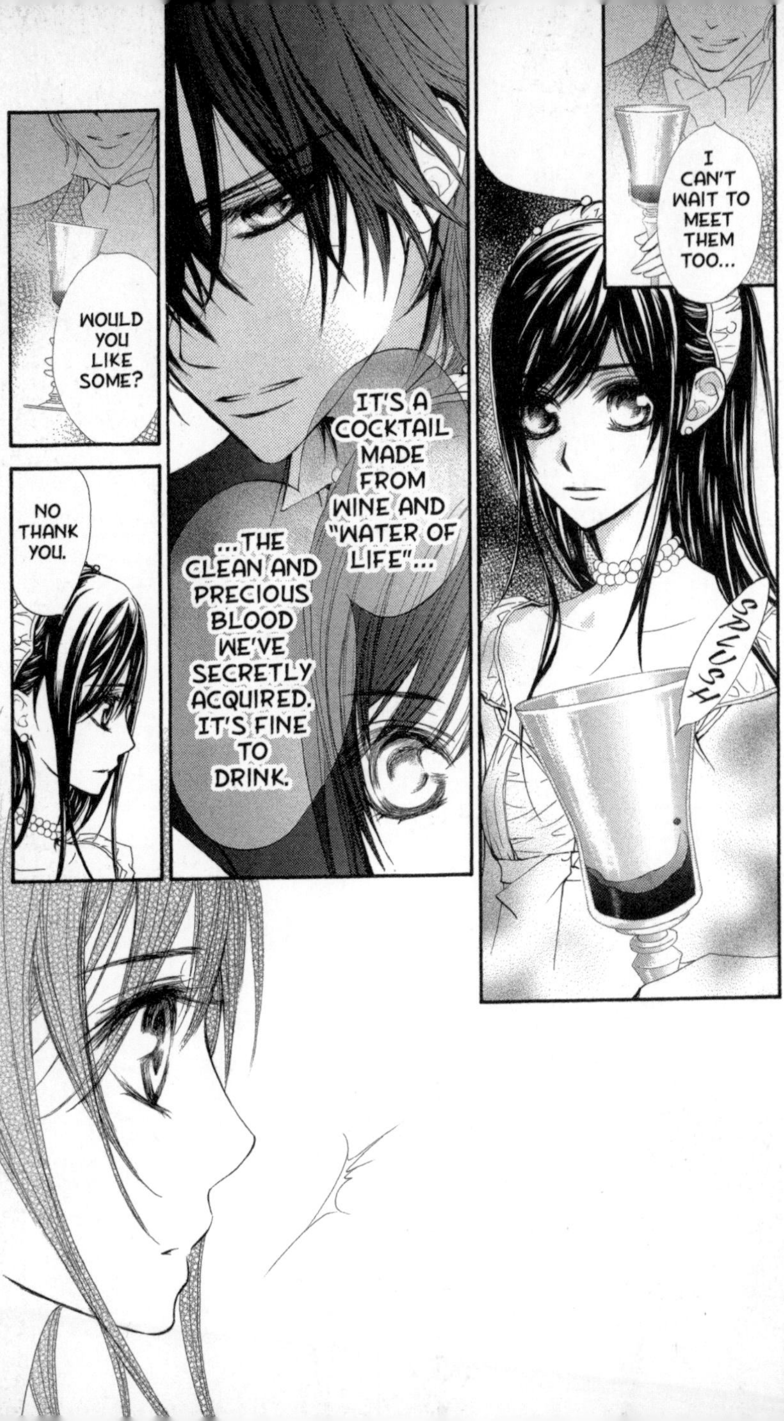
I CAN'T WAIT TO MEET THEM TOO...
SPLUSH
IT'S A COCKTAIL MADE FROM WINE AND "WATER OF LIFE"...
...THE CLEAN AND PRECIOUS BLOOD WE'VE SECRETLY ACQUIRED. IT'S FINE TO DRINK.
WOULD YOU LIKE SOME?
NO THANK YOU.

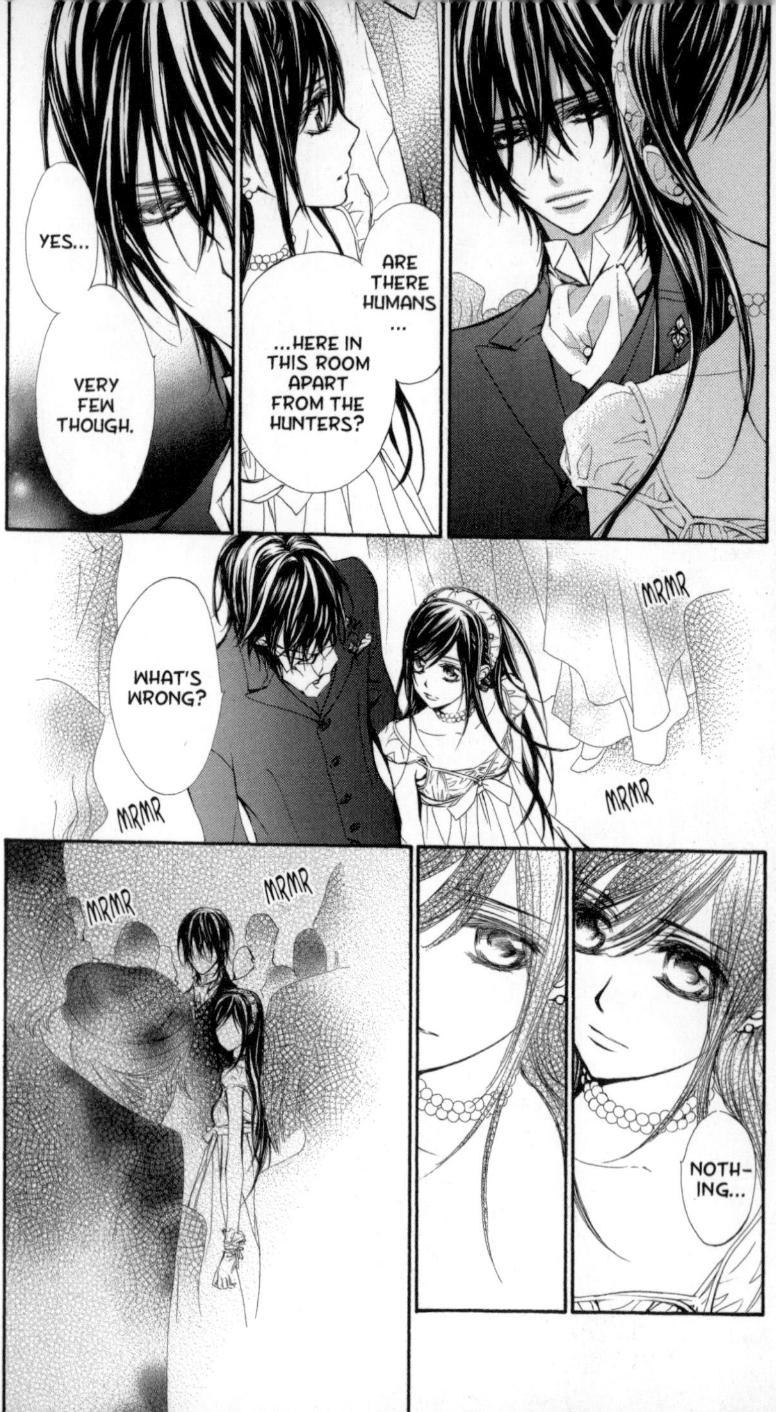
ARE THERE HUMANS ...
...HERE IN THIS ROOM APART FROM THE HUNTERS?
YES...
VERY FEW THOUGH.
MRMR
WHAT'S WRONG?
MRMR
MRMR
NOTH-ING...
MRMR
MRMR

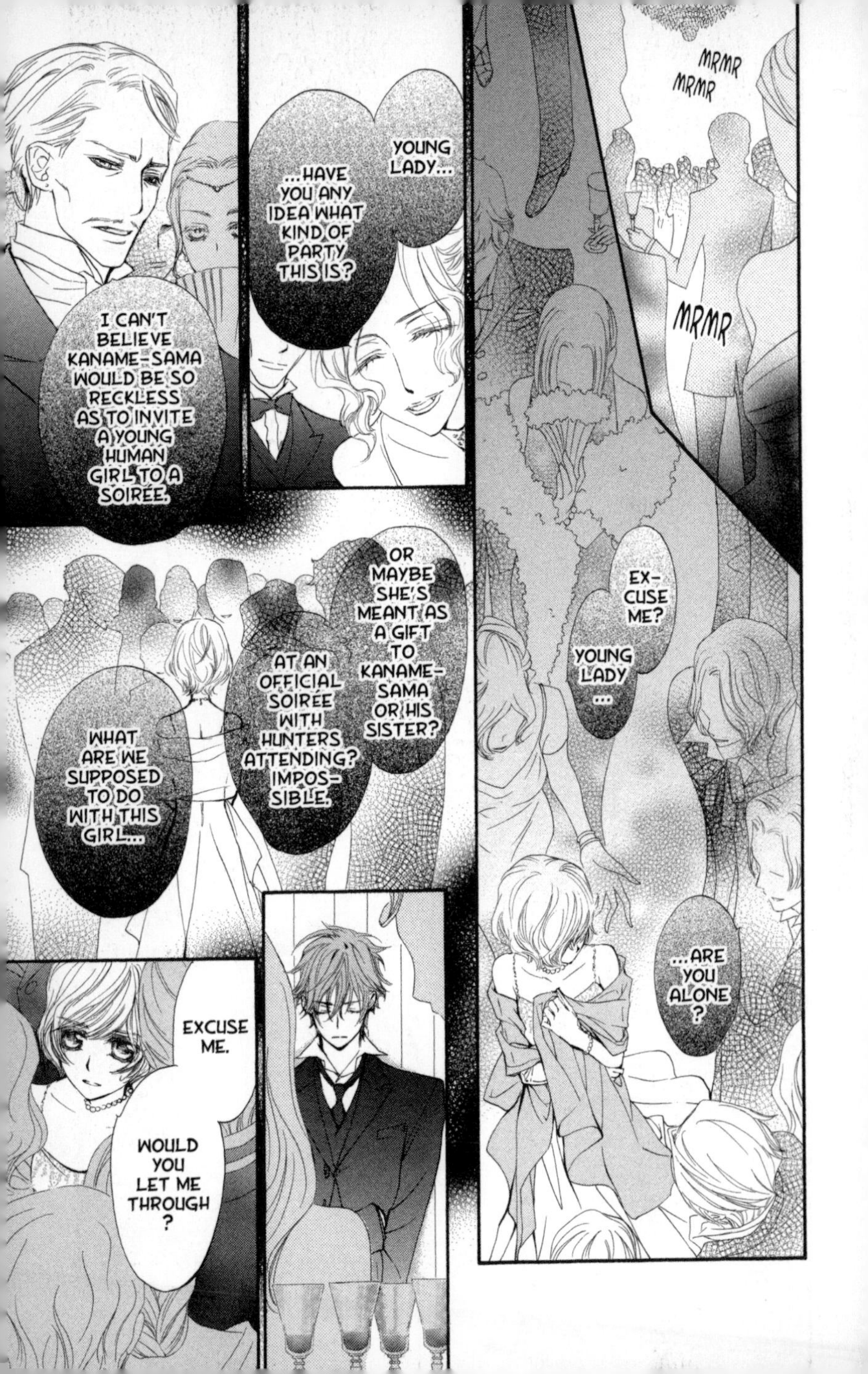
MRMR
MRMR
MRMR
EX-CUSE ME?
YOUNG LADY ...
...ARE YOU ALONE?
YOUNG LADY...
...HAVE YOU ANY IDEA WHAT KIND OF PARTY THIS IS?
I CAN'T BELIEVE KANAME-SAMA WOULD BE SO RECKLESS AS TO INVITE A YOUNG HUMAN GIRL TO A SOIRÉE.
OR MAYBE SHE'S MEANT AS A GIFT TO KANAME-SAMA OR HIS SISTER?
AT AN OFFICIAL SOIRÉE WITH HUNTERS ATTENDING? IMPOS-SIBLE.
WHAT ARE WE SUPPOSED TO DO WITH THIS GIRL...
EXCUSE ME.
WOULD YOU LET ME THROUGH?

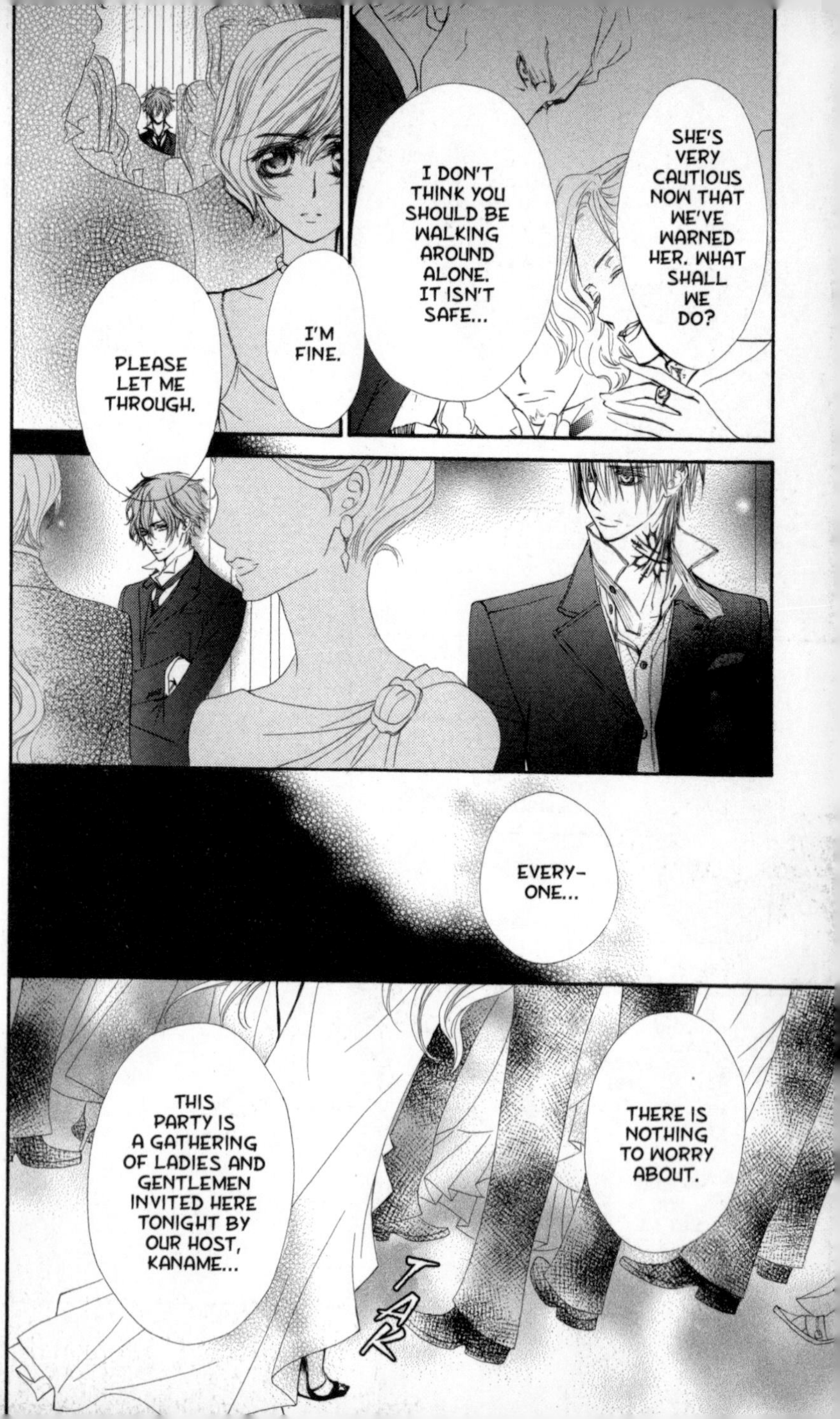
SHE'S VERY CAUTIOUS NOW THAT WE'VE WARNED HER. WHAT SHALL WE DO?
I DON'T THINK YOU SHOULD BE WALKING AROUND ALONE. IT ISN'T SAFE...
I'M FINE.
PLEASE LET ME THROUGH.
EVERY-ONE...
THERE IS NOTHING TO WORRY ABOUT.
THIS PARTY IS A GATHERING OF LADIES AND GENTLEMEN INVITED HERE TONIGHT BY OUR HOST, KANAME...
TAR

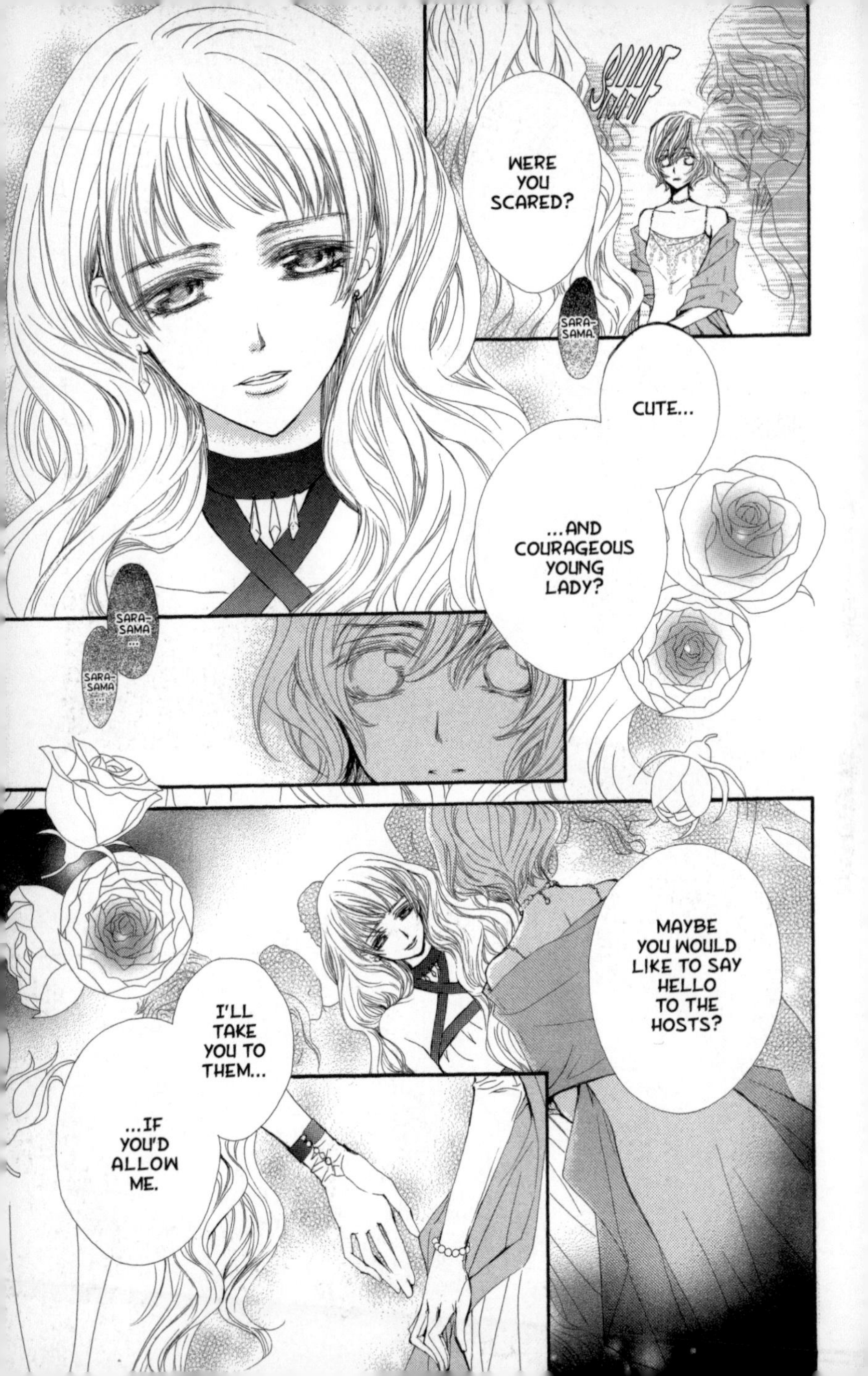
WERE YOU SCARED?
SARA-SAMA.
CUTE...
...AND COURAGEOUS YOUNG LADY?
SARA-SAMA...
SARA-SAMA...
MAYBE YOU WOULD LIKE TO SAY HELLO TO THE HOSTS?
I'LL TAKE YOU TO THEM...
...IF YOU'D ALLOW ME.

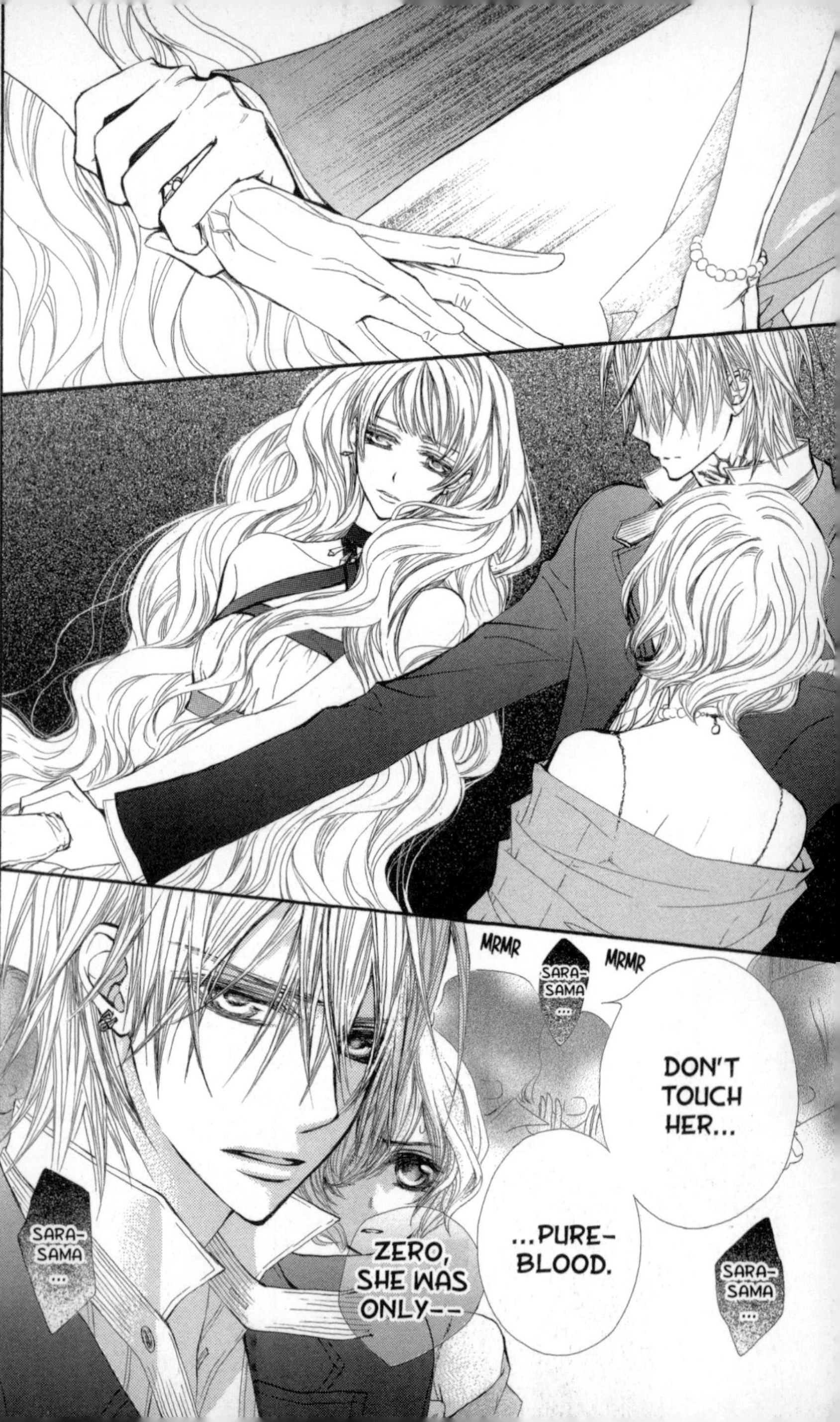
MRMR
SARA-SAMA...
MRMR
DON'T TOUCH HER...
SARA-SAMA...
...PURE-BLOOD.
ZERO, SHE WAS ONLY--
SARA-SAMA...

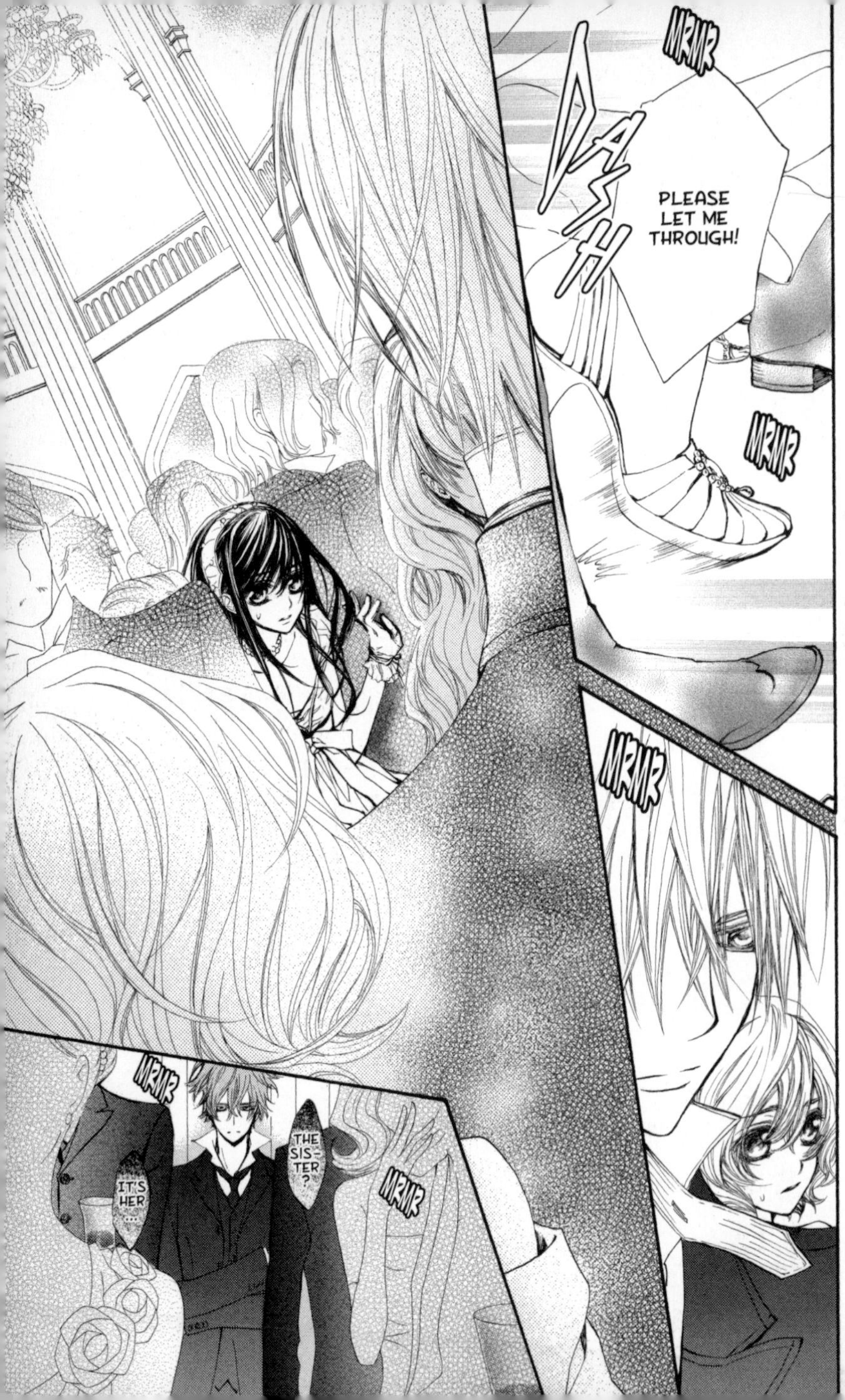
MRMR
DASH
PLEASE LET ME THROUGH!
MRMR
MRMR
MRMR
THE SISTER?
MRMR
IT'S HER...

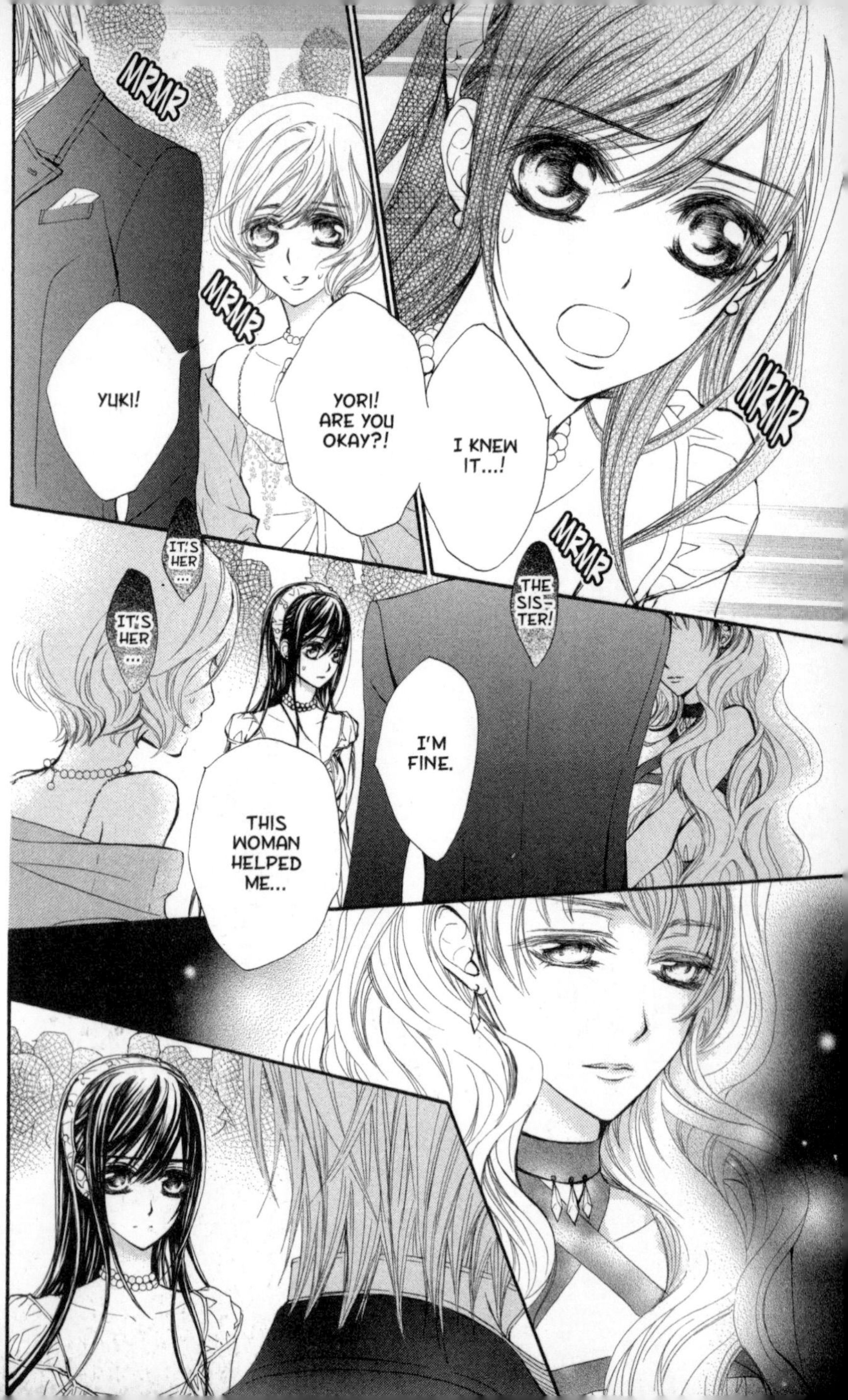
MRMR
I KNEW IT...!
MRMR
YORI! ARE YOU OKAY?!
MRMR
MRMR
YUKI!
THE SISTER!
I'M FINE.
IT'S HER...
IT'S HER...
THIS WOMAN HELPED ME...

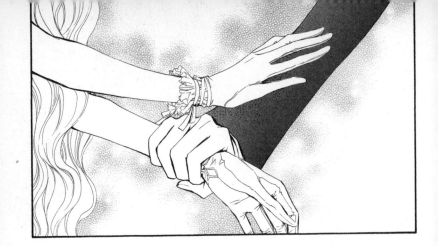

PLEASE LET GO OF HER HAND.

SHE'S AN IMPORTANT GUEST.

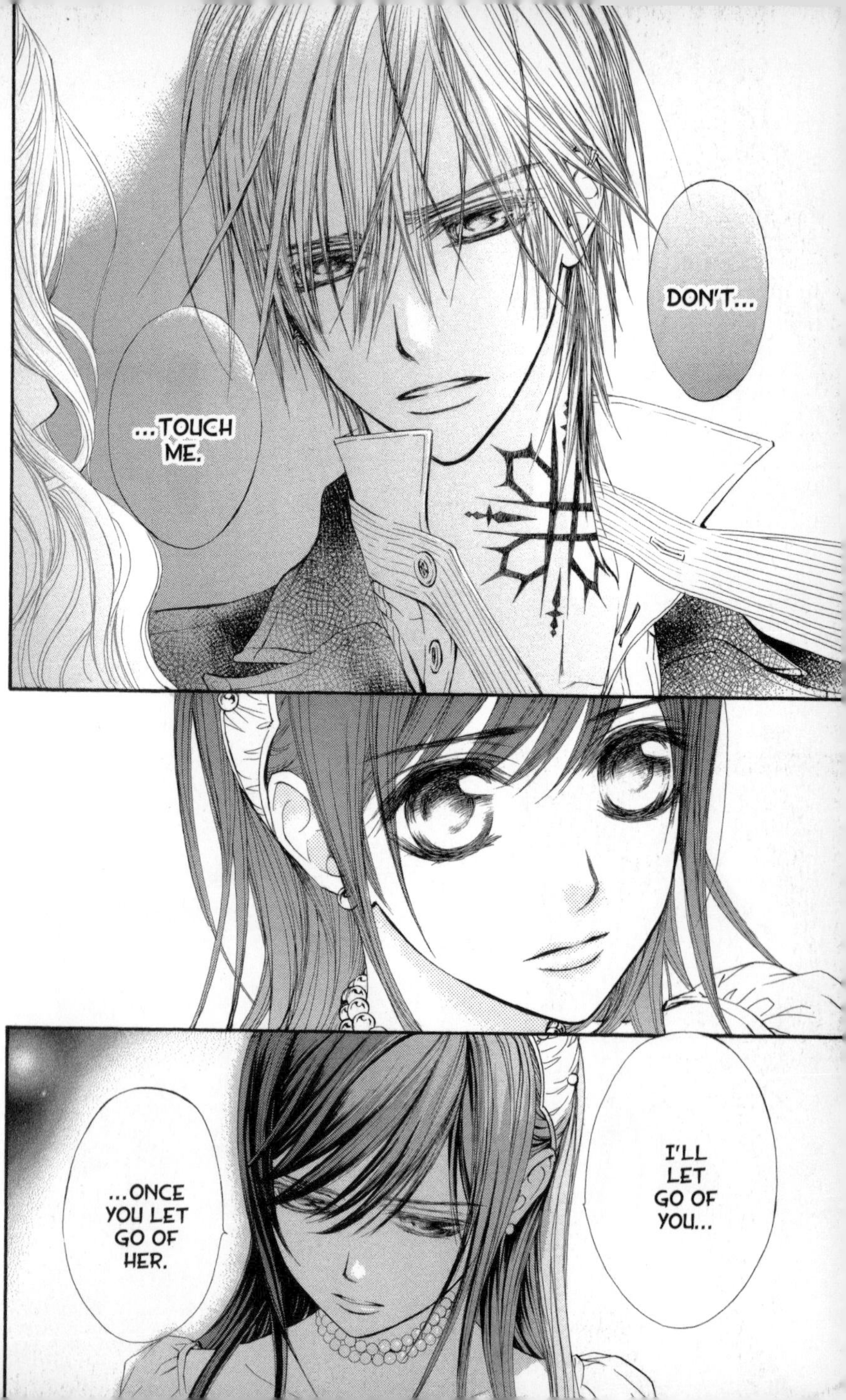
DON'T...
...TOUCH ME.
I'LL LET GO OF YOU...
...ONCE YOU LET GO OF HER.

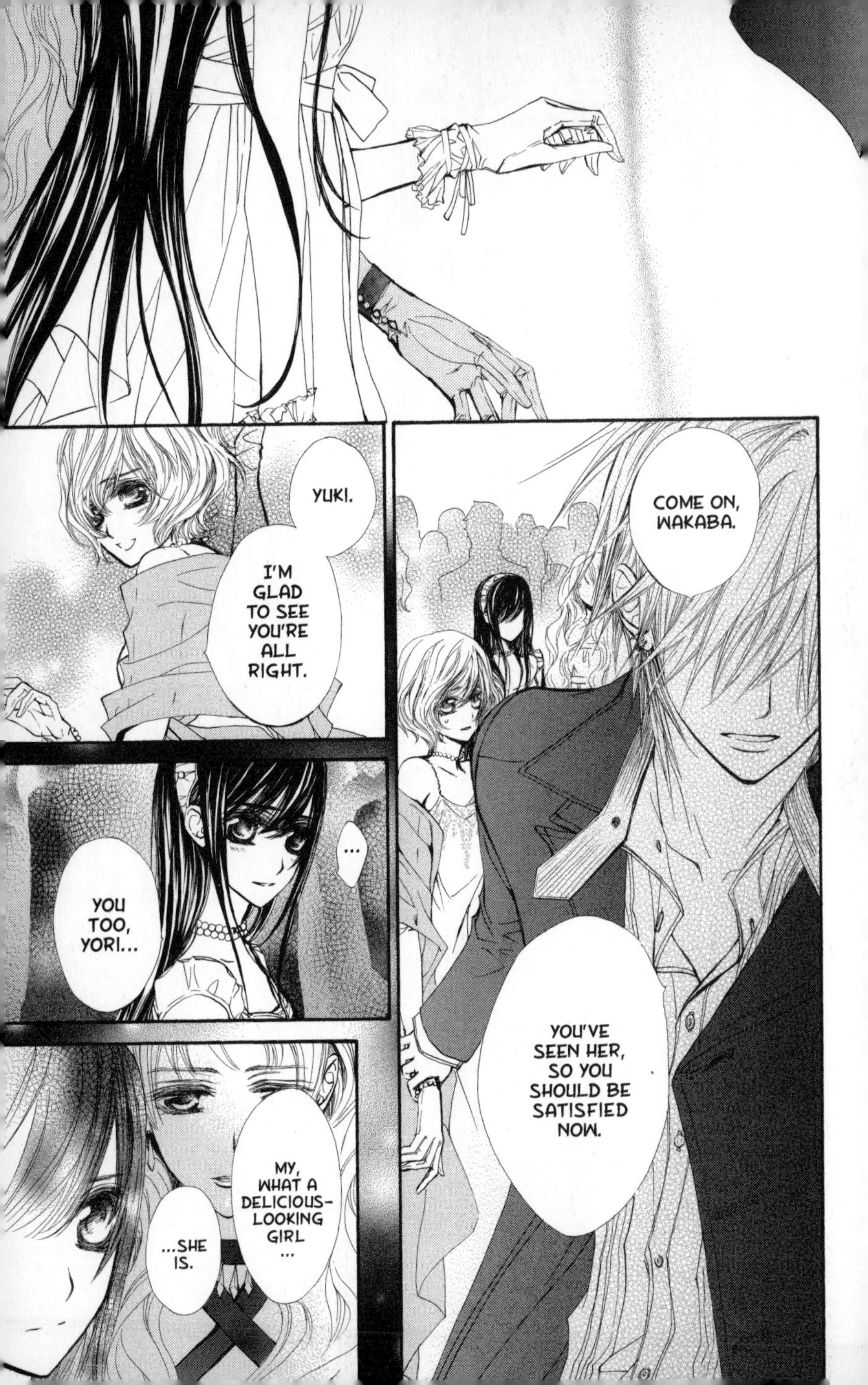
COME ON, WAKABA.
YOU'VE SEEN HER, SO YOU SHOULD BE SATISFIED NOW.
YUKI.
I'M GLAD TO SEE YOU'RE ALL RIGHT.
...
YOU TOO, YORI...
MY, WHAT A DELICIOUS-LOOKING GIRL ...
...SHE IS.

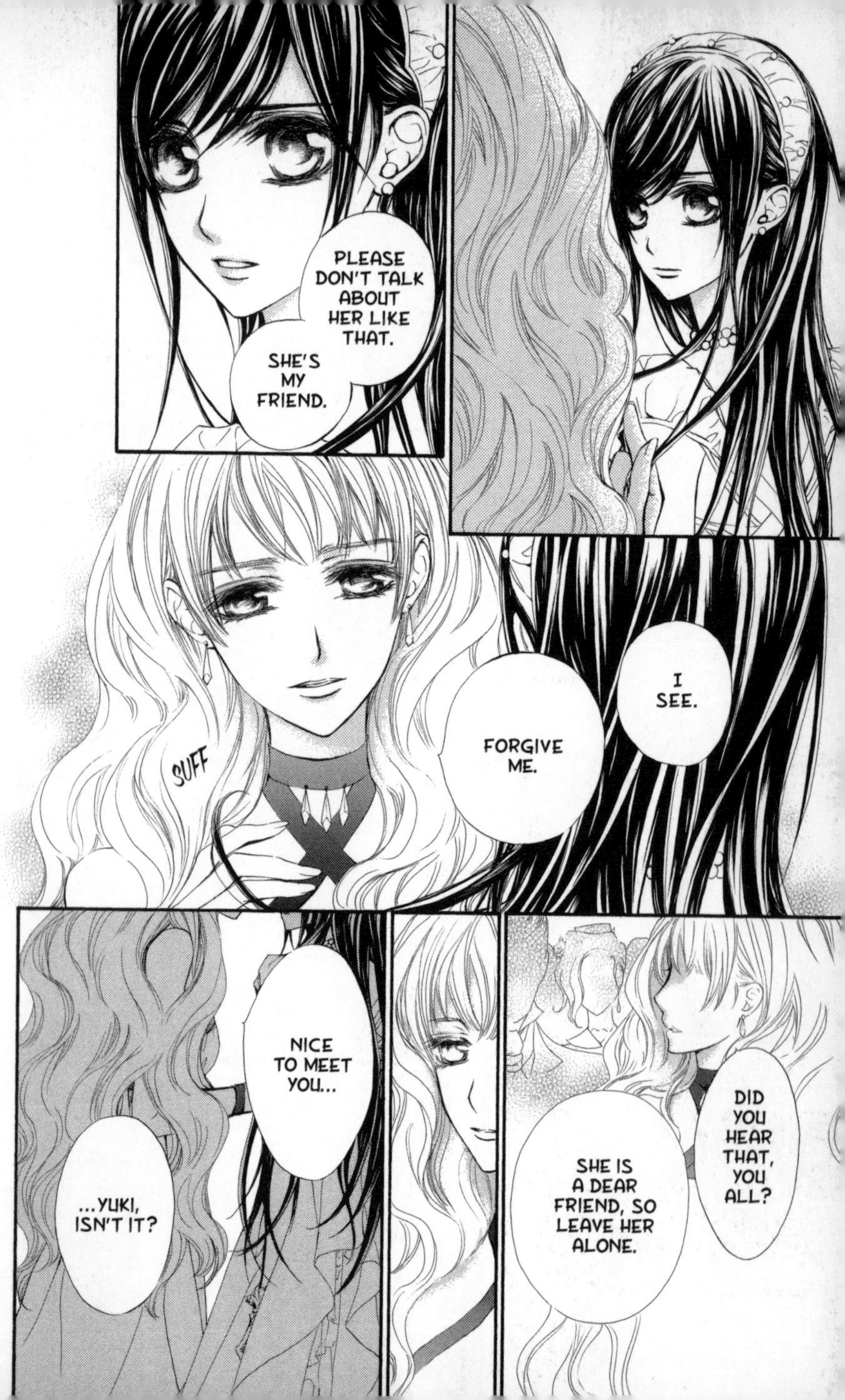
PLEASE DON'T TALK ABOUT HER LIKE THAT.
SHE'S MY FRIEND.
I SEE.
FORGIVE ME.
SUFF
DID YOU HEAR THAT, YOU ALL?
SHE IS A DEAR FRIEND, SO LEAVE HER ALONE.
NICE TO MEET YOU...
...YUKI, ISN'T IT?

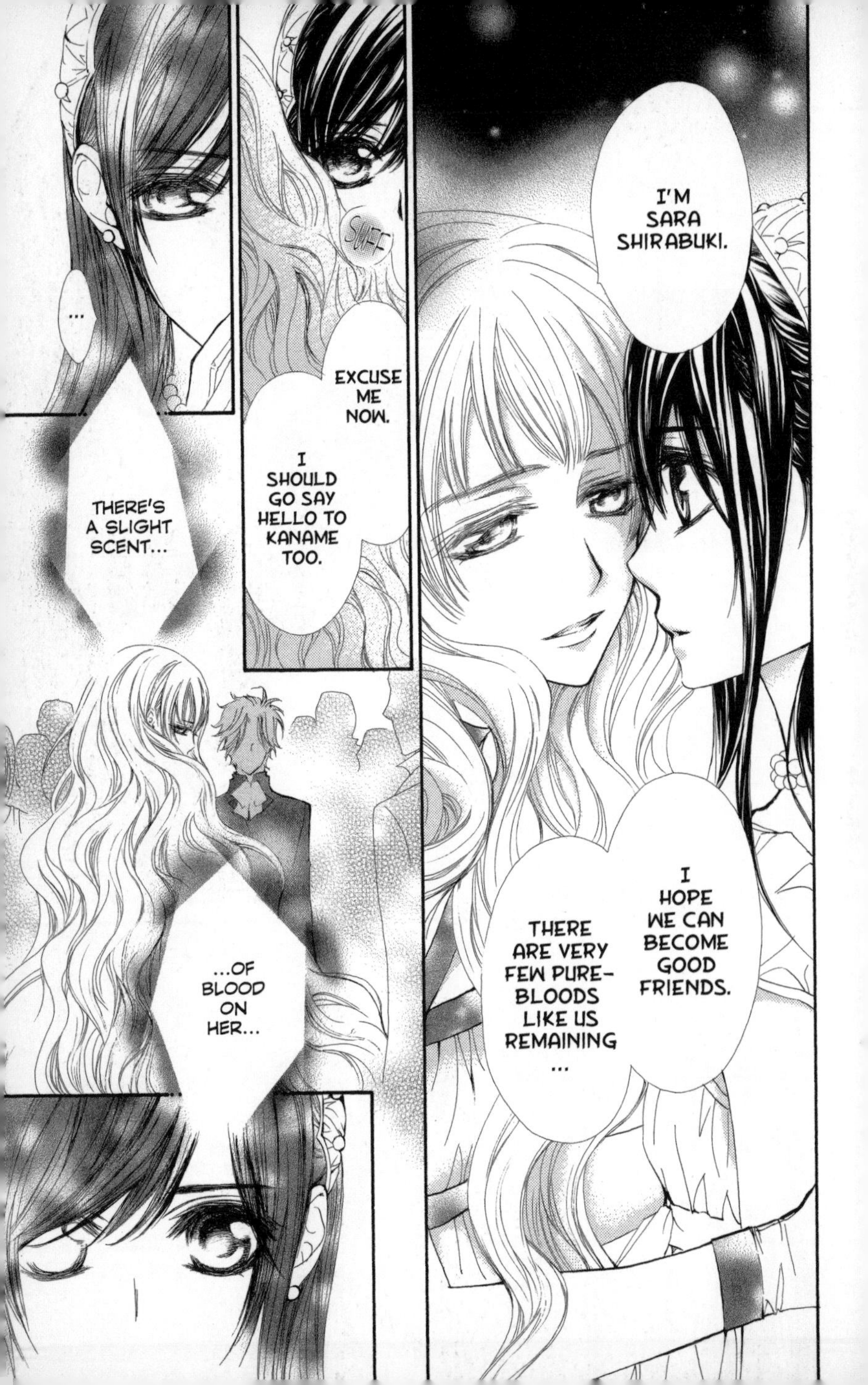
I'M SARA SHIRABUKI.
I HOPE WE CAN BECOME GOOD FRIENDS.
THERE ARE VERY FEW PURE-BLOODS LIKE US REMAINING ...
SNIFF
EXCUSE ME NOW.
I SHOULD GO SAY HELLO TO KANAME TOO.
...
THERE'S A SLIGHT SCENT...
...OF BLOOD ON HER...

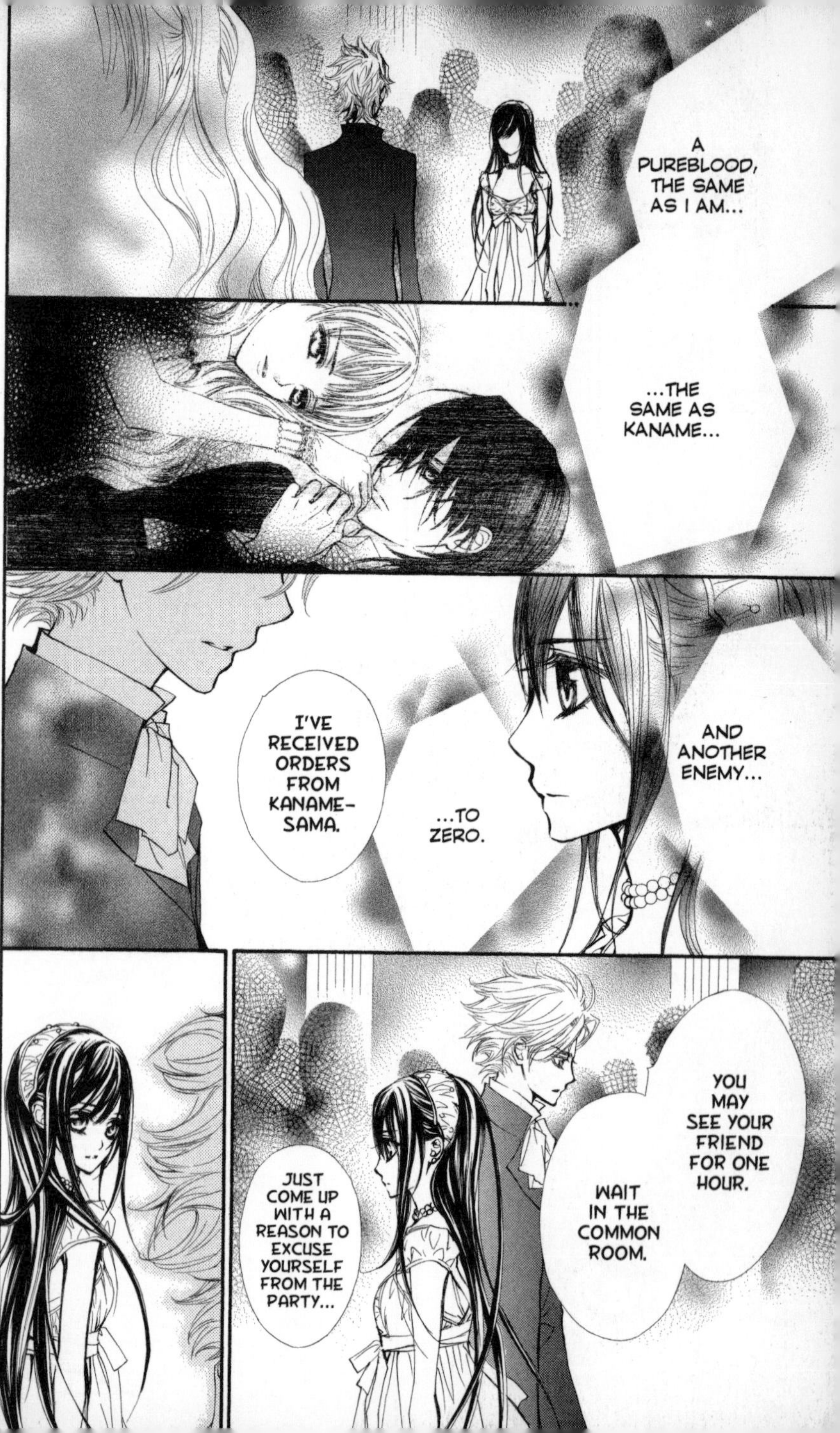
A PUREBLOOD, THE SAME AS I AM...
...THE SAME AS KANAME...
AND ANOTHER ENEMY...
...TO ZERO.
I'VE RECEIVED ORDERS FROM KANAME-SAMA.
YOU MAY SEE YOUR FRIEND FOR ONE HOUR.
WAIT IN THE COMMON ROOM.
JUST COME UP WITH A REASON TO EXCUSE YOURSELF FROM THE PARTY...

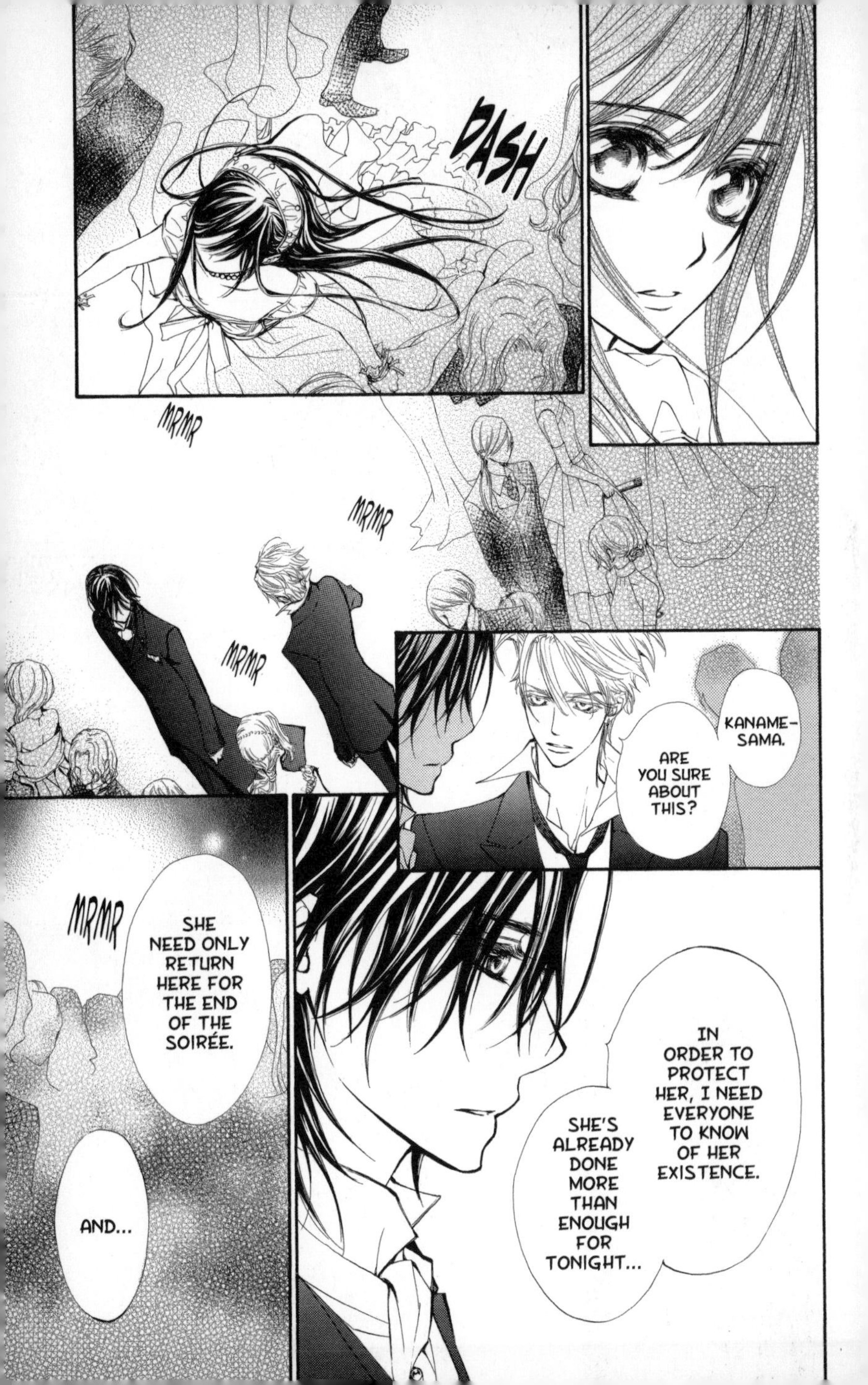
DASH
MRMR
MRMR
MRMR
KANAME-SAMA.
ARE YOU SURE ABOUT THIS?
IN ORDER TO PROTECT HER, I NEED EVERYONE TO KNOW OF HER EXISTENCE.
SHE'S ALREADY DONE MORE THAN ENOUGH FOR TONIGHT...
MRMR
SHE NEED ONLY RETURN HERE FOR THE END OF THE SOIRÉE.
AND...

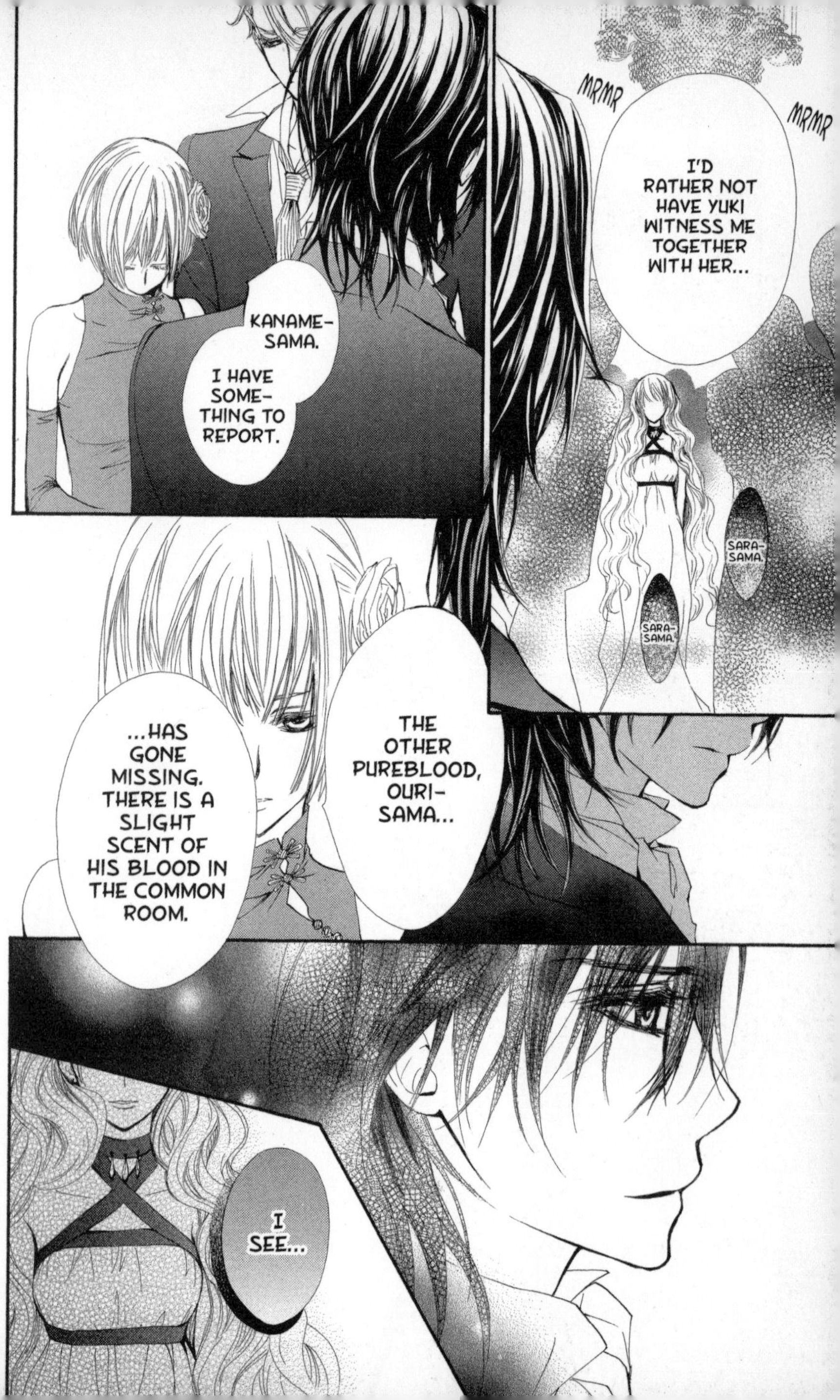
MRMR
MRMR
I'D RATHER NOT HAVE YUKI WITNESS ME TOGETHER WITH HER...
SARA-SAMA.
SARA-SAMA.
KANAME-SAMA.
I HAVE SOME-THING TO REPORT.
THE OTHER PUREBLOOD, OURI-SAMA...
...HAS GONE MISSING. THERE IS A SLIGHT SCENT OF HIS BLOOD IN THE COMMON ROOM.
I SEE...

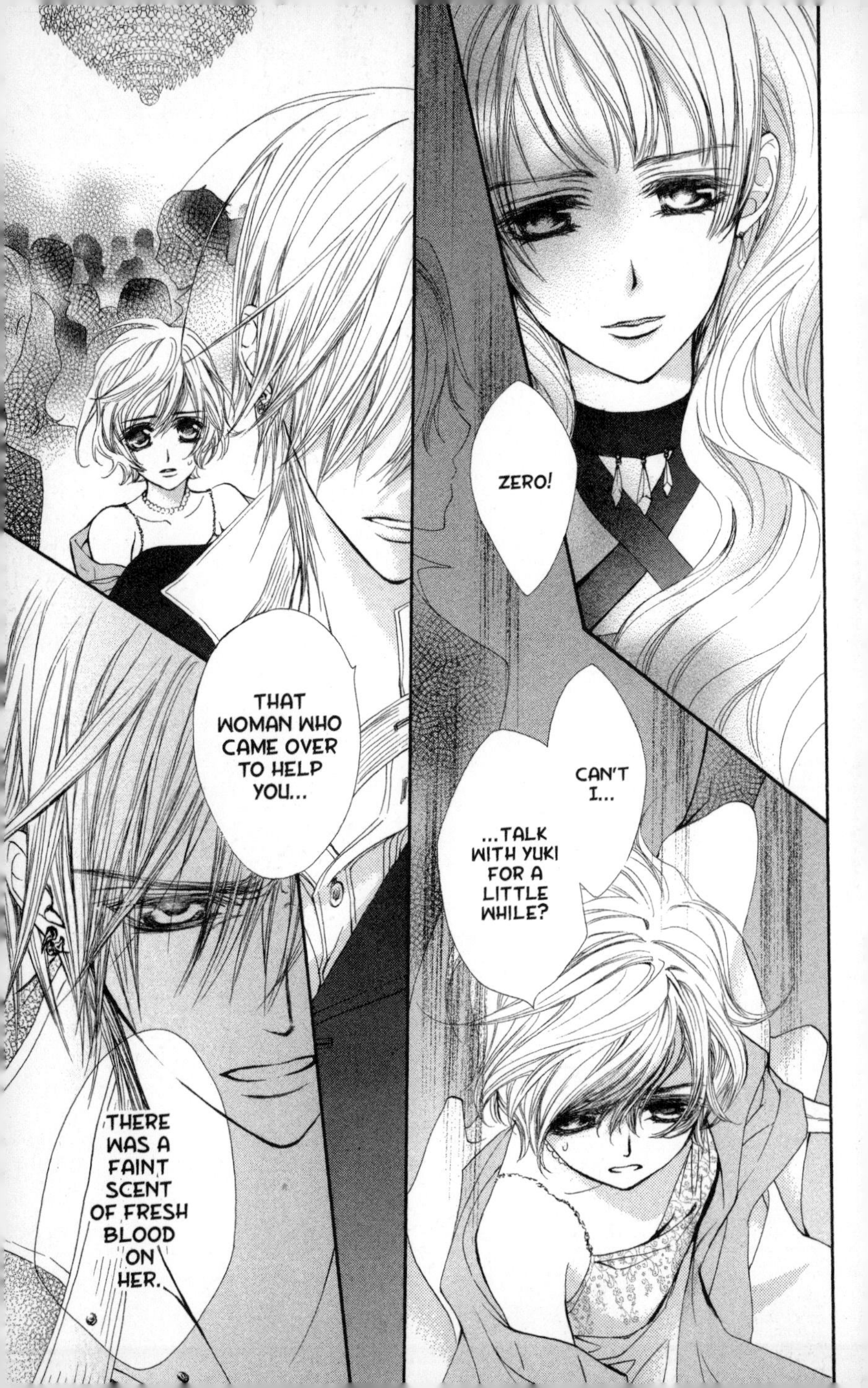
ZERO!
CAN'T I...
...TALK WITH YUKI FOR A LITTLE WHILE?
THAT WOMAN WHO CAME OVER TO HELP YOU...
THERE WAS A FAINT SCENT OF FRESH BLOOD ON HER.

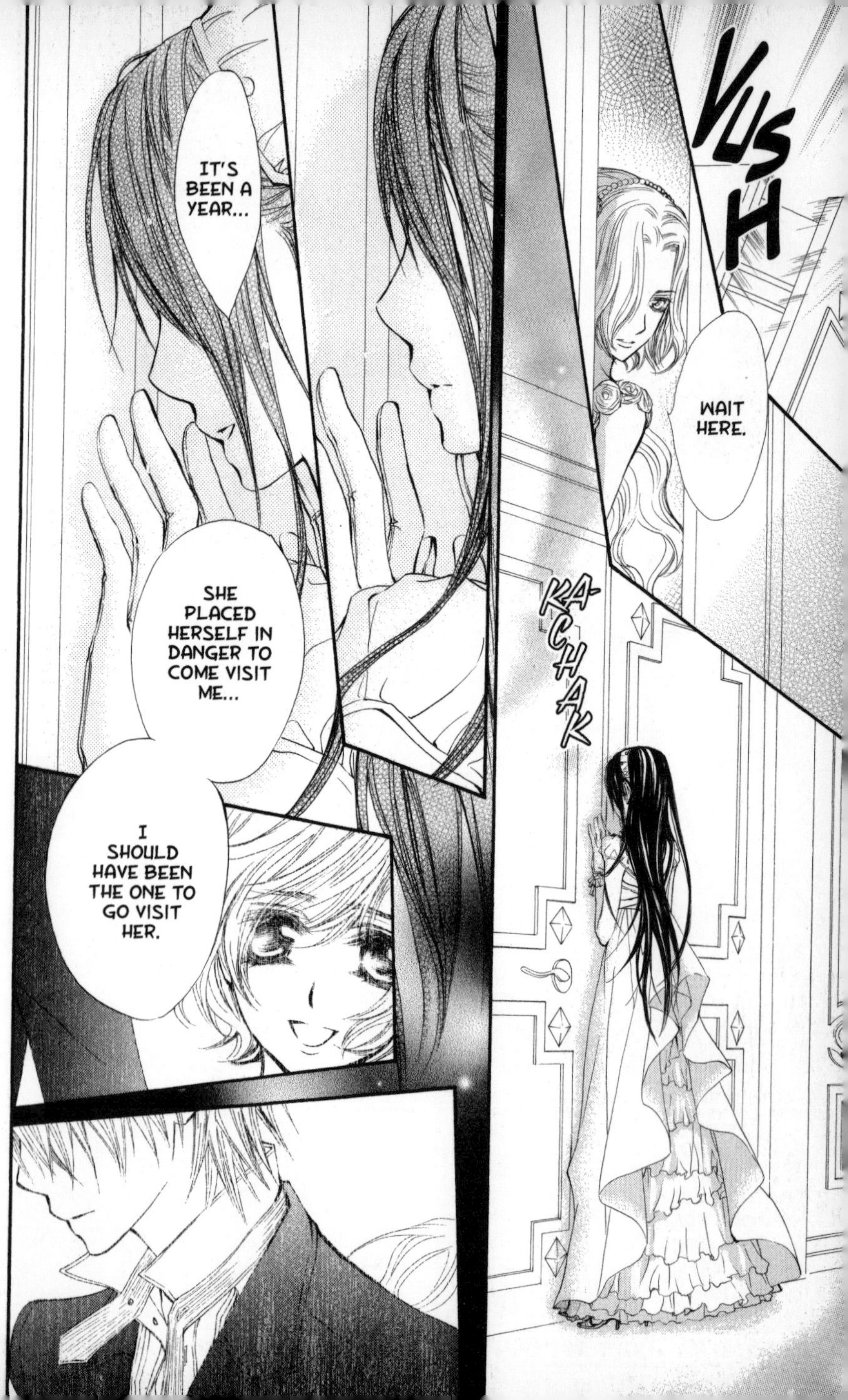
VUSH
WAIT HERE.
KA-CHAK
IT'S BEEN A YEAR...
SHE PLACED HERSELF IN DANGER TO COME VISIT ME...
I SHOULD HAVE BEEN THE ONE TO GO VISIT HER.

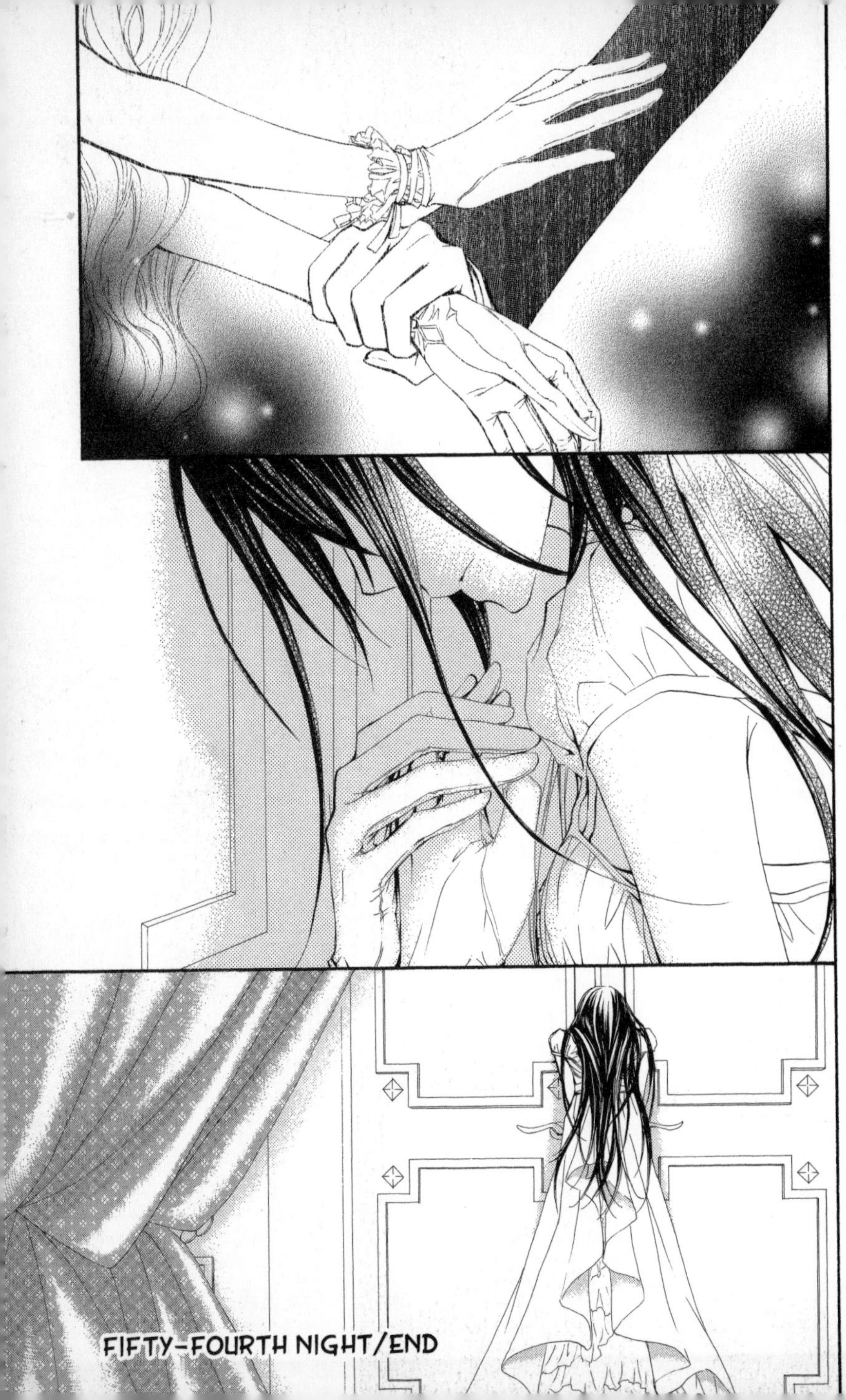
FIFTY-FOURTH NIGHT/END

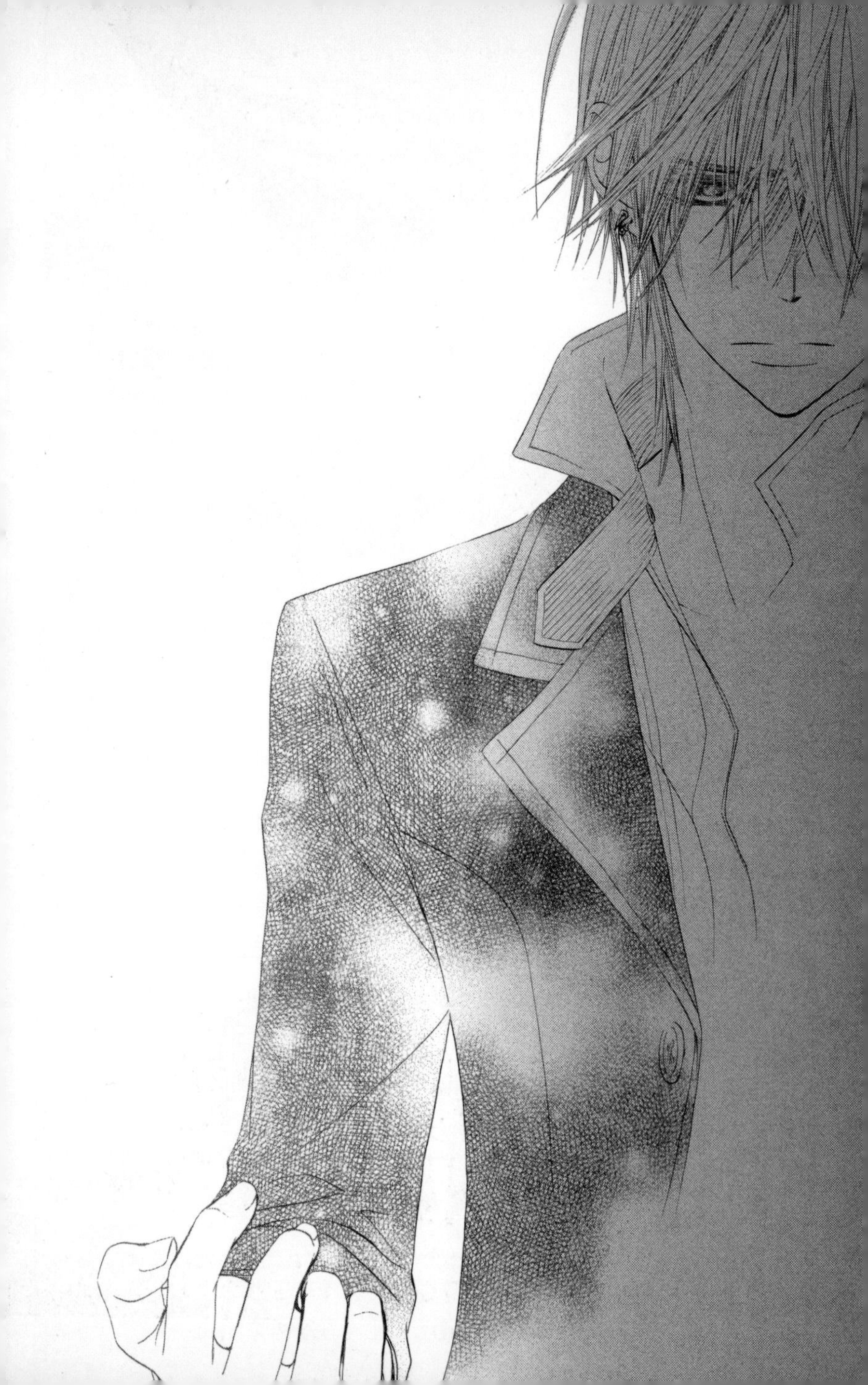

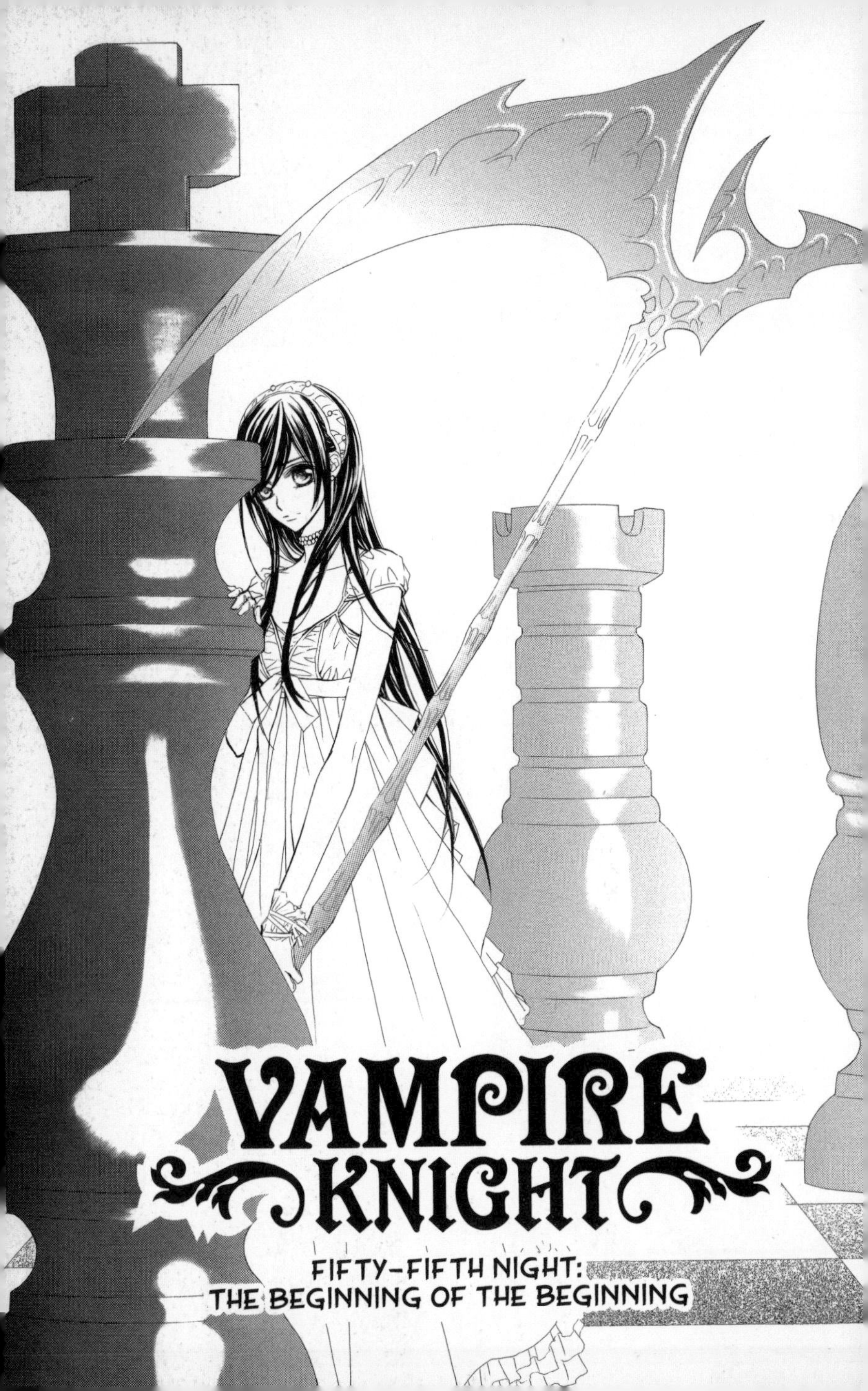
VAMPIRE KNIGHT
FIFTY-FIFTH NIGHT:
THE BEGINNING OF THE BEGINNING

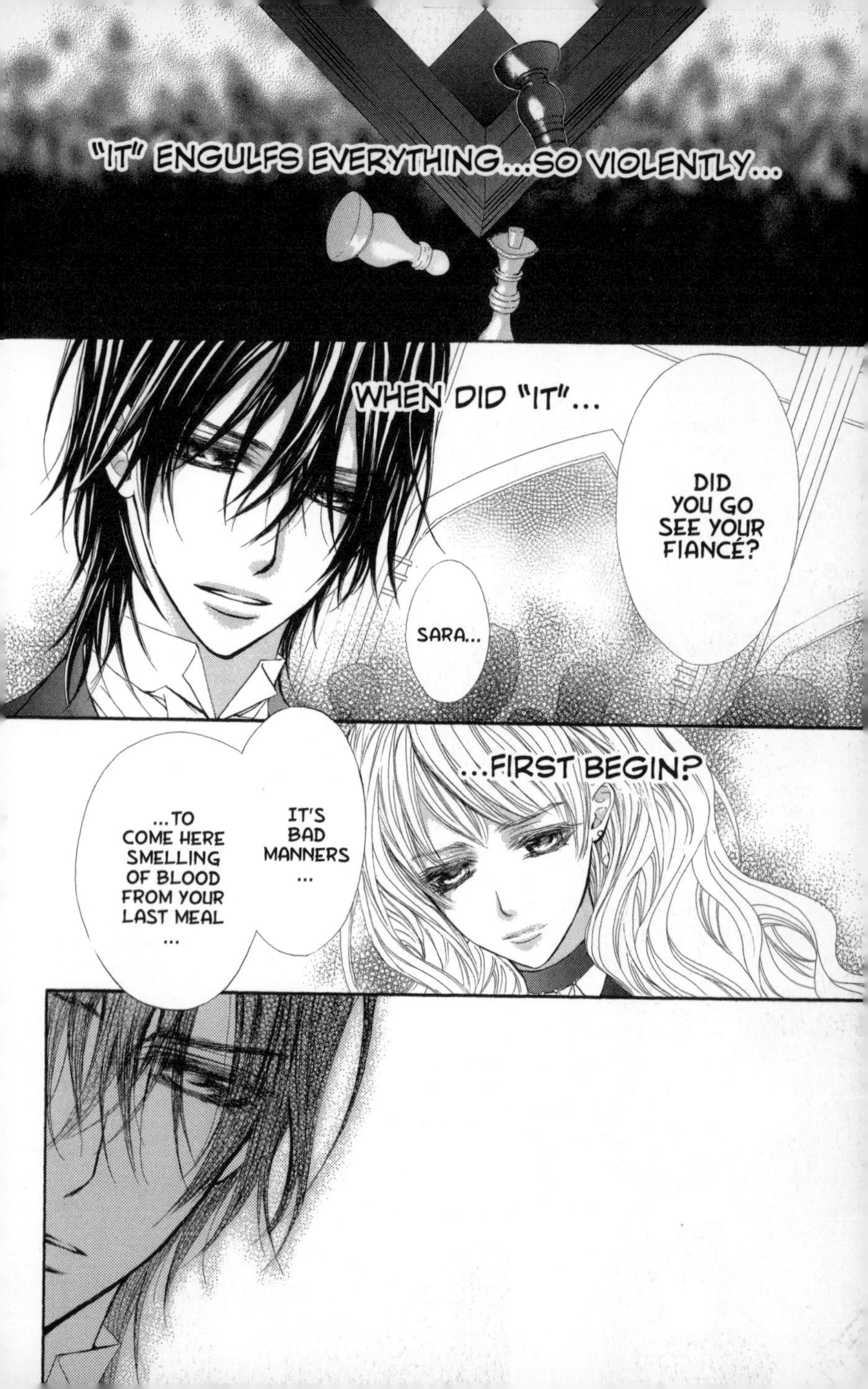
"IT" ENGULFS EVERYTHING...SO VIOLENTLY...
DID YOU GO SEE YOUR FIANCÉ?
WHEN DID "IT"...
SARA...
...FIRST BEGIN?
IT'S BAD MANNERS ...
...TO COME HERE SMELLING OF BLOOD FROM YOUR LAST MEAL ...

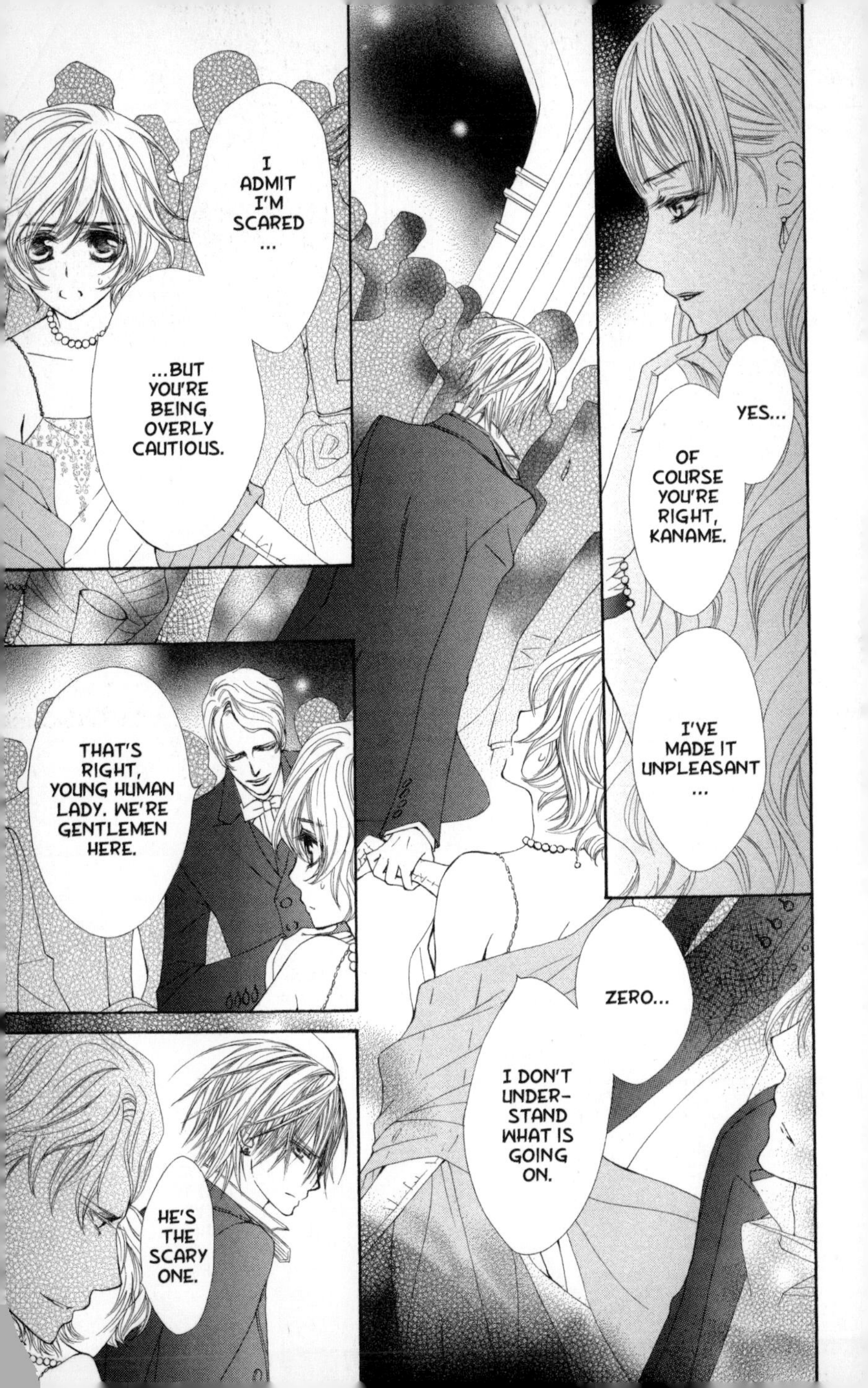
YES...
OF COURSE YOU'RE RIGHT, KANAME.
I'VE MADE IT UNPLEASANT...
I ADMIT I'M SCARED...
...BUT YOU'RE BEING OVERLY CAUTIOUS.
THAT'S RIGHT, YOUNG HUMAN LADY. WE'RE GENTLEMEN HERE.
ZERO...
I DON'T UNDER-STAND WHAT IS GOING ON.
HE'S THE SCARY ONE.

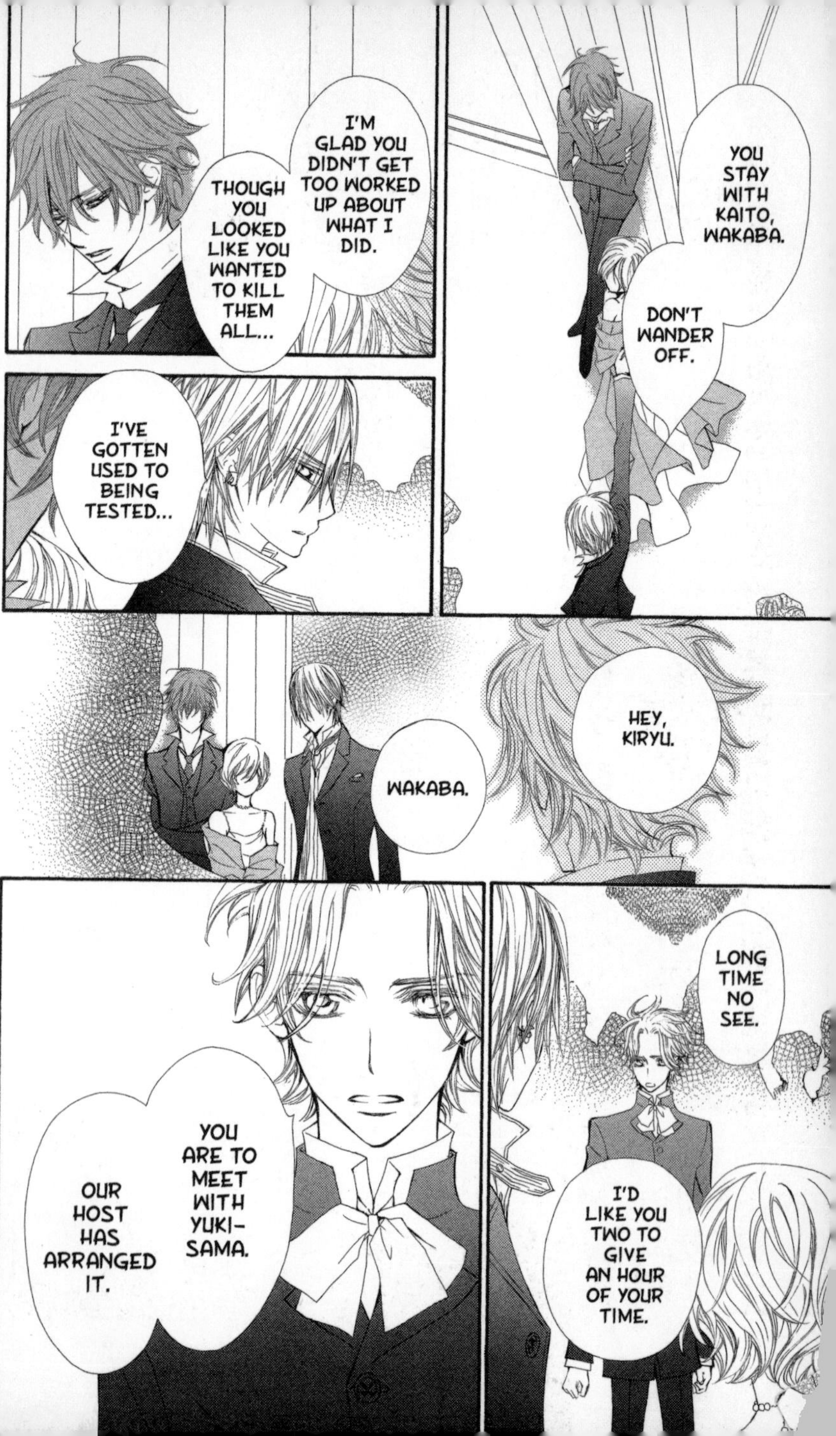
YOU STAY WITH KAITO, WAKABA.
DON'T WANDER OFF.
I'M GLAD YOU DIDN'T GET TOO WORKED UP ABOUT WHAT I DID.
THOUGH YOU LOOKED LIKE YOU WANTED TO KILL THEM ALL...
I'VE GOTTEN USED TO BEING TESTED...
HEY, KIRYU.
WAKABA.
LONG TIME NO SEE.
I'D LIKE YOU TWO TO GIVE AN HOUR OF YOUR TIME.
YOU ARE TO MEET WITH YUKI-SAMA.
OUR HOST HAS ARRANGED IT.

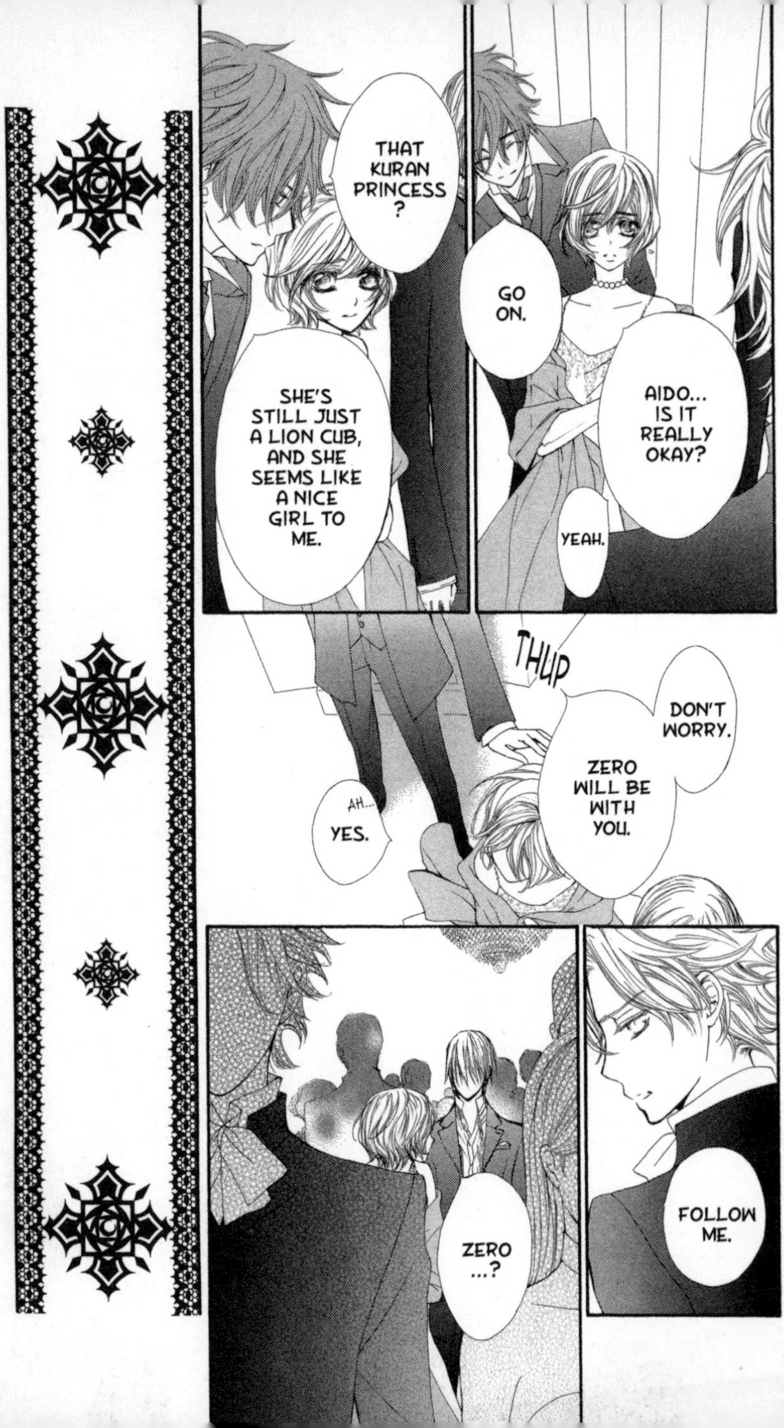
GO ON.
AIDO... IS IT REALLY OKAY?
YEAH.
THAT KURAN PRINCESS?
SHE'S STILL JUST A LION CUB, AND SHE SEEMS LIKE A NICE GIRL TO ME.
THUP
DON'T WORRY.
ZERO WILL BE WITH YOU.
AH... YES.
FOLLOW ME.
ZERO ...?

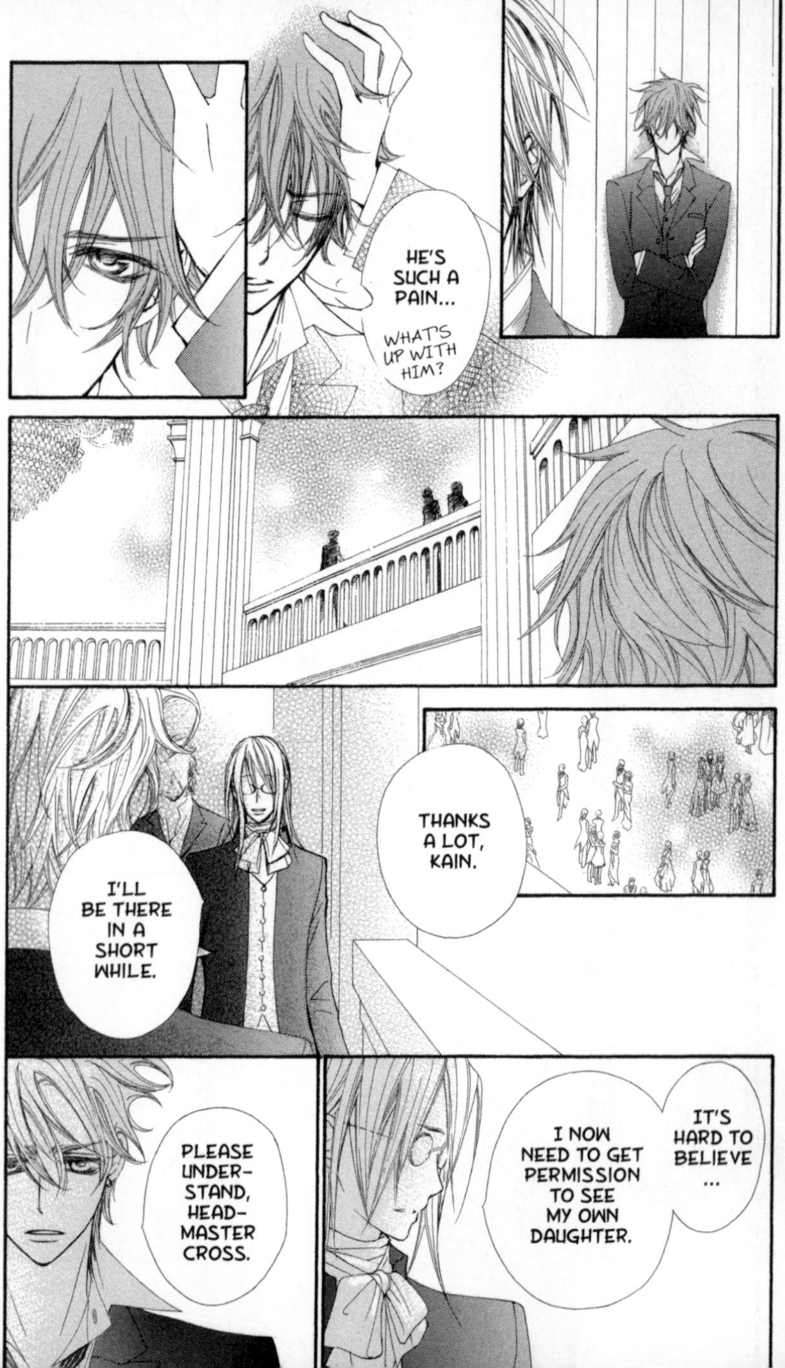
HE'S SUCH A PAIN...
WHAT'S UP WITH HIM?
THANKS A LOT, KAIN.
I'LL BE THERE IN A SHORT WHILE.
IT'S HARD TO BELIEVE ...
I NOW NEED TO GET PERMISSION TO SEE MY OWN DAUGHTER.
PLEASE UNDER-STAND, HEAD-MASTER CROSS.

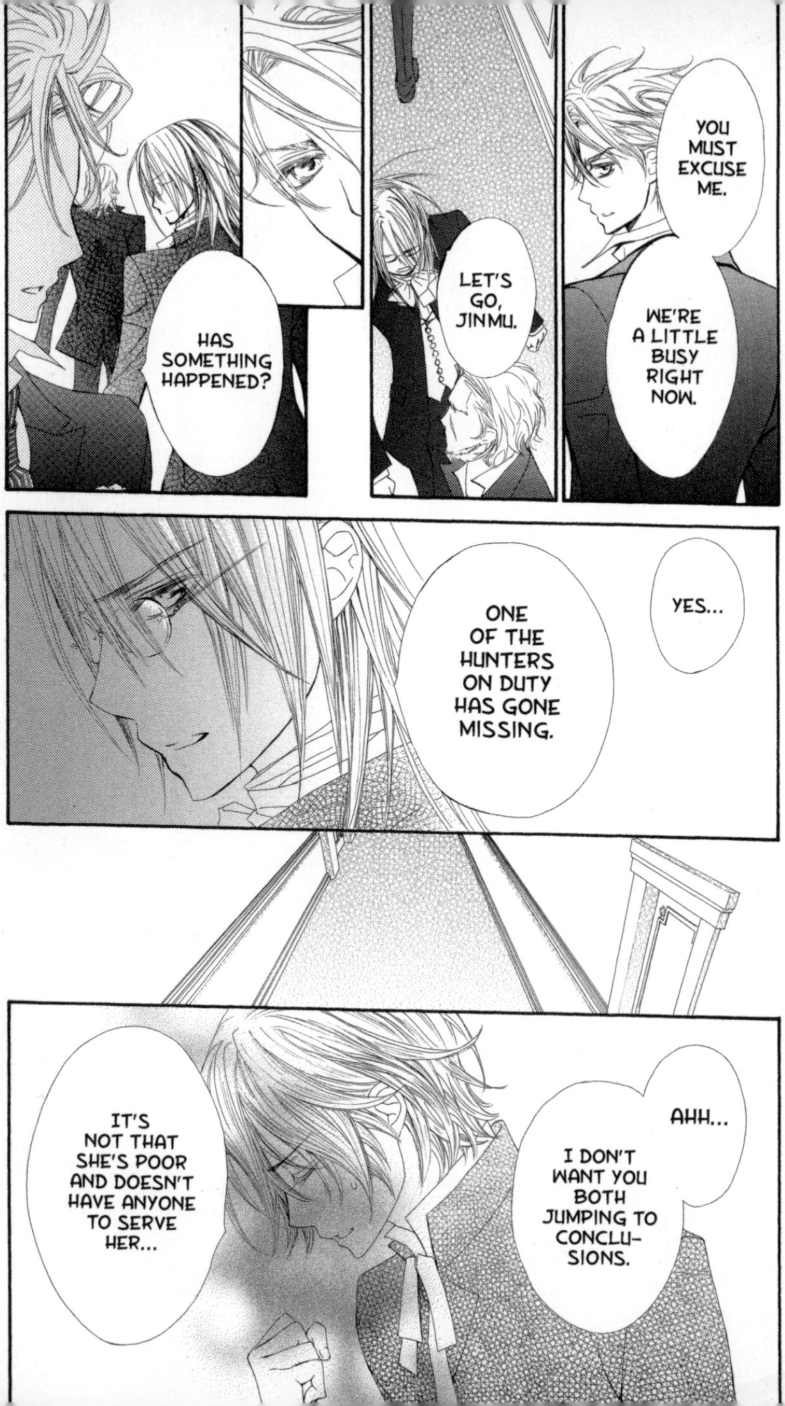
YOU MUST EXCUSE ME.
WE'RE A LITTLE BUSY RIGHT NOW.
LET'S GO, JINMU.
HAS SOMETHING HAPPENED?
YES...
ONE OF THE HUNTERS ON DUTY HAS GONE MISSING.
AHH...
I DON'T WANT YOU BOTH JUMPING TO CONCLU-SIONS.
IT'S NOT THAT SHE'S POOR AND DOESN'T HAVE ANYONE TO SERVE HER...

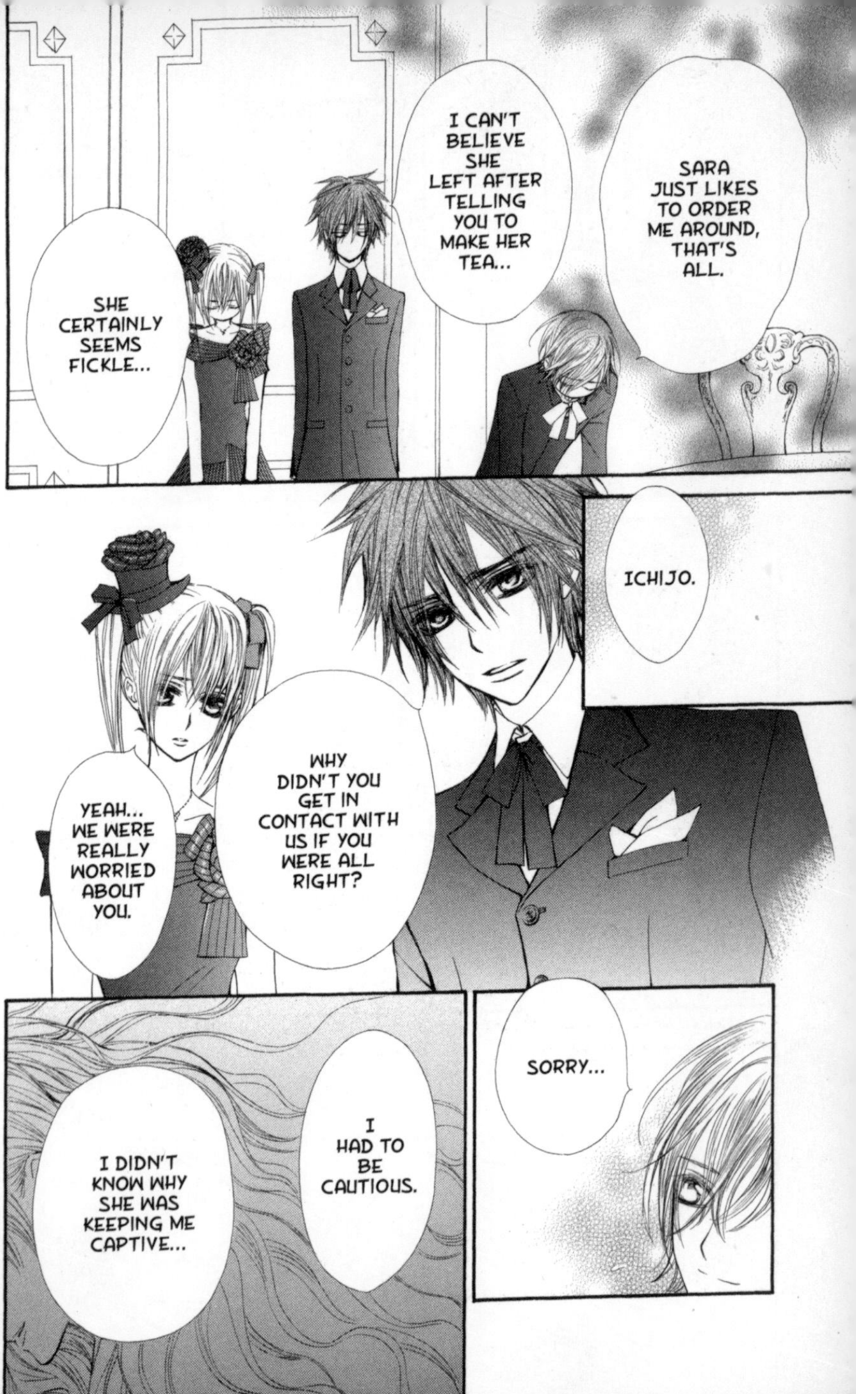
SARA JUST LIKES TO ORDER ME AROUND, THAT'S ALL.
I CAN'T BELIEVE SHE LEFT AFTER TELLING YOU TO MAKE HER TEA...
SHE CERTAINLY SEEMS FICKLE...
ICHIJO.
WHY DIDN'T YOU GET IN CONTACT WITH US IF YOU WERE ALL RIGHT?
YEAH... WE WERE REALLY WORRIED ABOUT YOU.
SORRY...
I HAD TO BE CAUTIOUS.
I DIDN'T KNOW WHY SHE WAS KEEPING ME CAPTIVE...

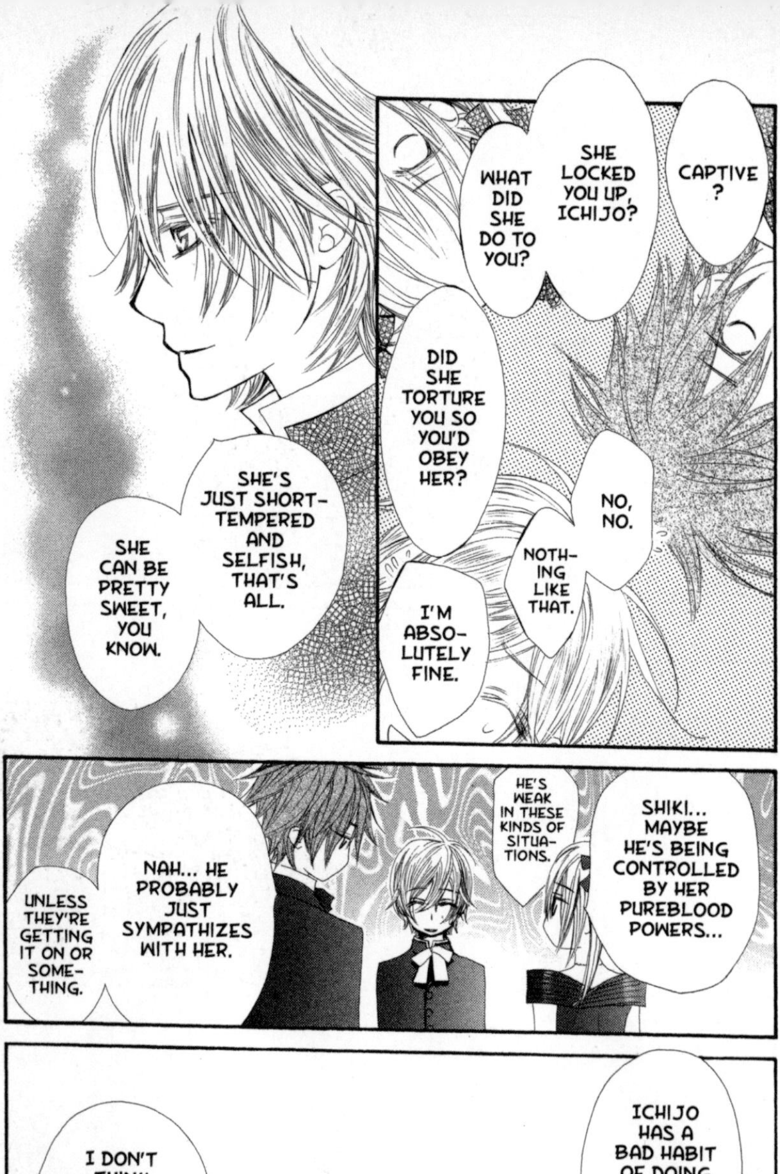
CAPTIVE?
SHE LOCKED YOU UP, ICHIJO?
WHAT DID SHE DO TO YOU?
DID SHE TORTURE YOU SO YOU'D OBEY HER?
NO, NO.
NOTHING LIKE THAT.
I'M ABSOLUTELY FINE.
SHE'S JUST SHORT-TEMPERED AND SELFISH, THAT'S ALL.
SHE CAN BE PRETTY SWEET, YOU KNOW.
SHIKI... MAYBE HE'S BEING CONTROLLED BY HER PUREBLOOD POWERS...
HE'S WEAK IN THESE KINDS OF SITUATIONS.
NAH... HE PROBABLY JUST SYMPATHIZES WITH HER.
UNLESS THEY'RE GETTING IT ON OR SOMETHING.
ICHIJO HAS A BAD HABIT OF DOING THIS...
I DON'T THINK IT'S BAD...

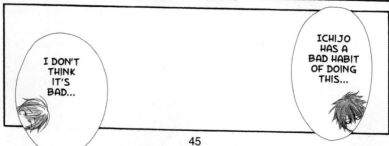

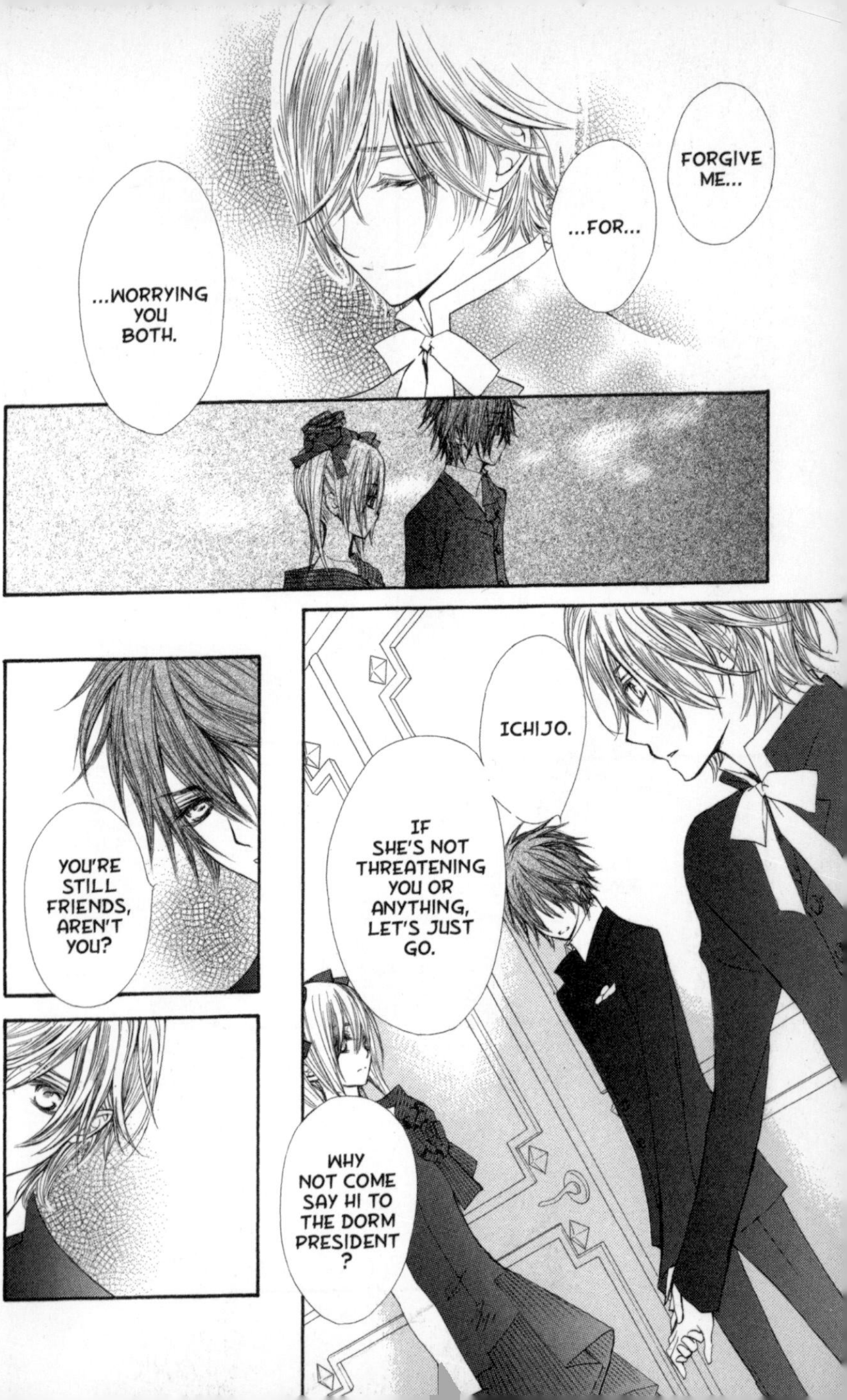
FORGIVE ME...
...FOR...
...WORRYING YOU BOTH.
ICHIJO.
IF SHE'S NOT THREATENING YOU OR ANYTHING, LET'S JUST GO.
WHY NOT COME SAY HI TO THE DORM PRESIDENT?
YOU'RE STILL FRIENDS, AREN'T YOU?

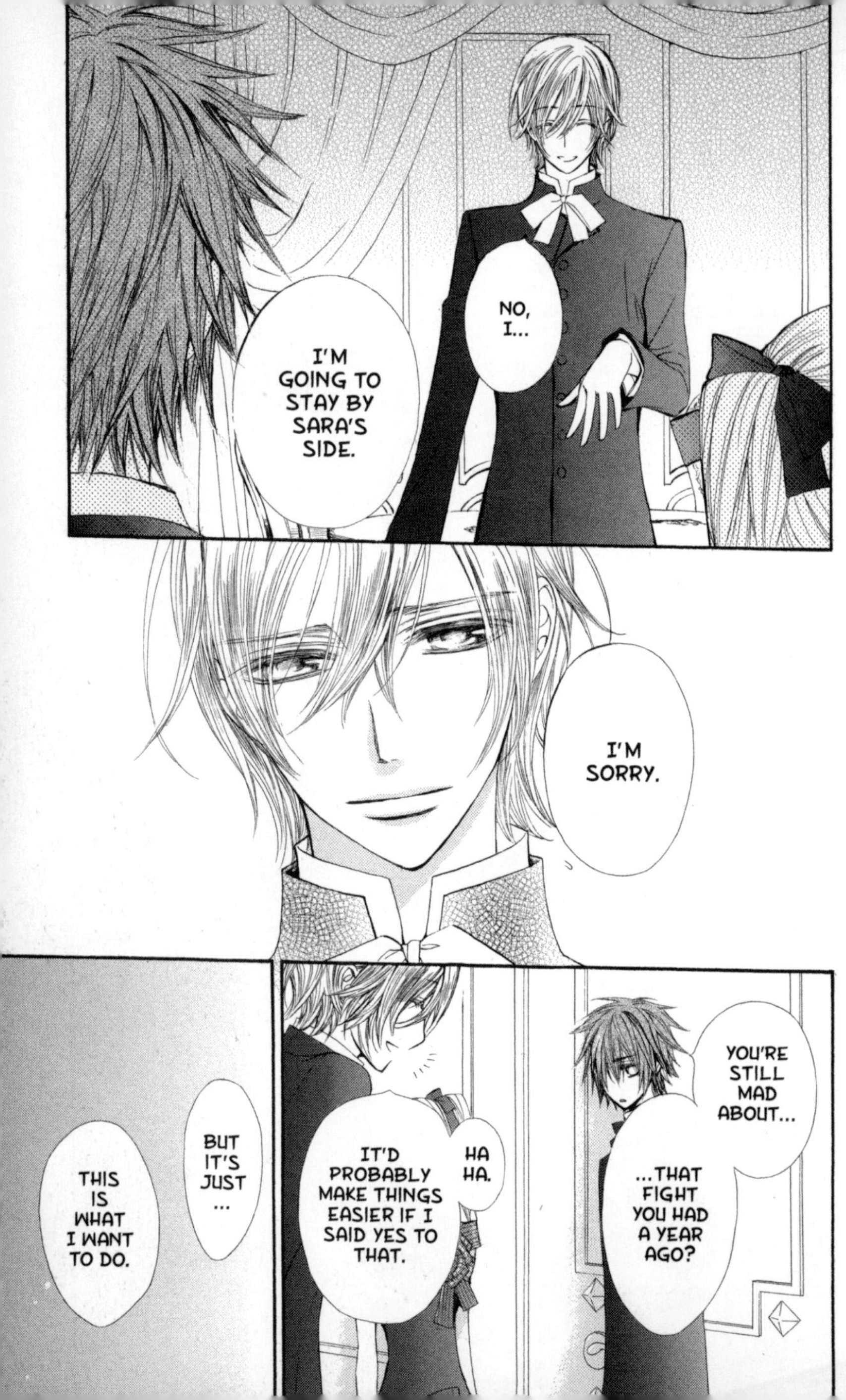
NO, I...
I'M GOING TO STAY BY SARA'S SIDE.
I'M SORRY.
YOU'RE STILL MAD ABOUT...
...THAT FIGHT YOU HAD A YEAR AGO?
HA HA.
IT'D PROBABLY MAKE THINGS EASIER IF I SAID YES TO THAT.
BUT IT'S JUST ...
THIS IS WHAT I WANT TO DO.

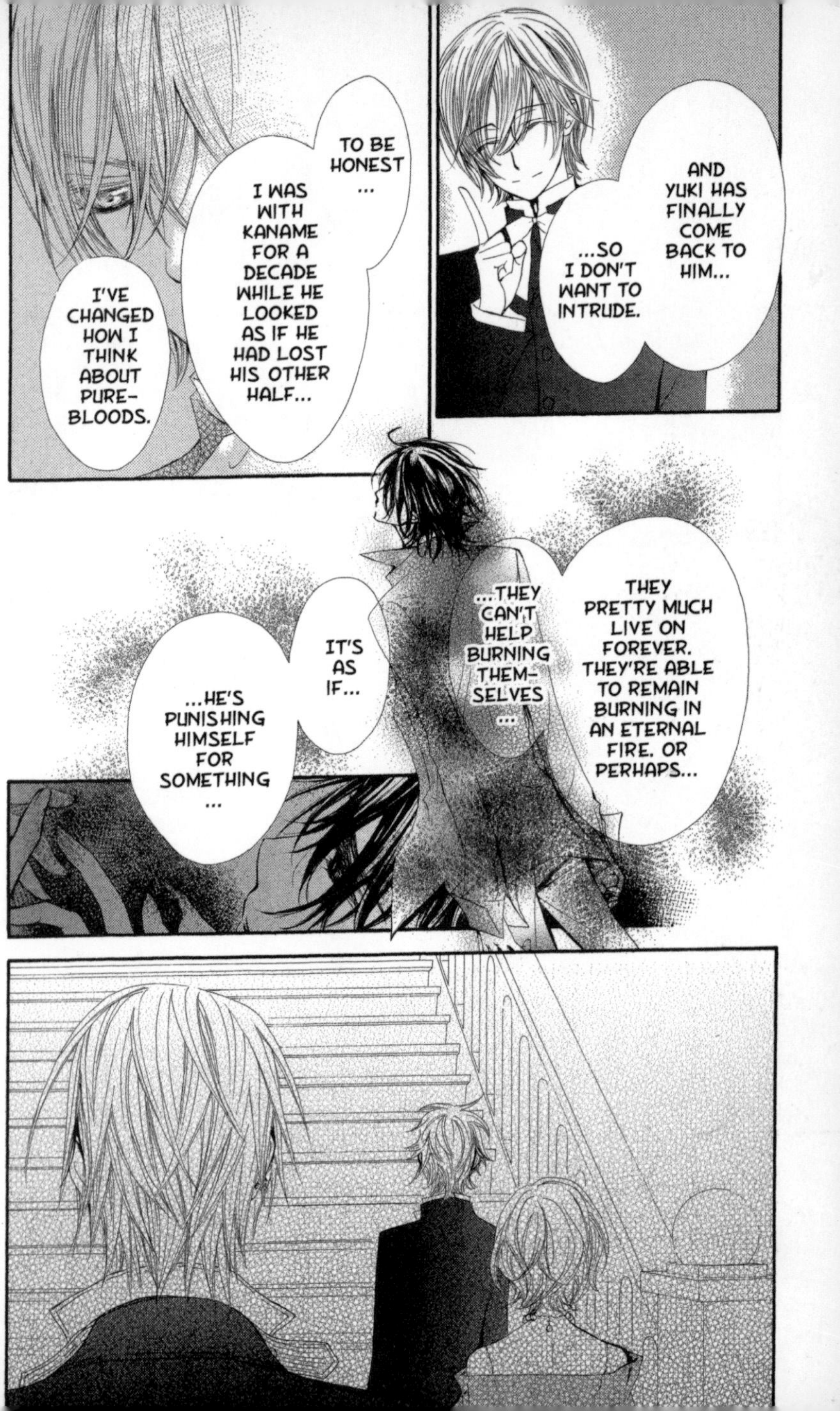
AND YUKI HAS FINALLY COME BACK TO HIM...
...SO I DON'T WANT TO INTRUDE.
TO BE HONEST...
I WAS WITH KANAME FOR A DECADE WHILE HE LOOKED AS IF HE HAD LOST HIS OTHER HALF...
I'VE CHANGED HOW I THINK ABOUT PURE-BLOODS.
THEY PRETTY MUCH LIVE ON FOREVER. THEY'RE ABLE TO REMAIN BURNING IN AN ETERNAL FIRE. OR PERHAPS...
...THEY CAN'T HELP BURNING THEM-SELVES...
IT'S AS IF...
...HE'S PUNISHING HIMSELF FOR SOMETHING...

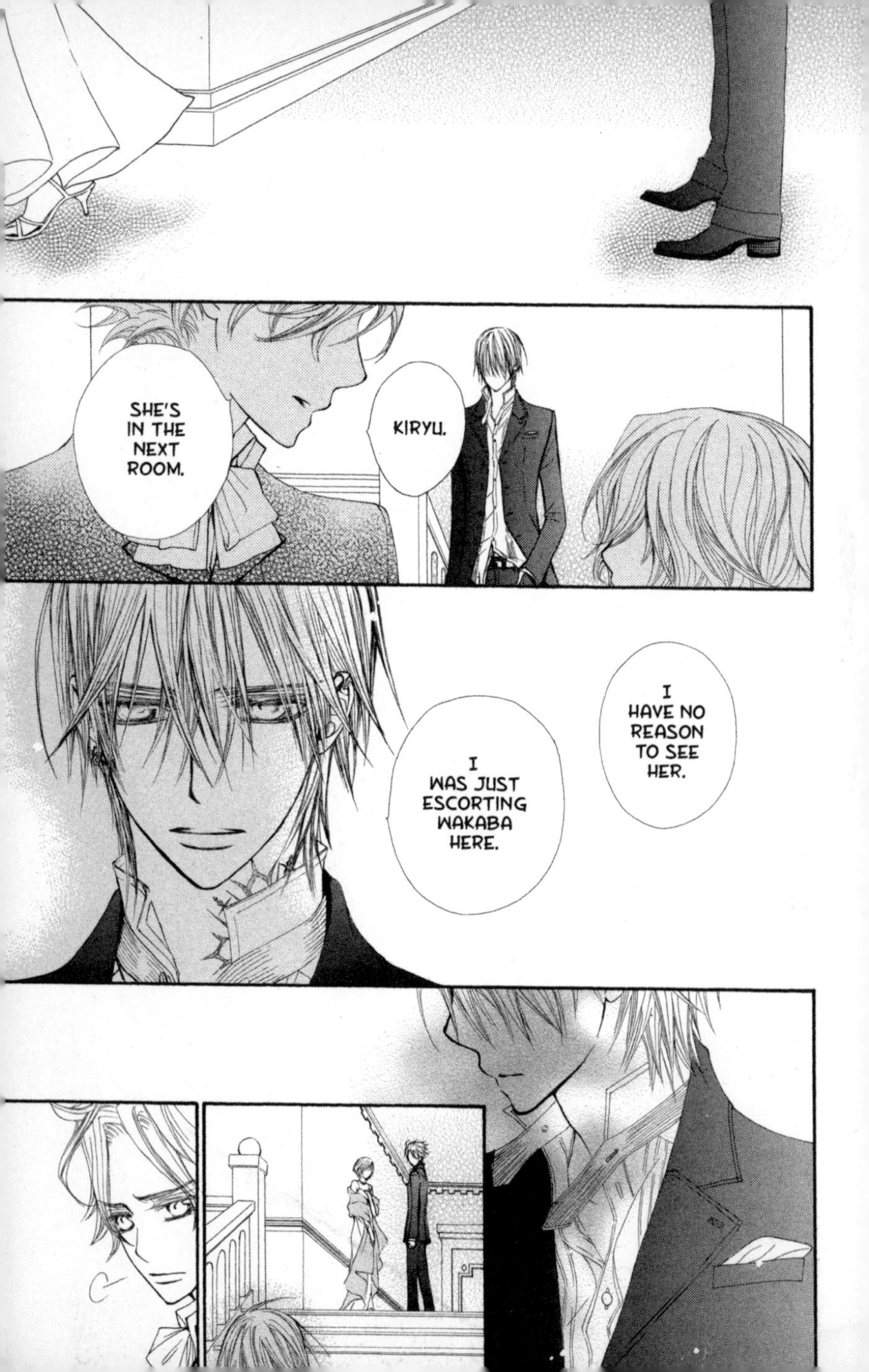
KIRYU.
SHE'S IN THE NEXT ROOM.
I HAVE NO REASON TO SEE HER.
I WAS JUST ESCORTING WAKABA HERE.

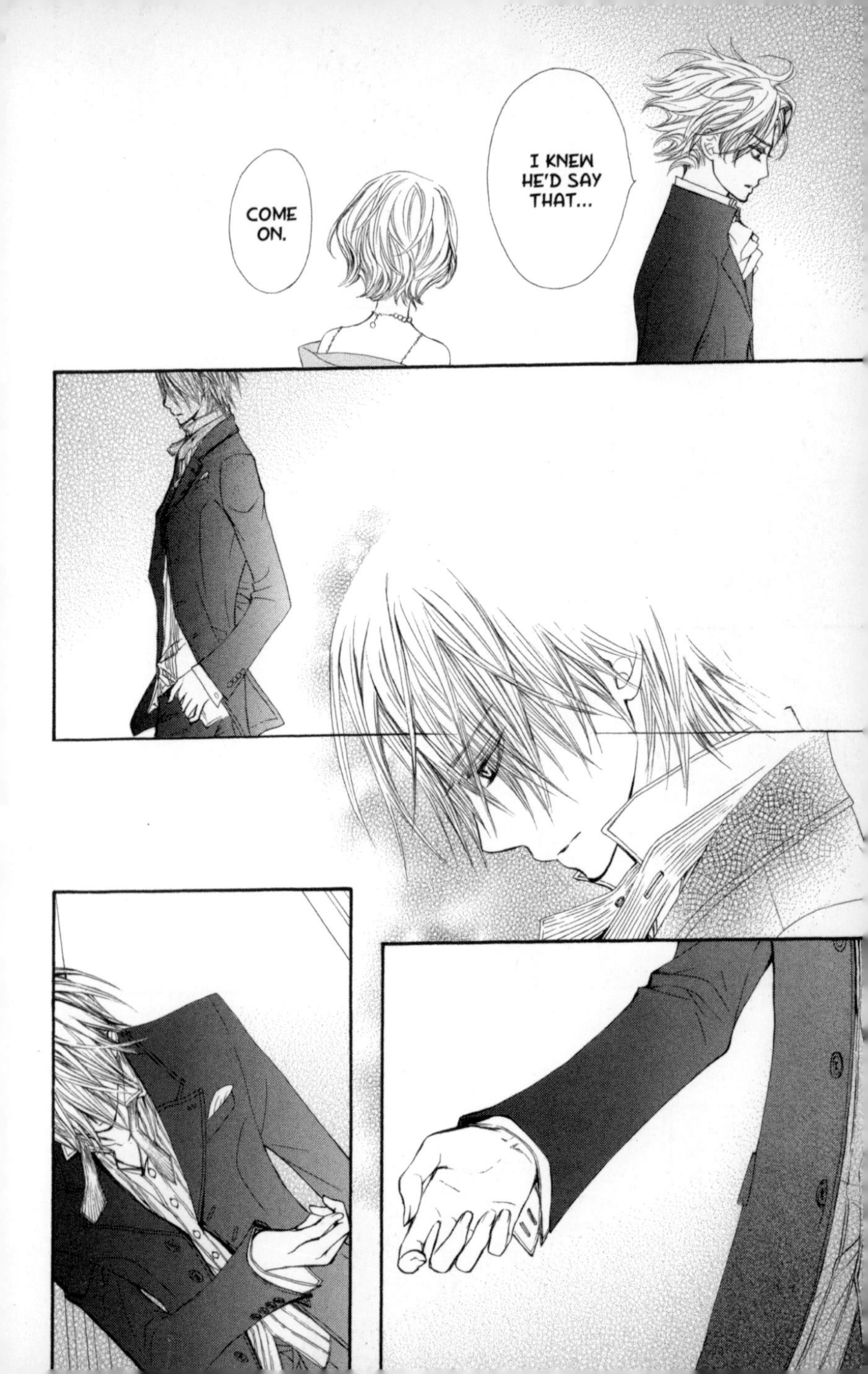
I KNEW HE'D SAY THAT...
COME ON.

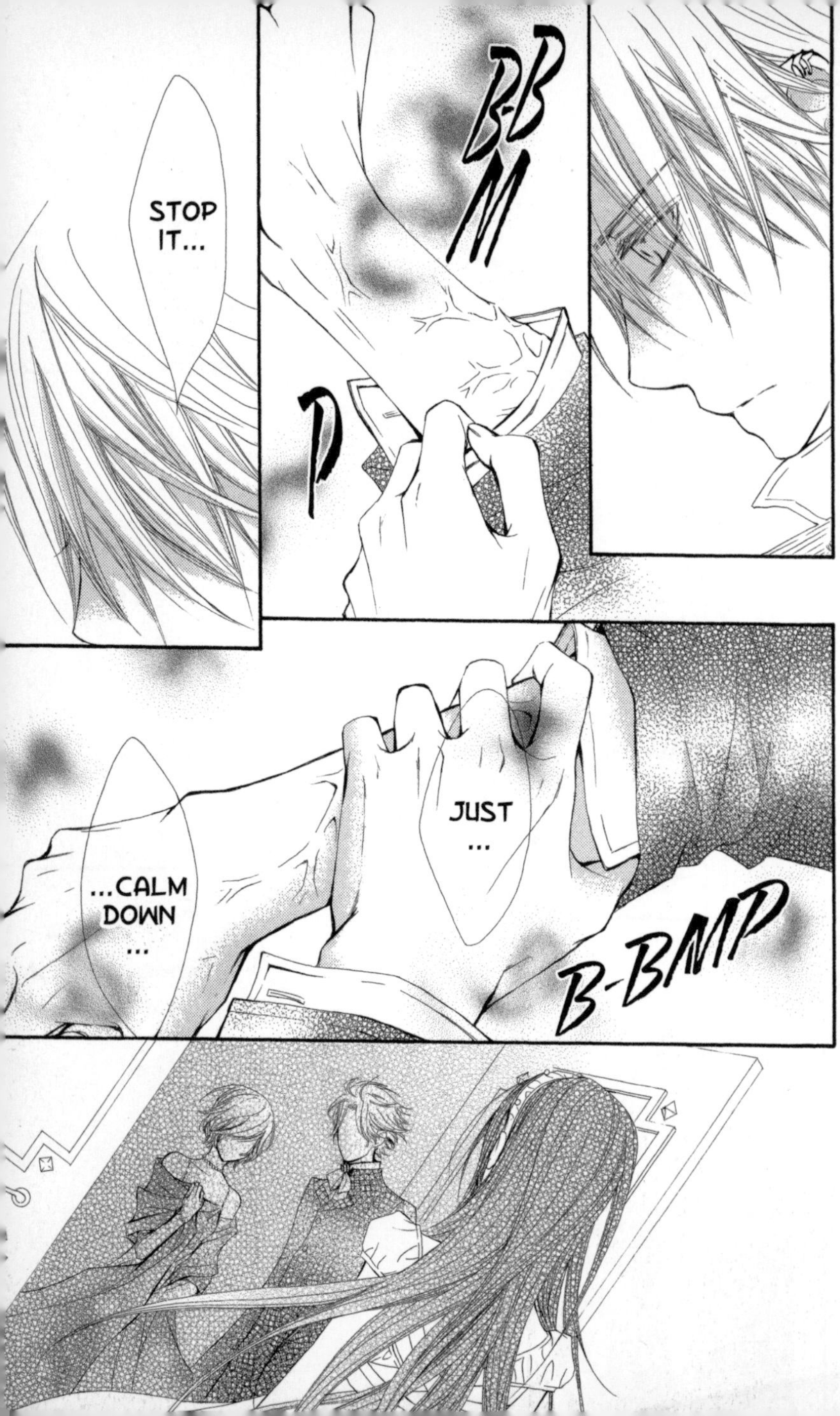

B-BM
P
STOP IT...
JUST ...
...CALM DOWN ...
B-BMP

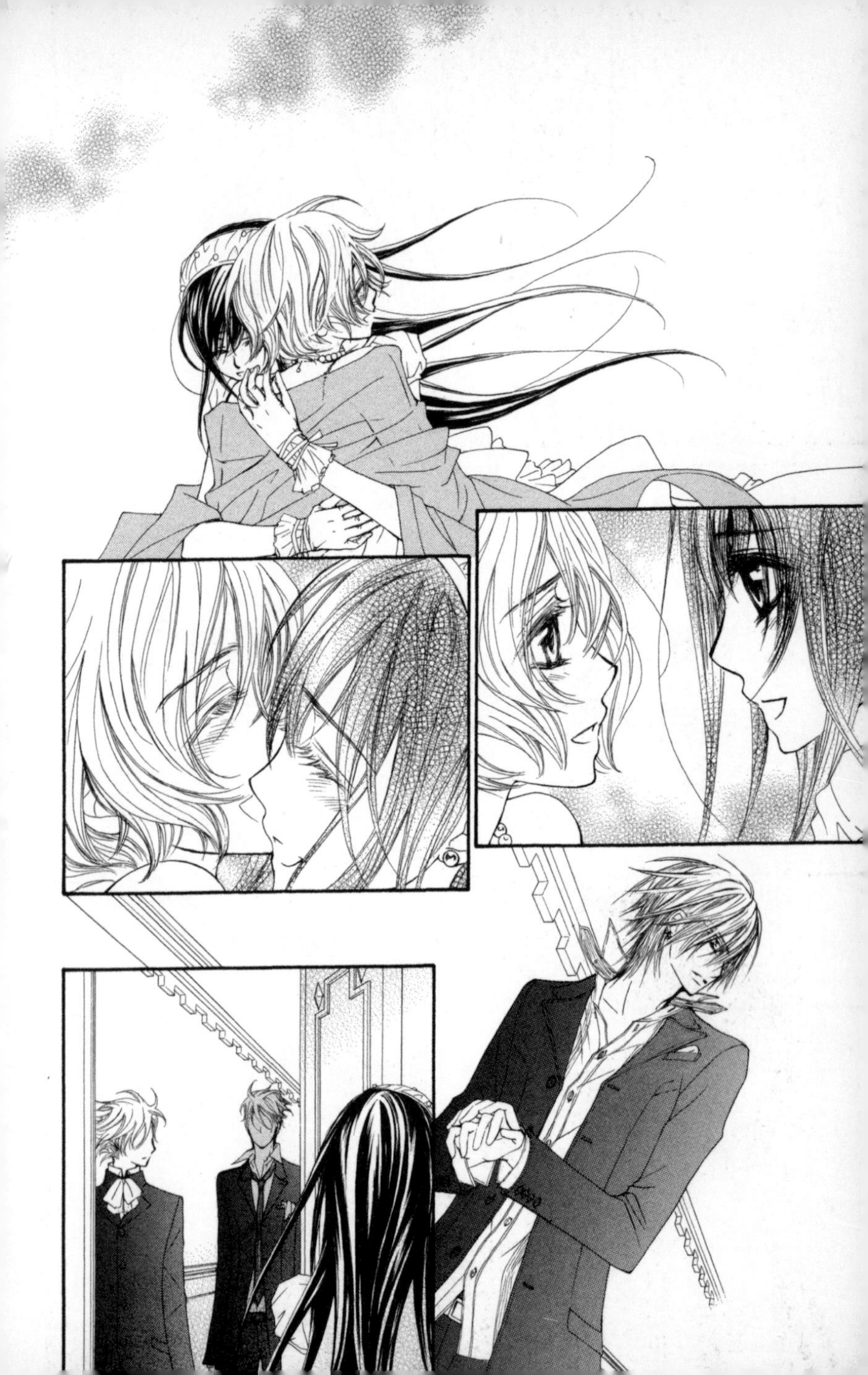

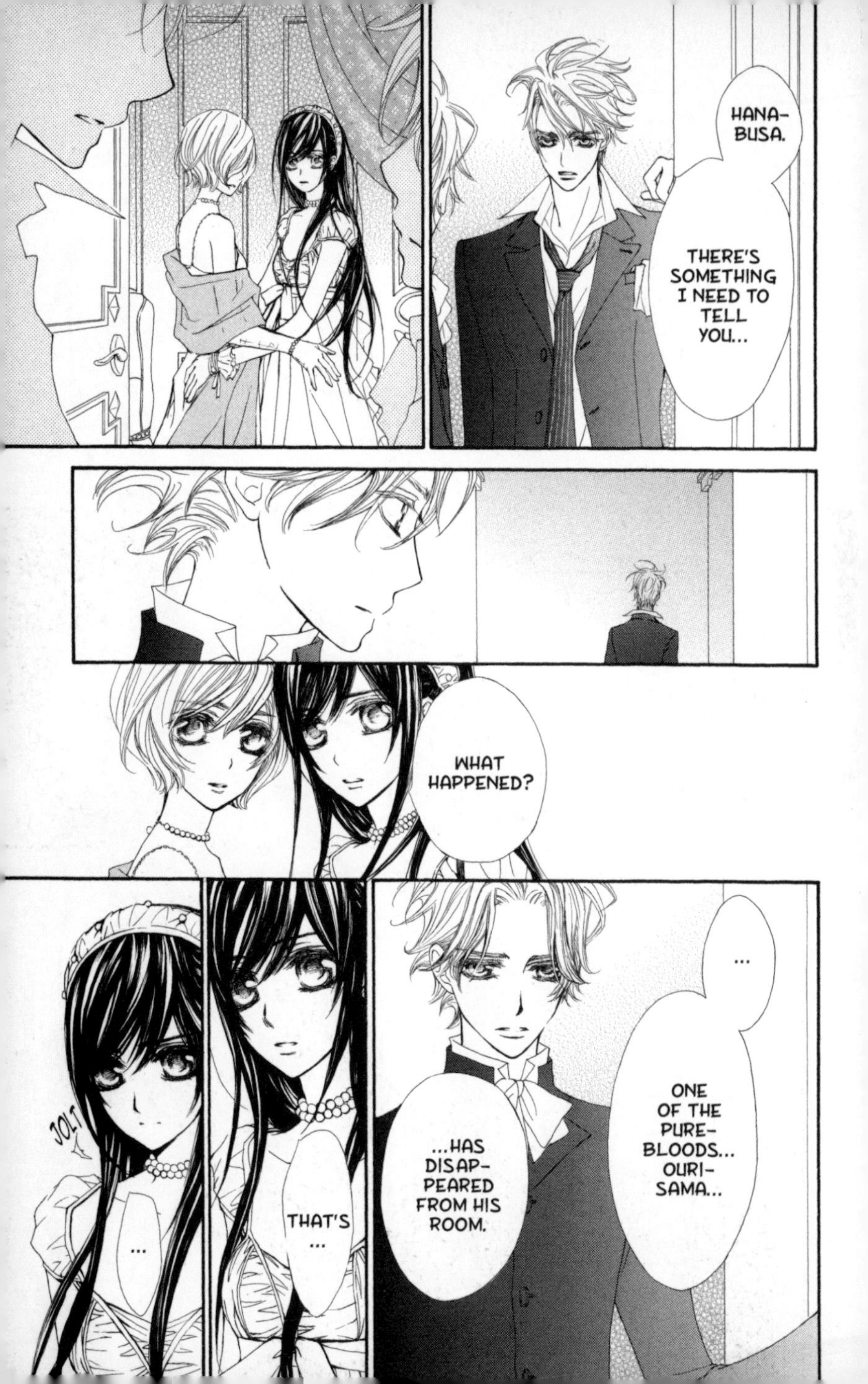
HANA-BUSA.
THERE'S SOMETHING I NEED TO TELL YOU...
WHAT HAPPENED?
...
ONE OF THE PURE-BLOODS... OURI-SAMA...
...HAS DISAP-PEARED FROM HIS ROOM.
THAT'S ...
JOLT
...

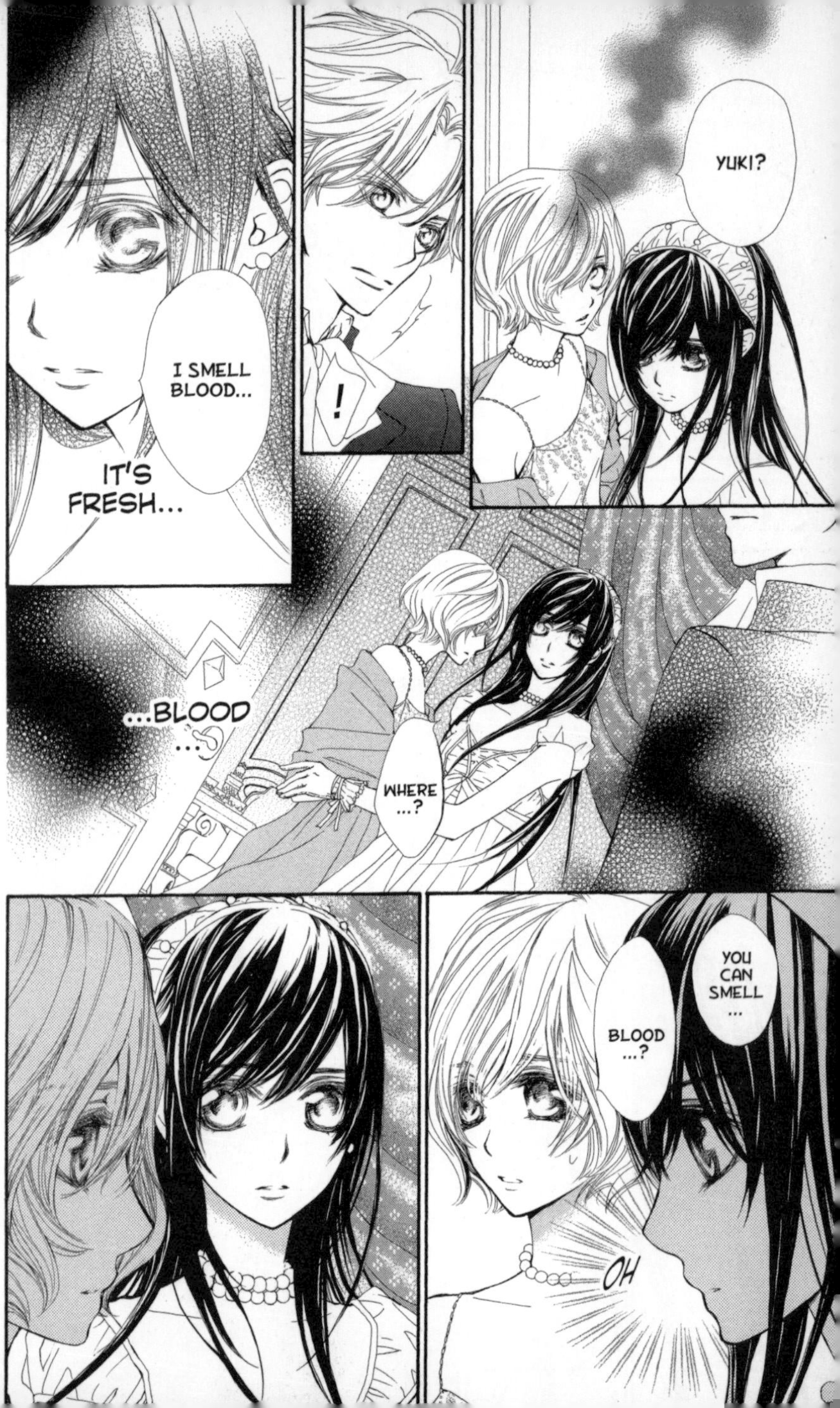
YUKI?
!
I SMELL BLOOD...
IT'S FRESH...
...BLOOD ...
WHERE ...?
YOU CAN SMELL ...
BLOOD ...?
OH

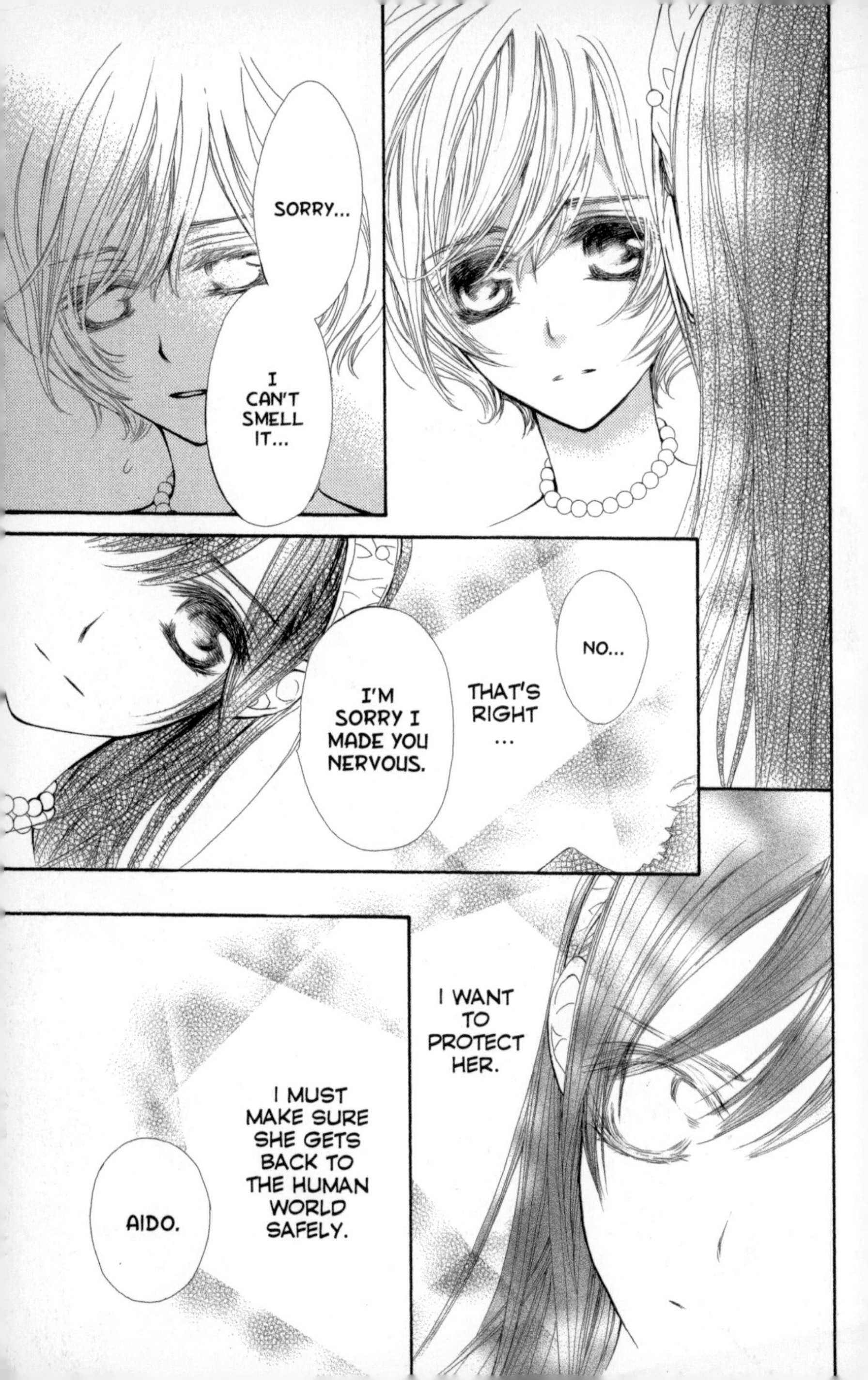
SORRY...
I CAN'T SMELL IT...
NO...
THAT'S RIGHT ...
I'M SORRY I MADE YOU NERVOUS.
I WANT TO PROTECT HER.
I MUST MAKE SURE SHE GETS BACK TO THE HUMAN WORLD SAFELY.
AIDO.

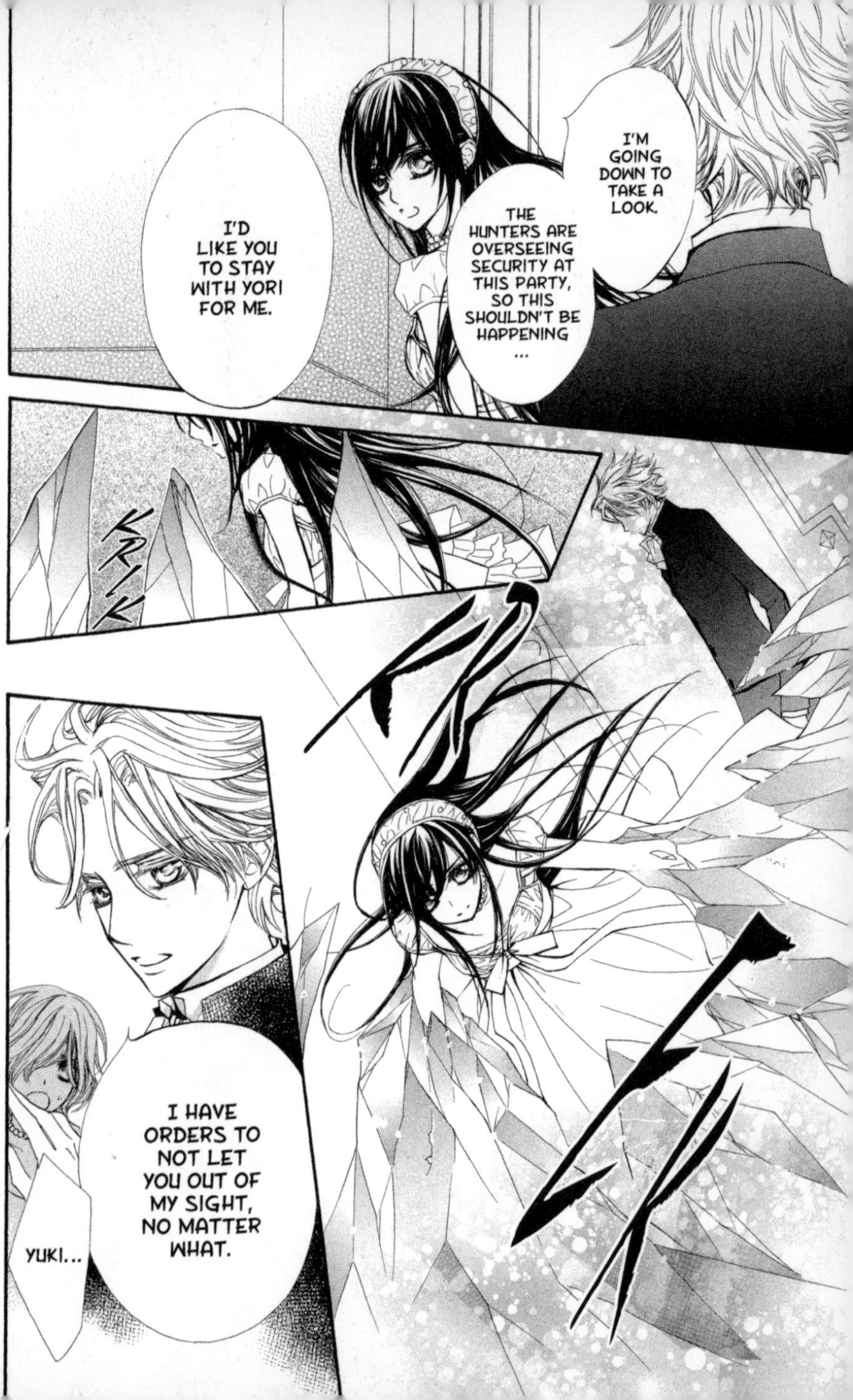
I'M GOING DOWN TO TAKE A LOOK.
THE HUNTERS ARE OVERSEEING SECURITY AT THIS PARTY, SO THIS SHOULDN'T BE HAPPENING ...
I'D LIKE YOU TO STAY WITH YORI FOR ME.
KRIK
I HAVE ORDERS TO NOT LET YOU OUT OF MY SIGHT, NO MATTER WHAT.
YUKI...

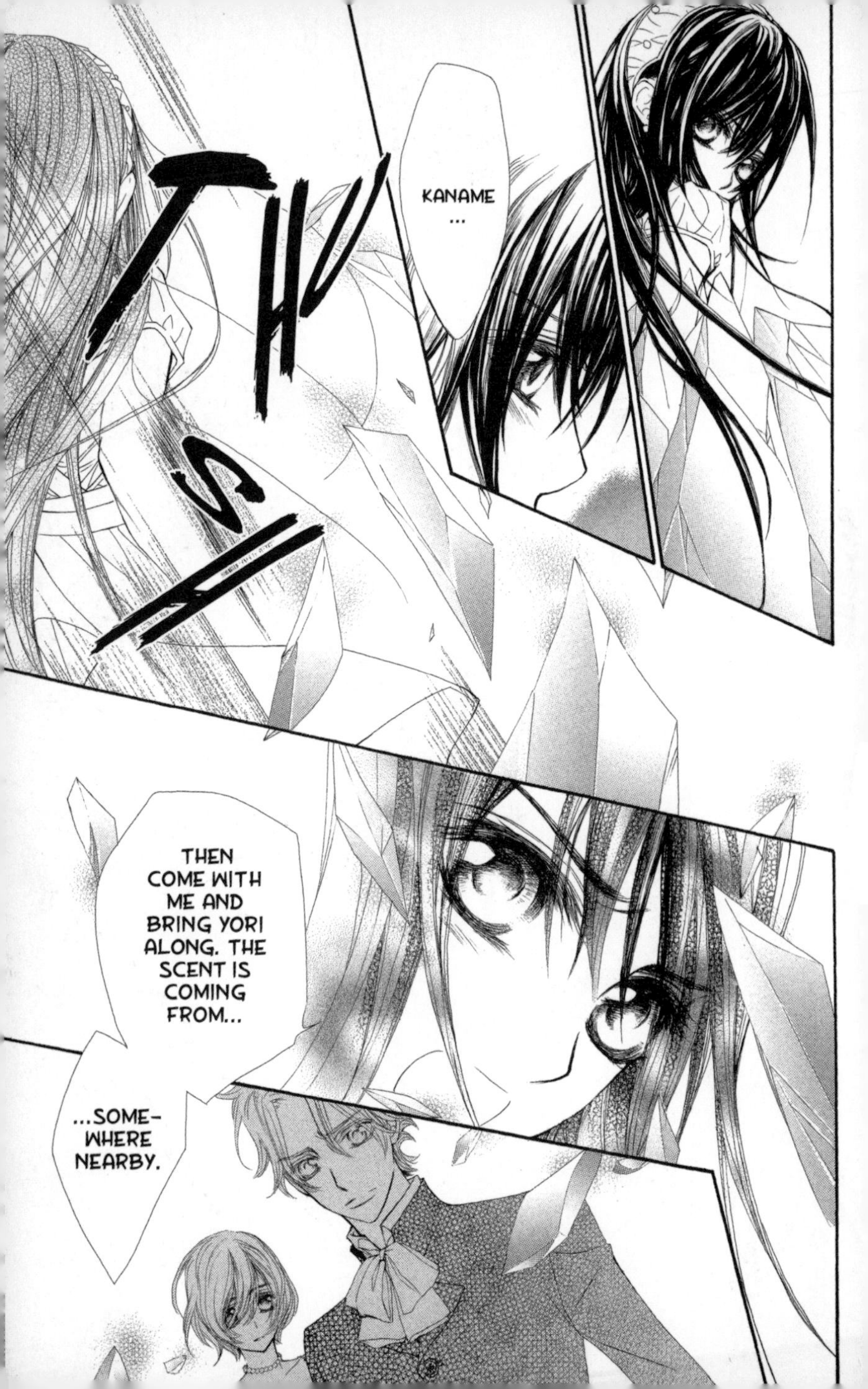
KANAME ...
THWSH
THEN COME WITH ME AND BRING YORI ALONG. THE SCENT IS COMING FROM...
...SOME-WHERE NEARBY.

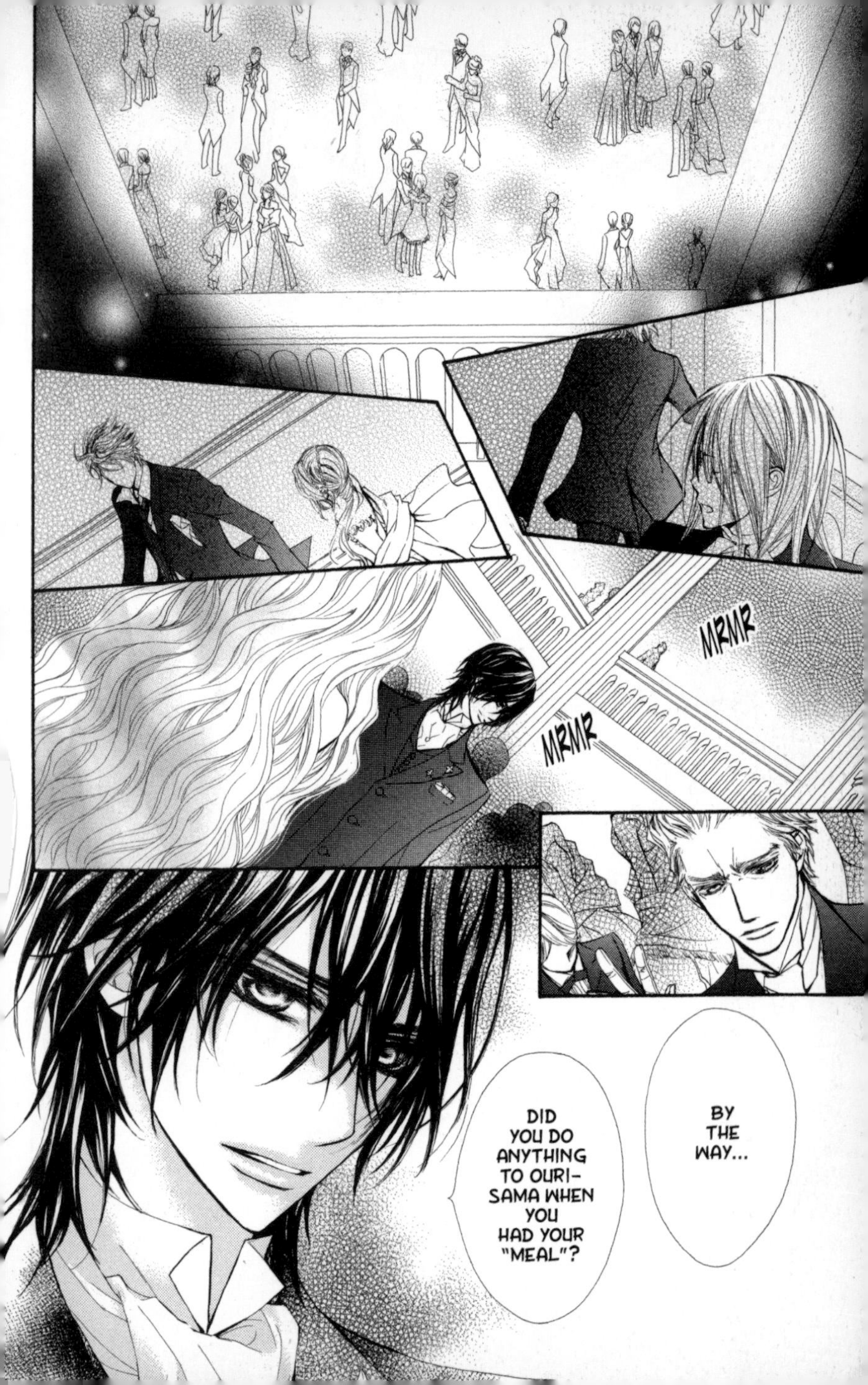
MRMR
MRMR
BY THE WAY...
DID YOU DO ANYTHING TO OURI-SAMA WHEN YOU HAD YOUR "MEAL"?

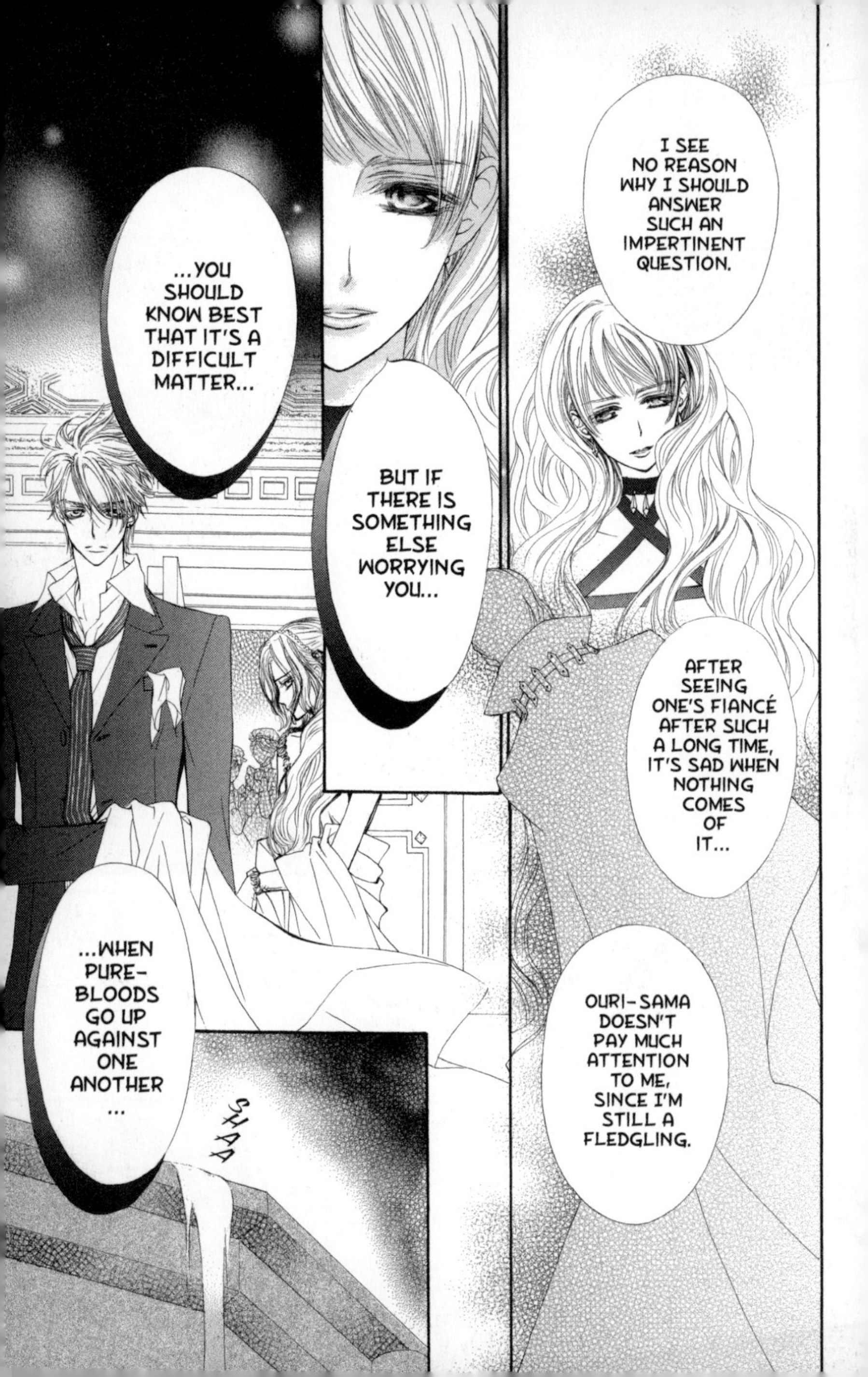
I SEE NO REASON WHY I SHOULD ANSWER SUCH AN IMPERTINENT QUESTION.
AFTER SEEING ONE'S FIANCÉ AFTER SUCH A LONG TIME, IT'S SAD WHEN NOTHING COMES OF IT...
OURI-SAMA DOESN'T PAY MUCH ATTENTION TO ME, SINCE I'M STILL A FLEDGLING.
BUT IF THERE IS SOMETHING ELSE WORRYING YOU...
...YOU SHOULD KNOW BEST THAT IT'S A DIFFICULT MATTER...
...WHEN PURE-BLOODS GO UP AGAINST ONE ANOTHER ...
SHAA

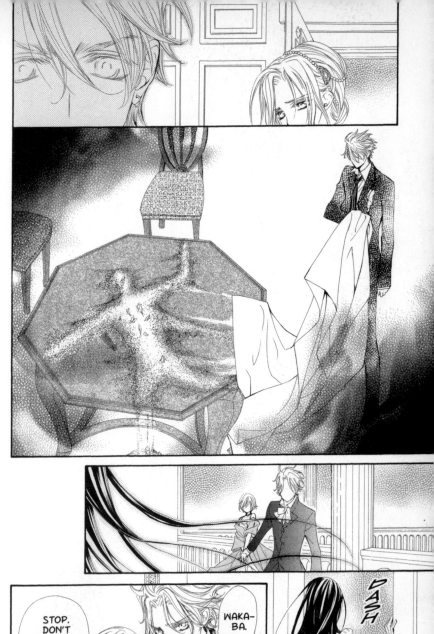

STOP. DON'T COME ANY CLOSER.

WAKA-BA.

DASH

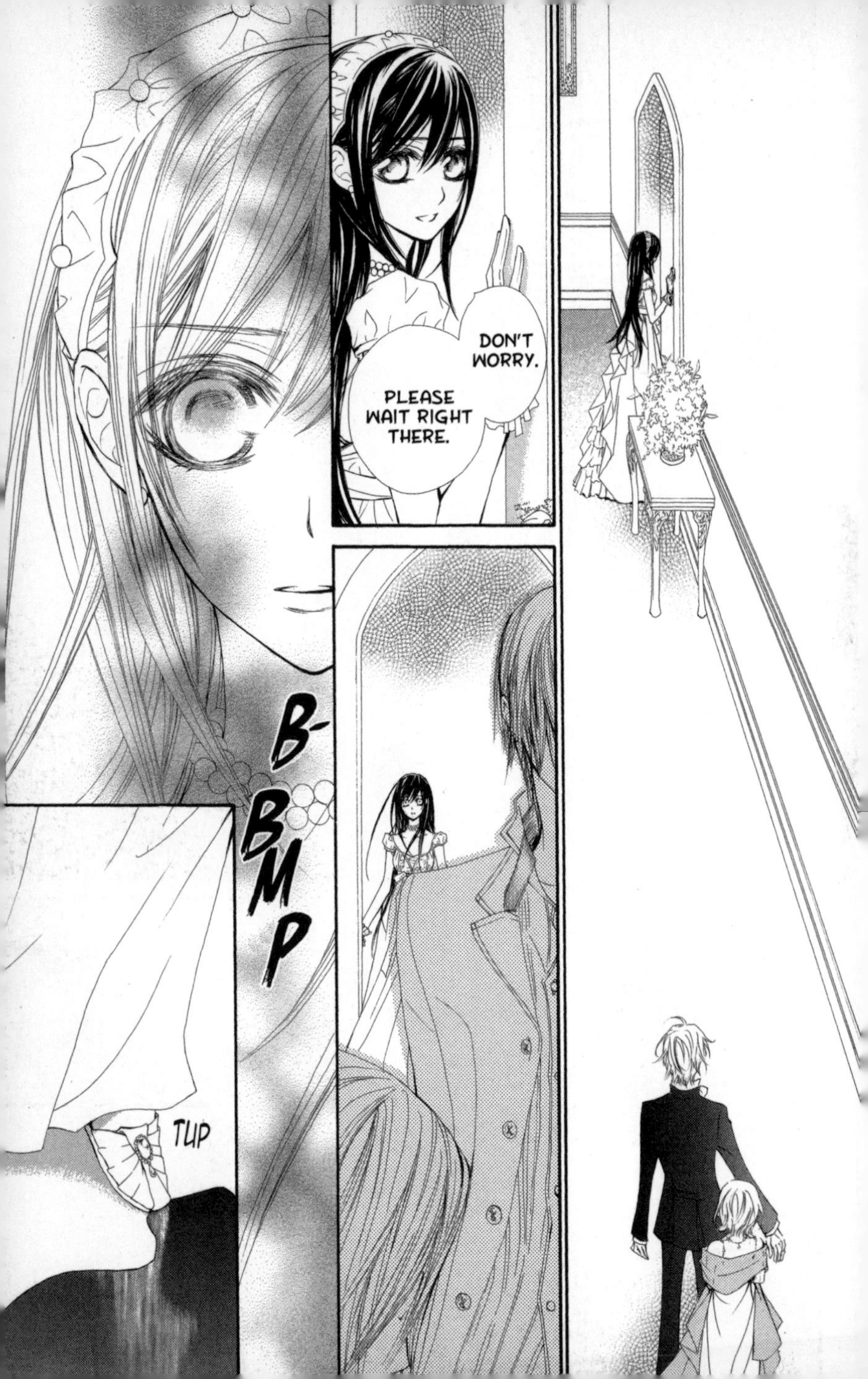
DON'T WORRY.
PLEASE WAIT RIGHT THERE.
B-BUMP
TUP

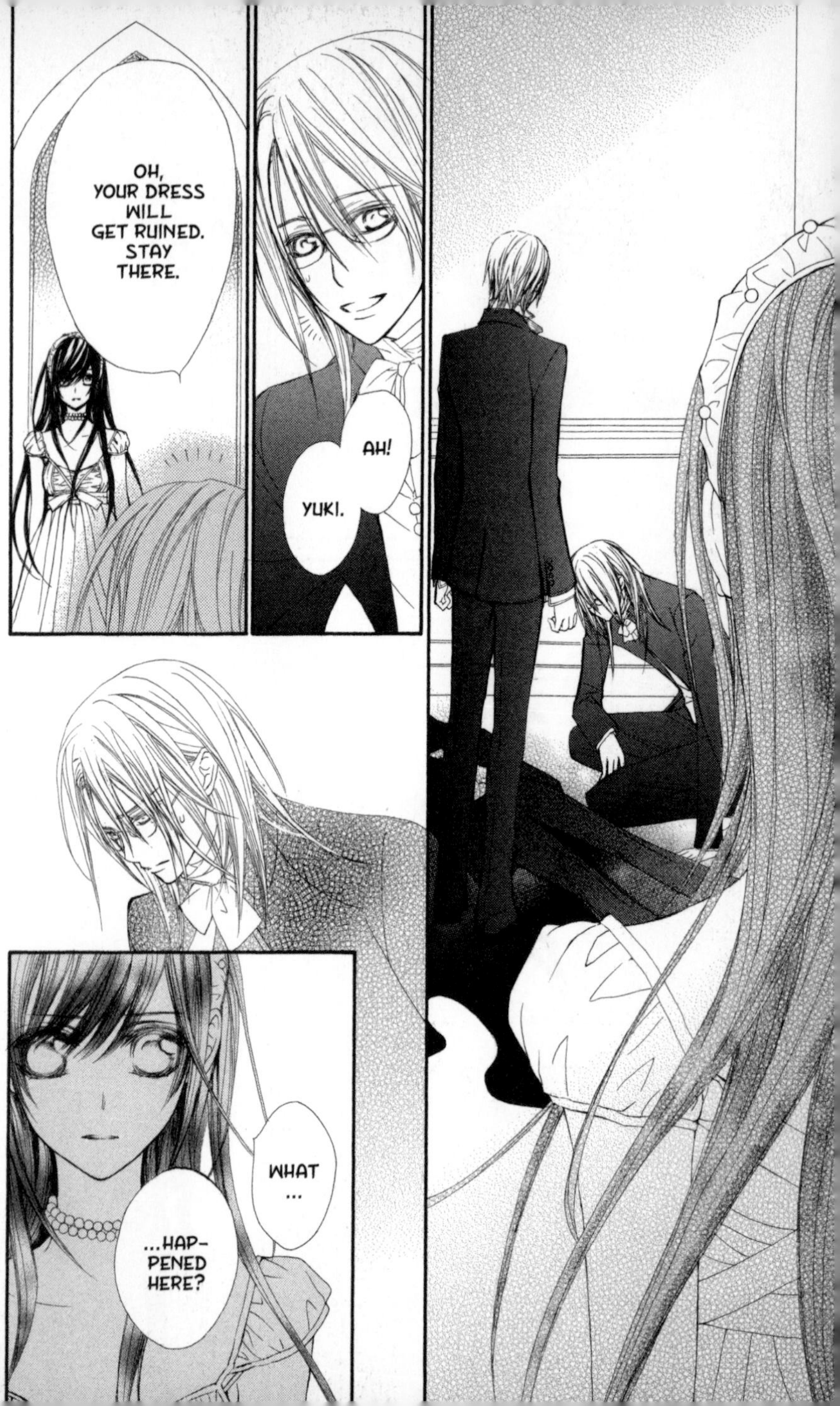
AH!
YUKI.
OH, YOUR DRESS WILL GET RUINED. STAY THERE.
WHAT ...
...HAP-PENED HERE?

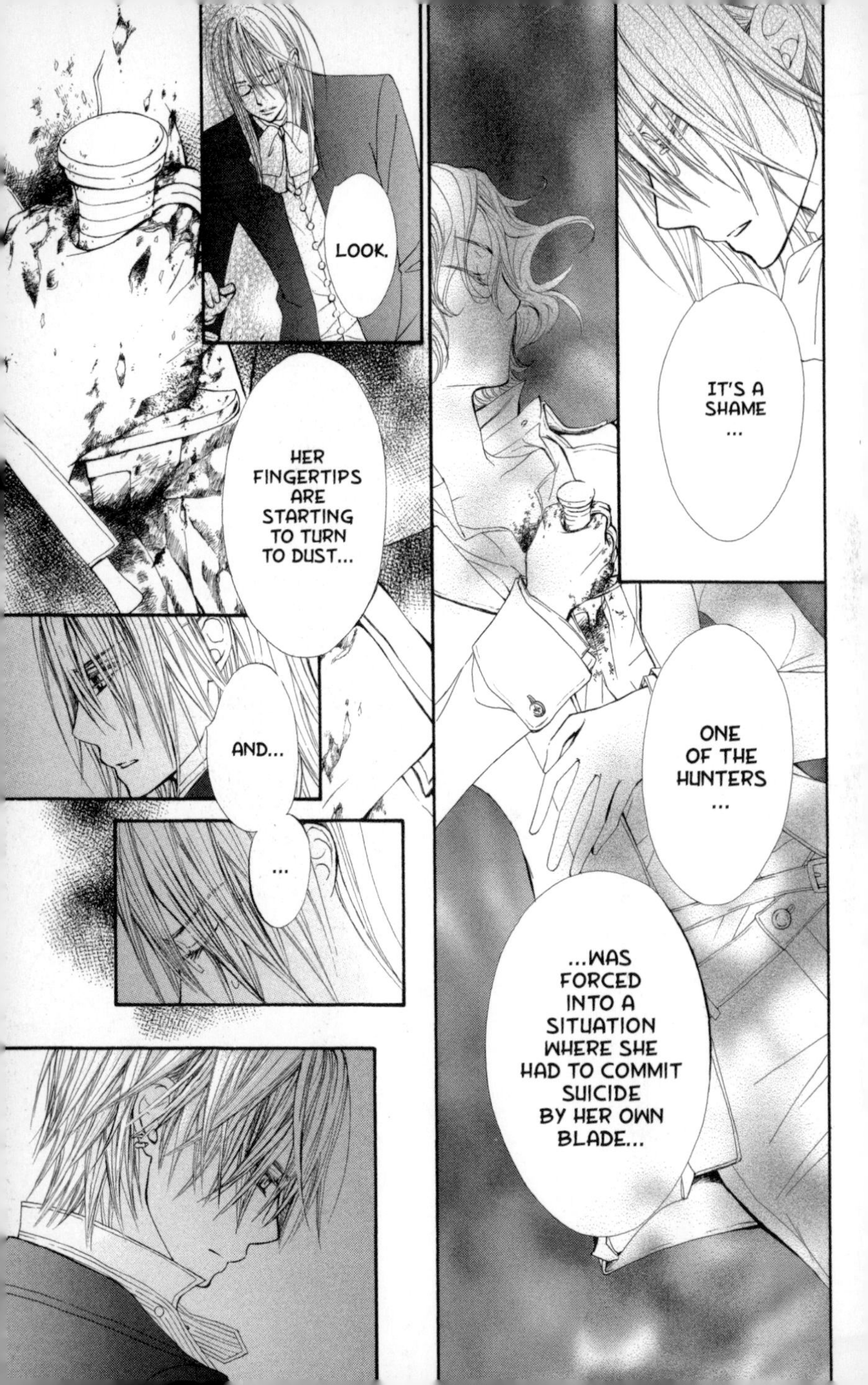
IT'S A SHAME ...
ONE OF THE HUNTERS ...
...WAS FORCED INTO A SITUATION WHERE SHE HAD TO COMMIT SUICIDE BY HER OWN BLADE...
LOOK.
HER FINGERTIPS ARE STARTING TO TURN TO DUST...
AND...
...

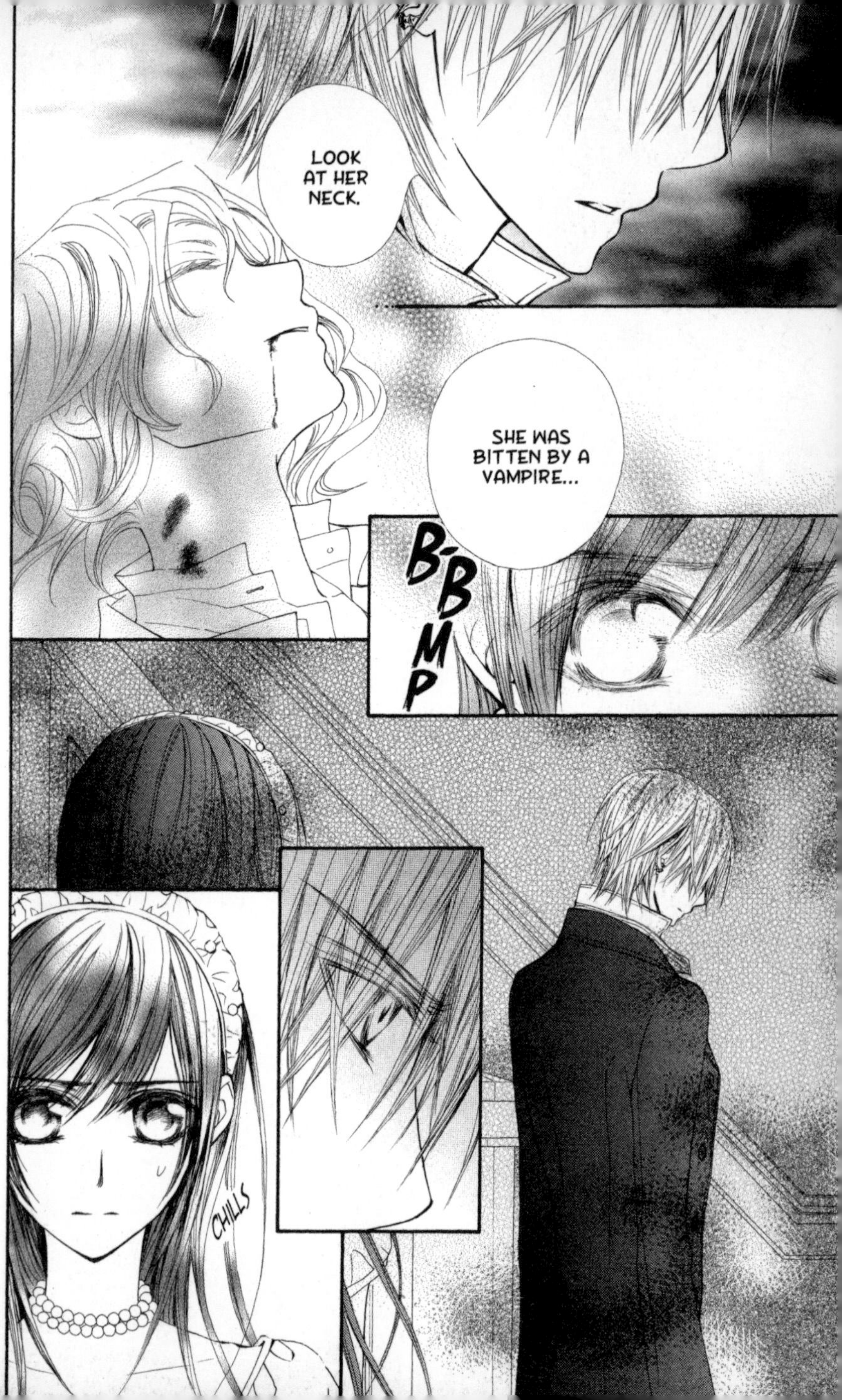
LOOK AT HER NECK.
SHE WAS BITTEN BY A VAMPIRE...
B-BMP
CHILLS

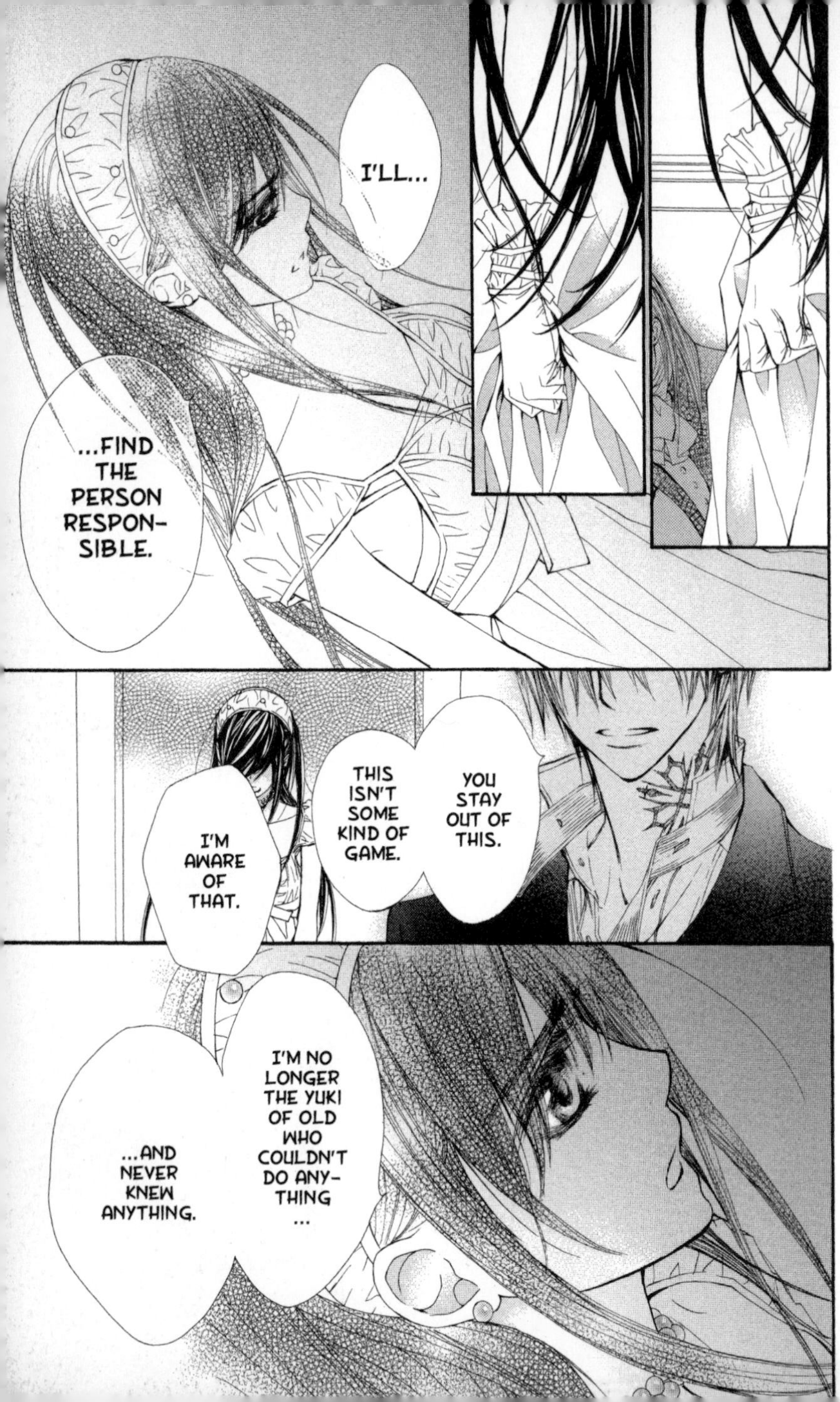
I'LL...
...FIND THE PERSON RESPONSIBLE.
YOU STAY OUT OF THIS.
THIS ISN'T SOME KIND OF GAME.
I'M AWARE OF THAT.
I'M NO LONGER THE YUKI OF OLD WHO COULDN'T DO ANYTHING...
...AND NEVER KNEW ANYTHING.

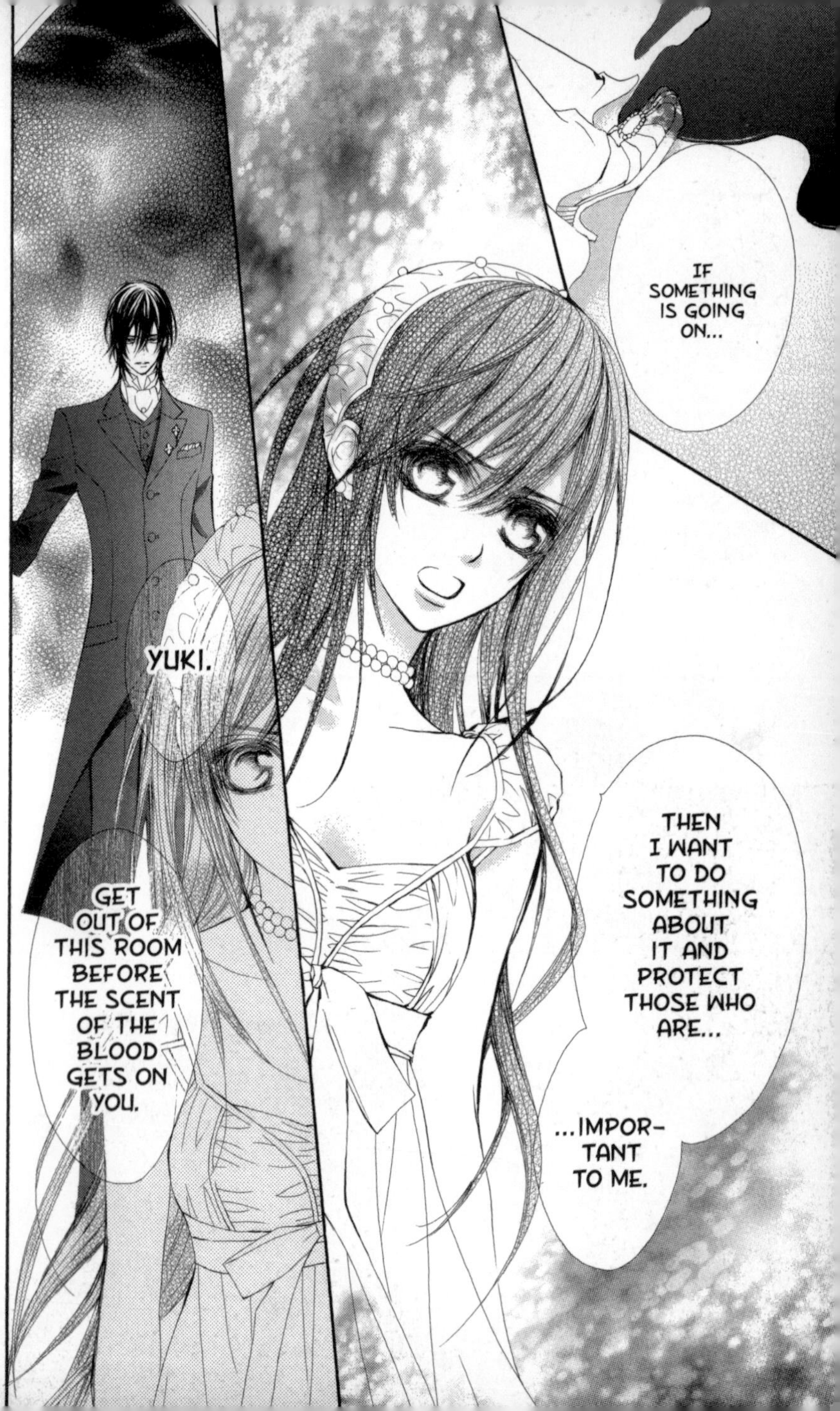
IF SOMETHING IS GOING ON...
THEN I WANT TO DO SOMETHING ABOUT IT AND PROTECT THOSE WHO ARE...
...IMPOR-TANT TO ME.
YUKI.
GET OUT OF THIS ROOM BEFORE THE SCENT OF THE BLOOD GETS ON YOU.

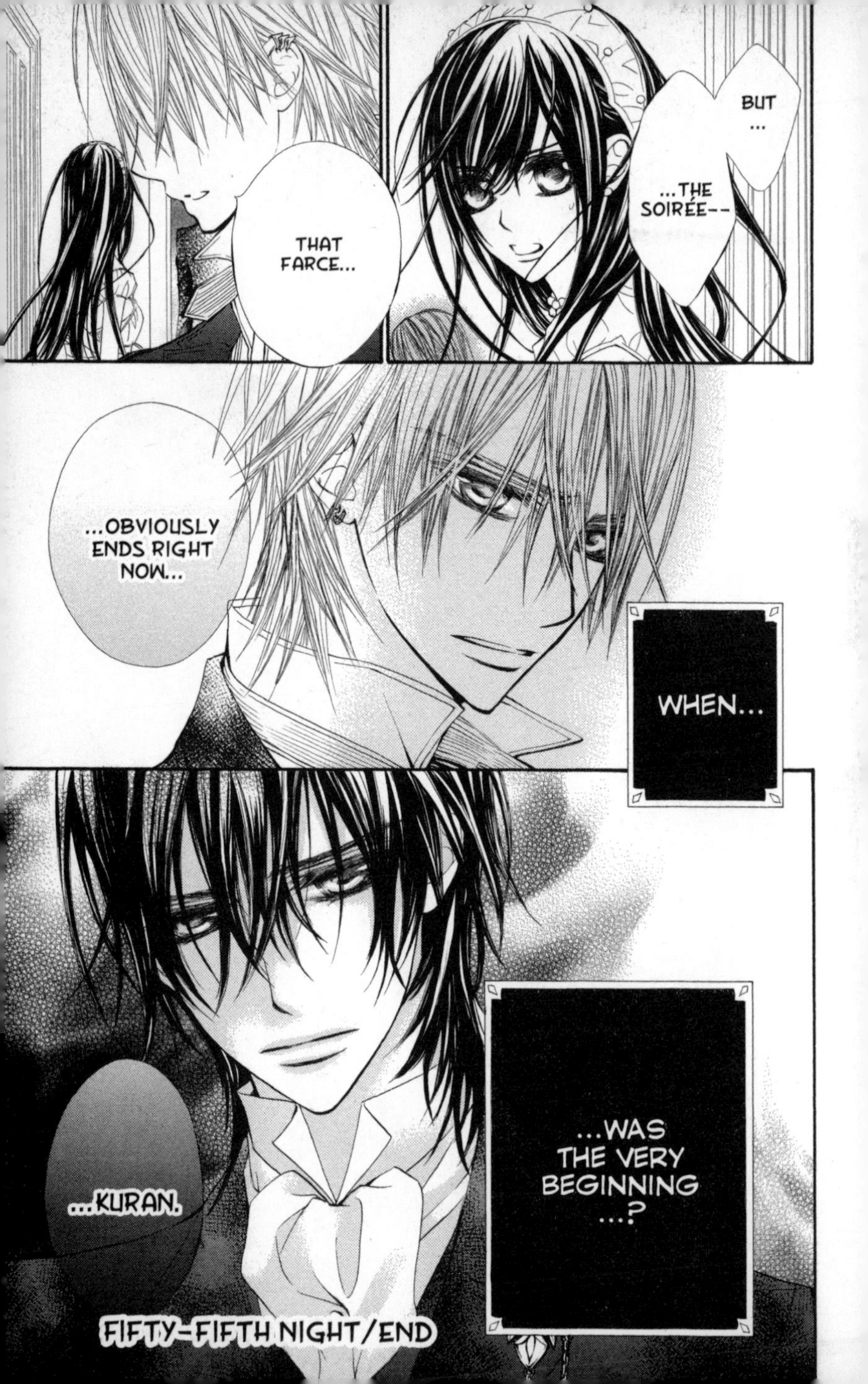
BUT ...
...THE SOIRÉE--
THAT FARCE...
...OBVIOUSLY ENDS RIGHT NOW...
WHEN...
...KURAN.
...WAS THE VERY BEGINNING ...?
FIFTY-FIFTH NIGHT/END

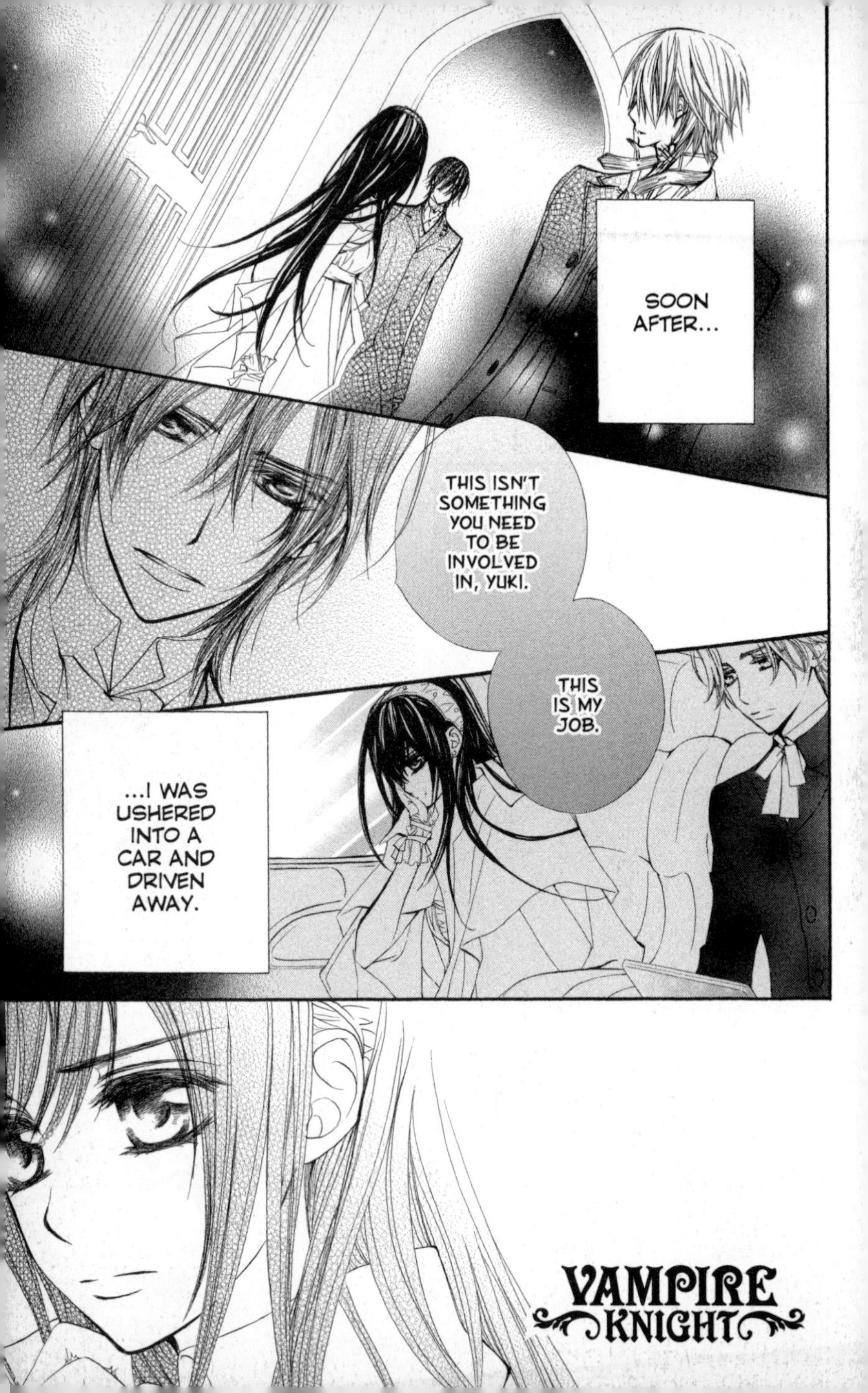
SOON AFTER...
THIS ISN'T SOMETHING YOU NEED TO BE INVOLVED IN, YUKI.
THIS IS MY JOB.
...I WAS USHERED INTO A CAR AND DRIVEN AWAY.
VAMPIRE KNIGHT

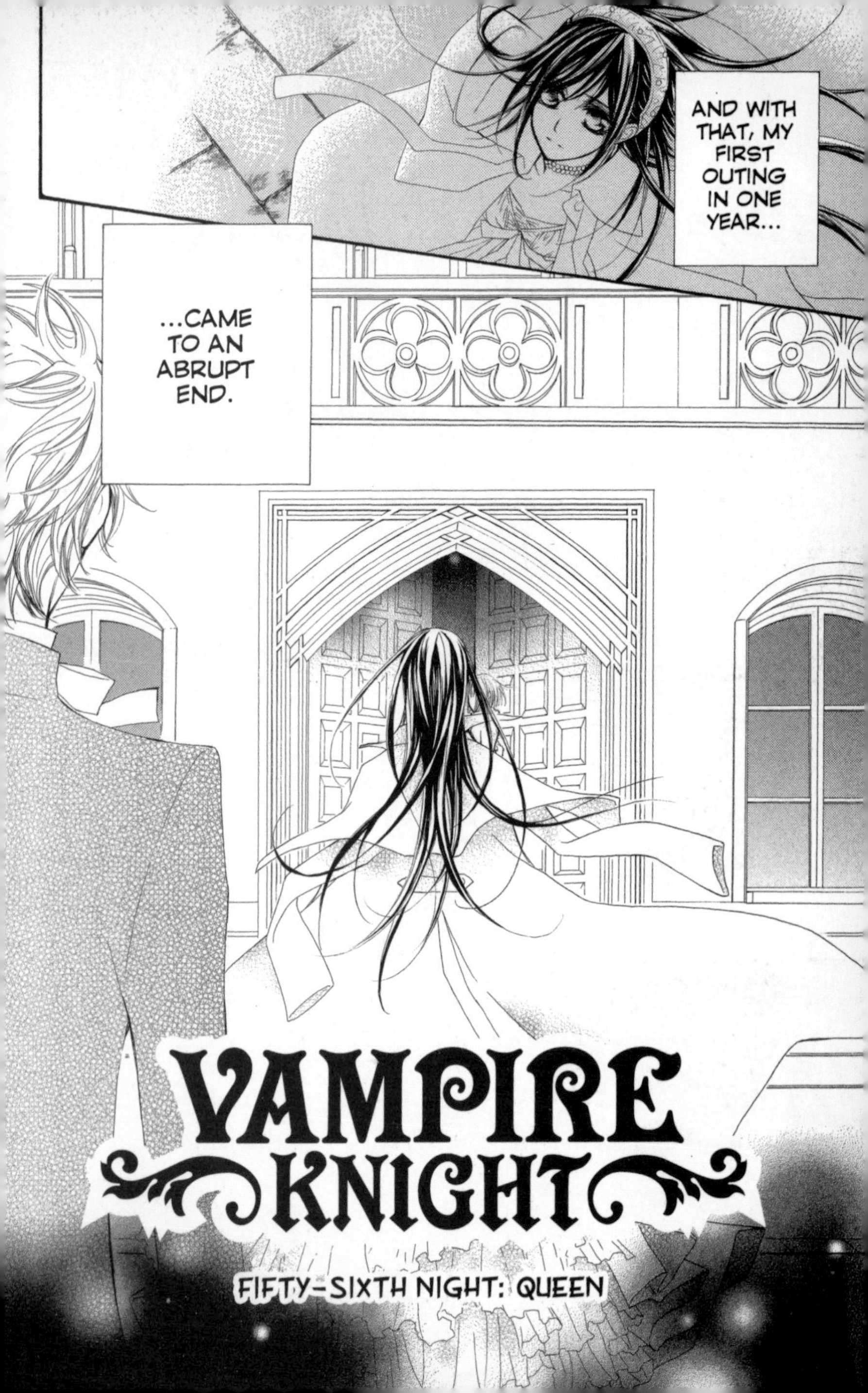
AND WITH THAT, MY FIRST OUTING IN ONE YEAR...
...CAME TO AN ABRUPT END.
VAMPIRE KNIGHT
FIFTY-SIXTH NIGHT: QUEEN

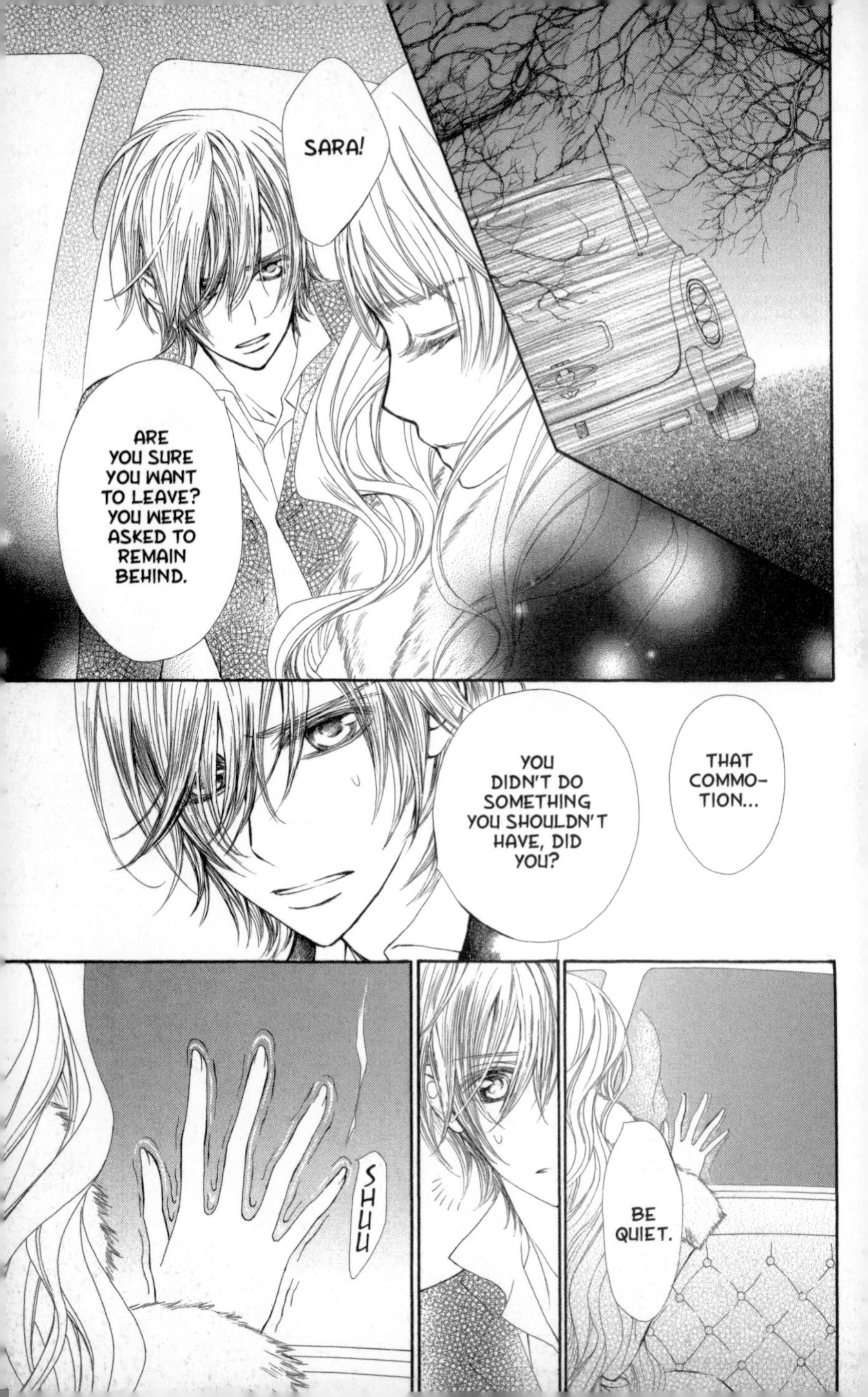
SARA!
ARE YOU SURE YOU WANT TO LEAVE? YOU WERE ASKED TO REMAIN BEHIND.
THAT COMMO-TION...
YOU DIDN'T DO SOMETHING YOU SHOULDN'T HAVE, DID YOU?
BE QUIET.
SHUU

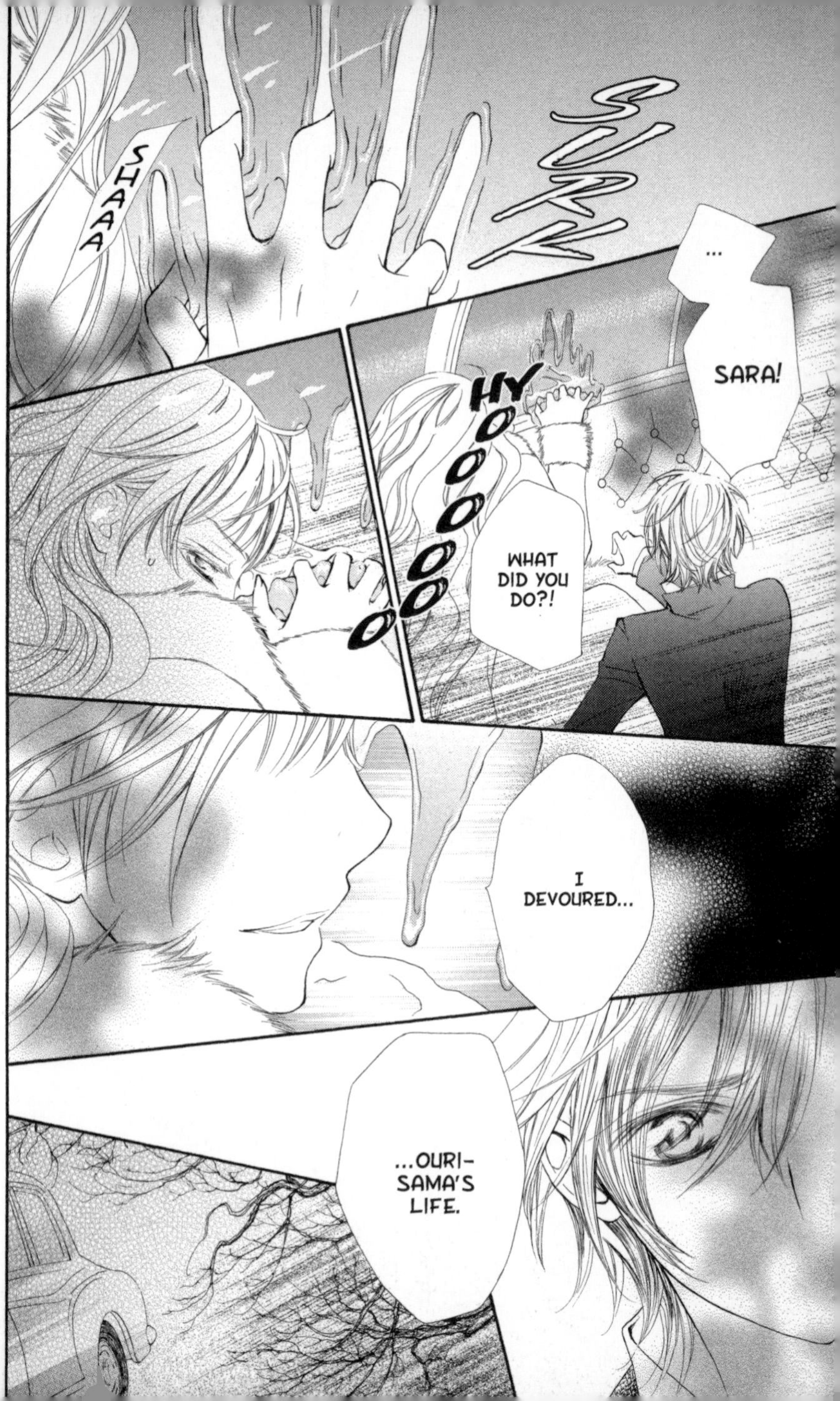
SURK
SHAAAA
...
SARA!
WHAT DID YOU DO?!
HYOOOOOOOOOO
I DEVOURED...
...OURI-SAMA'S LIFE.

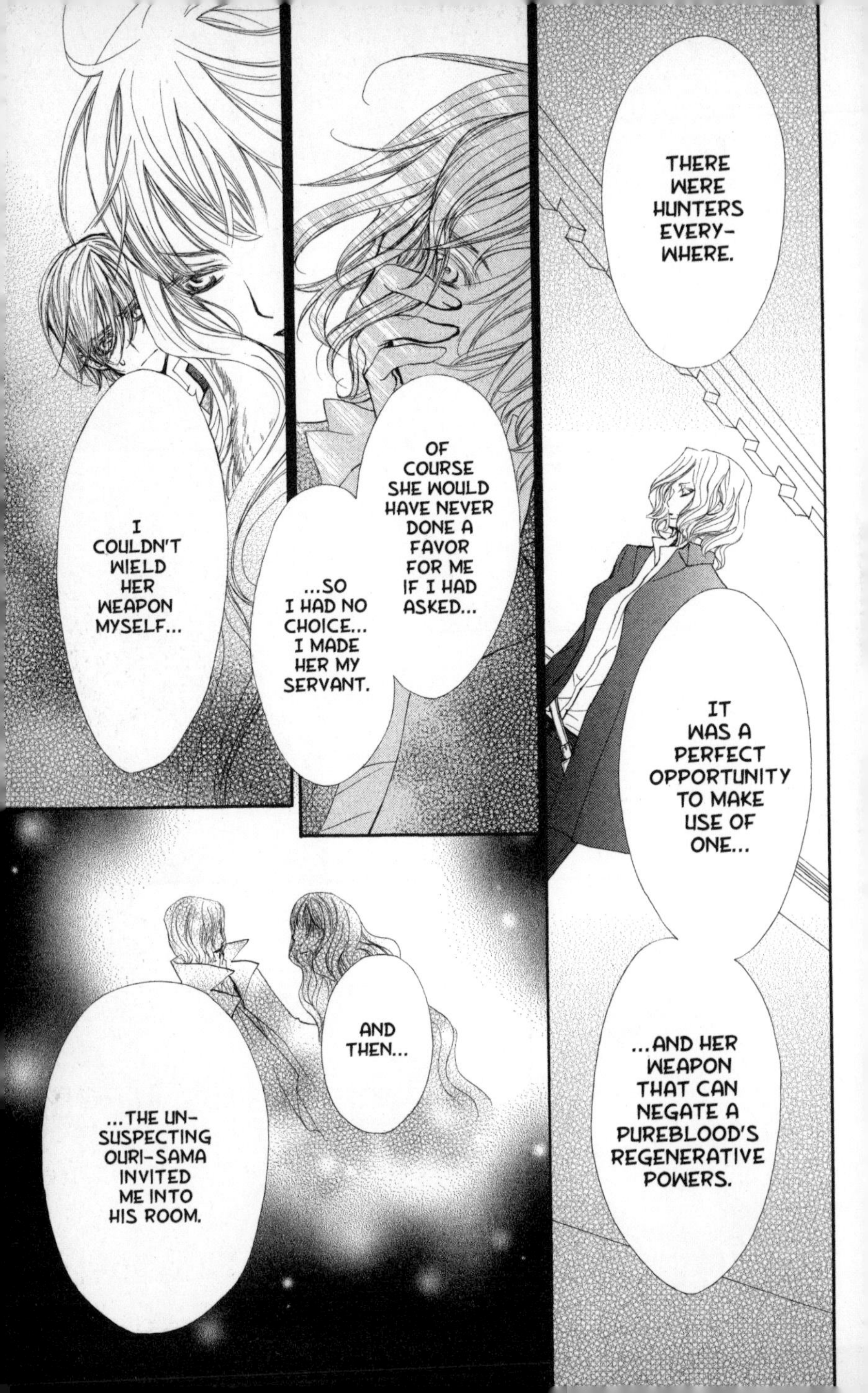
THERE WERE HUNTERS EVERY-WHERE.
IT WAS A PERFECT OPPORTUNITY TO MAKE USE OF ONE...
...AND HER WEAPON THAT CAN NEGATE A PUREBLOOD'S REGENERATIVE POWERS.
OF COURSE SHE WOULD HAVE NEVER DONE A FAVOR FOR ME IF I HAD ASKED...
...SO I HAD NO CHOICE... I MADE HER MY SERVANT.
I COULDN'T WIELD HER WEAPON MYSELF...
AND THEN...
...THE UN-SUSPECTING OURI-SAMA INVITED ME INTO HIS ROOM.

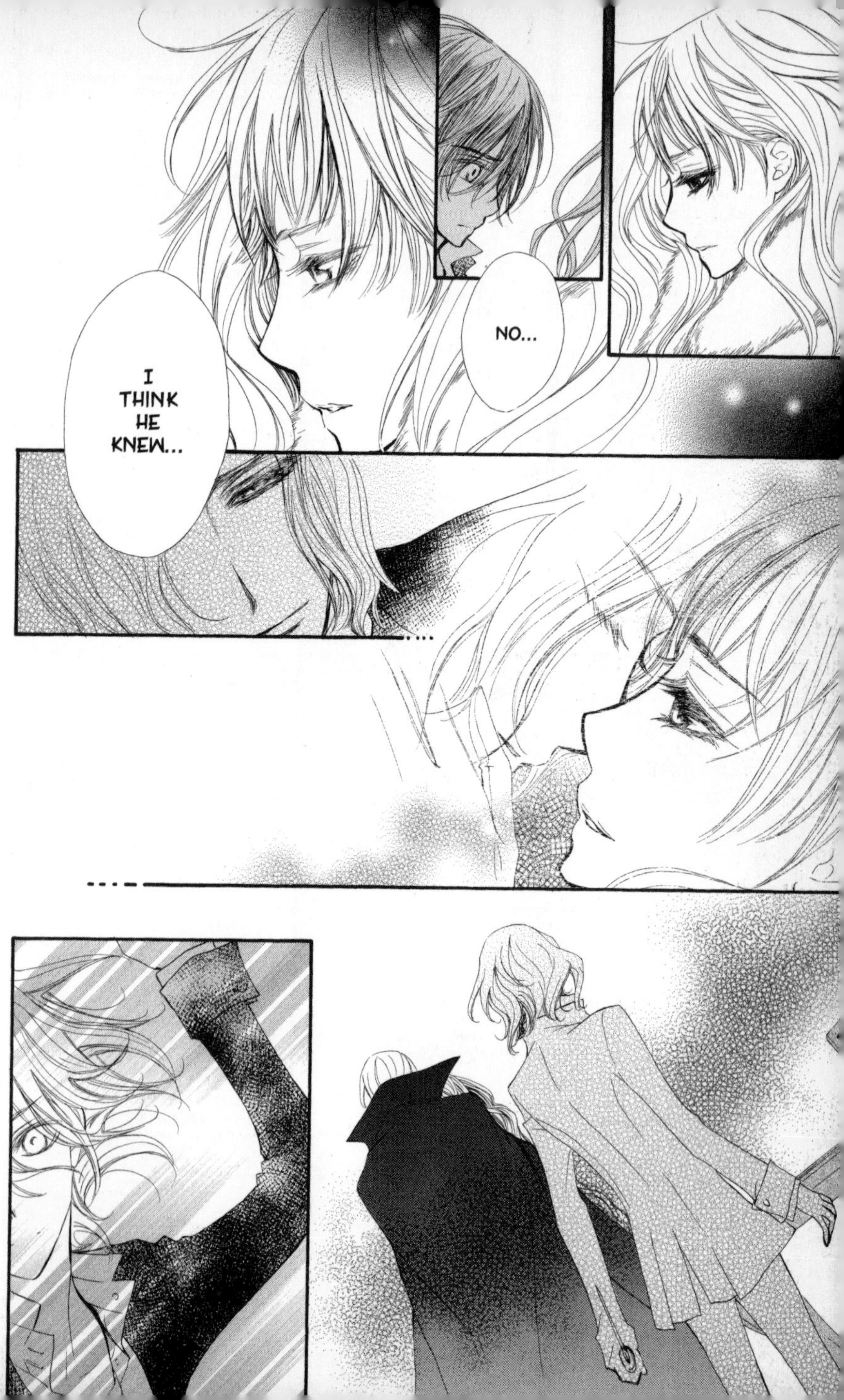
NO...
I THINK HE KNEW...

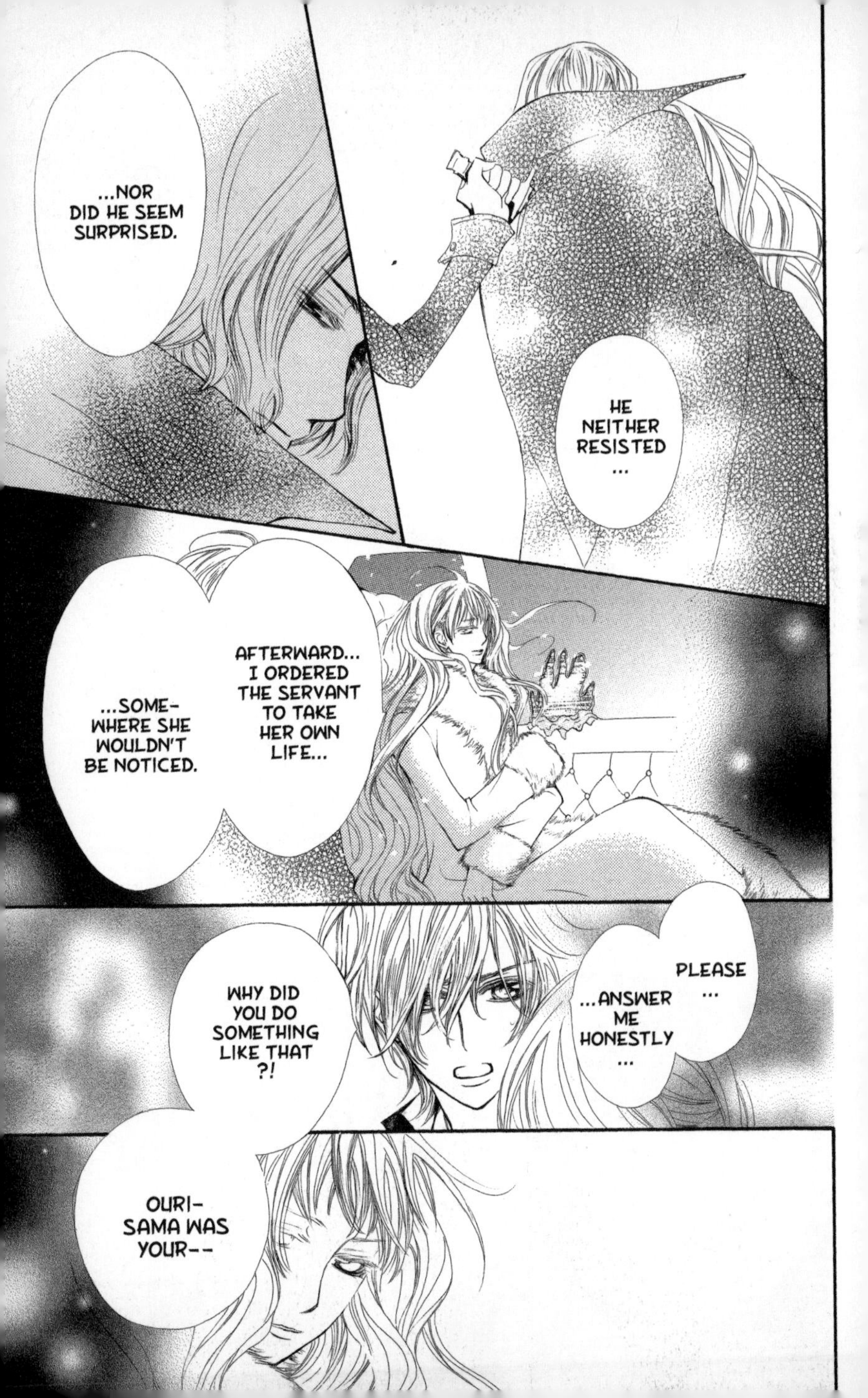
HE NEITHER RESISTED...
...NOR DID HE SEEM SURPRISED.
AFTERWARD... I ORDERED THE SERVANT TO TAKE HER OWN LIFE...
...SOMEWHERE SHE WOULDN'T BE NOTICED.
PLEASE...
...ANSWER ME HONESTLY...
WHY DID YOU DO SOMETHING LIKE THAT?!
OURI-SAMA WAS YOUR--

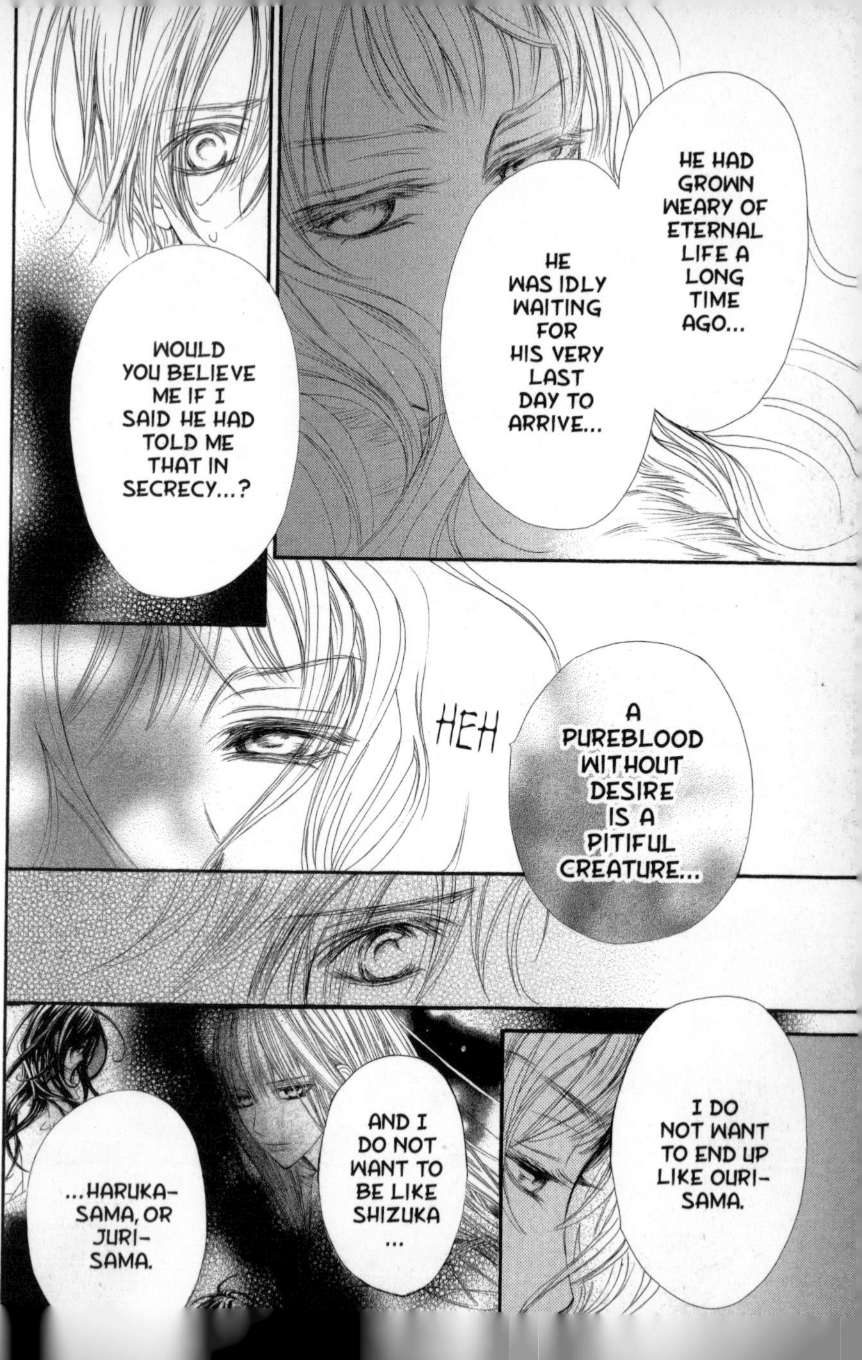
HE HAD GROWN WEARY OF ETERNAL LIFE A LONG TIME AGO...
HE WAS IDLY WAITING FOR HIS VERY LAST DAY TO ARRIVE...
WOULD YOU BELIEVE ME IF I SAID HE HAD TOLD ME THAT IN SECRECY...?
A PUREBLOOD WITHOUT DESIRE IS A PITIFUL CREATURE...
HEH
I DO NOT WANT TO END UP LIKE OURI-SAMA.
AND I DO NOT WANT TO BE LIKE SHIZUKA ...
...HARUKA-SAMA, OR JURI-SAMA.

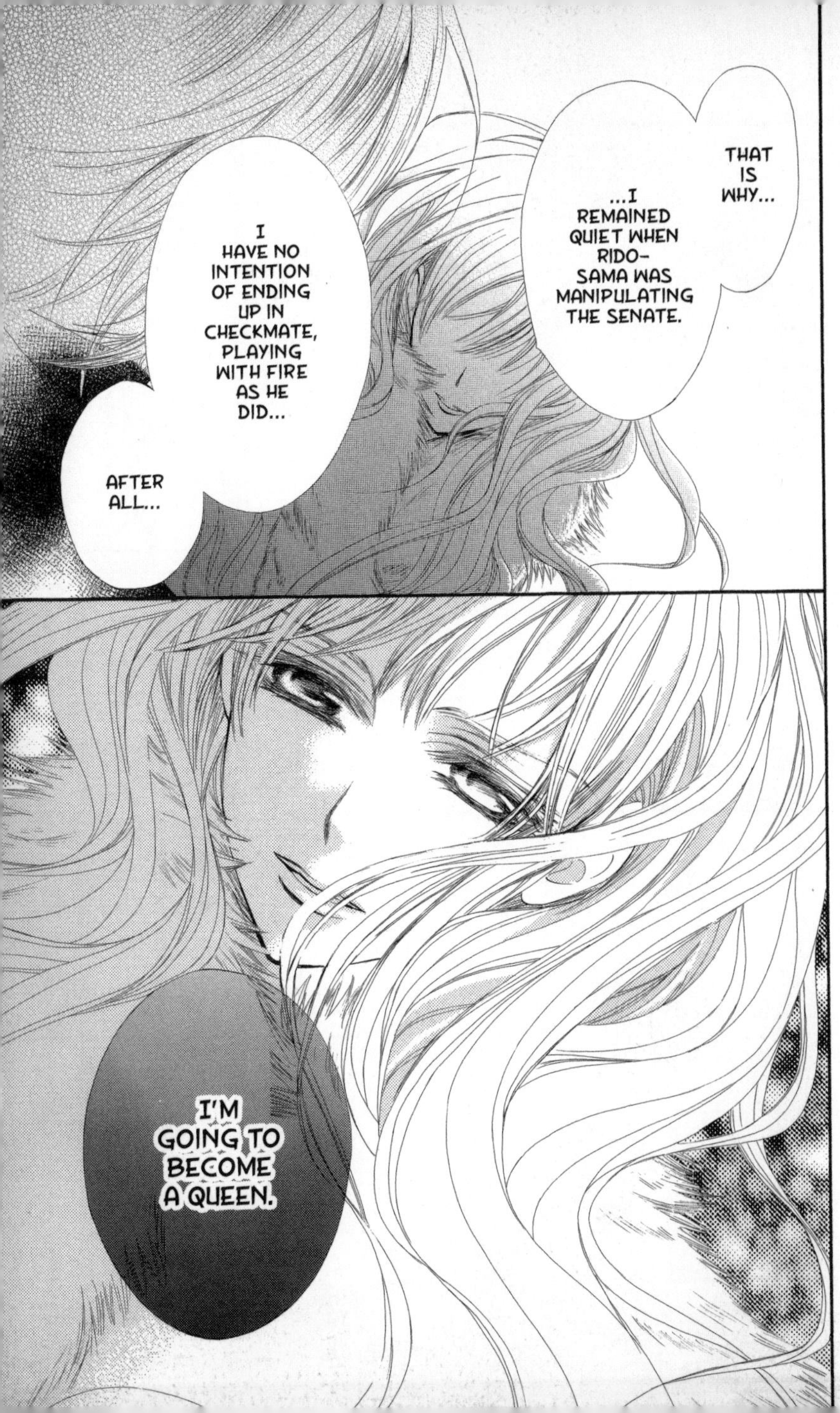
THAT IS WHY...
...I REMAINED QUIET WHEN RIDO-SAMA WAS MANIPULATING THE SENATE.
I HAVE NO INTENTION OF ENDING UP IN CHECKMATE, PLAYING WITH FIRE AS HE DID...
AFTER ALL...
I'M GOING TO BECOME A QUEEN.

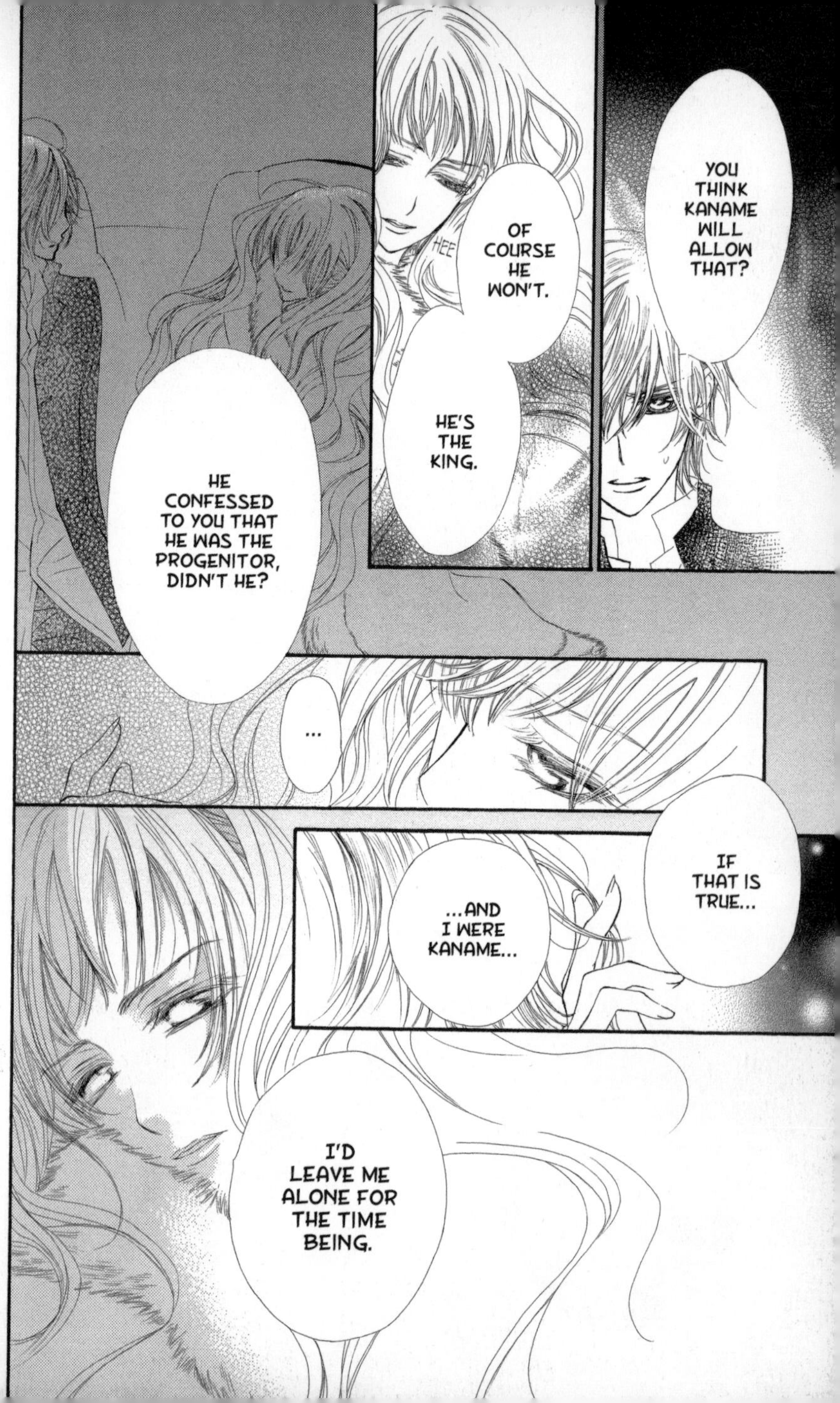
YOU THINK KANAME WILL ALLOW THAT?
OF COURSE HE WON'T.
HEE
HE'S THE KING.
HE CONFESSED TO YOU THAT HE WAS THE PROGENITOR, DIDN'T HE?
...
IF THAT IS TRUE...
...AND I WERE KANAME...
I'D LEAVE ME ALONE FOR THE TIME BEING.

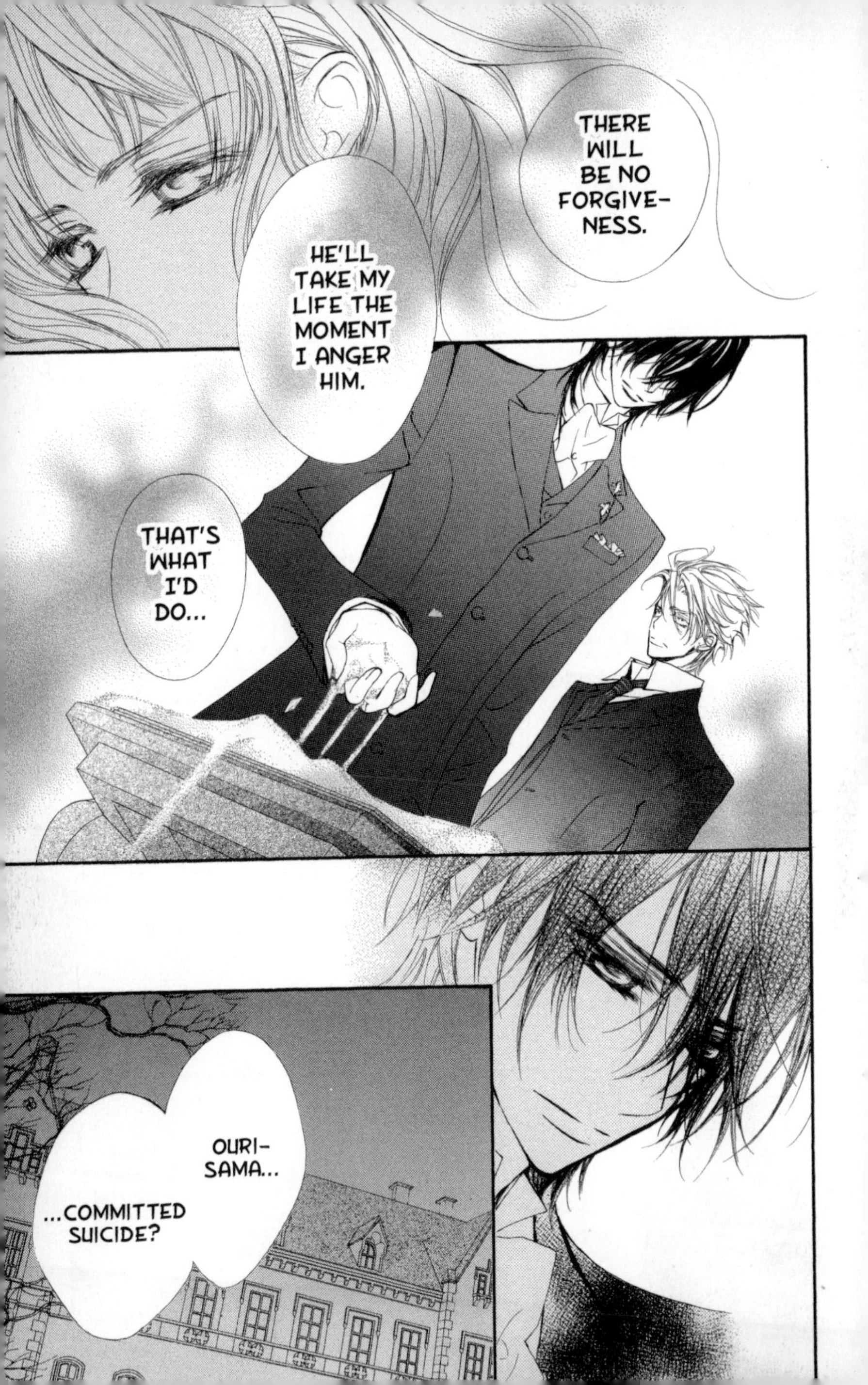
THERE WILL BE NO FORGIVE-NESS.
HE'LL TAKE MY LIFE THE MOMENT I ANGER HIM.
THAT'S WHAT I'D DO...
OURI-SAMA...
...COMMITTED SUICIDE?

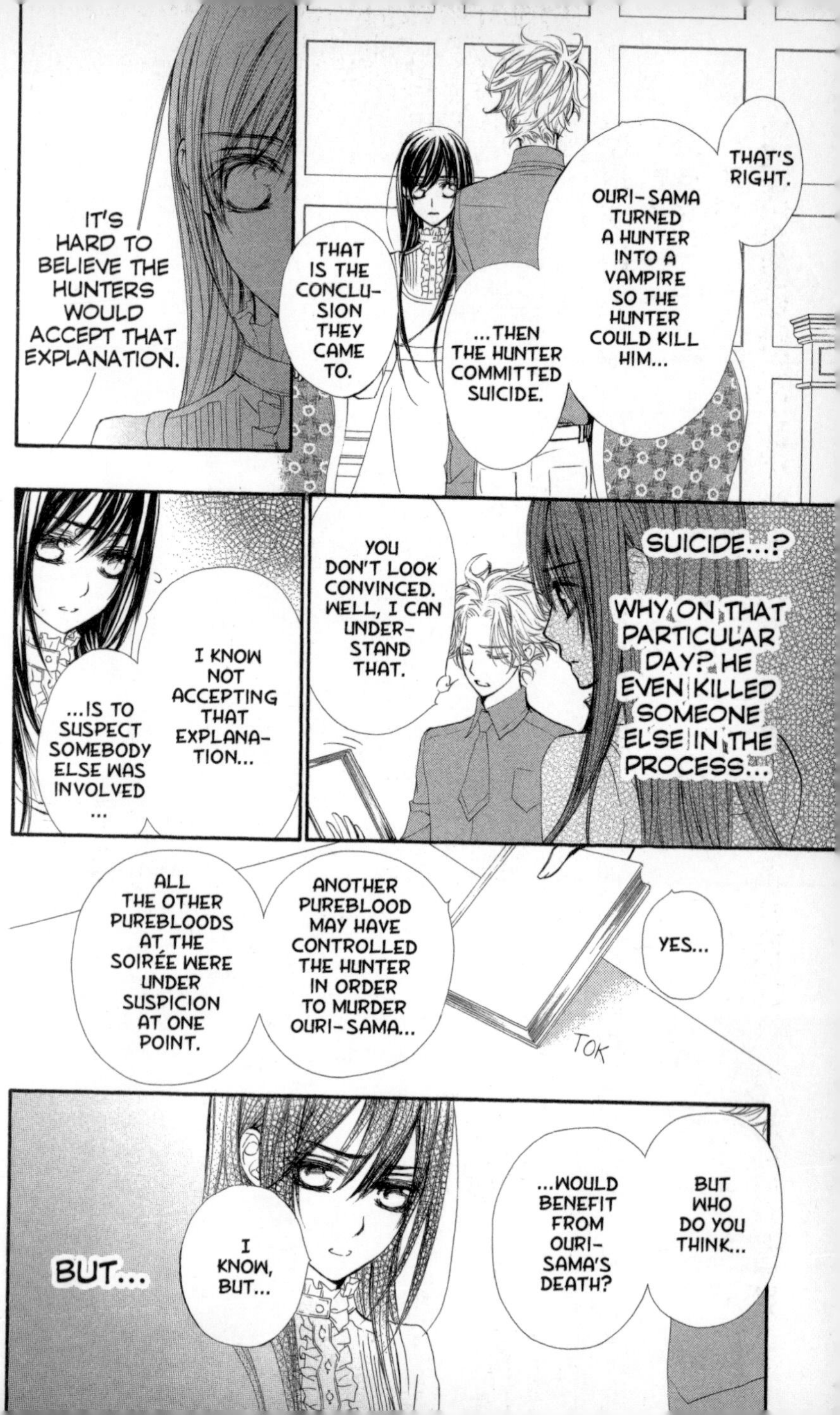
THAT'S RIGHT.
OURI-SAMA TURNED A HUNTER INTO A VAMPIRE SO THE HUNTER COULD KILL HIM...
...THEN THE HUNTER COMMITTED SUICIDE.
THAT IS THE CONCLUSION THEY CAME TO.
IT'S HARD TO BELIEVE THE HUNTERS WOULD ACCEPT THAT EXPLANATION.
SUICIDE...?
WHY ON THAT PARTICULAR DAY? HE EVEN KILLED SOMEONE ELSE IN THE PROCESS...
YOU DON'T LOOK CONVINCED. WELL, I CAN UNDERSTAND THAT.
I KNOW NOT ACCEPTING THAT EXPLANATION...
...IS TO SUSPECT SOMEBODY ELSE WAS INVOLVED...
YES...
TOK
ANOTHER PUREBLOOD MAY HAVE CONTROLLED THE HUNTER IN ORDER TO MURDER OURI-SAMA...
ALL THE OTHER PUREBLOODS AT THE SOIRÉE WERE UNDER SUSPICION AT ONE POINT.
BUT WHO DO YOU THINK...
...WOULD BENEFIT FROM OURI-SAMA'S DEATH?
I KNOW, BUT...
BUT...

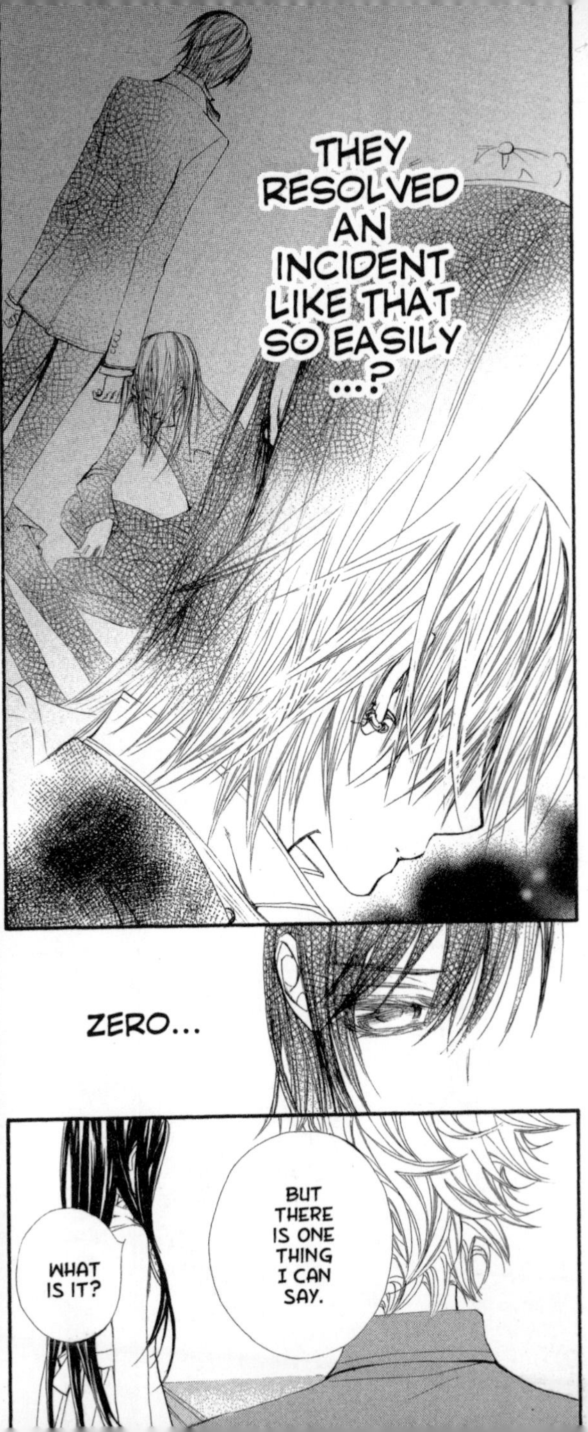
THEY RESOLVED AN INCIDENT LIKE THAT SO EASILY ...?
ZERO...
BUT THERE IS ONE THING I CAN SAY.
WHAT IS IT?

Questions Answered Corner ♡

Q: Is the vampire who was up to no good in Twenty-Fourth Night and the vampire standing behind Kaname-sama in Fifty-Third Night the same person?
A: Th...that's right! I tried my best with my feeble skills as I wanted someone to notice...? I'm so surprised that somebody actually did! (I leave it up to you to imagine what they did to him...M;) But I'm really glad.♡

Q: Please teach me how to draw cool-looking boys!
A: I don't know if this will answer your question, but I used to continuously do sketches of Kevin Costner (the actor) when I was in high school just because he had great bone structure...♡ I seriously believe that the good looks of a boy lie in his bone structure! So imagine his bones! Beneath that young skin is a robust bone structure unlike that of a girl. (I'm so envious...) If you're asking about "cool" as in "facial structure," then I think it boils down to doing research. I'm still in the midst of my research too. After all, artistic trends continue to change all the time. M;

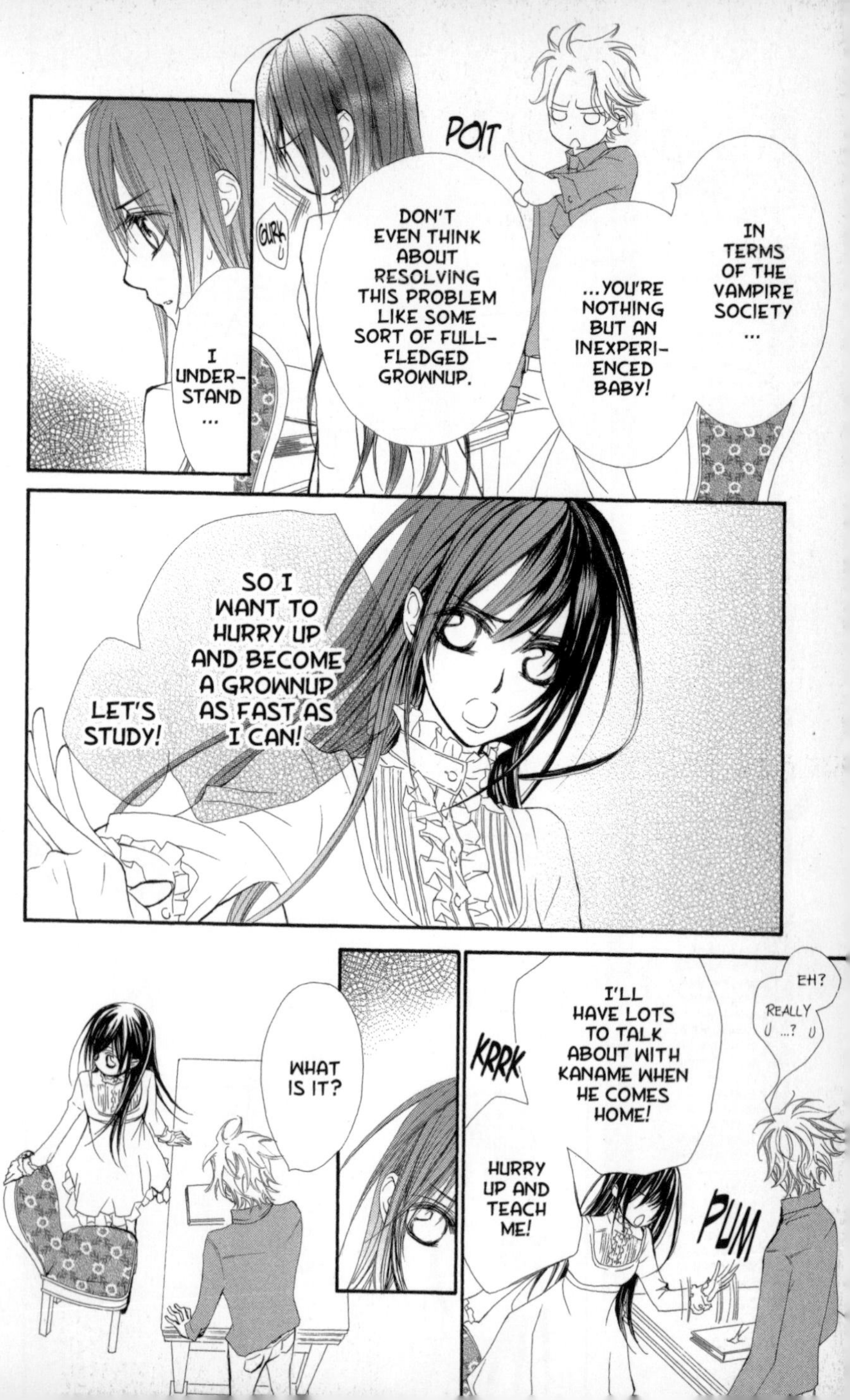
POIT
IN TERMS OF THE VAMPIRE SOCIETY...
...YOU'RE NOTHING BUT AN INEXPERIENCED BABY!
DON'T EVEN THINK ABOUT RESOLVING THIS PROBLEM LIKE SOME SORT OF FULL-FLEDGED GROWNUP.
GURK
I UNDERSTAND...
SO I WANT TO HURRY UP AND BECOME A GROWNUP AS FAST AS I CAN!
LET'S STUDY!
EH? REALLY...?
I'LL HAVE LOTS TO TALK ABOUT WITH KANAME WHEN HE COMES HOME!
KRRK
HURRY UP AND TEACH ME!
PUM
WHAT IS IT?

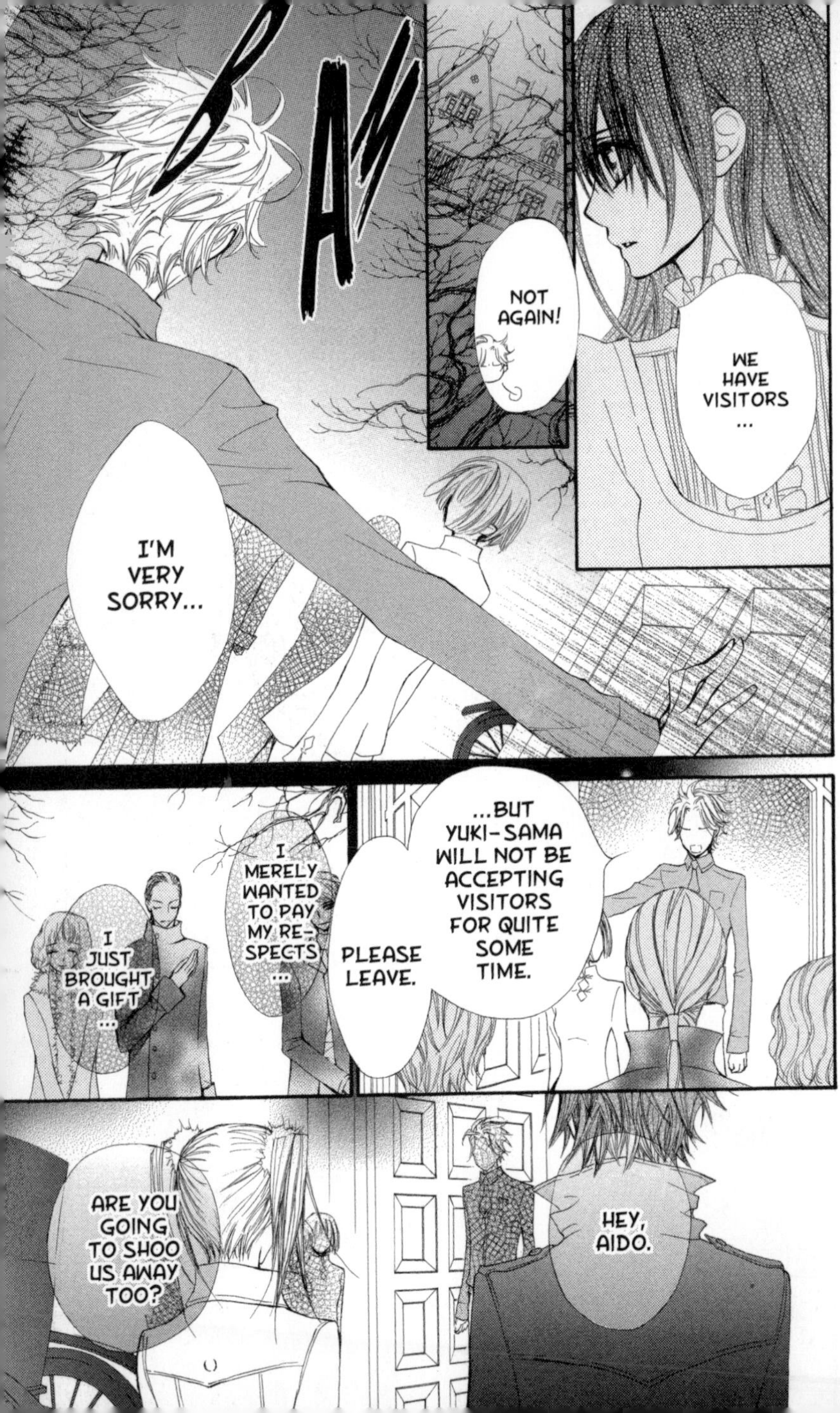
WE HAVE VISITORS ...
NOT AGAIN!
BAM
I'M VERY SORRY...
...BUT YUKI-SAMA WILL NOT BE ACCEPTING VISITORS FOR QUITE SOME TIME.
PLEASE LEAVE.
I MERELY WANTED TO PAY MY RE-SPECTS ...
I JUST BROUGHT A GIFT ...
HEY, AIDO.
ARE YOU GOING TO SHOO US AWAY TOO?

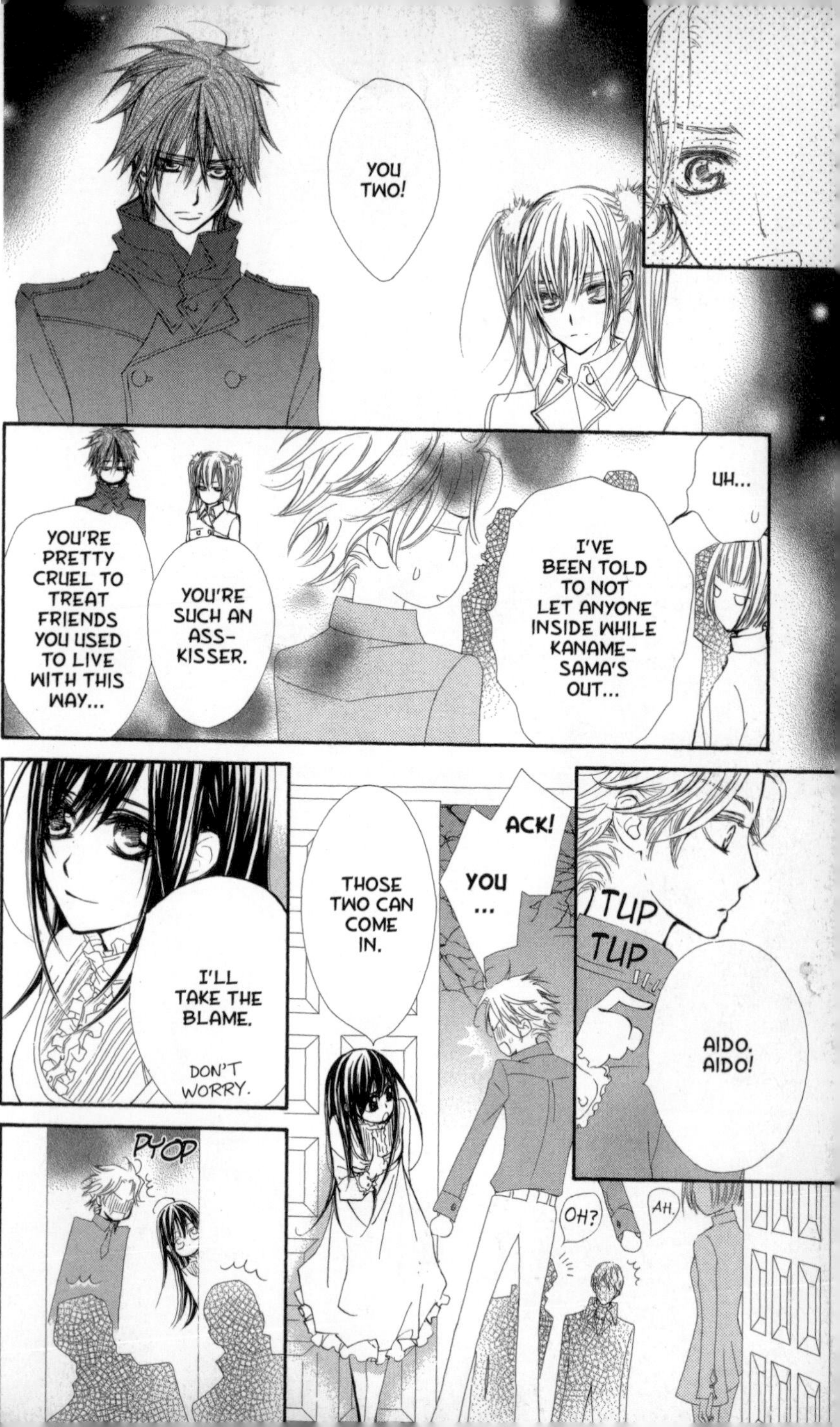
YOU TWO!
UH...
I'VE BEEN TOLD TO NOT LET ANYONE INSIDE WHILE KANAME-SAMA'S OUT...
YOU'RE SUCH AN ASS-KISSER.
YOU'RE PRETTY CRUEL TO TREAT FRIENDS YOU USED TO LIVE WITH THIS WAY...
TUP
TUP
AIDO. AIDO!
ACK!
YOU ...
THOSE TWO CAN COME IN.
AH.
OH?
I'LL TAKE THE BLAME.
DON'T WORRY.
PYOP

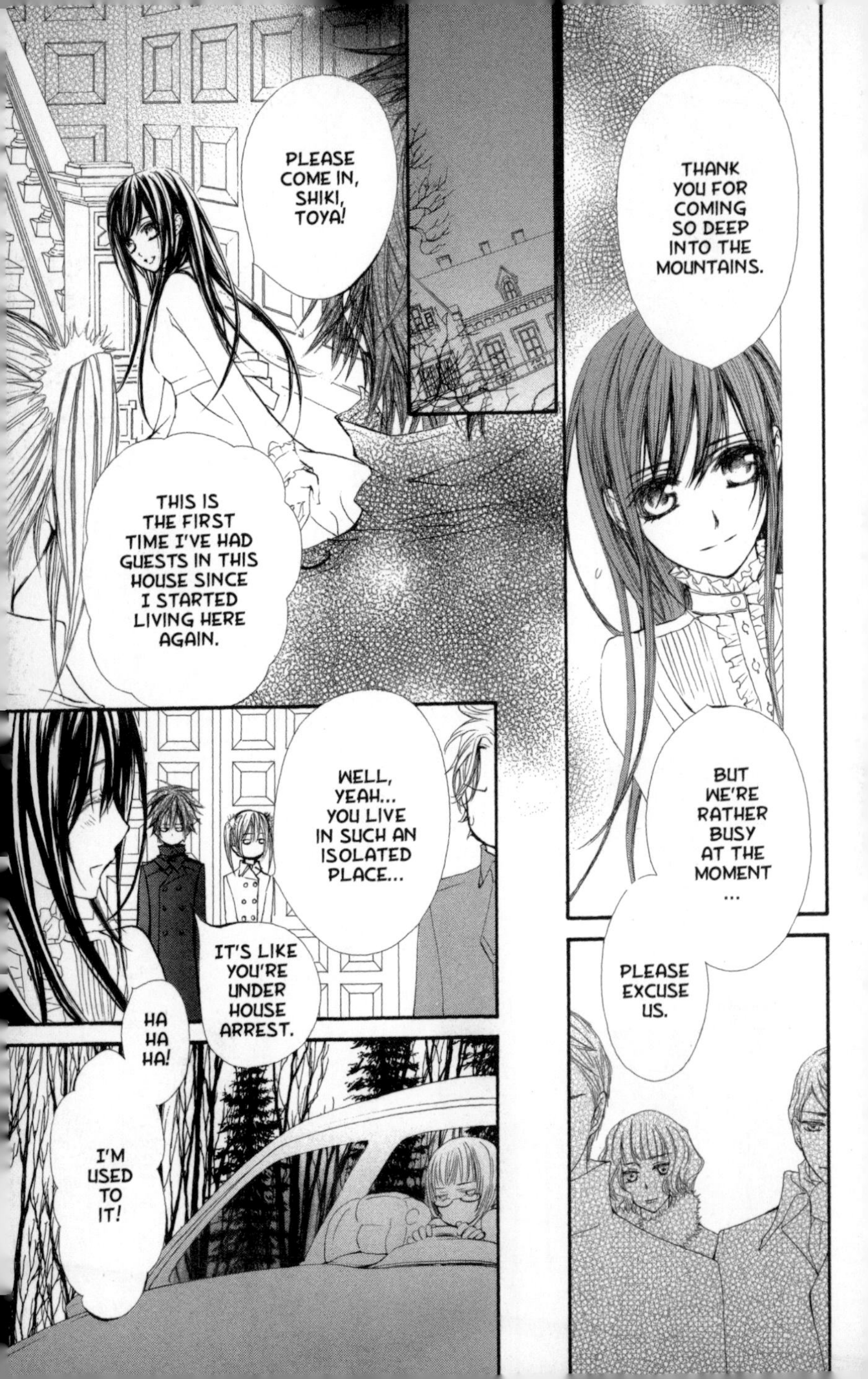
THANK YOU FOR COMING SO DEEP INTO THE MOUNTAINS.
BUT WE'RE RATHER BUSY AT THE MOMENT...
PLEASE EXCUSE US.
PLEASE COME IN, SHIKI, TOYA!
THIS IS THE FIRST TIME I'VE HAD GUESTS IN THIS HOUSE SINCE I STARTED LIVING HERE AGAIN.
WELL, YEAH... YOU LIVE IN SUCH AN ISOLATED PLACE...
IT'S LIKE YOU'RE UNDER HOUSE ARREST.
HA HA HA!
I'M USED TO IT!

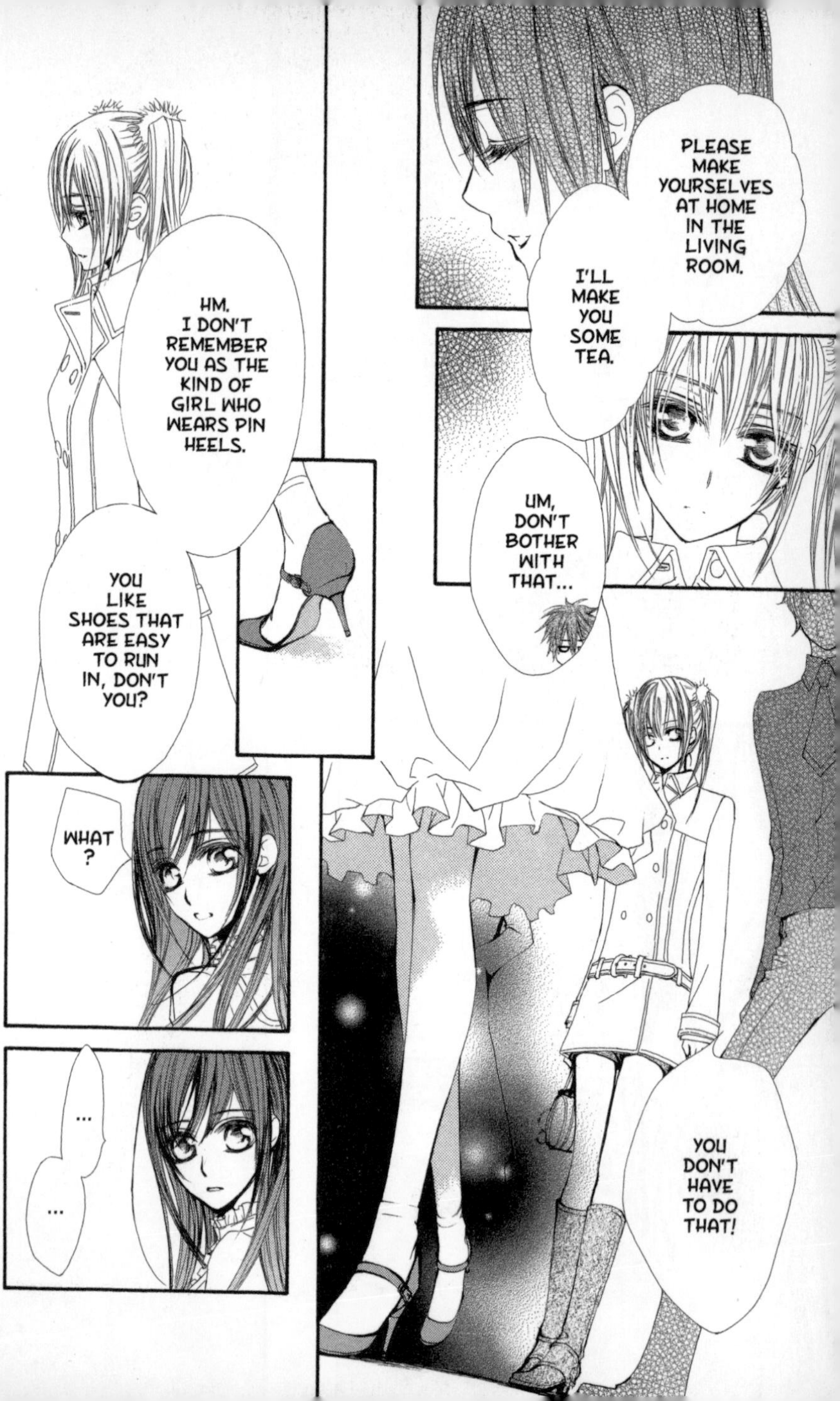
PLEASE MAKE YOURSELVES AT HOME IN THE LIVING ROOM.
I'LL MAKE YOU SOME TEA.
UM, DON'T BOTHER WITH THAT...
YOU DON'T HAVE TO DO THAT!
HM. I DON'T REMEMBER YOU AS THE KIND OF GIRL WHO WEARS PIN HEELS.
YOU LIKE SHOES THAT ARE EASY TO RUN IN, DON'T YOU?
WHAT?
...
...

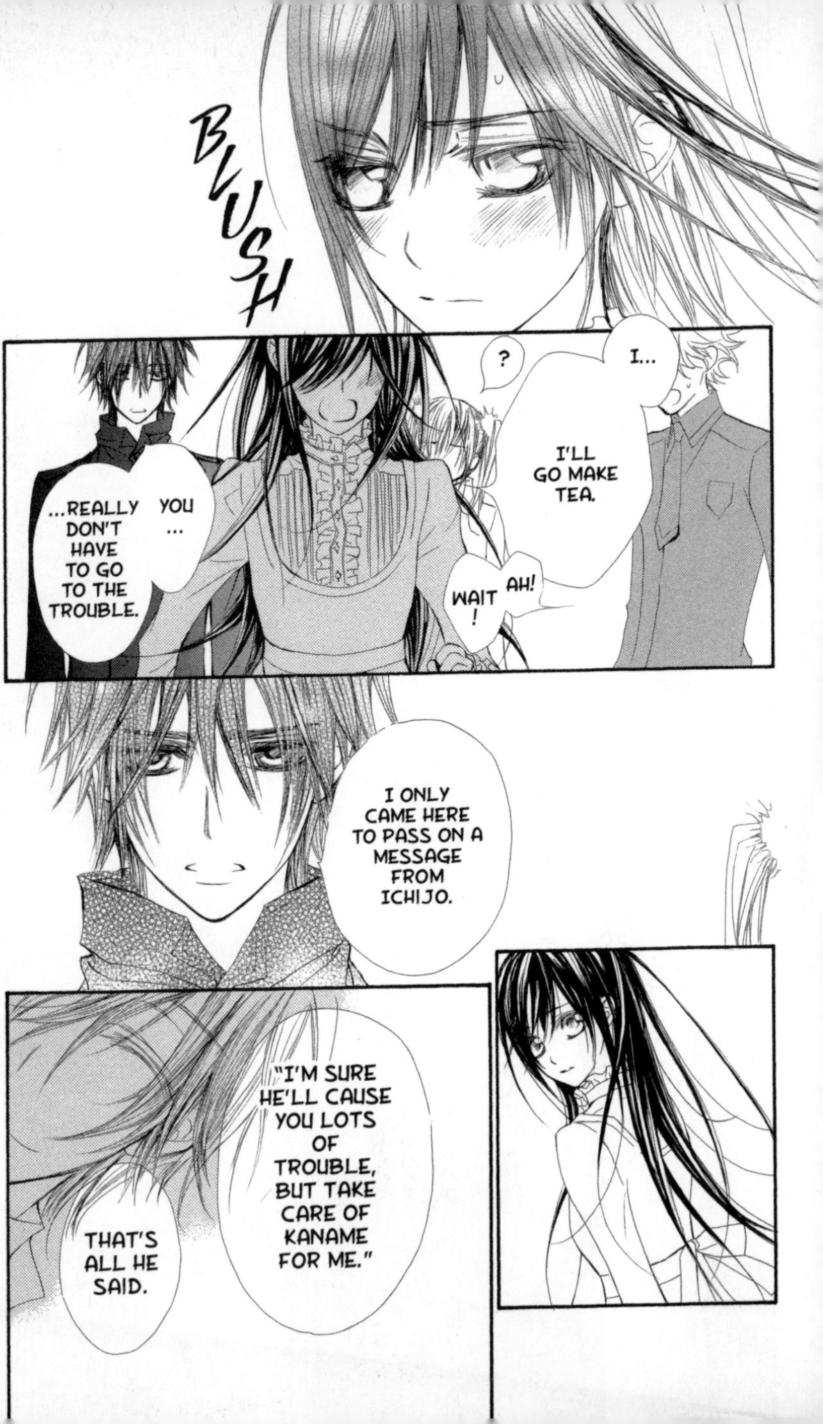
BLUSH
I...
?
I'LL GO MAKE TEA.
YOU ...
...REALLY DON'T HAVE TO GO TO THE TROUBLE.
AH!
WAIT!
I ONLY CAME HERE TO PASS ON A MESSAGE FROM ICHIJO.
"I'M SURE HE'LL CAUSE YOU LOTS OF TROUBLE, BUT TAKE CARE OF KANAME FOR ME."
THAT'S ALL HE SAID.

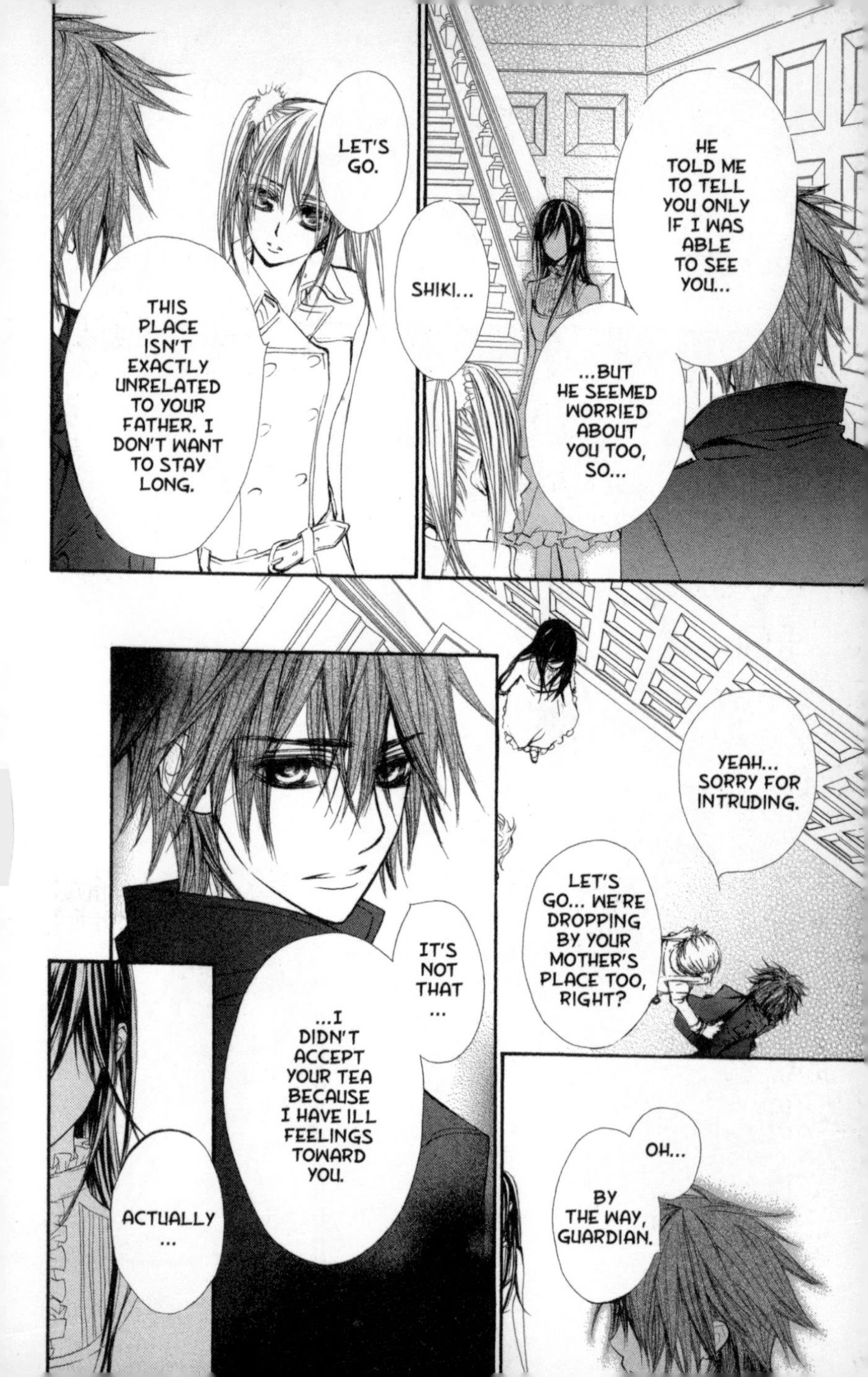
HE TOLD ME TO TELL YOU ONLY IF I WAS ABLE TO SEE YOU...
...BUT HE SEEMED WORRIED ABOUT YOU TOO, SO...
SHIKI...
LET'S GO.
THIS PLACE ISN'T EXACTLY UNRELATED TO YOUR FATHER. I DON'T WANT TO STAY LONG.
YEAH... SORRY FOR INTRUDING.
LET'S GO... WE'RE DROPPING BY YOUR MOTHER'S PLACE TOO, RIGHT?
OH...
BY THE WAY, GUARDIAN.
IT'S NOT THAT ...
...I DIDN'T ACCEPT YOUR TEA BECAUSE I HAVE ILL FEELINGS TOWARD YOU.
ACTUALLY ...

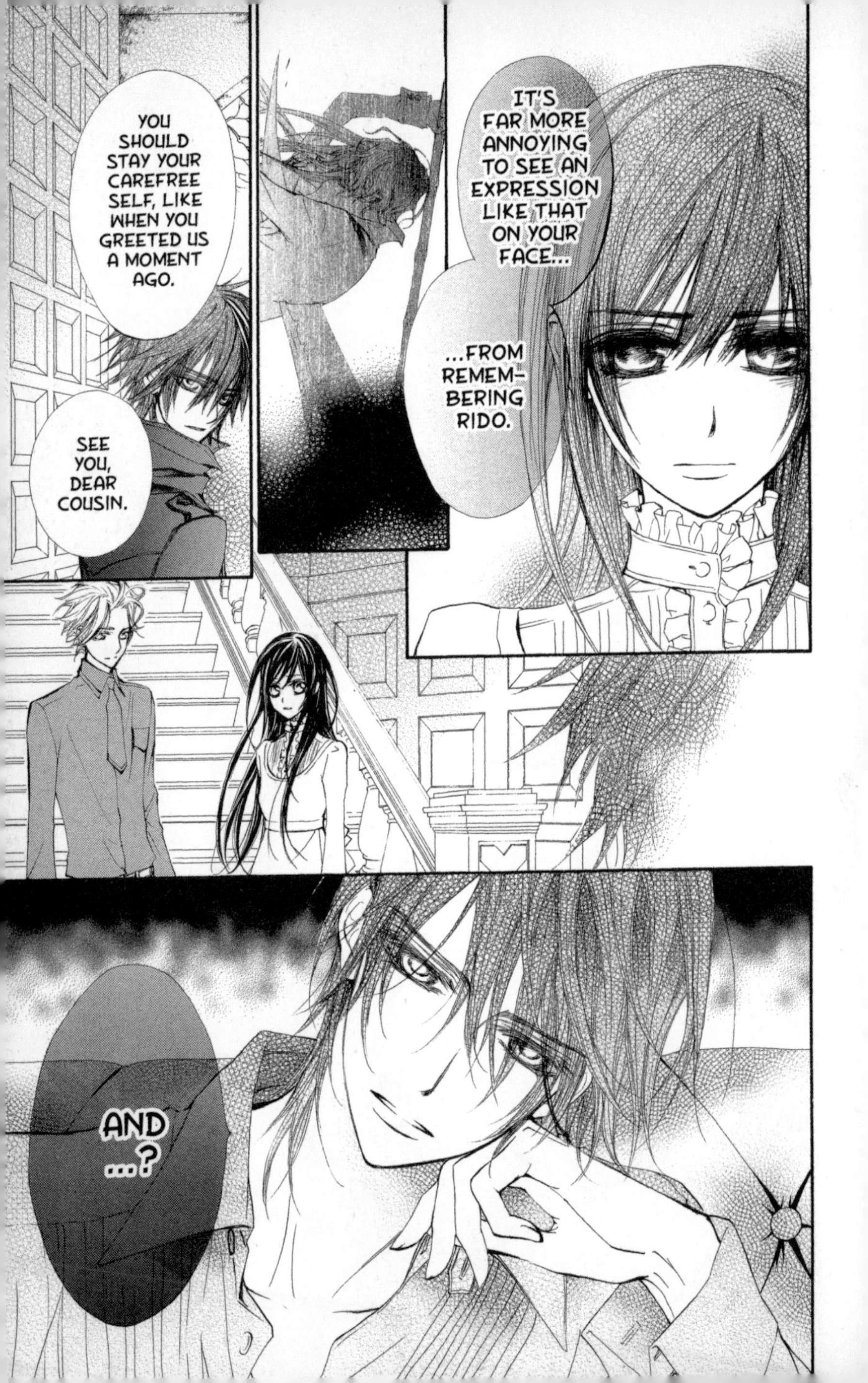
IT'S FAR MORE ANNOYING TO SEE AN EXPRESSION LIKE THAT ON YOUR FACE...
...FROM REMEM-BERING RIDO.
YOU SHOULD STAY YOUR CAREFREE SELF, LIKE WHEN YOU GREETED US A MOMENT AGO.
SEE YOU, DEAR COUSIN.
AND ...?

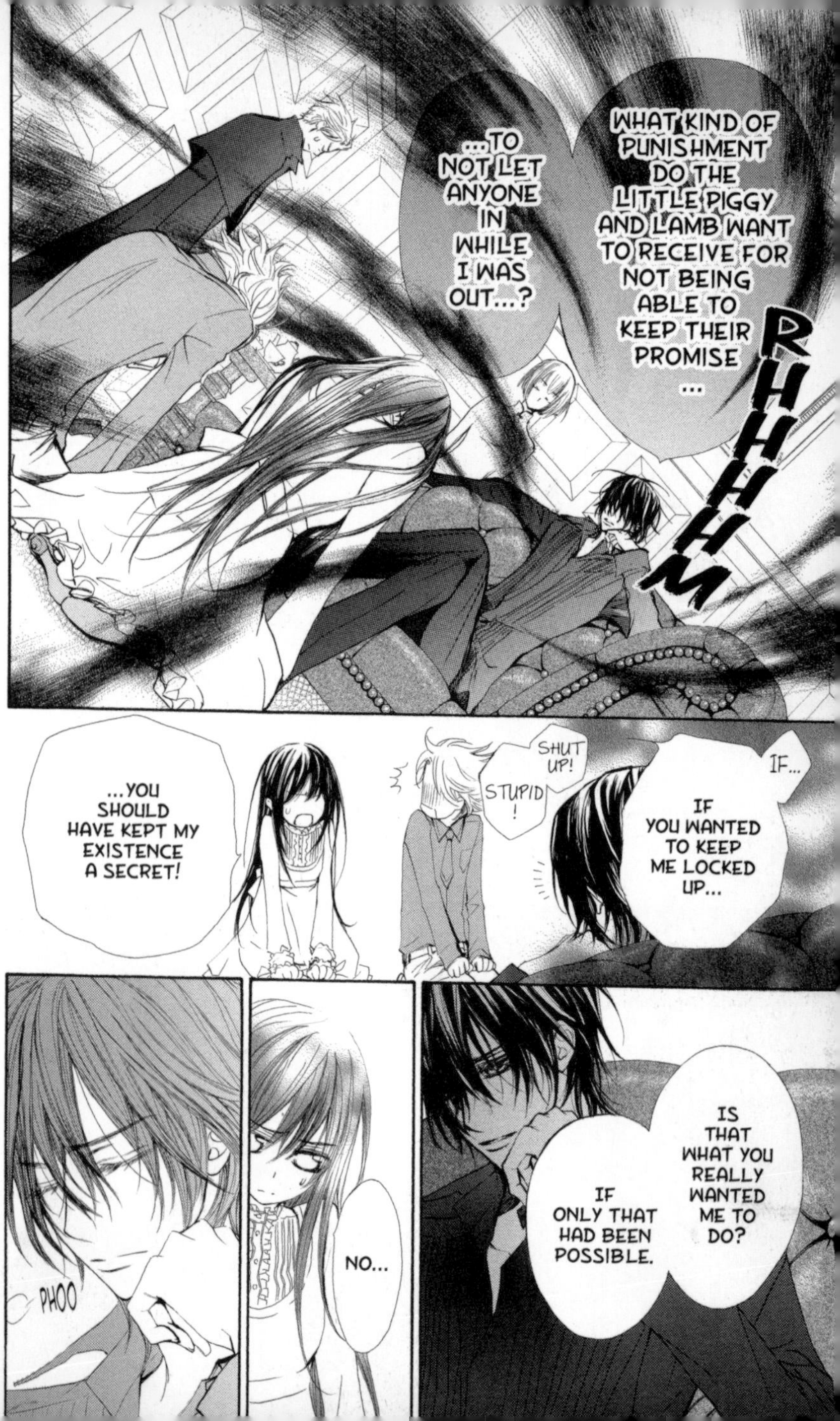

WHAT KIND OF PUNISHMENT DO THE LITTLE PIGGY AND LAMB WANT TO RECEIVE FOR NOT BEING ABLE TO KEEP THEIR PROMISE ...
...TO NOT LET ANYONE IN WHILE I WAS OUT...?
RHHHHM
IF...
IF YOU WANTED TO KEEP ME LOCKED UP...
SHUT UP!
STUPID!
...YOU SHOULD HAVE KEPT MY EXISTENCE A SECRET!
IS THAT WHAT YOU REALLY WANTED ME TO DO?
IF ONLY THAT HAD BEEN POSSIBLE.
NO...
PHOO

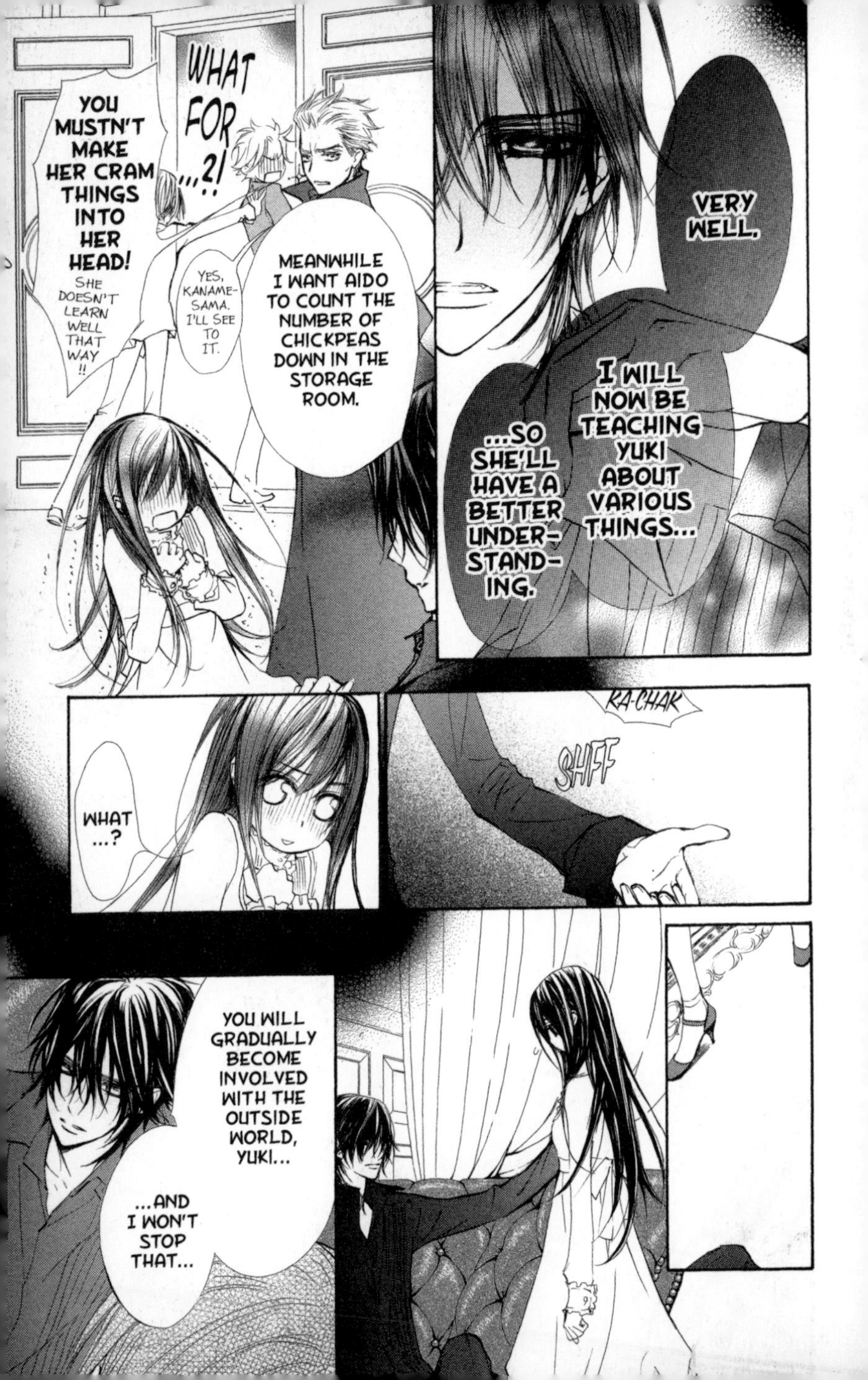
VERY WELL.
I WILL NOW BE TEACHING YUKI ABOUT VARIOUS THINGS...
...SO SHE'LL HAVE A BETTER UNDER-STANDING.
MEANWHILE I WANT AIDO TO COUNT THE NUMBER OF CHICKPEAS DOWN IN THE STORAGE ROOM.
YES, KANAME-SAMA. I'LL SEE TO IT.
WHAT FOR ...?!
YOU MUSTN'T MAKE HER CRAM THINGS INTO HER HEAD!
SHE DOESN'T LEARN WELL THAT WAY !!
RA-CHAK
SHFF
WHAT ...?
YOU WILL GRADUALLY BECOME INVOLVED WITH THE OUTSIDE WORLD, YUKI...
...AND I WON'T STOP THAT...

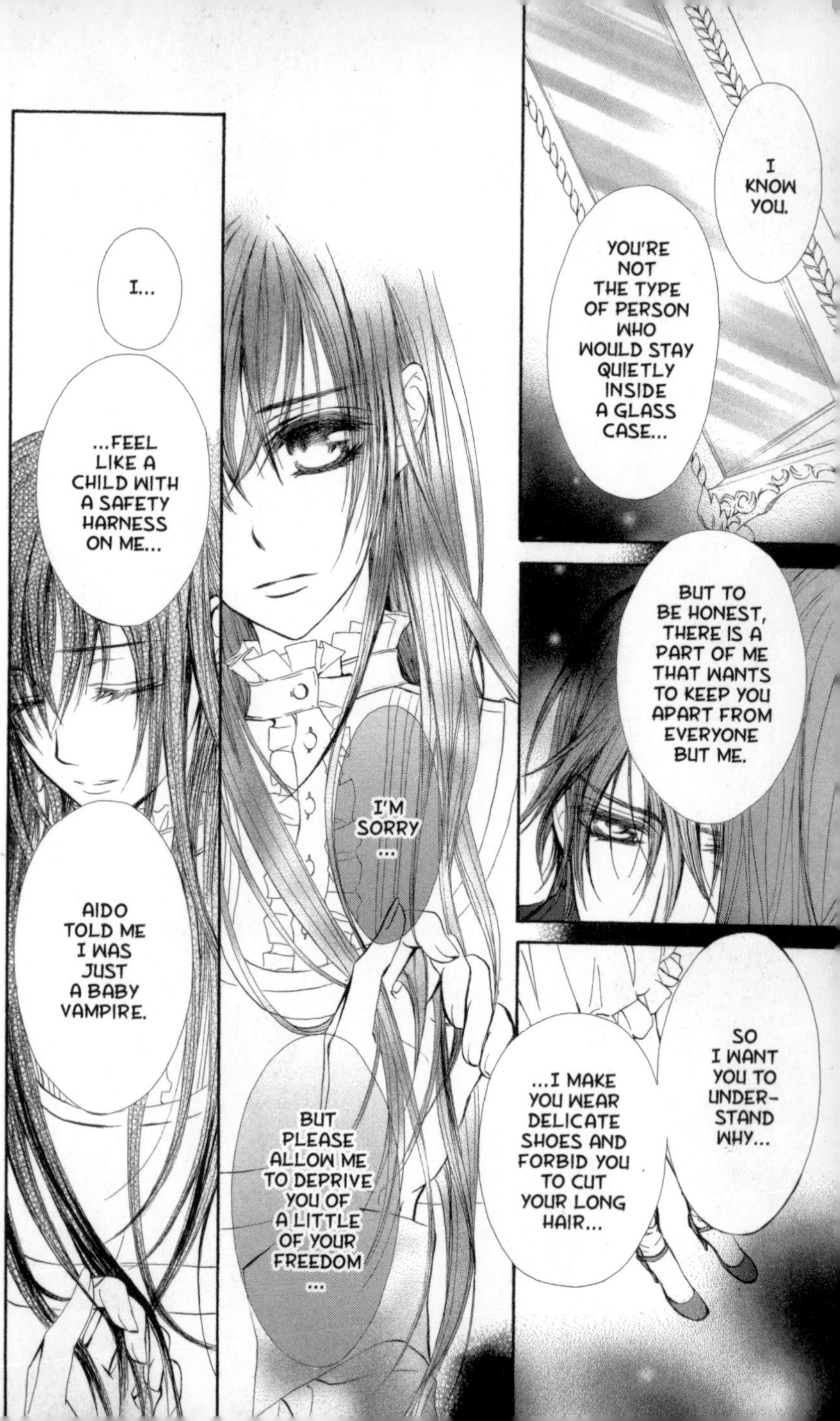
I KNOW YOU.
YOU'RE NOT THE TYPE OF PERSON WHO WOULD STAY QUIETLY INSIDE A GLASS CASE...
BUT TO BE HONEST, THERE IS A PART OF ME THAT WANTS TO KEEP YOU APART FROM EVERYONE BUT ME.
SO I WANT YOU TO UNDER-STAND WHY...
...I MAKE YOU WEAR DELICATE SHOES AND FORBID YOU TO CUT YOUR LONG HAIR...
I'M SORRY...
BUT PLEASE ALLOW ME TO DEPRIVE YOU OF A LITTLE OF YOUR FREEDOM...
I...
...FEEL LIKE A CHILD WITH A SAFETY HARNESS ON ME...
AIDO TOLD ME I WAS JUST A BABY VAMPIRE.

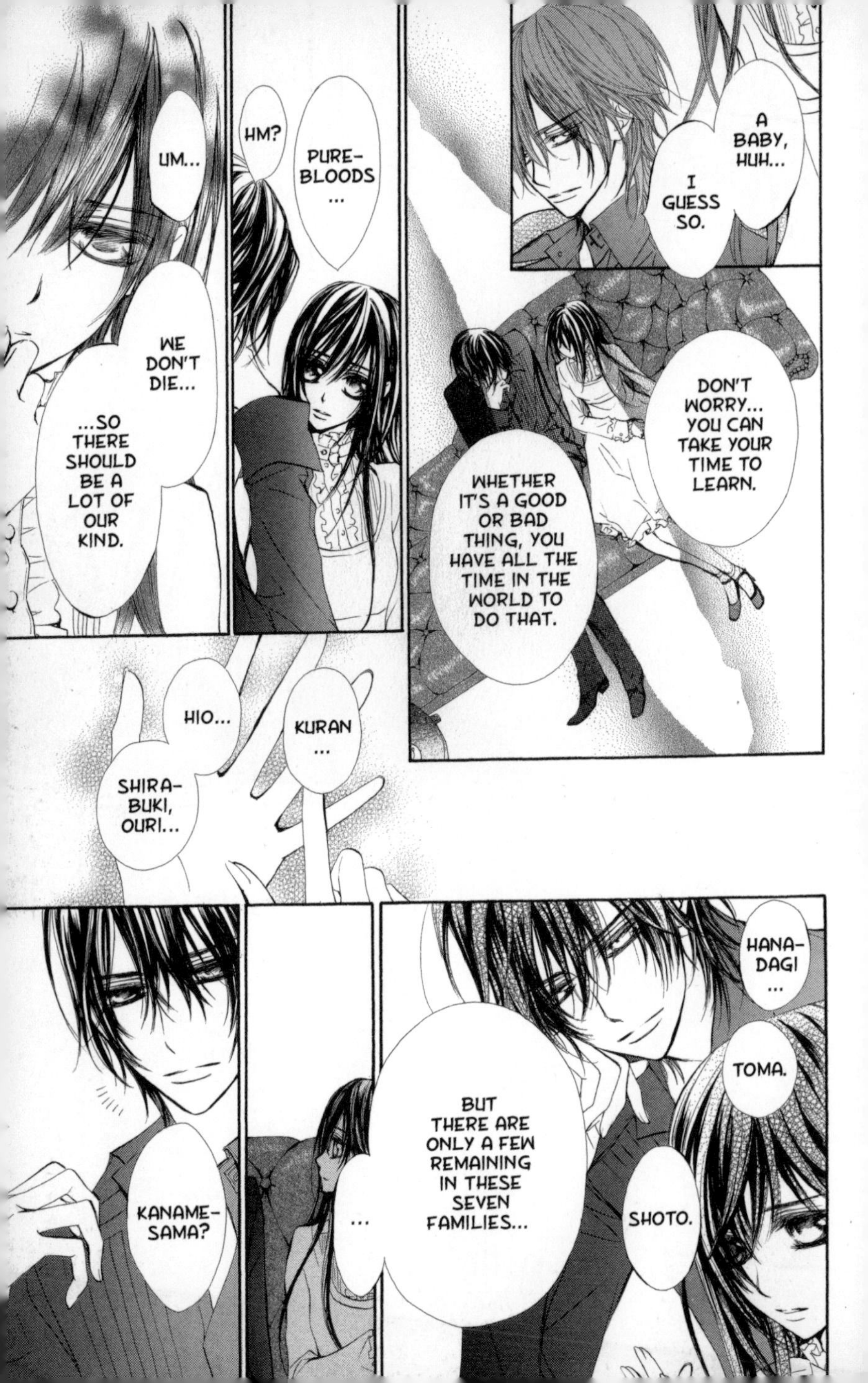
A BABY, HUH...
I GUESS SO.
DON'T WORRY... YOU CAN TAKE YOUR TIME TO LEARN.
WHETHER IT'S A GOOD OR BAD THING, YOU HAVE ALL THE TIME IN THE WORLD TO DO THAT.
PURE-BLOODS...
HM?
UM...
WE DON'T DIE...
...SO THERE SHOULD BE A LOT OF OUR KIND.
KURAN...
HIO...
SHIRA-BUKI, OURI...
HANA-DAGI...
TOMA.
SHOTO.
BUT THERE ARE ONLY A FEW REMAINING IN THESE SEVEN FAMILIES...
...
KANAME-SAMA?

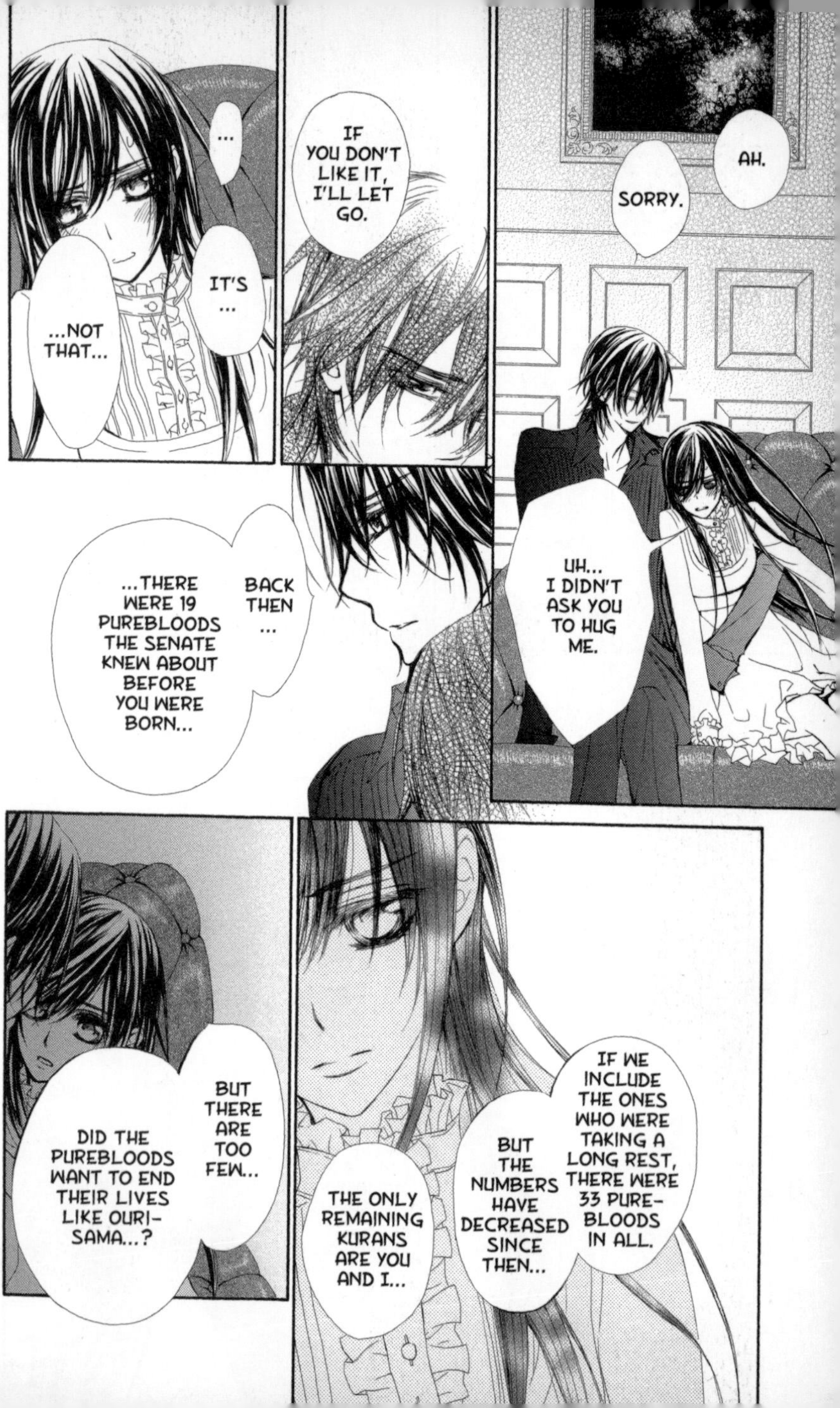
AH.
SORRY.
UH... I DIDN'T ASK YOU TO HUG ME.
IF YOU DON'T LIKE IT, I'LL LET GO.
...
IT'S...
...NOT THAT...
BACK THEN...
...THERE WERE 19 PUREBLOODS THE SENATE KNEW ABOUT BEFORE YOU WERE BORN...
IF WE INCLUDE THE ONES WHO WERE TAKING A LONG REST, THERE WERE 33 PURE-BLOODS IN ALL.
BUT THE NUMBERS HAVE DECREASED SINCE THEN...
THE ONLY REMAINING KURANS ARE YOU AND I...
BUT THERE ARE TOO FEW...
DID THE PUREBLOODS WANT TO END THEIR LIVES LIKE OURI-SAMA...?

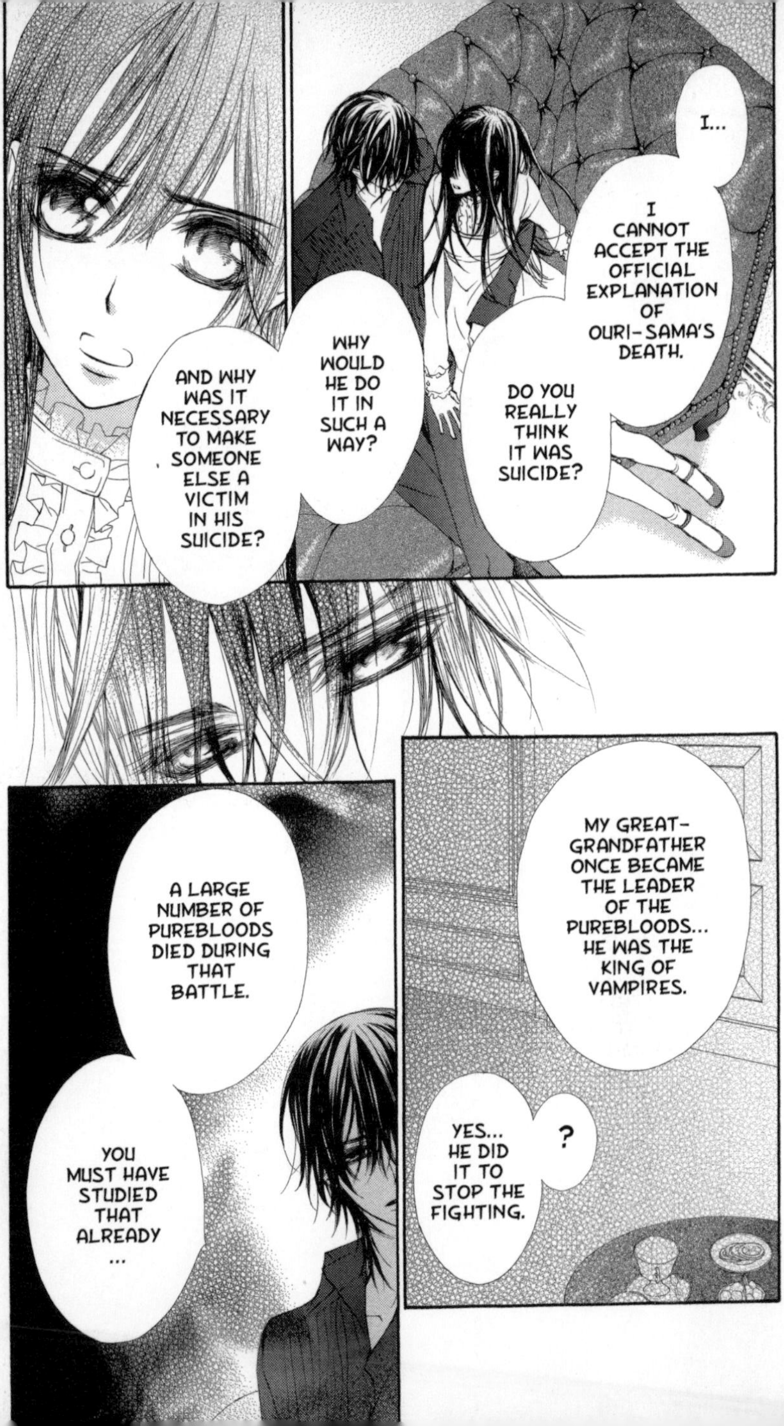
I...
I CANNOT ACCEPT THE OFFICIAL EXPLANATION OF OURI-SAMA'S DEATH.
DO YOU REALLY THINK IT WAS SUICIDE?
WHY WOULD HE DO IT IN SUCH A WAY?
AND WHY WAS IT NECESSARY TO MAKE SOMEONE ELSE A VICTIM IN HIS SUICIDE?
MY GREAT-GRANDFATHER ONCE BECAME THE LEADER OF THE PUREBLOODS... HE WAS THE KING OF VAMPIRES.
?
YES... HE DID IT TO STOP THE FIGHTING.
A LARGE NUMBER OF PUREBLOODS DIED DURING THAT BATTLE.
YOU MUST HAVE STUDIED THAT ALREADY ...

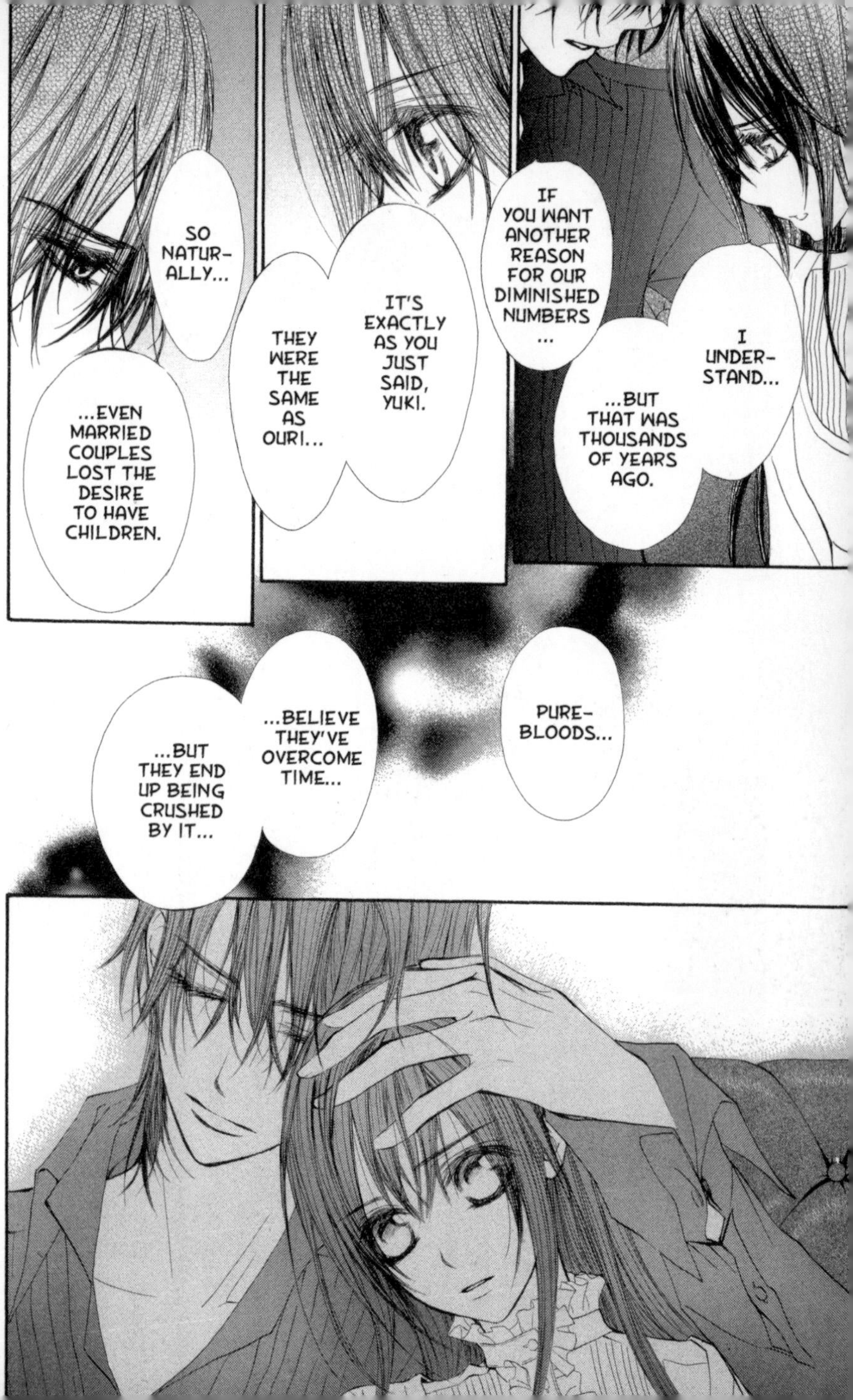
I UNDERSTAND...
...BUT THAT WAS THOUSANDS OF YEARS AGO.
IF YOU WANT ANOTHER REASON FOR OUR DIMINISHED NUMBERS...
IT'S EXACTLY AS YOU JUST SAID, YUKI.
THEY WERE THE SAME AS OURI...
SO NATURALLY...
...EVEN MARRIED COUPLES LOST THE DESIRE TO HAVE CHILDREN.
PUREBLOODS...
...BELIEVE THEY'VE OVERCOME TIME...
...BUT THEY END UP BEING CRUSHED BY IT...

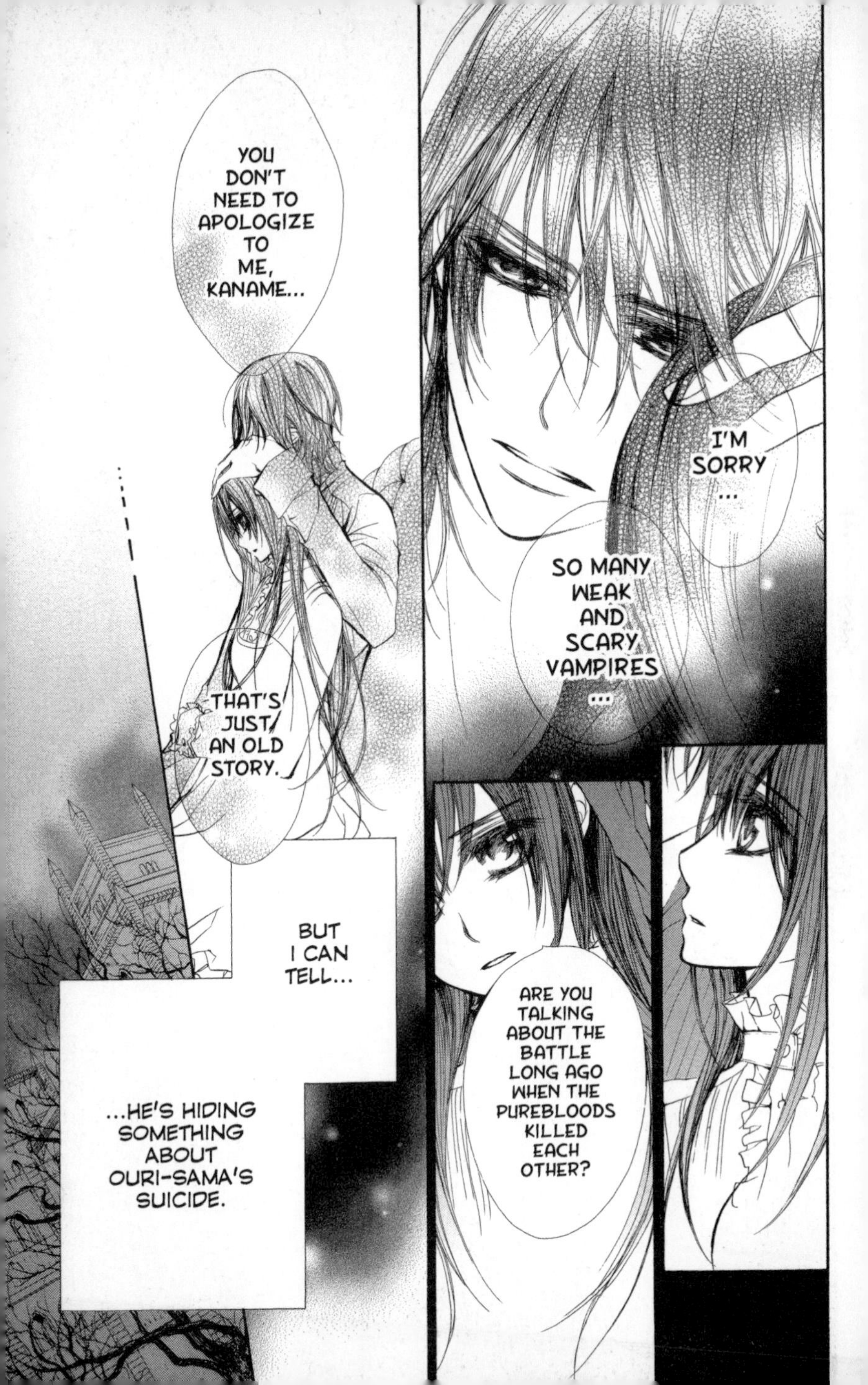
I'M SORRY...
SO MANY WEAK AND SCARY VAMPIRES...
ARE YOU TALKING ABOUT THE BATTLE LONG AGO WHEN THE PUREBLOODS KILLED EACH OTHER?
YOU DON'T NEED TO APOLOGIZE TO ME, KANAME...
...
THAT'S JUST AN OLD STORY.
BUT I CAN TELL...
...HE'S HIDING SOMETHING ABOUT OURI-SAMA'S SUICIDE.

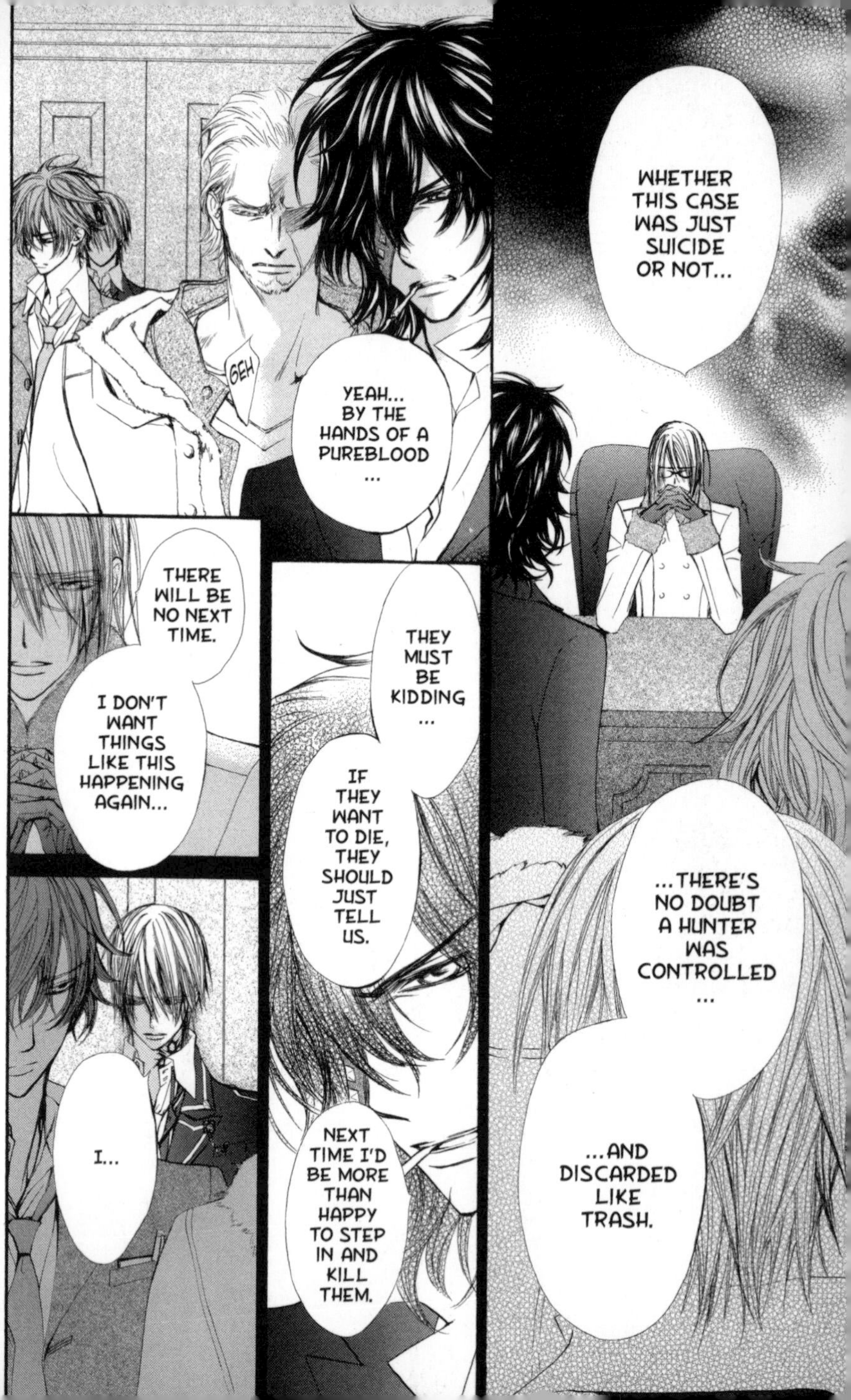
WHETHER THIS CASE WAS JUST SUICIDE OR NOT...
...THERE'S NO DOUBT A HUNTER WAS CONTROLLED...
...AND DISCARDED LIKE TRASH.
YEAH... BY THE HANDS OF A PUREBLOOD...
GEH
THEY MUST BE KIDDING...
IF THEY WANT TO DIE, THEY SHOULD JUST TELL US.
NEXT TIME I'D BE MORE THAN HAPPY TO STEP IN AND KILL THEM.
THERE WILL BE NO NEXT TIME.
I DON'T WANT THINGS LIKE THIS HAPPENING AGAIN...
I...

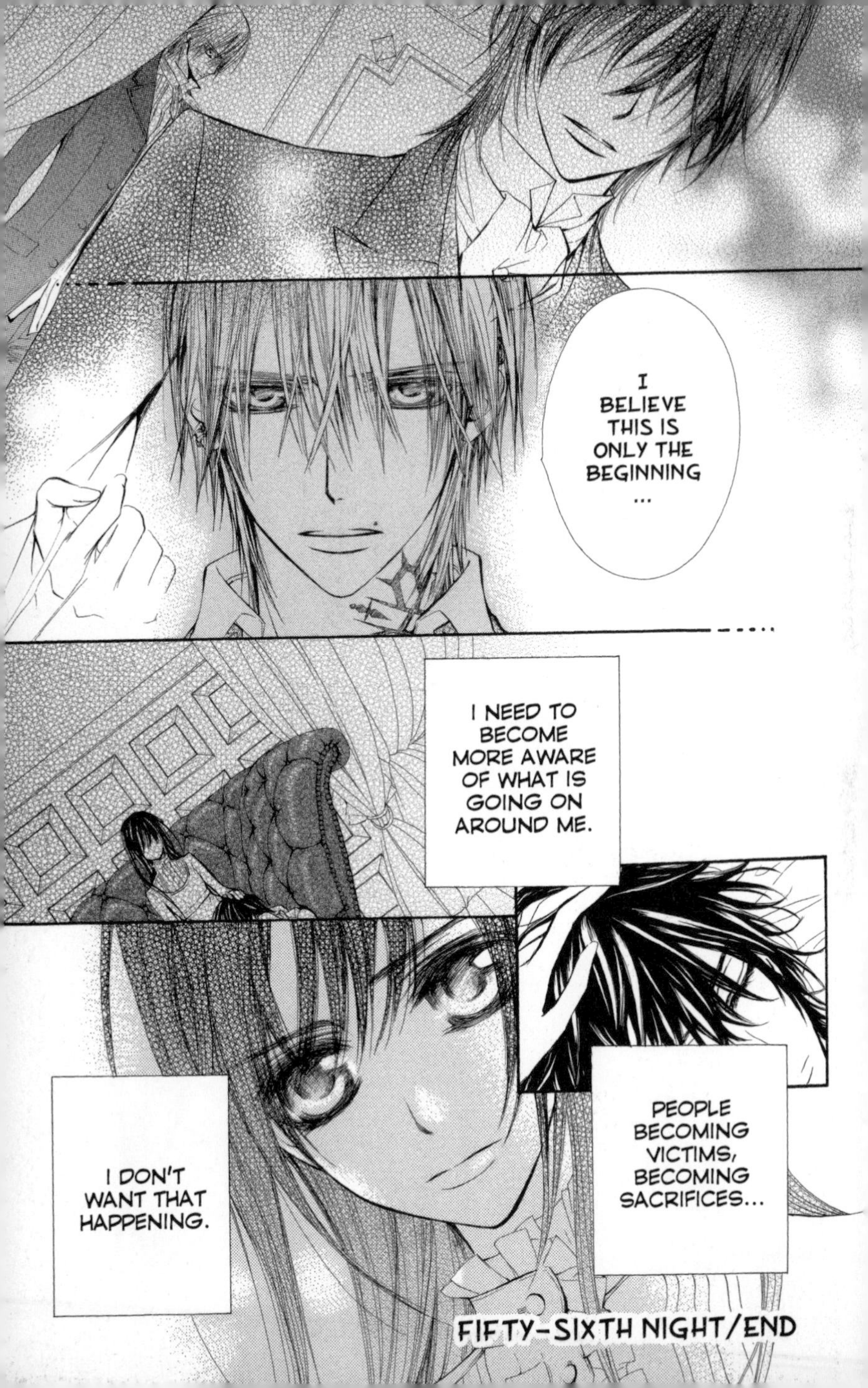
I BELIEVE THIS IS ONLY THE BEGINNING...
I NEED TO BECOME MORE AWARE OF WHAT IS GOING ON AROUND ME.
PEOPLE BECOMING VICTIMS, BECOMING SACRIFICES...
I DON'T WANT THAT HAPPENING.
FIFTY-SIXTH NIGHT/END

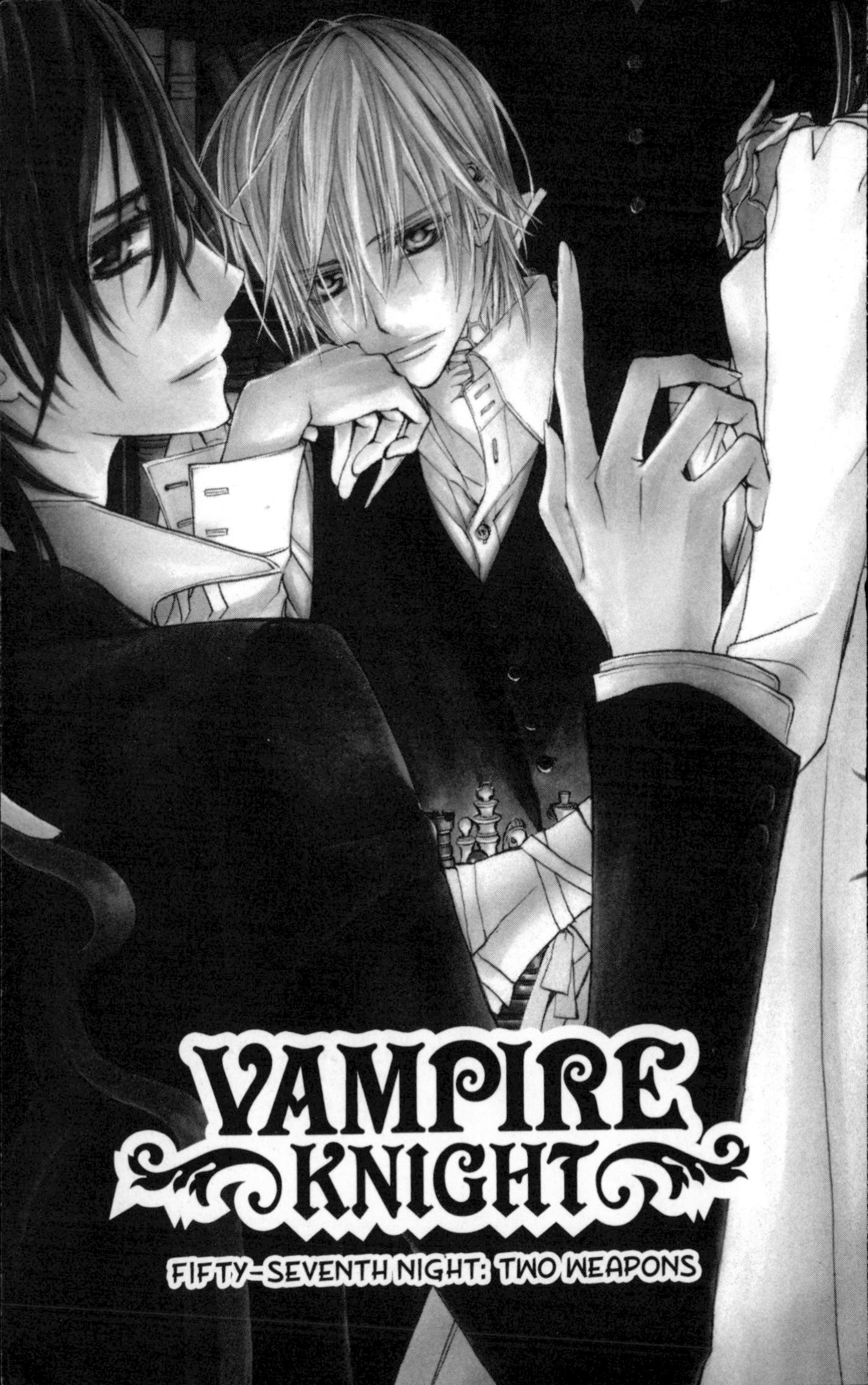
VAMPIRE KNIGHT
FIFTY-SEVENTH NIGHT: TWO WEAPONS

AIDO, MEANWHILE...

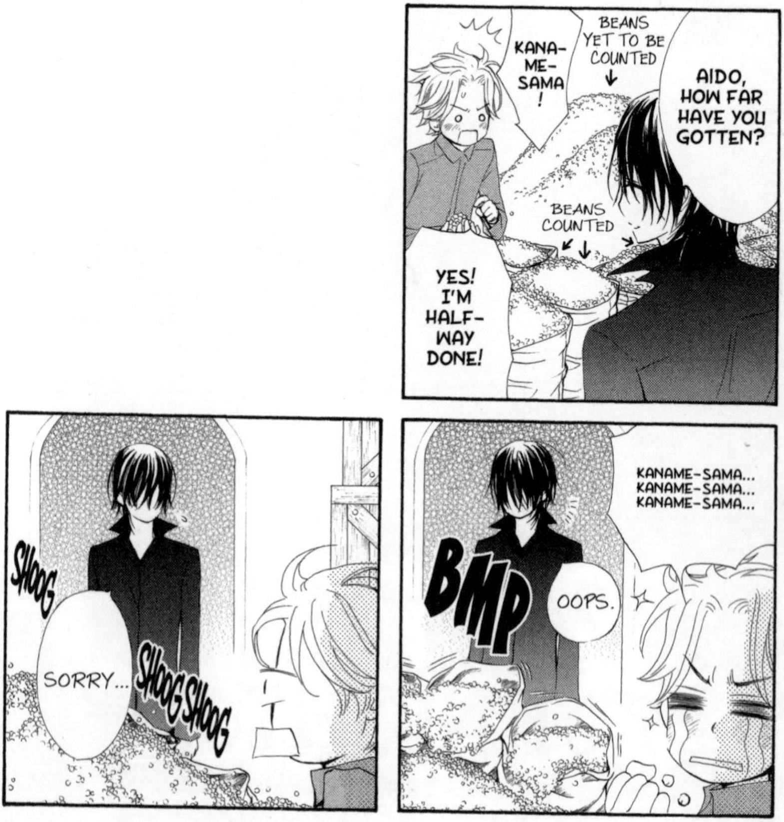
AIDO, HOW FAR HAVE YOU GOTTEN?
BEANS YET TO BE COUNTED
KANAME-SAMA!
BEANS COUNTED
YES! I'M HALF-WAY DONE!
KANAME-SAMA... KANAME-SAMA... KANAME-SAMA...
OOPS.
BMP
SHOOG SHOOG
SHOOG
SORRY...

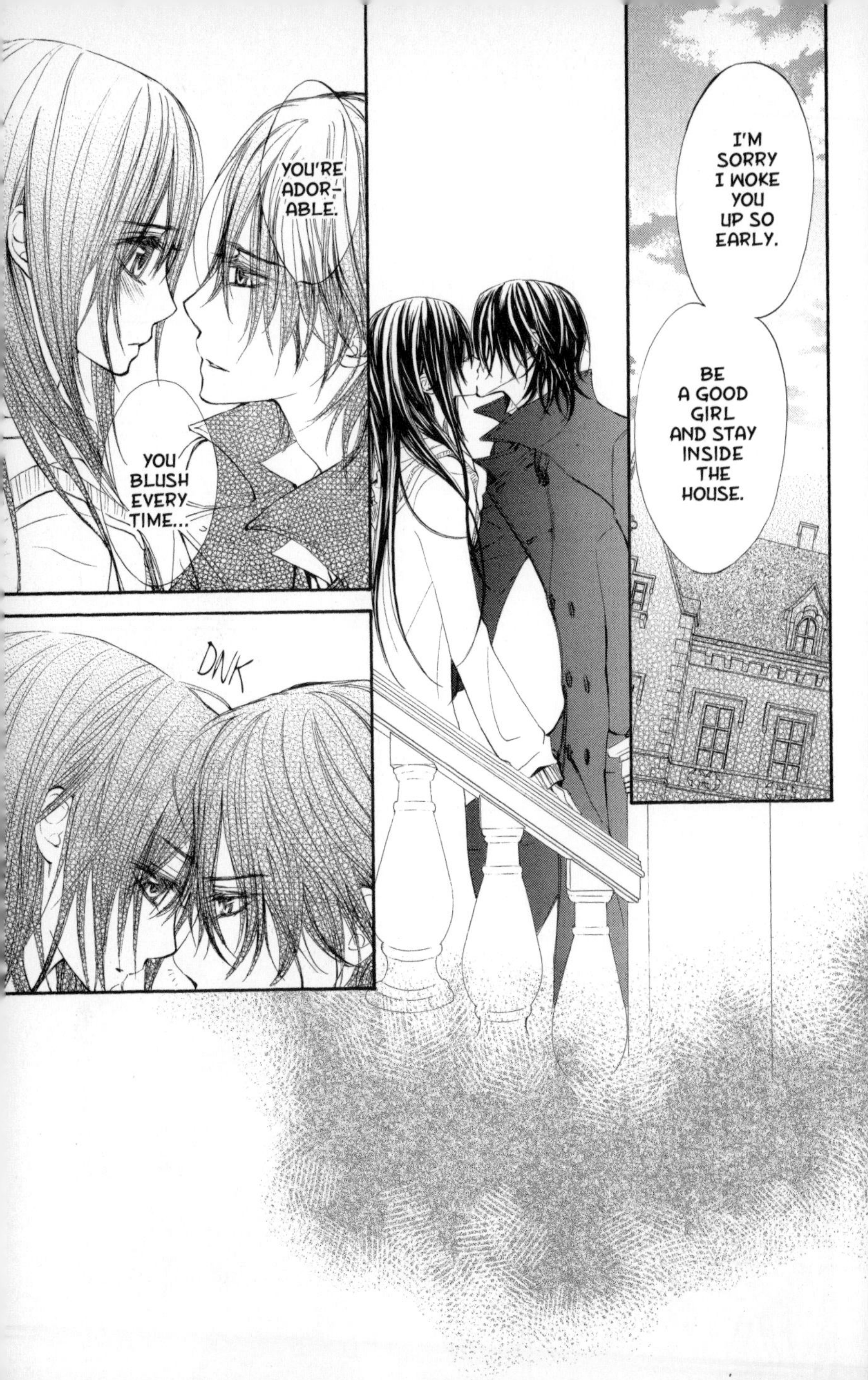
I'M SORRY I WOKE YOU UP SO EARLY.
BE A GOOD GIRL AND STAY INSIDE THE HOUSE.
YOU'RE ADORABLE.
YOU BLUSH EVERY TIME...
DNK

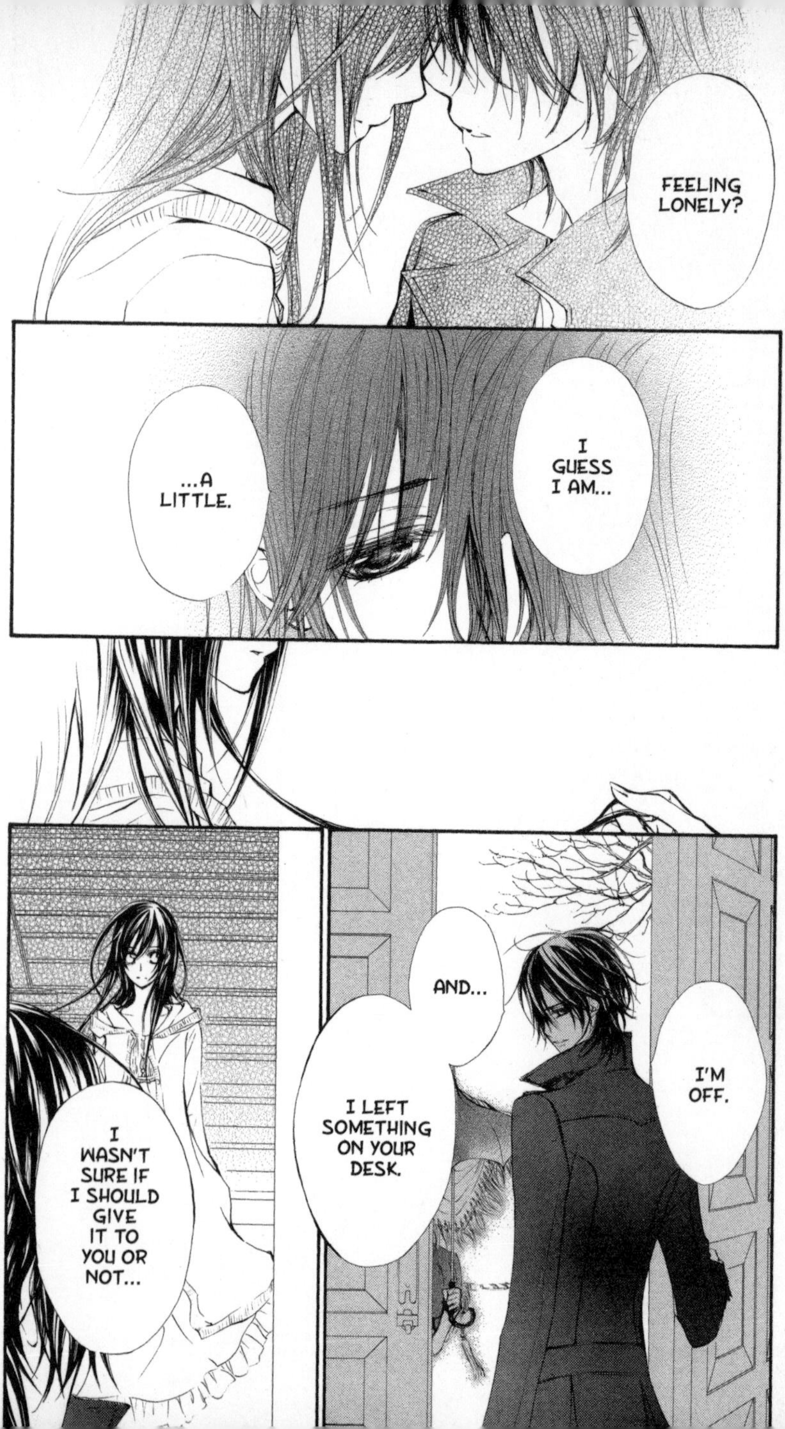
FEELING LONELY?
I GUESS I AM...
...A LITTLE.
I'M OFF.
AND...
I LEFT SOMETHING ON YOUR DESK.
I WASN'T SURE IF I SHOULD GIVE IT TO YOU OR NOT...

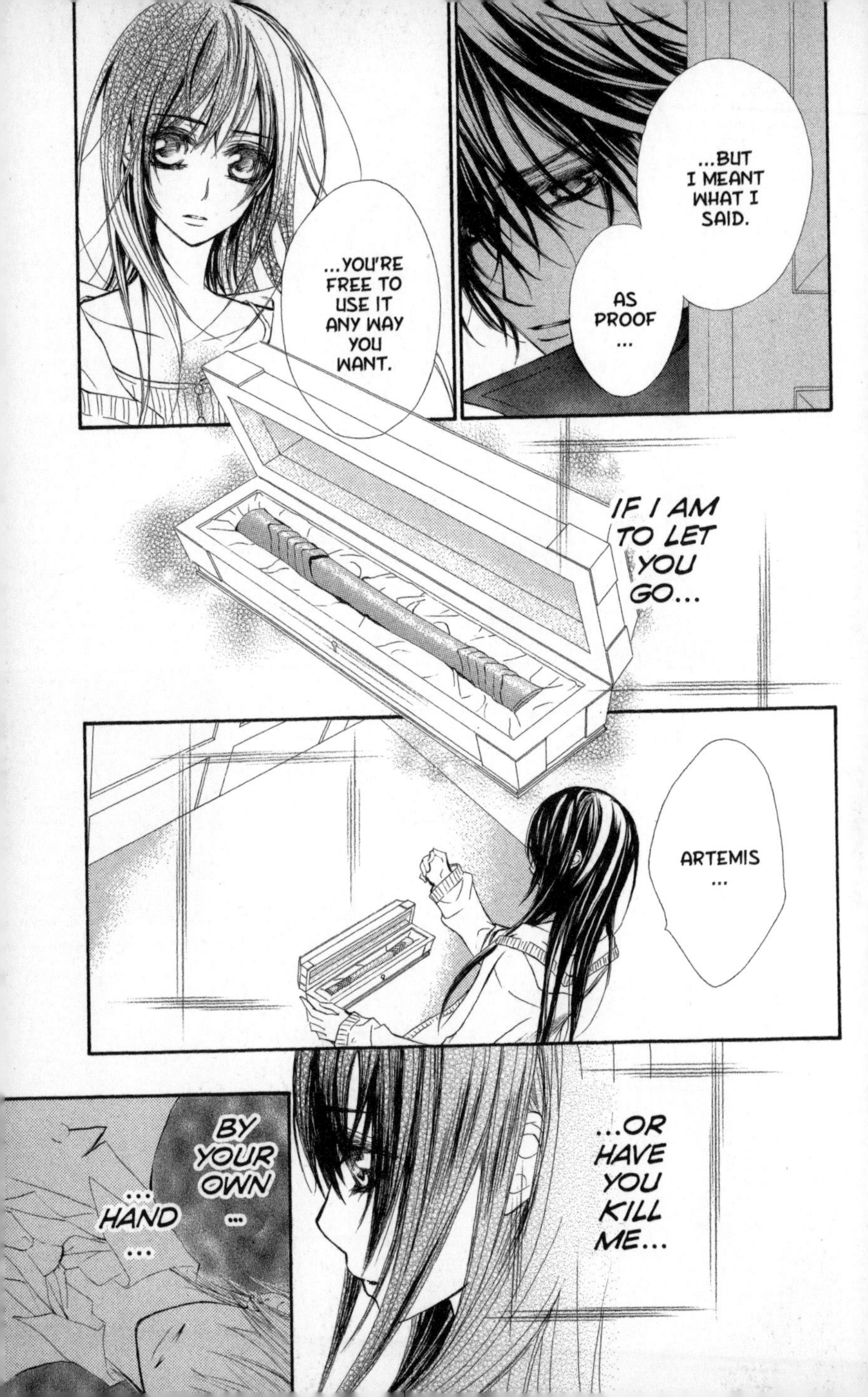
...BUT I MEANT WHAT I SAID.
AS PROOF ...
...YOU'RE FREE TO USE IT ANY WAY YOU WANT.
IF I AM TO LET YOU GO...
ARTEMIS ...
...OR HAVE YOU KILL ME...
BY YOUR OWN ...
... HAND ...

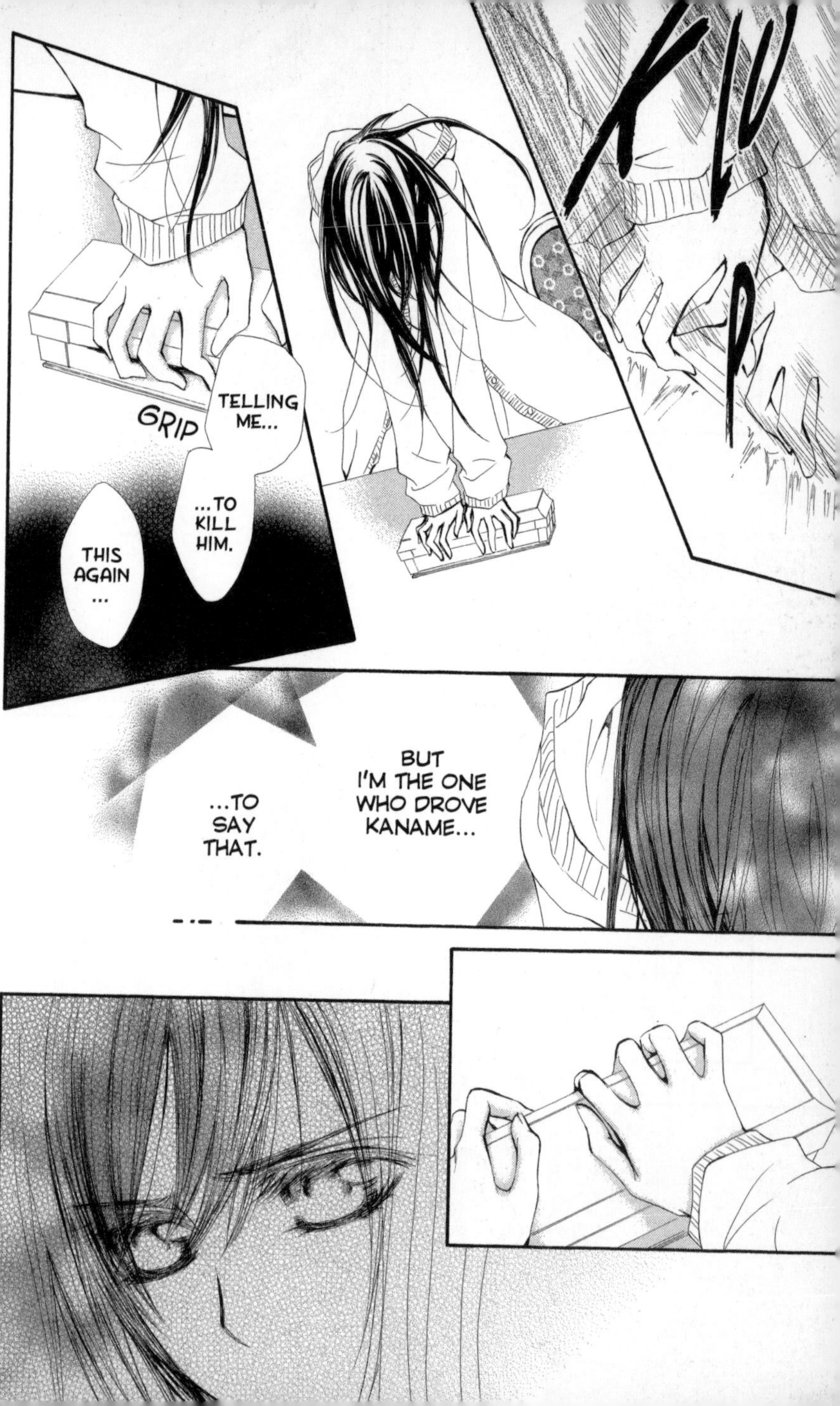
TELLING ME...
GRIP
...TO KILL HIM.
THIS AGAIN...
BUT I'M THE ONE WHO DROVE KANAME...
...TO SAY THAT.

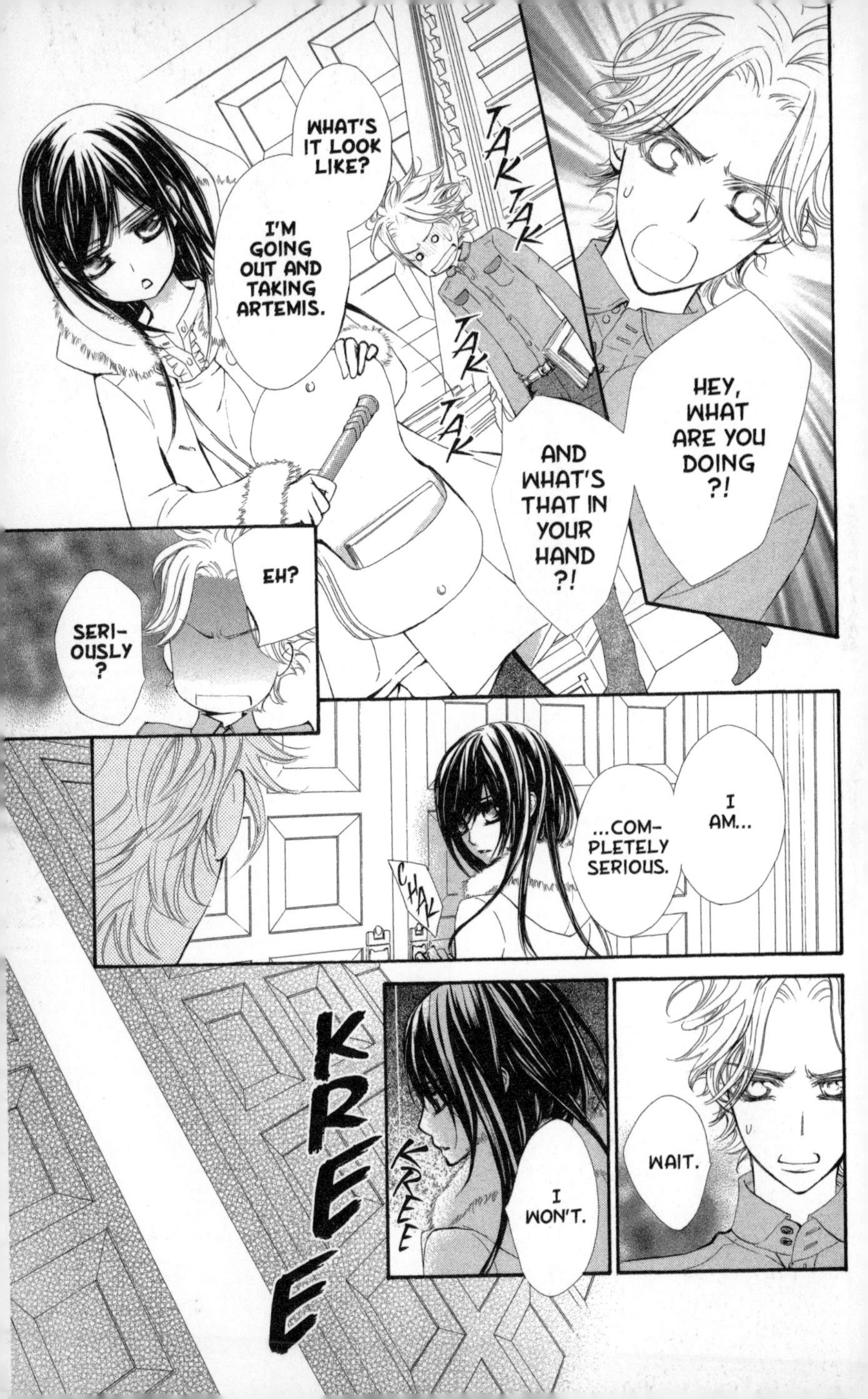
HEY, WHAT ARE YOU DOING ?!
AND WHAT'S THAT IN YOUR HAND ?!
TAK TAK
TAK
TAK
WHAT'S IT LOOK LIKE?
I'M GOING OUT AND TAKING ARTEMIS.
EH?
SERI-OUSLY ?
I AM...
...COM-PLETELY SERIOUS.
CHAK
WAIT.
I WON'T.
KREE
KREEE

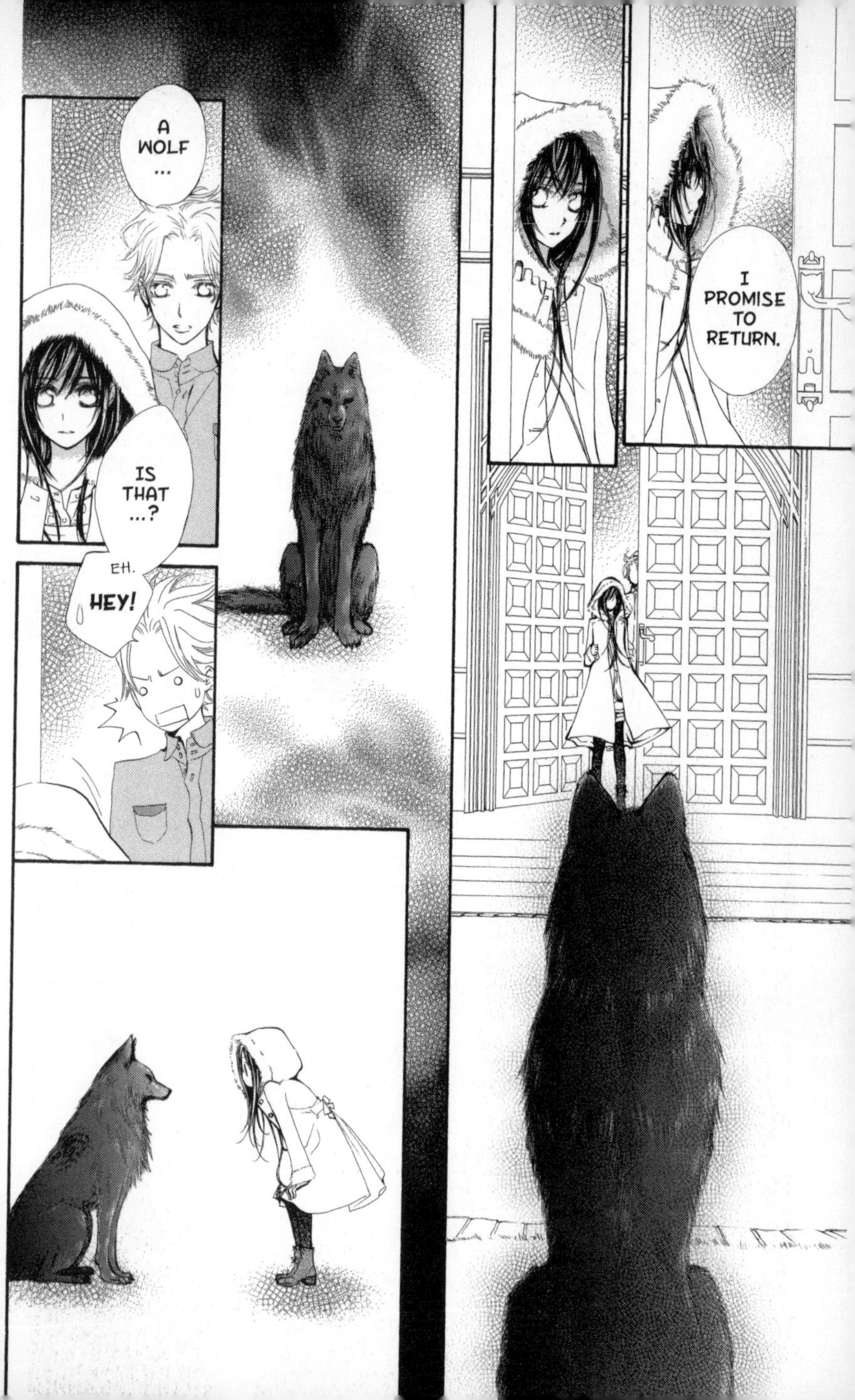
I PROMISE TO RETURN.
A WOLF ...
IS THAT ...?
EH.
HEY!

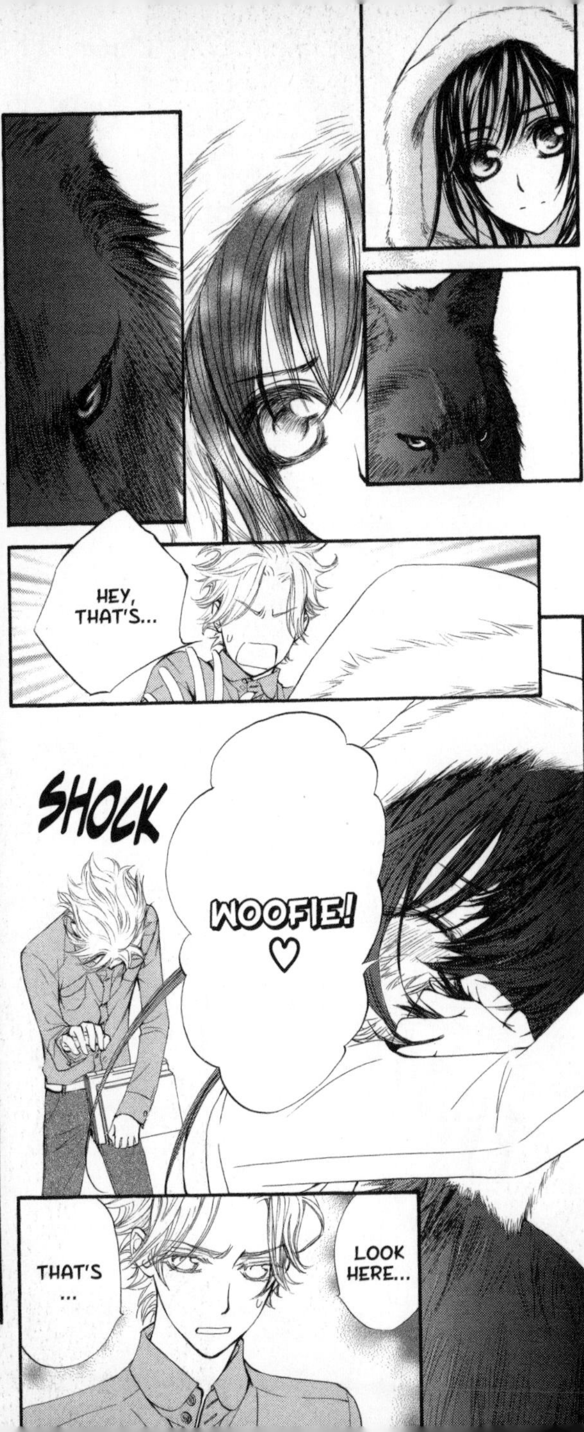
HEY, THAT'S...
WOOFIE! ♥
SHOCK
LOOK HERE...
THAT'S ...

If you want to create a certain atmosphere, imagine that you're a professional photographer and try to capture the perfect moment of the subject you want to shoot. That's what I do. A moment that makes you think, "This is it!" (Especially when I'm drawing Aram and Zero...) Do you think this...will be of any help to you?

Q: Is Kaname-sama a pervert?

A: I just have to answer a question like this when you ask it so seriously... Because it's so fun. I admit he is treated like a joke in the fanbook. But I would like to answer this question earnestly. Both my editor and I share the same feelings about this. And those feelings...do not have much to do with the fact that we know how the story is going to end. In other words, it is the same feeling all the readers are probably gradually starting to feel as well... But there is one thing I would like to say! There is love in it (for me, the creator of this series). There is love in it... Isn't there, Dear Editor...?

◎ Thank you very much for all the questions!! I'm sorry I was only able to answer a few. 3

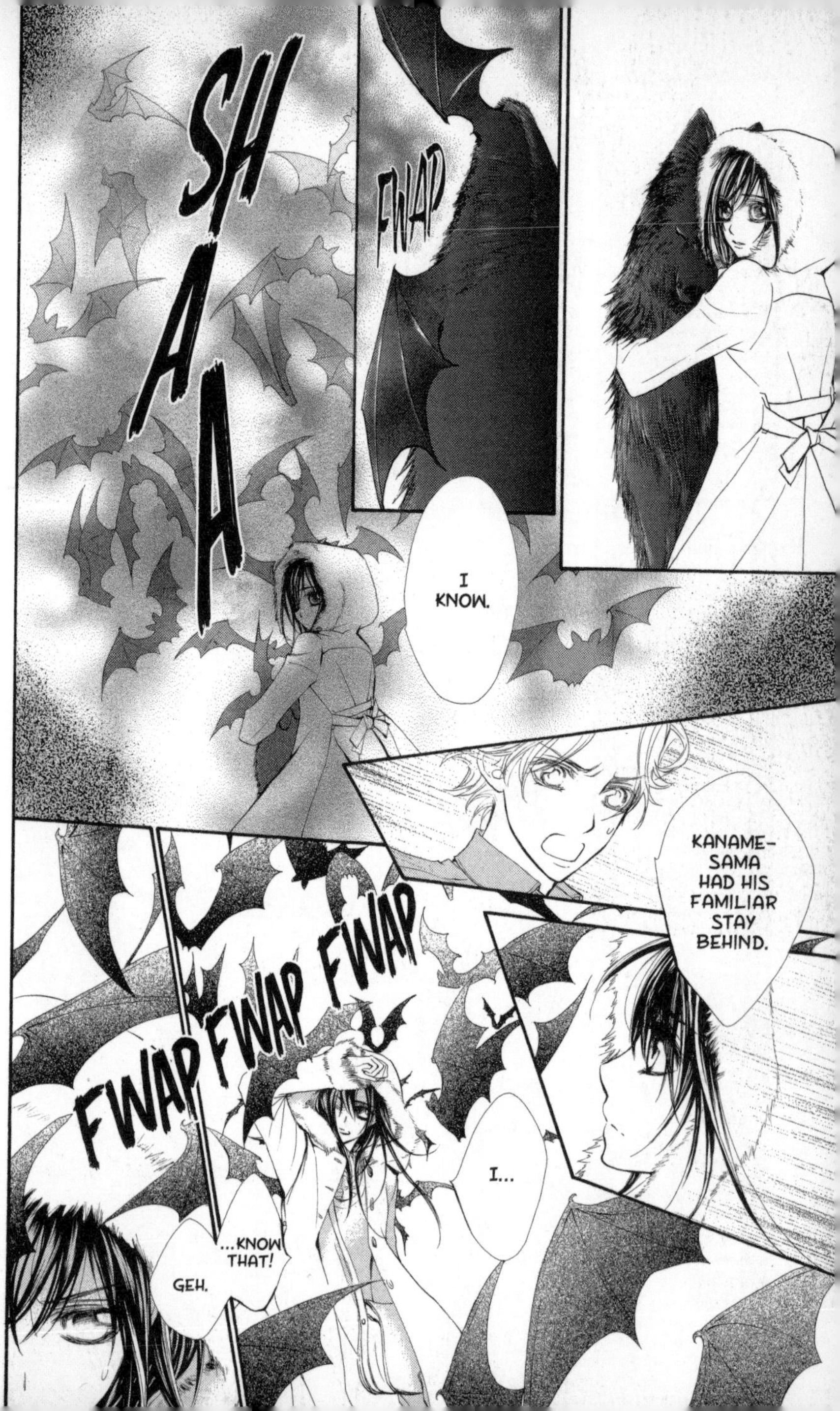
FWAP
SHAAA
I KNOW.
KANAME-SAMA HAD HIS FAMILIAR STAY BEHIND.
I...
...KNOW THAT!
FWAP FWAP FWAP
GEH.

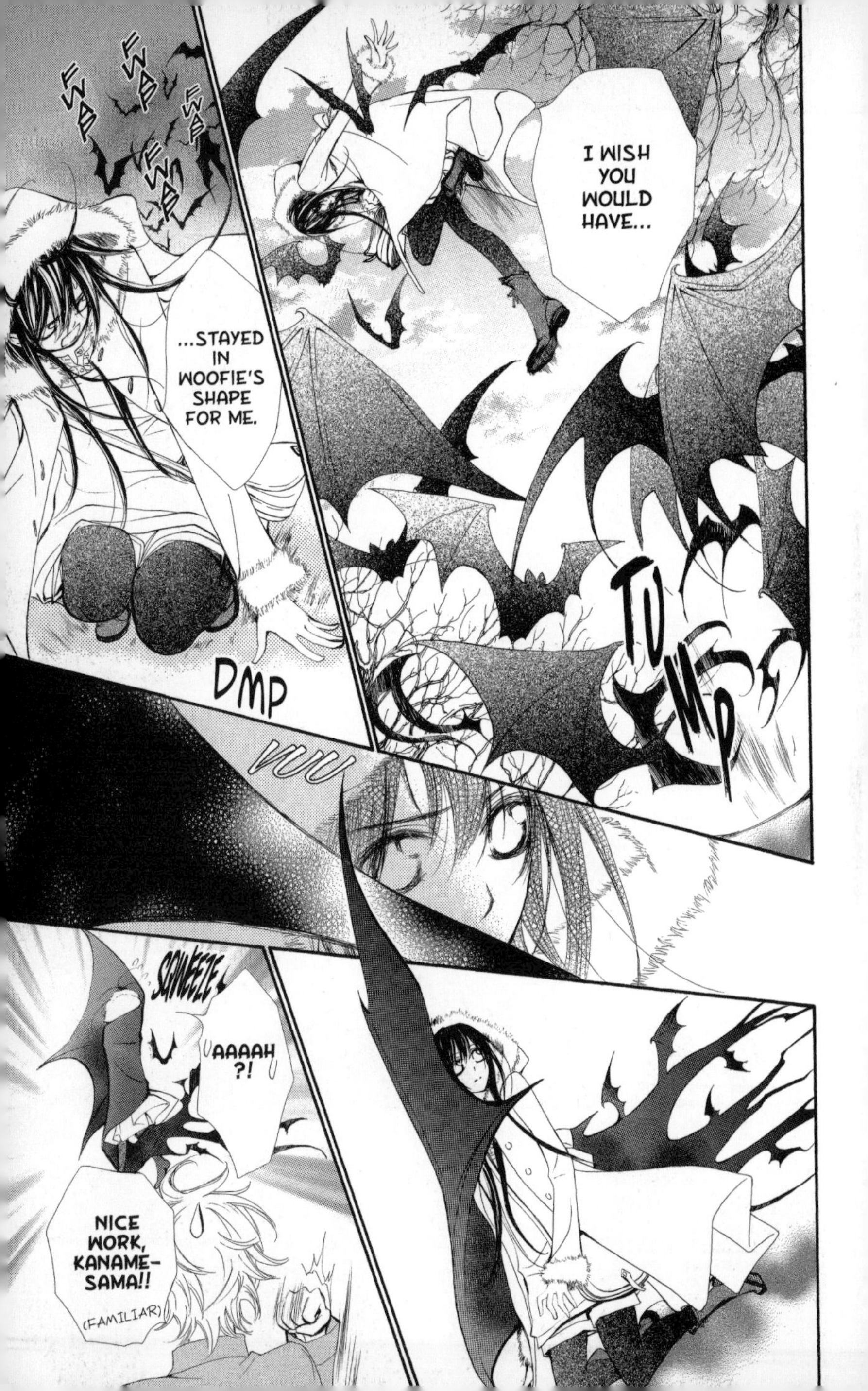
I WISH YOU WOULD HAVE...
TUMP
FWP FWP FWP FWP
...STAYED IN WOOFIE'S SHAPE FOR ME.
DMP
VUU
SQWEEZE
AAAAH?!
NICE WORK, KANAME-SAMA!!
(FAMILIAR)

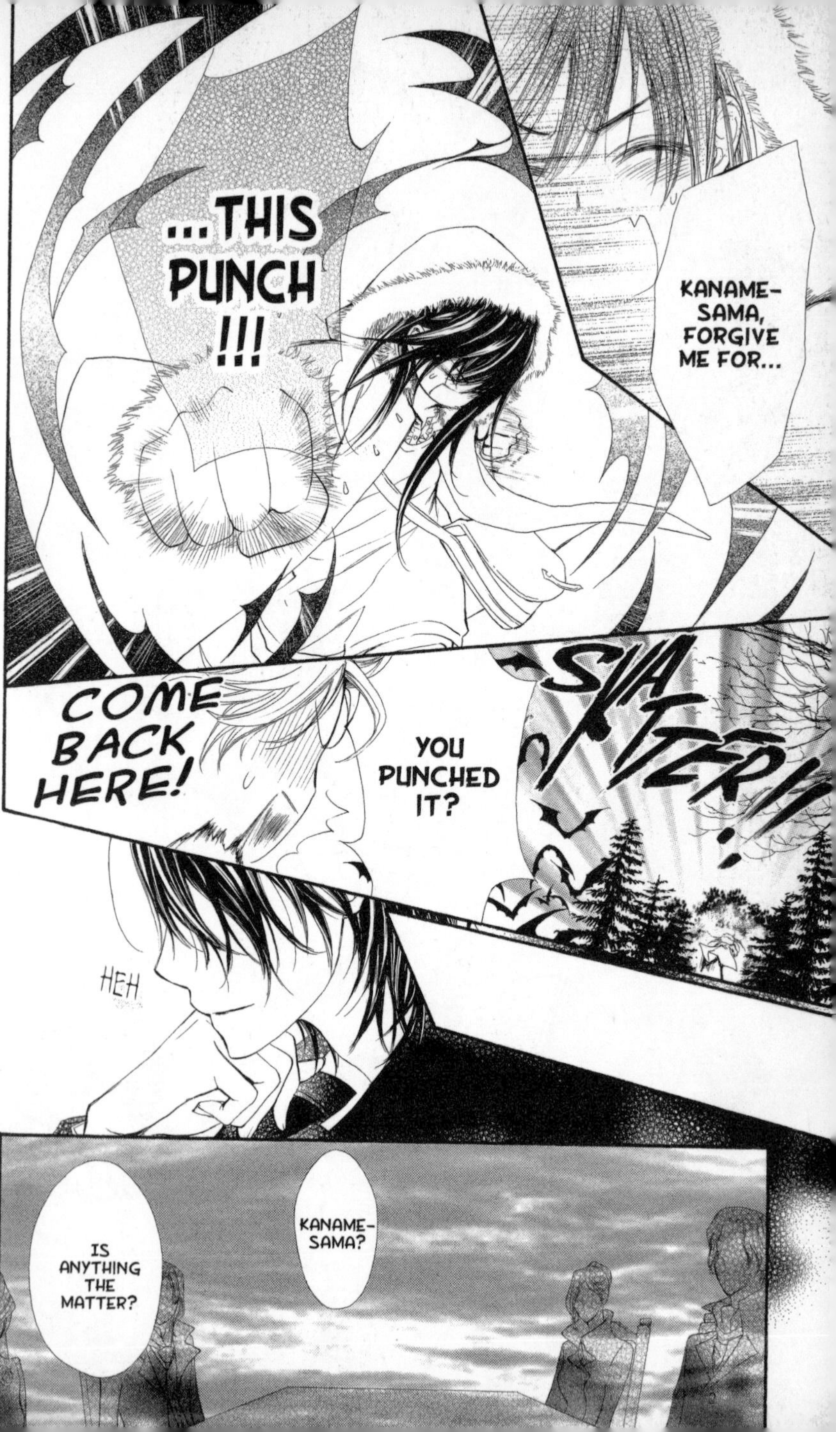
KANAME-SAMA, FORGIVE ME FOR...
...THIS PUNCH!!!
SPLATTER!!
YOU PUNCHED IT?
COME BACK HERE!
HEH
KANAME-SAMA?
IS ANYTHING THE MATTER?

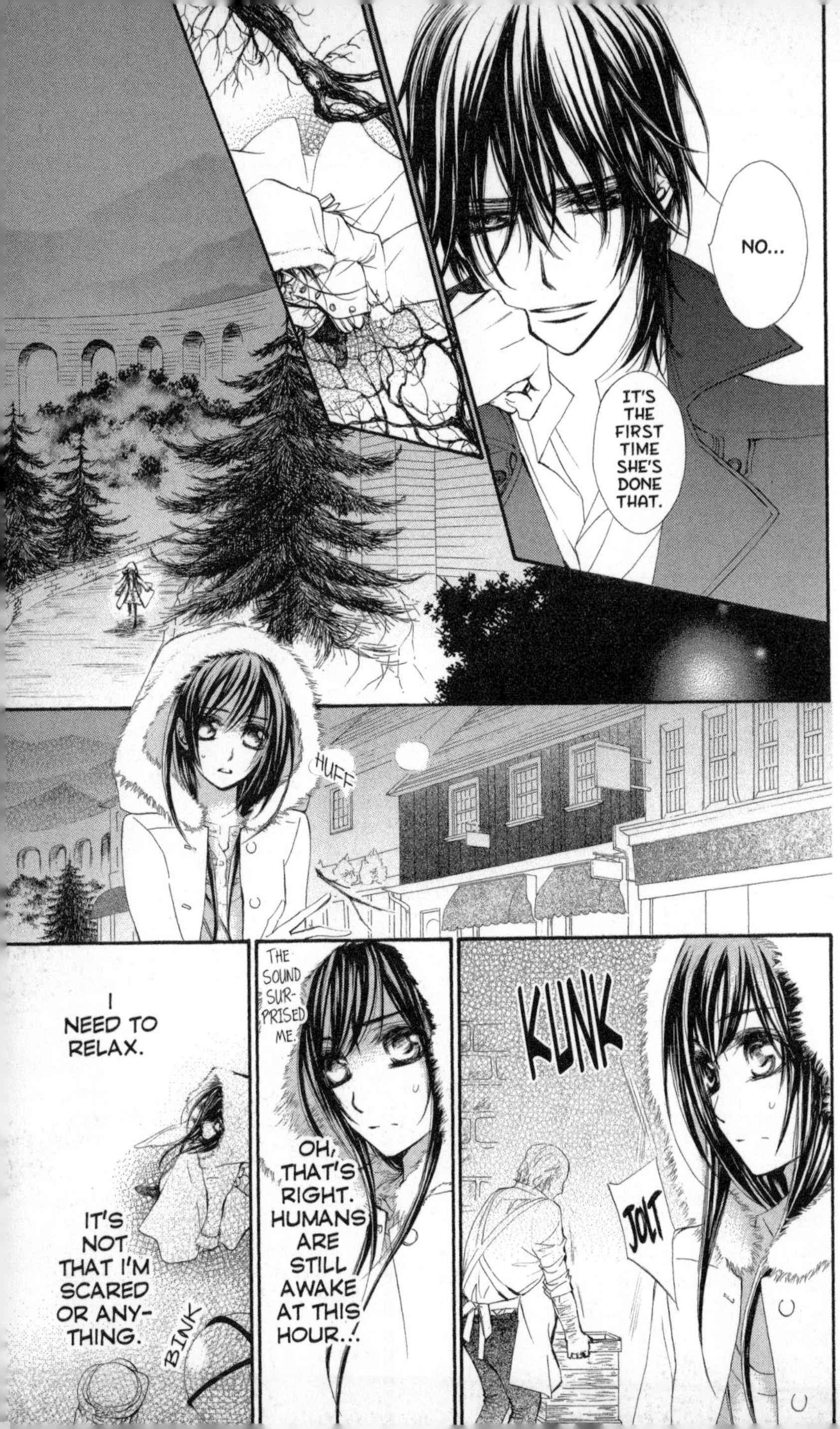
NO...
IT'S THE FIRST TIME SHE'S DONE THAT.
HUFF
KUNK
JOLT
THE SOUND SUR-PRISED ME.
OH, THAT'S RIGHT. HUMANS ARE STILL AWAKE AT THIS HOUR...
I NEED TO RELAX.
IT'S NOT THAT I'M SCARED OR ANY-THING.
BINK

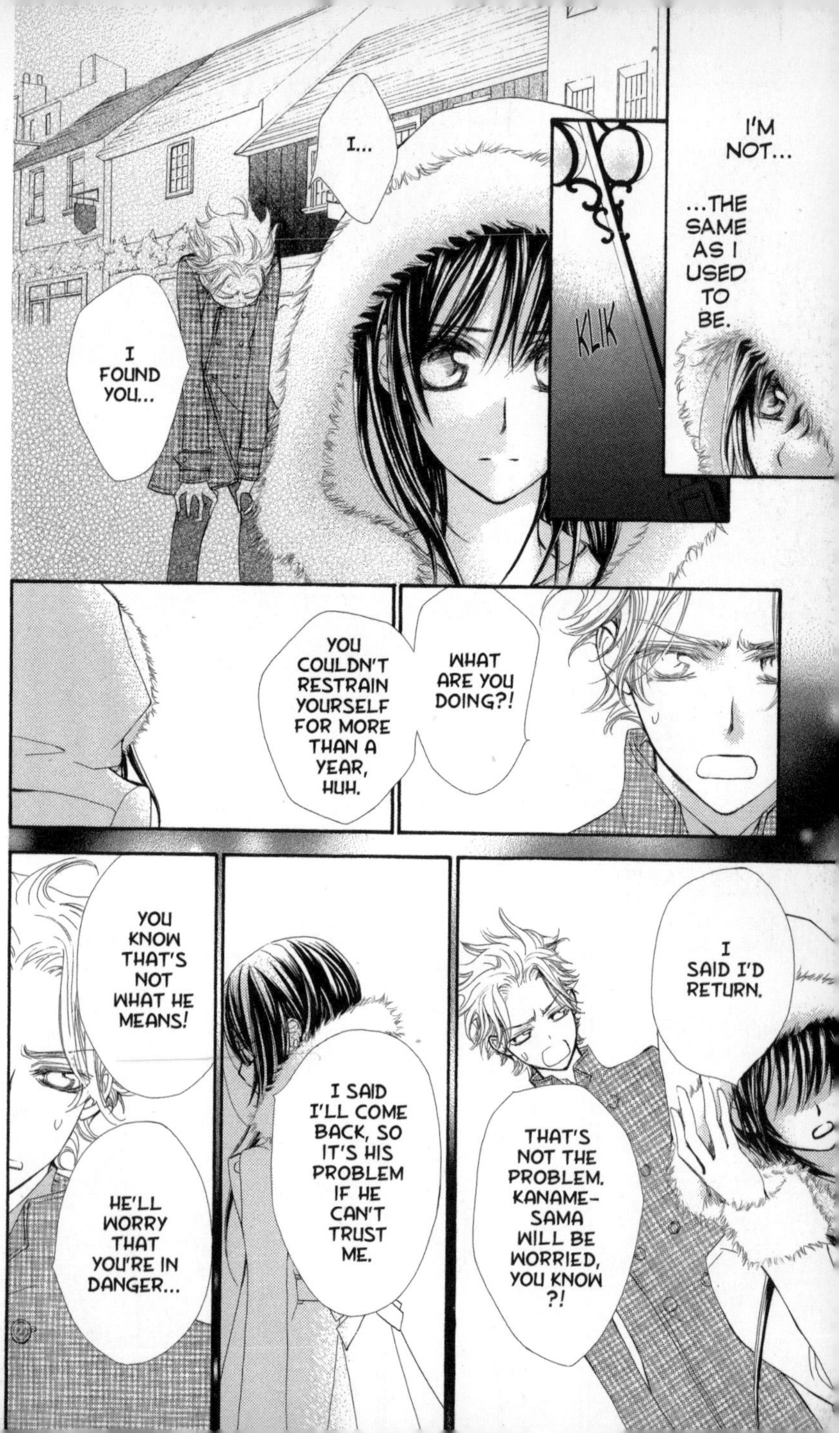
I'M NOT...
...THE SAME AS I USED TO BE.
KLIK
I...
I FOUND YOU...
WHAT ARE YOU DOING?!
YOU COULDN'T RESTRAIN YOURSELF FOR MORE THAN A YEAR, HUH.
I SAID I'D RETURN.
THAT'S NOT THE PROBLEM. KANAME-SAMA WILL BE WORRIED, YOU KNOW?!
I SAID I'LL COME BACK, SO IT'S HIS PROBLEM IF HE CAN'T TRUST ME.
YOU KNOW THAT'S NOT WHAT HE MEANS!
HE'LL WORRY THAT YOU'RE IN DANGER...

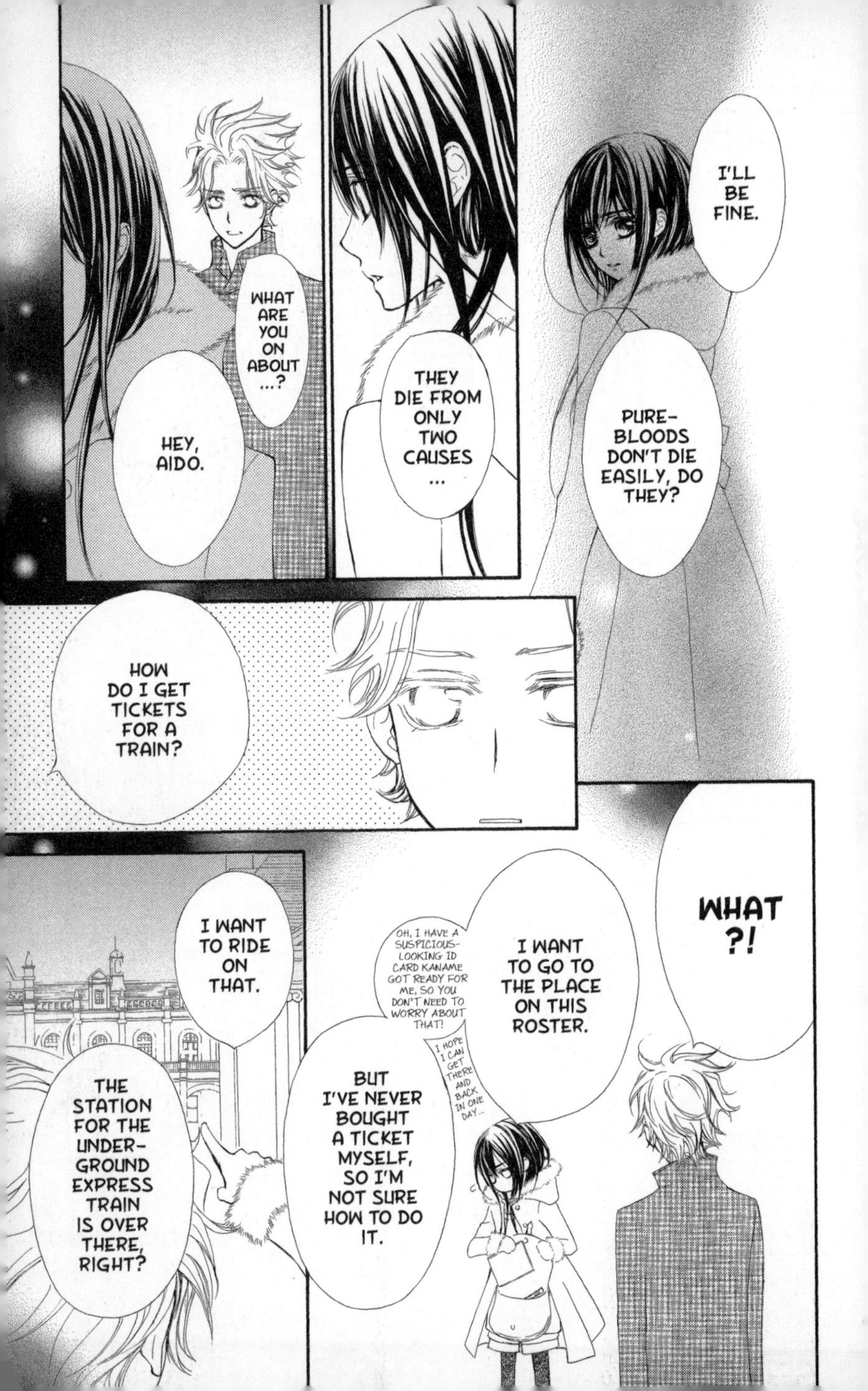
I'LL BE FINE.
PURE-BLOODS DON'T DIE EASILY, DO THEY?
THEY DIE FROM ONLY TWO CAUSES...
WHAT ARE YOU ON ABOUT...?
HEY, AIDO.
HOW DO I GET TICKETS FOR A TRAIN?
WHAT?!
I WANT TO GO TO THE PLACE ON THIS ROSTER.
OH, I HAVE A SUSPICIOUS-LOOKING ID CARD KANAME GOT READY FOR ME, SO YOU DON'T NEED TO WORRY ABOUT THAT!
I HOPE I CAN GET THERE AND BACK IN ONE DAY...
BUT I'VE NEVER BOUGHT A TICKET MYSELF, SO I'M NOT SURE HOW TO DO IT.
I WANT TO RIDE ON THAT.
THE STATION FOR THE UNDER-GROUND EXPRESS TRAIN IS OVER THERE, RIGHT?

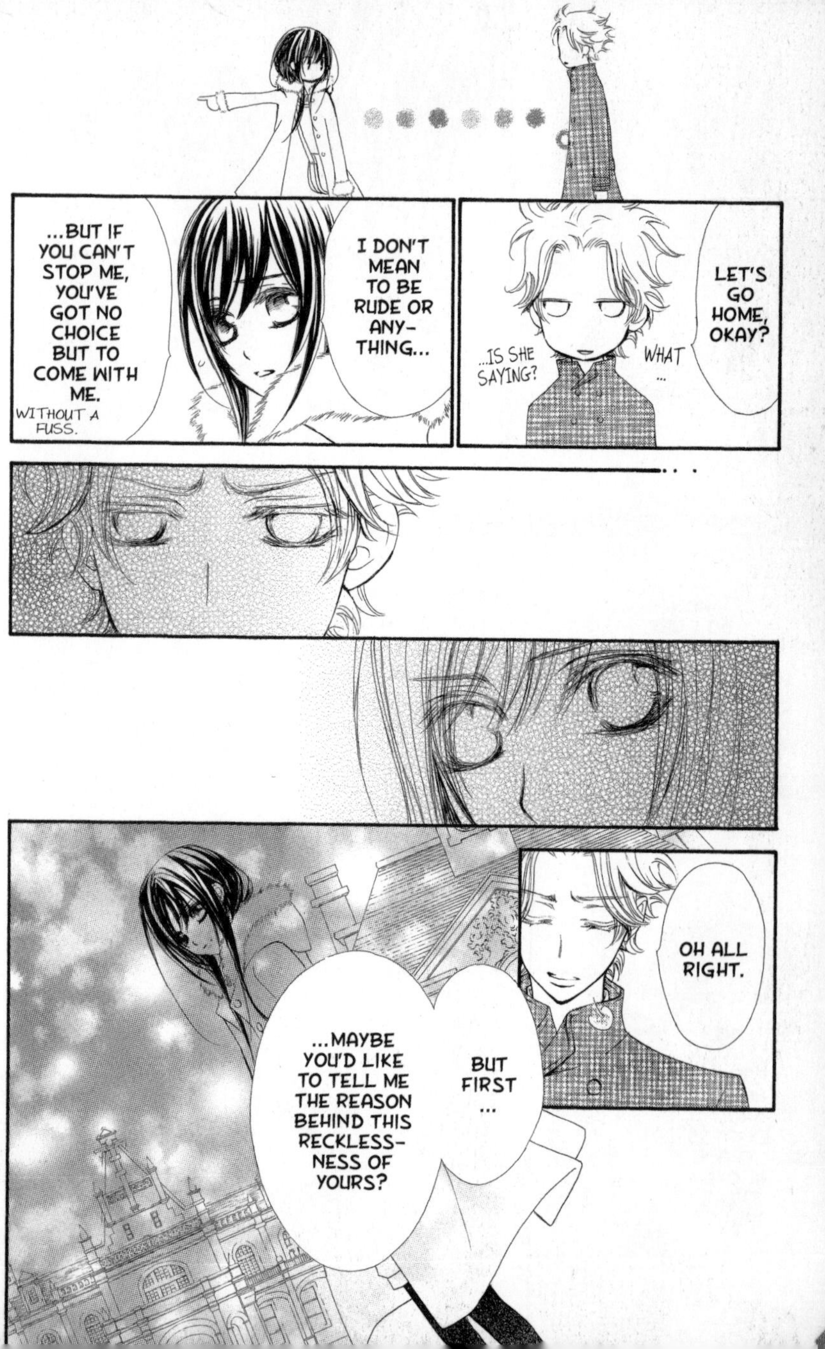
LET'S GO HOME, OKAY?
WHAT ...
...IS SHE SAYING?
I DON'T MEAN TO BE RUDE OR ANY-THING...
...BUT IF YOU CAN'T STOP ME, YOU'VE GOT NO CHOICE BUT TO COME WITH ME.
WITHOUT A FUSS.
OH ALL RIGHT.
BUT FIRST ...
...MAYBE YOU'D LIKE TO TELL ME THE REASON BEHIND THIS RECKLESS-NESS OF YOURS?

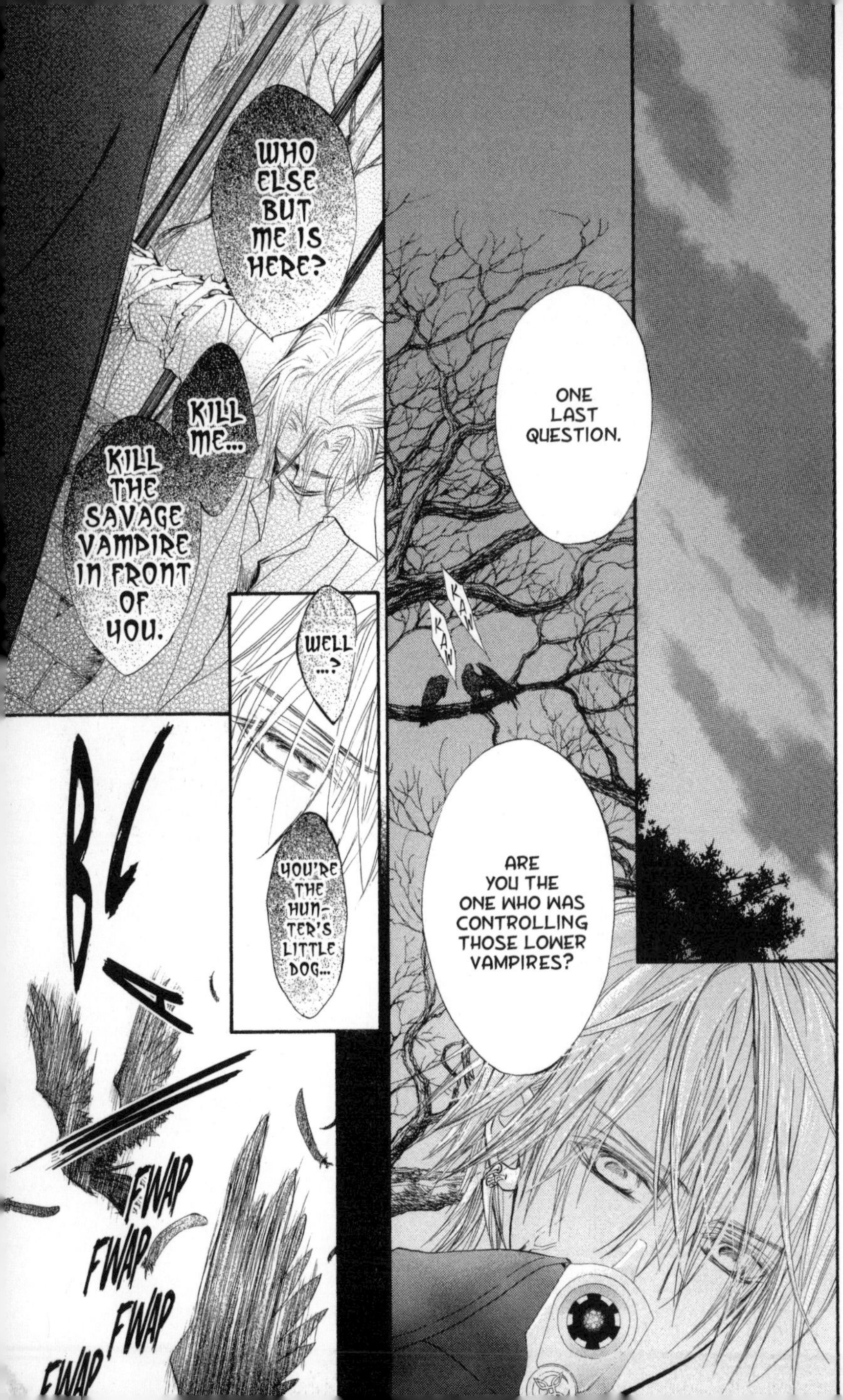
ONE LAST QUESTION.
KAW
KAW
ARE YOU THE ONE WHO WAS CONTROLLING THOSE LOWER VAMPIRES?
WHO ELSE BUT ME IS HERE?
KILL ME...
KILL THE SAVAGE VAMPIRE IN FRONT OF YOU.
WELL ...?
YOU'RE THE HUN-TER'S LITTLE DOG...
BLA
FWAP
FWAP
FWAP
FWAP

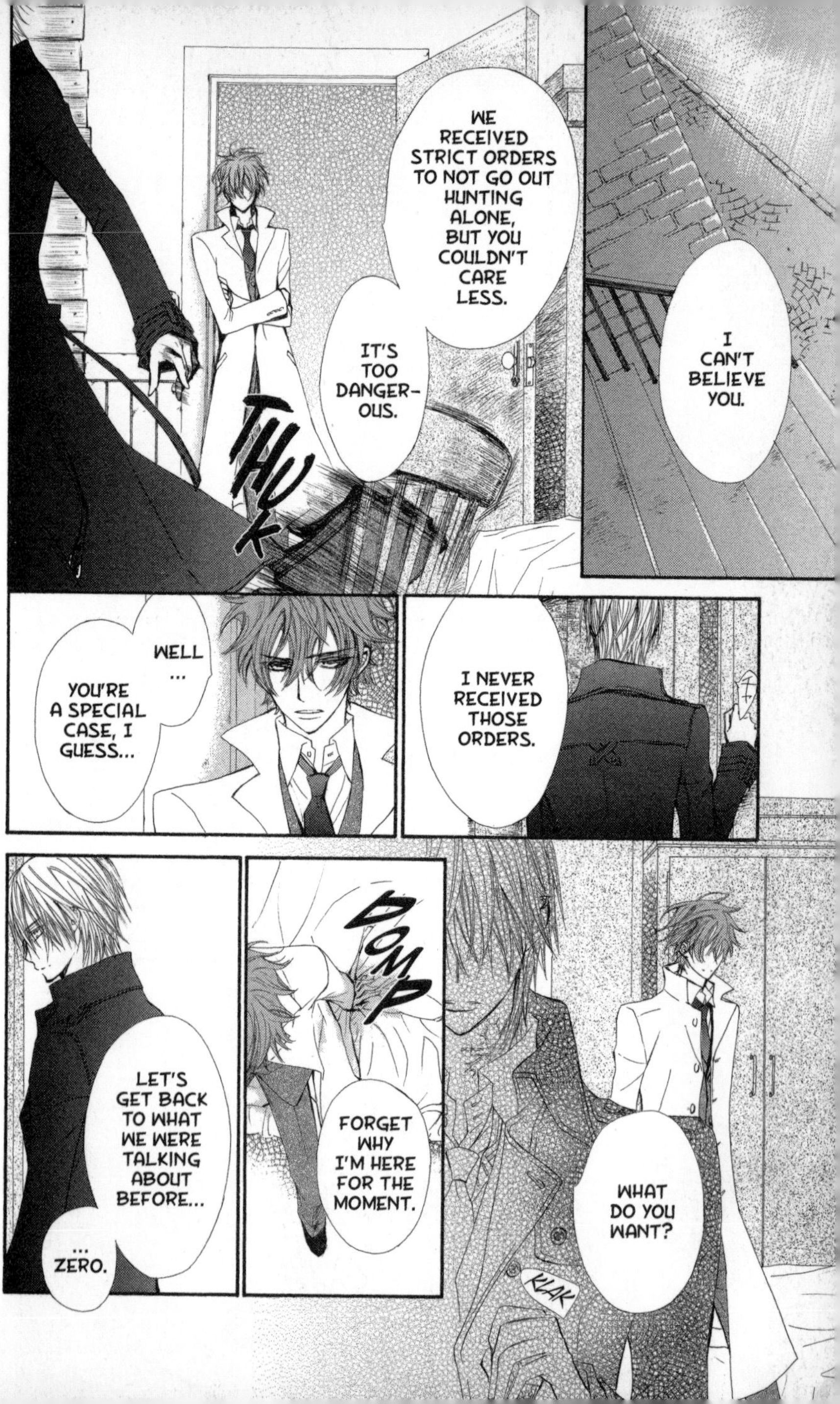
I CAN'T BELIEVE YOU.
WE RECEIVED STRICT ORDERS TO NOT GO OUT HUNTING ALONE, BUT YOU COULDN'T CARE LESS.
IT'S TOO DANGER-OUS.
THUNK
I NEVER RECEIVED THOSE ORDERS.
WELL ...
YOU'RE A SPECIAL CASE, I GUESS...
WHAT DO YOU WANT?
KLAK
DOMP
FORGET WHY I'M HERE FOR THE MOMENT.
LET'S GET BACK TO WHAT WE WERE TALKING ABOUT BEFORE...
... ZERO.

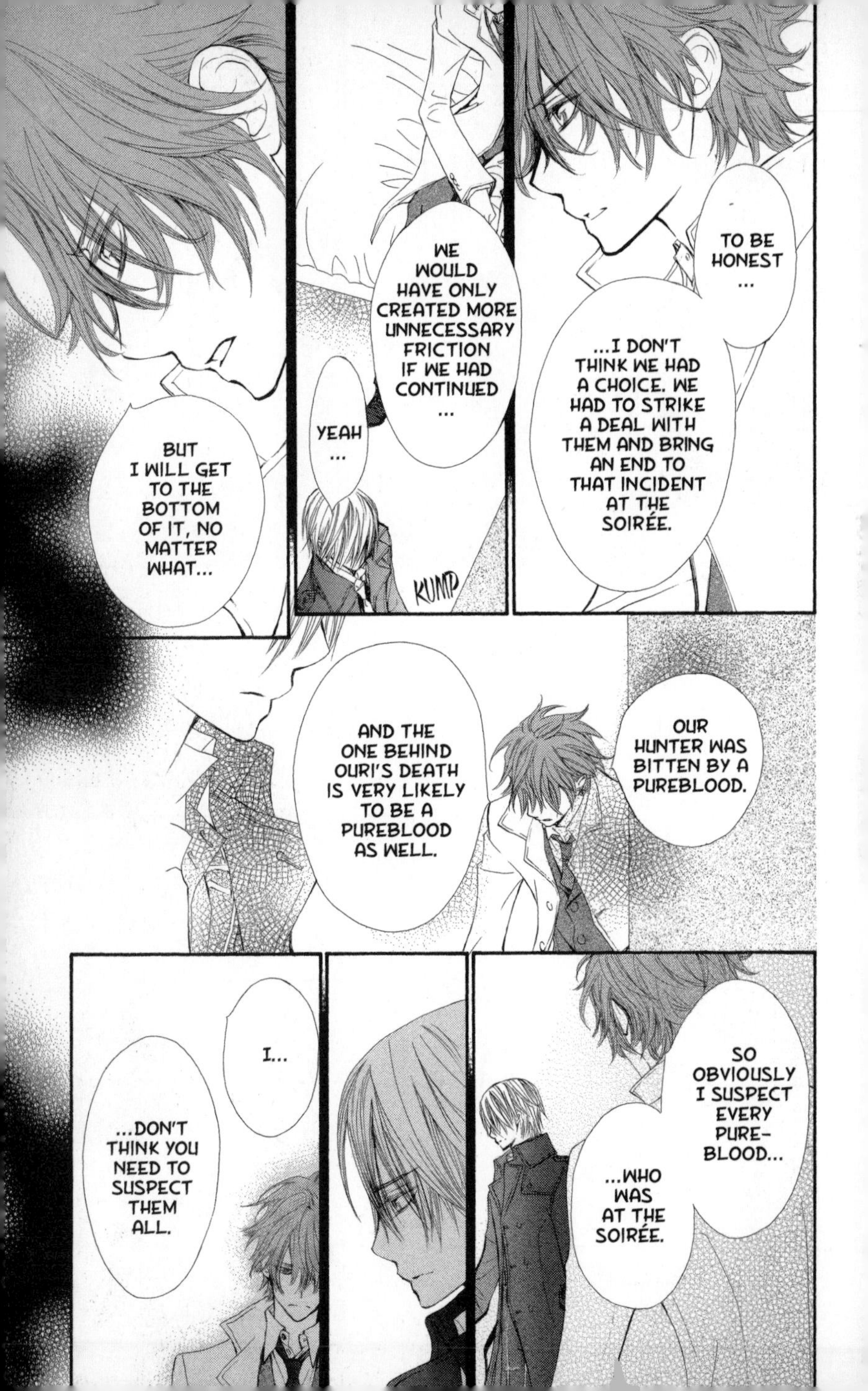
TO BE HONEST ...
...I DON'T THINK WE HAD A CHOICE. WE HAD TO STRIKE A DEAL WITH THEM AND BRING AN END TO THAT INCIDENT AT THE SOIRÉE.
WE WOULD HAVE ONLY CREATED MORE UNNECESSARY FRICTION IF WE HAD CONTINUED ...
YEAH ...
KUMP
BUT I WILL GET TO THE BOTTOM OF IT, NO MATTER WHAT...
OUR HUNTER WAS BITTEN BY A PUREBLOOD.
AND THE ONE BEHIND OURI'S DEATH IS VERY LIKELY TO BE A PUREBLOOD AS WELL.
SO OBVIOUSLY I SUSPECT EVERY PURE-BLOOD...
...WHO WAS AT THE SOIRÉE.
I...
...DON'T THINK YOU NEED TO SUSPECT THEM ALL.

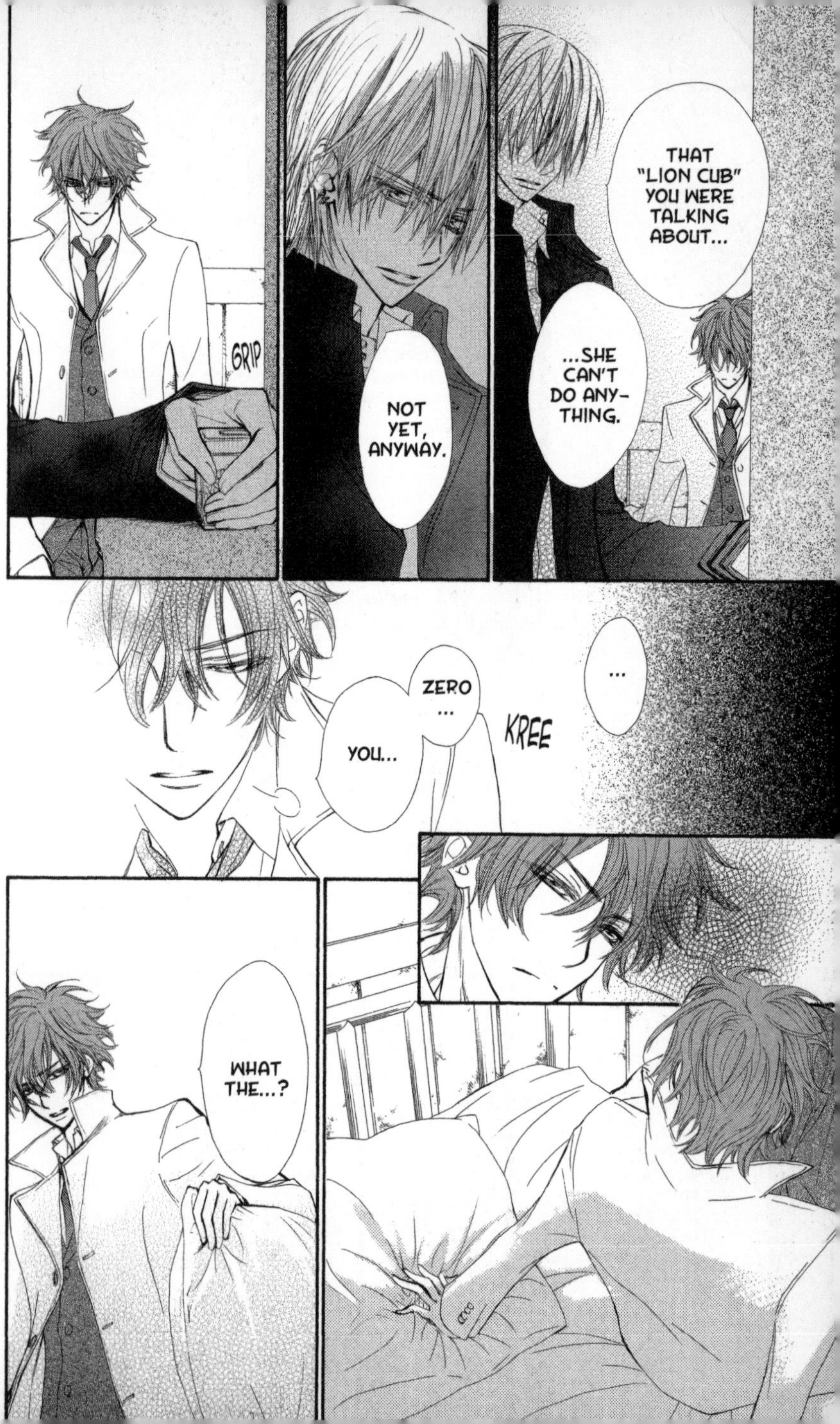
THAT "LION CUB" YOU WERE TALKING ABOUT...
...SHE CAN'T DO ANYTHING.
NOT YET, ANYWAY.
GRIP
...
KREE
ZERO...
YOU...
WHAT THE...?

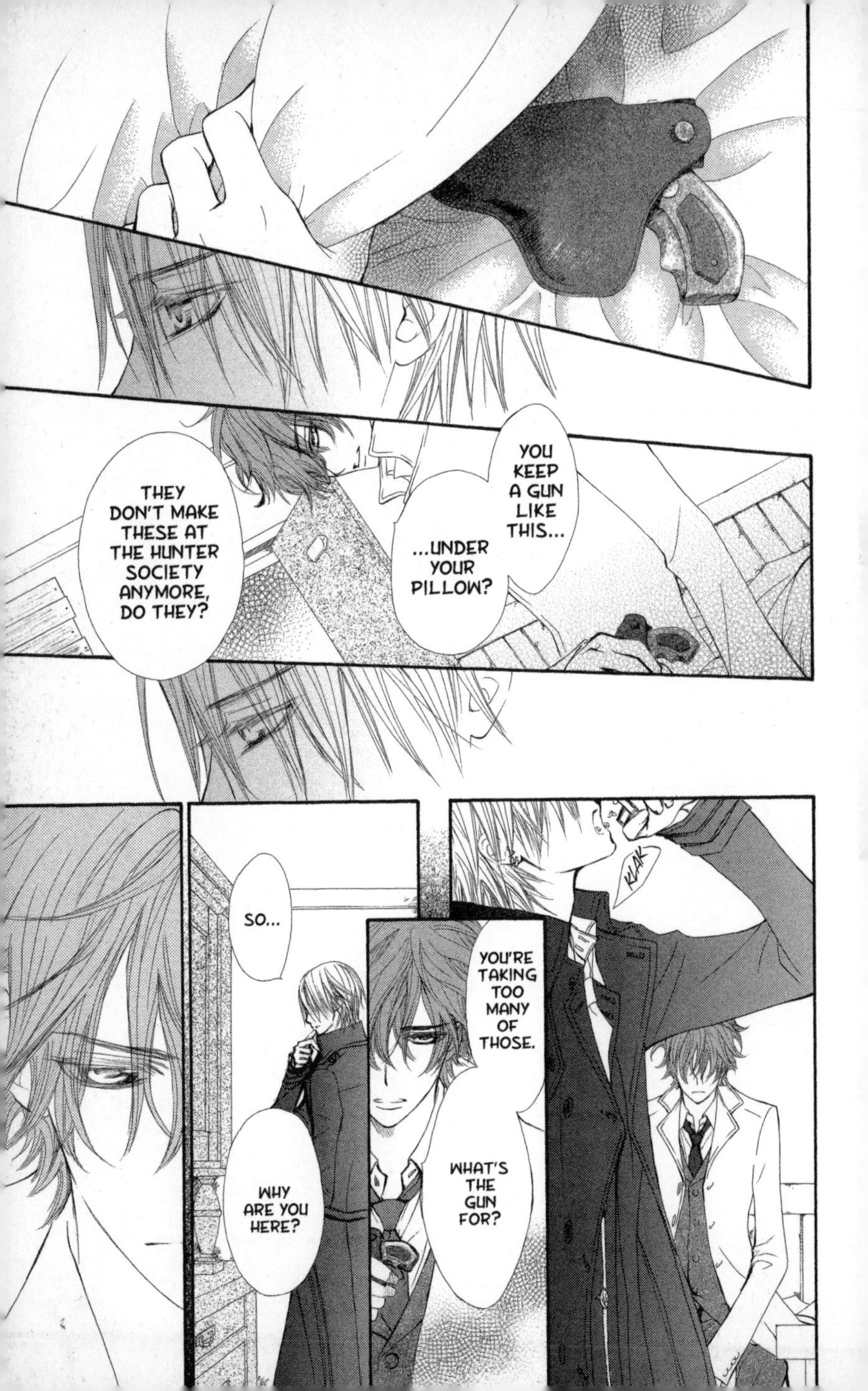
YOU KEEP A GUN LIKE THIS...
...UNDER YOUR PILLOW?
THEY DON'T MAKE THESE AT THE HUNTER SOCIETY ANYMORE, DO THEY?
KLAK
YOU'RE TAKING TOO MANY OF THOSE.
WHAT'S THE GUN FOR?
SO...
WHY ARE YOU HERE?

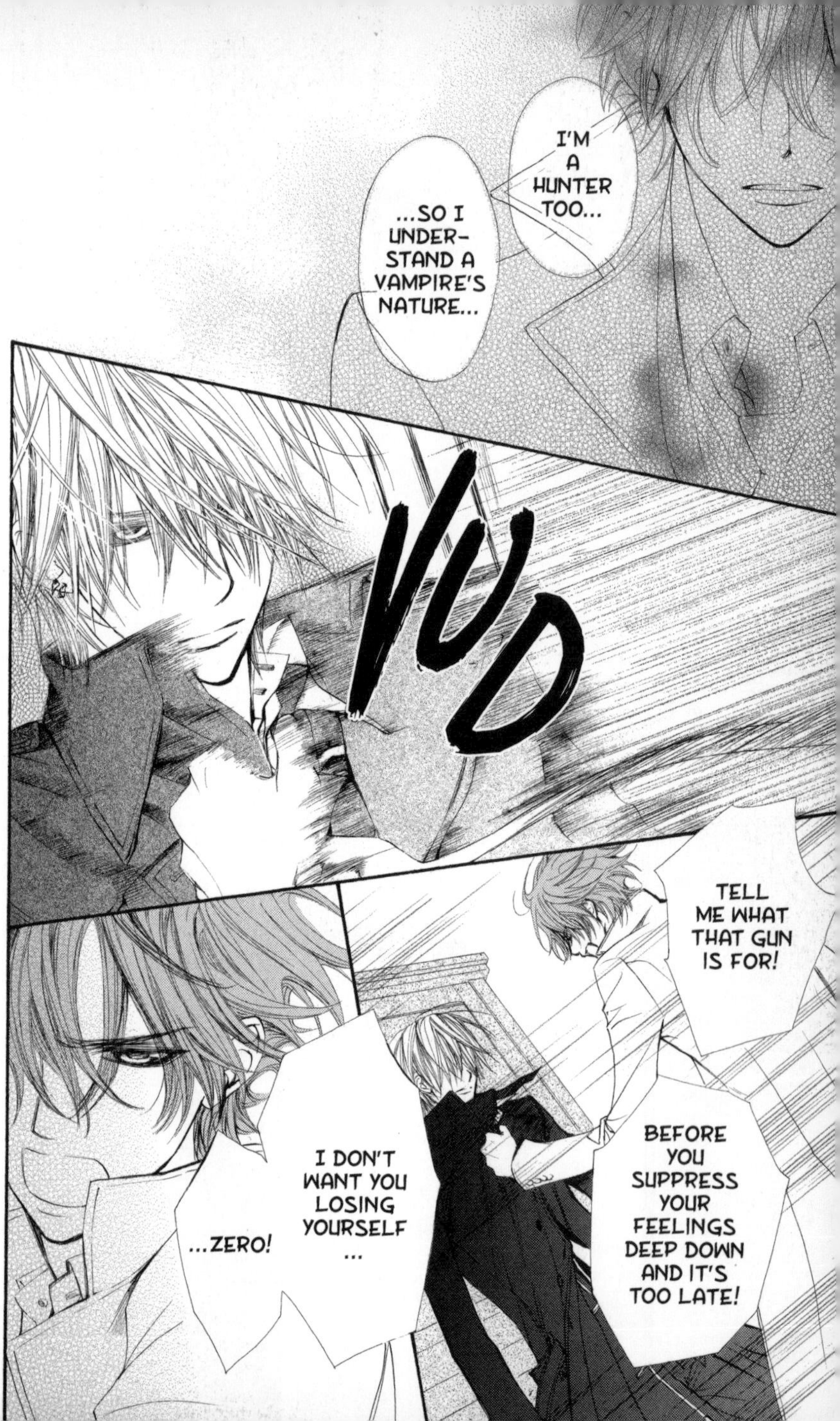
I'M A HUNTER TOO...
...SO I UNDER-STAND A VAMPIRE'S NATURE...
VUD
TELL ME WHAT THAT GUN IS FOR!
BEFORE YOU SUPPRESS YOUR FEELINGS DEEP DOWN AND IT'S TOO LATE!
I DON'T WANT YOU LOSING YOURSELF ...
...ZERO!

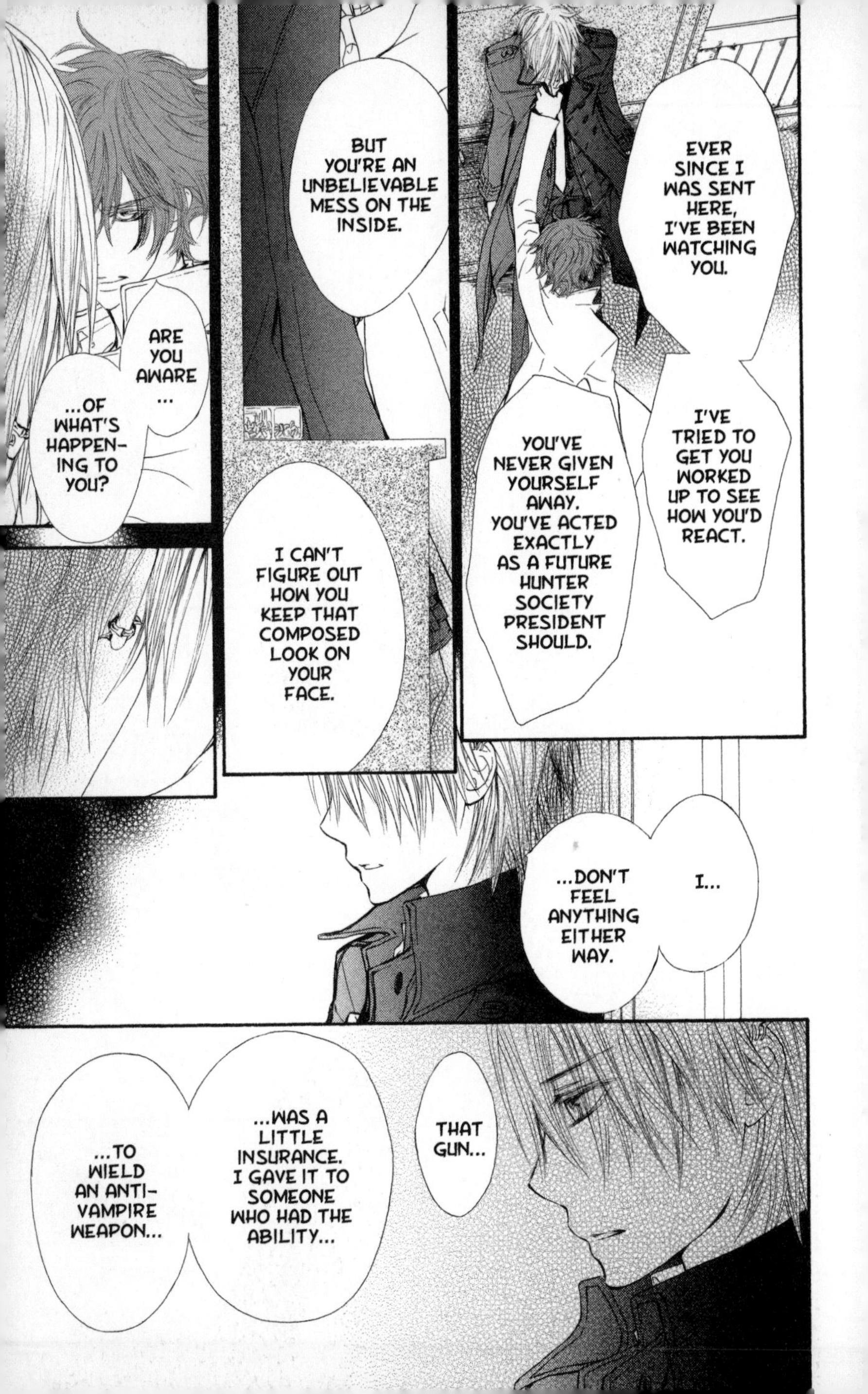
EVER SINCE I WAS SENT HERE, I'VE BEEN WATCHING YOU.
I'VE TRIED TO GET YOU WORKED UP TO SEE HOW YOU'D REACT.
YOU'VE NEVER GIVEN YOURSELF AWAY. YOU'VE ACTED EXACTLY AS A FUTURE HUNTER SOCIETY PRESIDENT SHOULD.
BUT YOU'RE AN UNBELIEVABLE MESS ON THE INSIDE.
I CAN'T FIGURE OUT HOW YOU KEEP THAT COMPOSED LOOK ON YOUR FACE.
ARE YOU AWARE...
...OF WHAT'S HAPPEN-ING TO YOU?
I...
...DON'T FEEL ANYTHING EITHER WAY.
THAT GUN...
...WAS A LITTLE INSURANCE. I GAVE IT TO SOMEONE WHO HAD THE ABILITY...
...TO WIELD AN ANTI-VAMPIRE WEAPON...

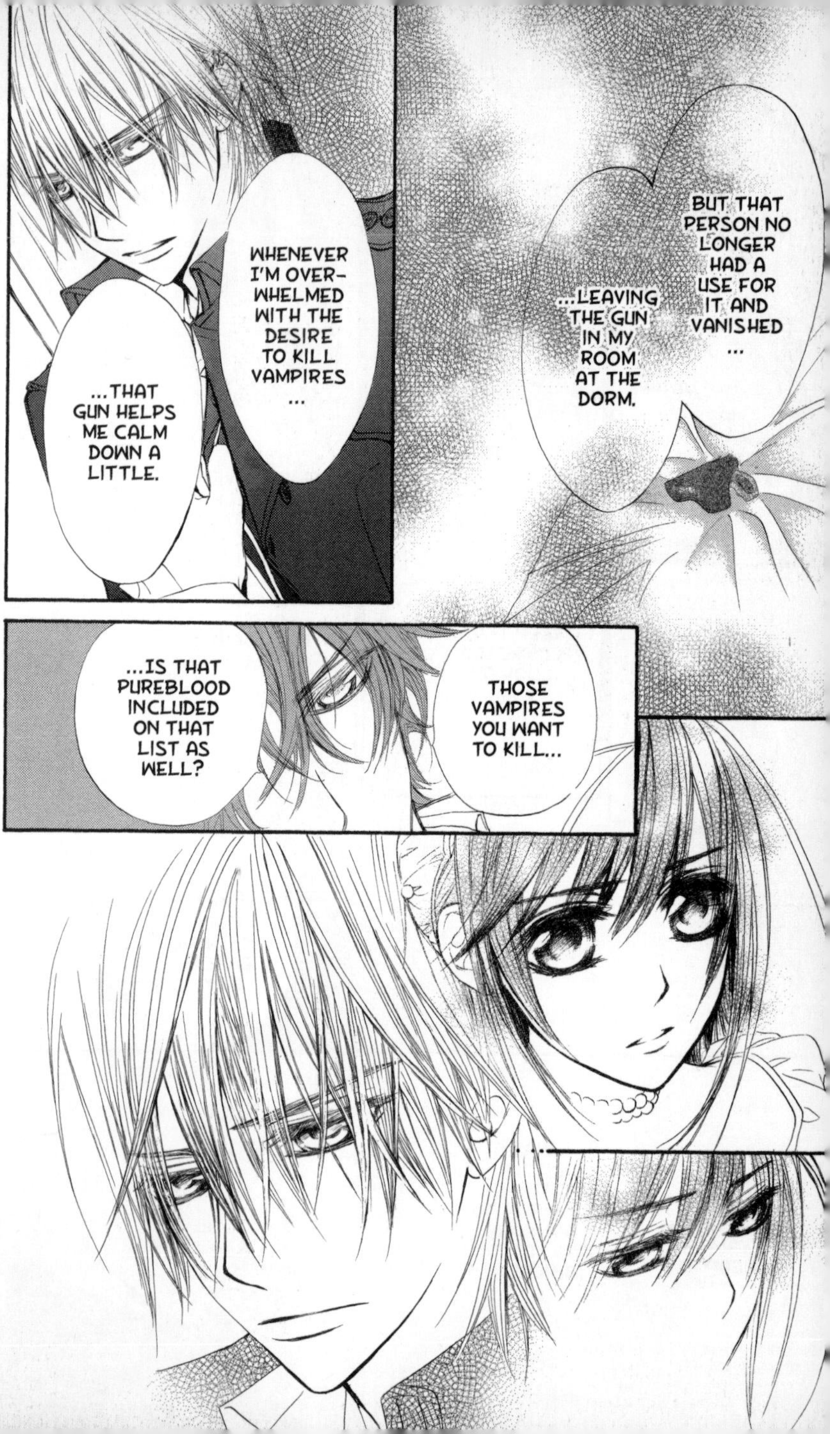
BUT THAT PERSON NO LONGER HAD A USE FOR IT AND VANISHED...
...LEAVING THE GUN IN MY ROOM AT THE DORM.
WHENEVER I'M OVER-WHELMED WITH THE DESIRE TO KILL VAMPIRES...
...THAT GUN HELPS ME CALM DOWN A LITTLE.
THOSE VAMPIRES YOU WANT TO KILL...
...IS THAT PUREBLOOD INCLUDED ON THAT LIST AS WELL?
...

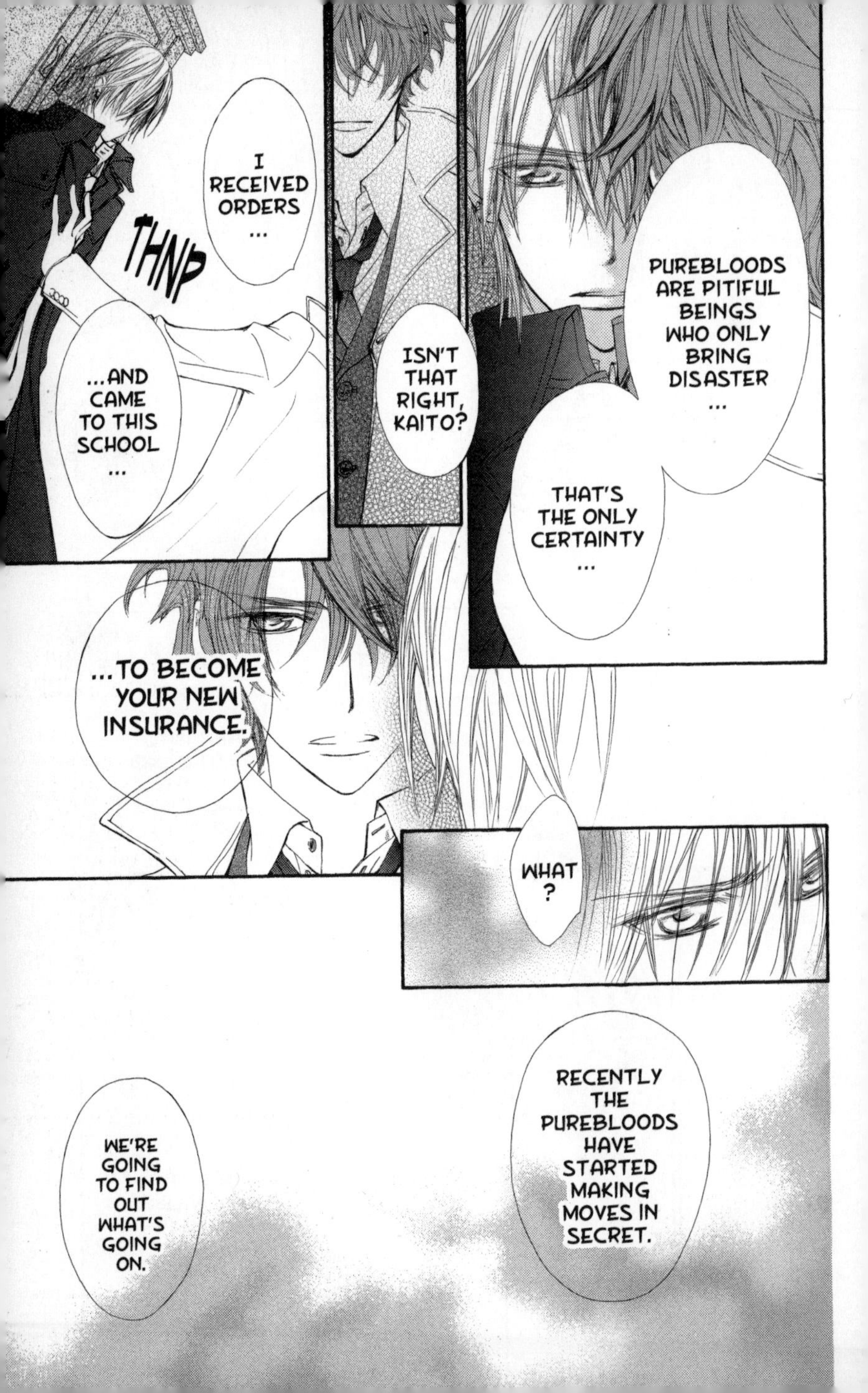
PUREBLOODS ARE PITIFUL BEINGS WHO ONLY BRING DISASTER...
THAT'S THE ONLY CERTAINTY...
ISN'T THAT RIGHT, KAITO?
I RECEIVED ORDERS...
THNP
...AND CAME TO THIS SCHOOL...
...TO BECOME YOUR NEW INSURANCE.
WHAT?
RECENTLY THE PUREBLOODS HAVE STARTED MAKING MOVES IN SECRET.
WE'RE GOING TO FIND OUT WHAT'S GOING ON.

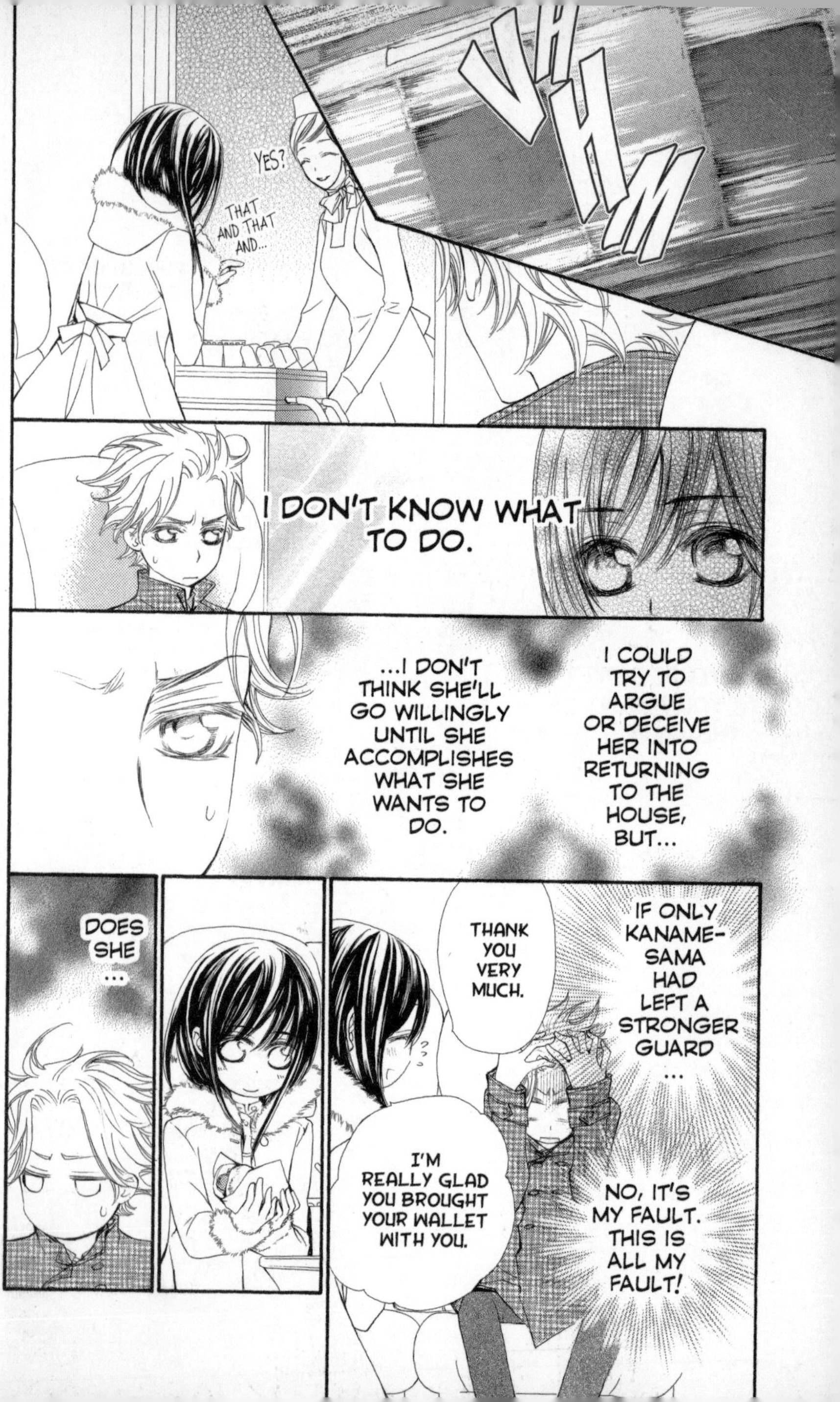
VAHM
YES?
THAT AND THAT AND...
I DON'T KNOW WHAT TO DO.
I COULD TRY TO ARGUE OR DECEIVE HER INTO RETURNING TO THE HOUSE, BUT...
...I DON'T THINK SHE'LL GO WILLINGLY UNTIL SHE ACCOMPLISHES WHAT SHE WANTS TO DO.
IF ONLY KANAME-SAMA HAD LEFT A STRONGER GUARD...
THANK YOU VERY MUCH.
NO, IT'S MY FAULT. THIS IS ALL MY FAULT!
I'M REALLY GLAD YOU BROUGHT YOUR WALLET WITH YOU.
DOES SHE...

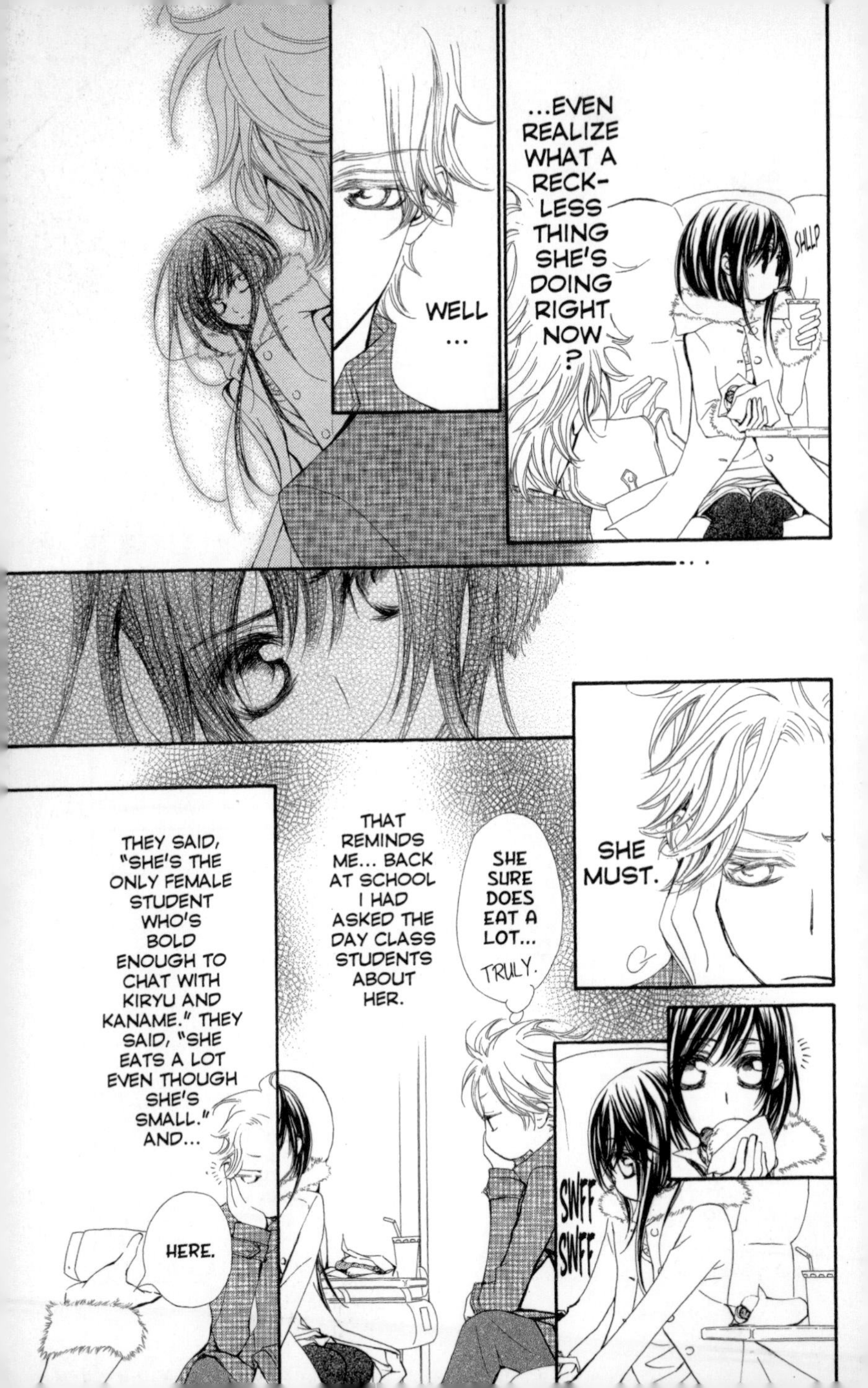

...EVEN REALIZE WHAT A RECK-LESS THING SHE'S DOING RIGHT NOW?
SHLLP
WELL ...
SHE MUST.
SHE SURE DOES EAT A LOT...
TRULY.
THAT REMINDS ME... BACK AT SCHOOL I HAD ASKED THE DAY CLASS STUDENTS ABOUT HER.
SWFF SWFF
THEY SAID, "SHE'S THE ONLY FEMALE STUDENT WHO'S BOLD ENOUGH TO CHAT WITH KIRYU AND KANAME." THEY SAID, "SHE EATS A LOT EVEN THOUGH SHE'S SMALL." AND...
HERE.

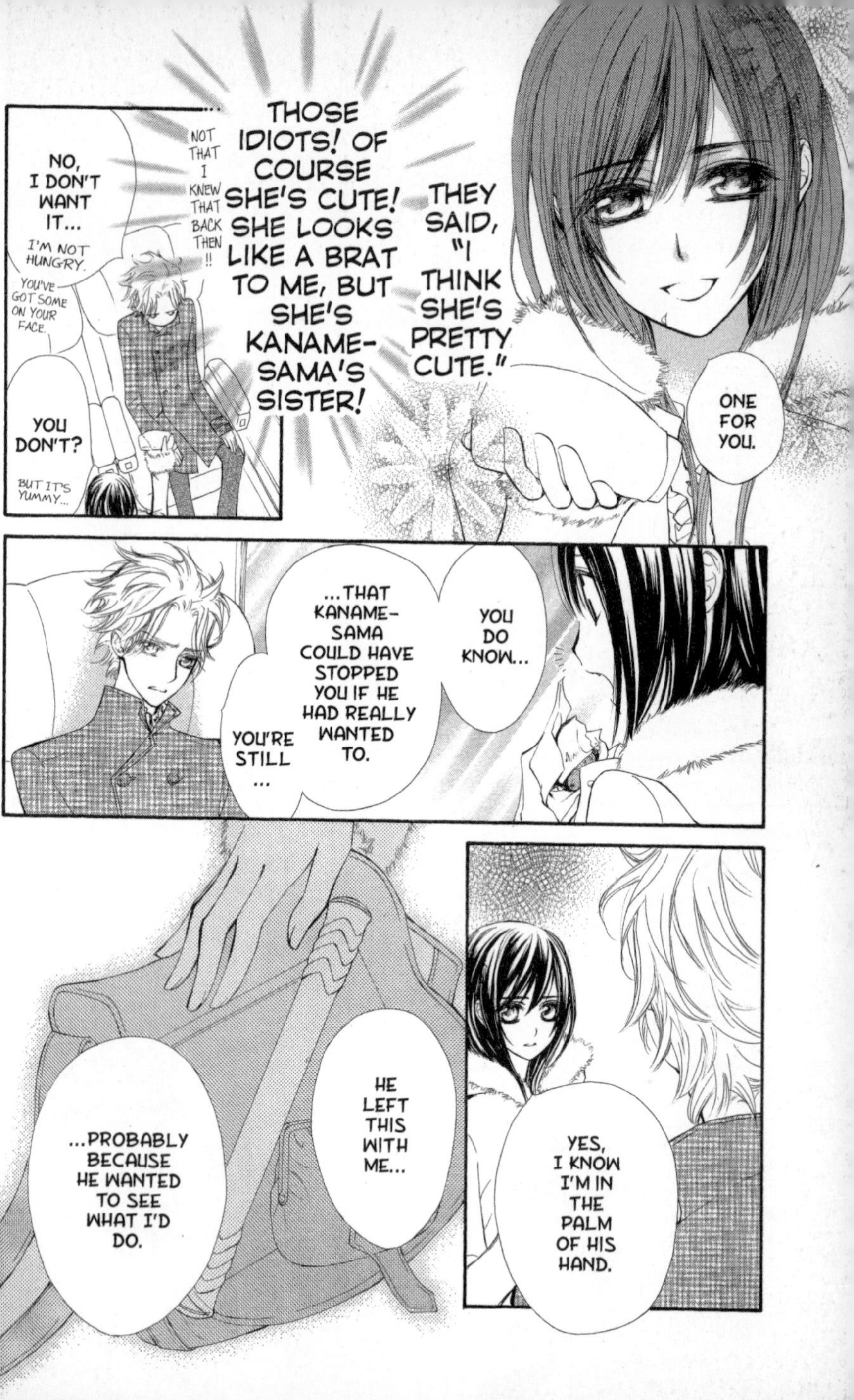
ONE FOR YOU.
THEY SAID, "I THINK SHE'S PRETTY CUTE."
THOSE IDIOTS! OF COURSE SHE'S CUTE! SHE LOOKS LIKE A BRAT TO ME, BUT SHE'S KANAME-SAMA'S SISTER!
NOT THAT I KNEW THAT BACK THEN!!
NO, I DON'T WANT IT...
I'M NOT HUNGRY.
YOU'VE GOT SOME ON YOUR FACE.
YOU DON'T?
BUT IT'S YUMMY...
YOU DO KNOW...
...THAT KANAME-SAMA COULD HAVE STOPPED YOU IF HE HAD REALLY WANTED TO.
YOU'RE STILL ...
YES, I KNOW I'M IN THE PALM OF HIS HAND.
HE LEFT THIS WITH ME...
...PROBABLY BECAUSE HE WANTED TO SEE WHAT I'D DO.

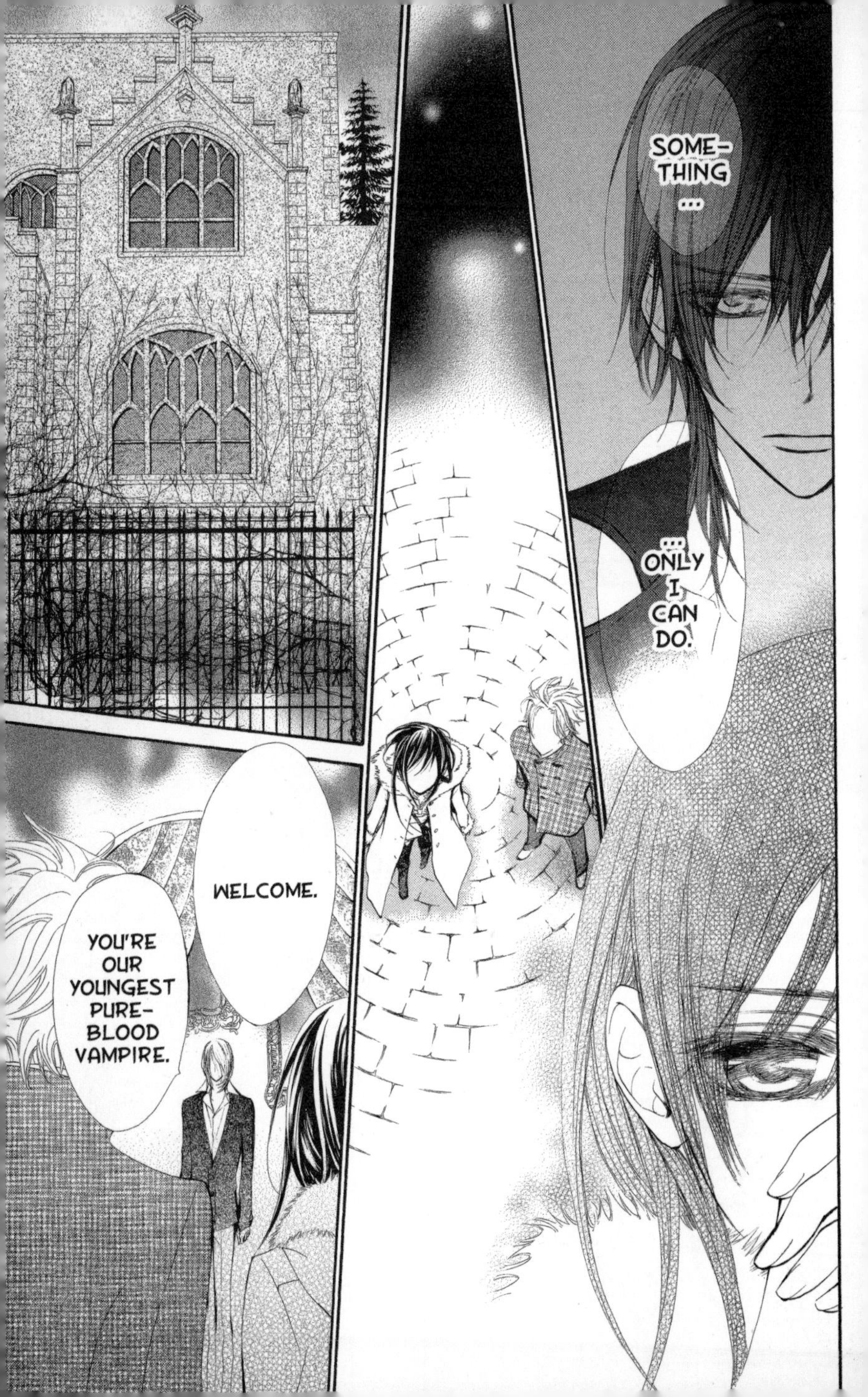
SOME-THING ...
... ONLY I CAN DO.
WELCOME.
YOU'RE OUR YOUNGEST PURE-BLOOD VAMPIRE.

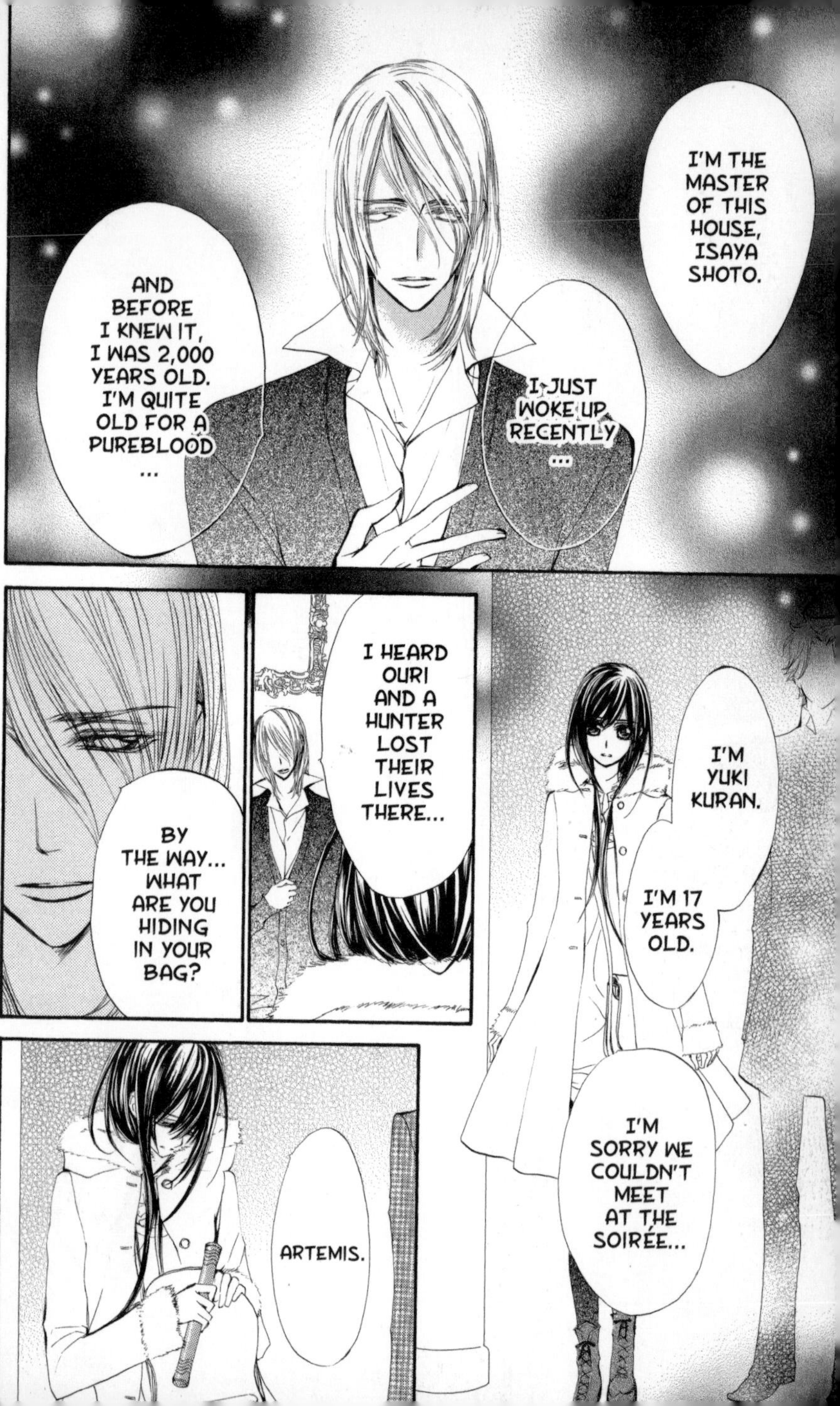
I'M THE MASTER OF THIS HOUSE, ISAYA SHOTO.
I JUST WOKE UP RECENTLY...
AND BEFORE I KNEW IT, I WAS 2,000 YEARS OLD. I'M QUITE OLD FOR A PUREBLOOD...
I'M YUKI KURAN.
I'M 17 YEARS OLD.
I'M SORRY WE COULDN'T MEET AT THE SOIRÉE...
I HEARD OURI AND A HUNTER LOST THEIR LIVES THERE...
BY THE WAY... WHAT ARE YOU HIDING IN YOUR BAG?
ARTEMIS.

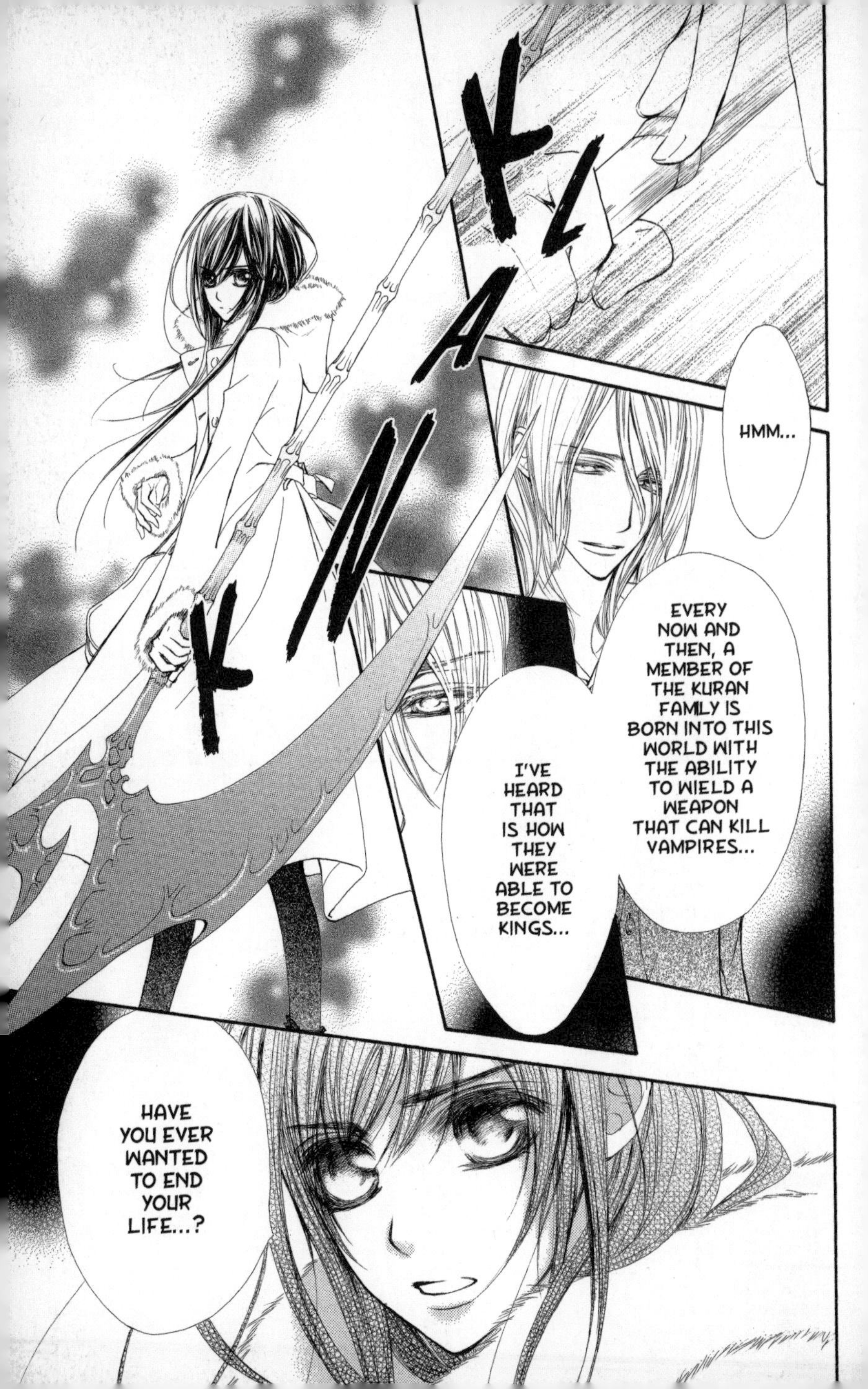
HMM...
EVERY NOW AND THEN, A MEMBER OF THE KURAN FAMILY IS BORN INTO THIS WORLD WITH THE ABILITY TO WIELD A WEAPON THAT CAN KILL VAMPIRES...
I'VE HEARD THAT IS HOW THEY WERE ABLE TO BECOME KINGS...
KLANK
HAVE YOU EVER WANTED TO END YOUR LIFE...?

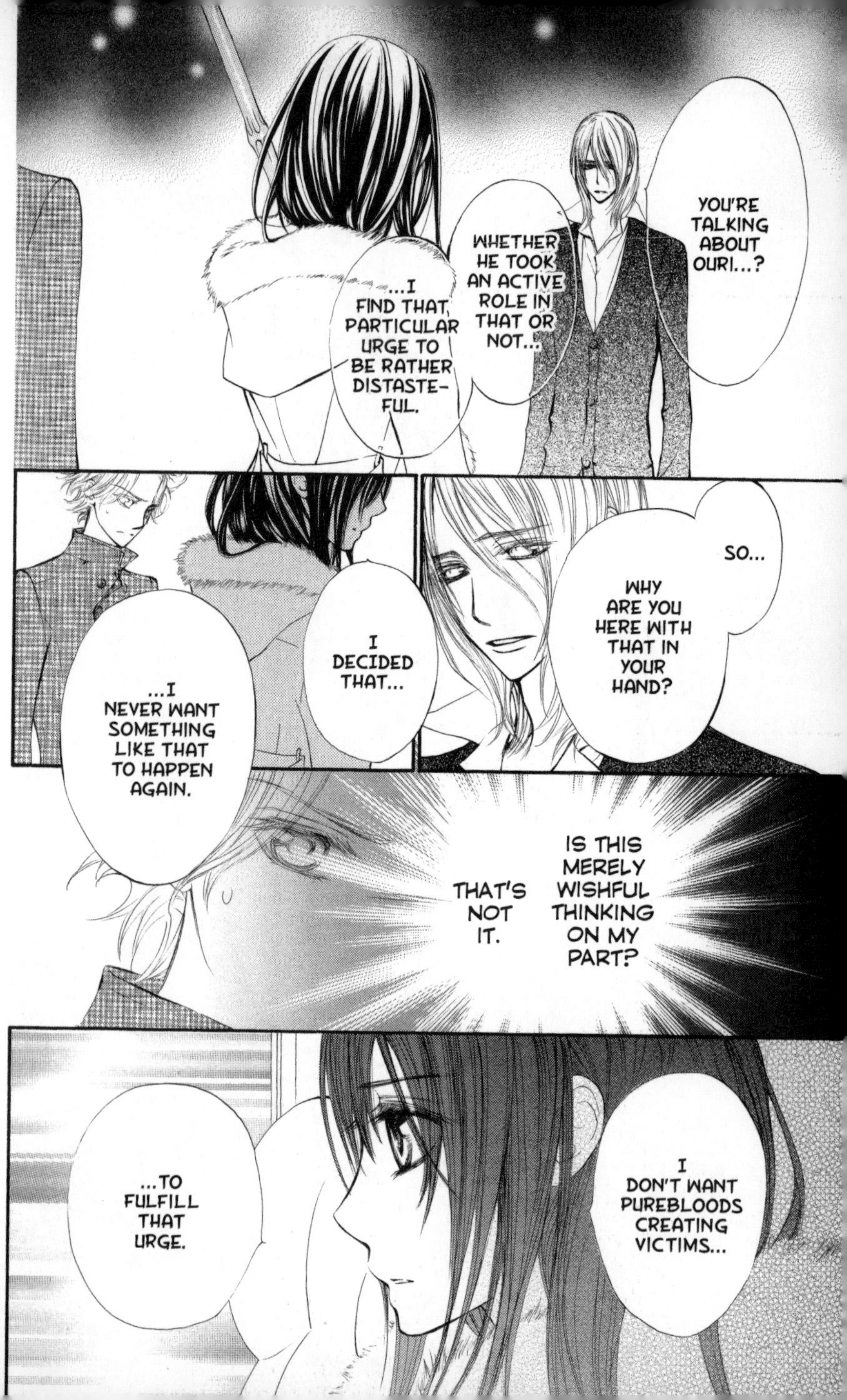
YOU'RE TALKING ABOUT OURI...?
WHETHER HE TOOK AN ACTIVE ROLE IN THAT OR NOT...
...I FIND THAT PARTICULAR URGE TO BE RATHER DISTASTE-FUL.
SO...
WHY ARE YOU HERE WITH THAT IN YOUR HAND?
I DECIDED THAT...
...I NEVER WANT SOMETHING LIKE THAT TO HAPPEN AGAIN.
IS THIS MERELY WISHFUL THINKING ON MY PART?
THAT'S NOT IT.
I DON'T WANT PUREBLOODS CREATING VICTIMS...
...TO FULFILL THAT URGE.

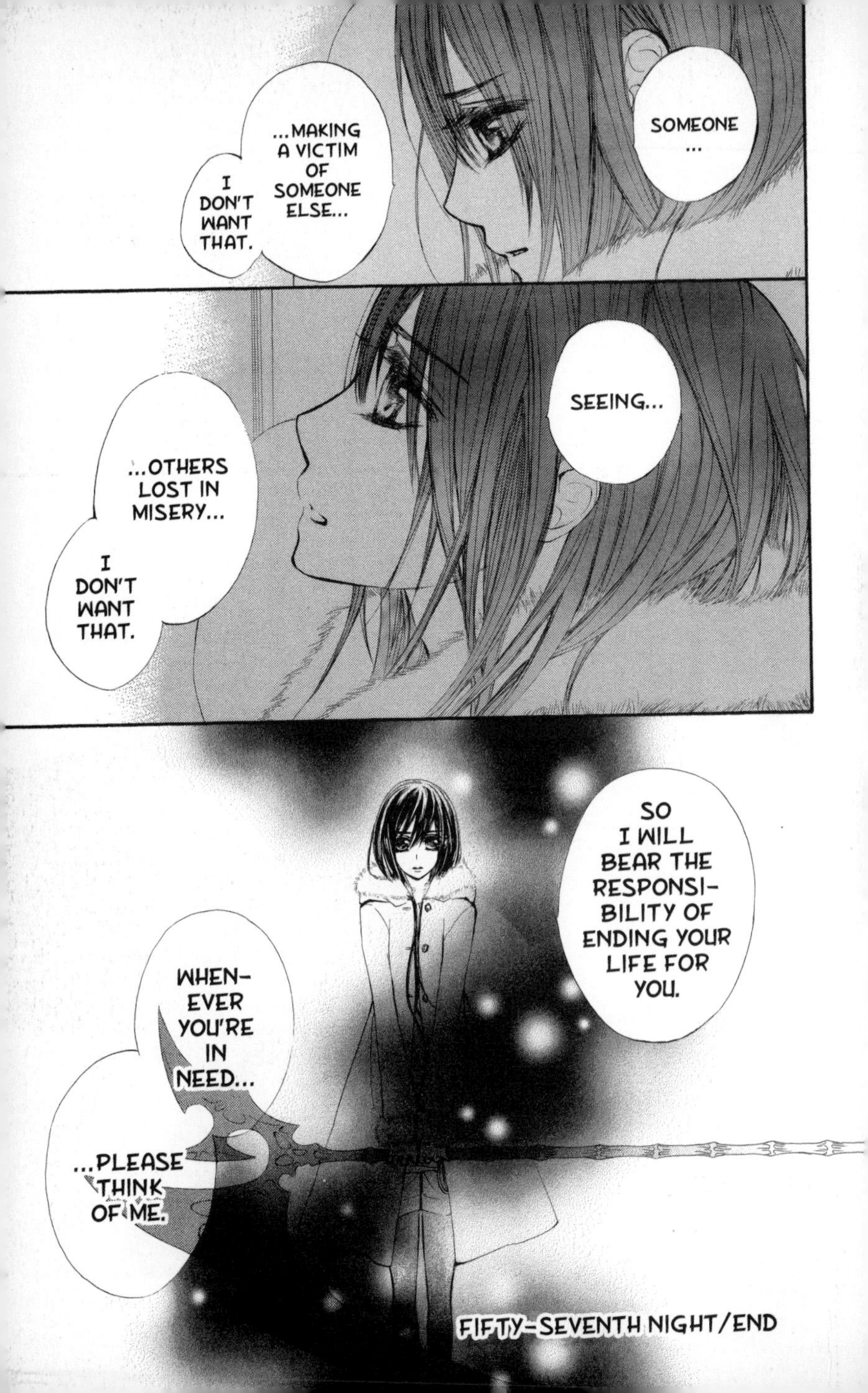
SOMEONE ...
...MAKING A VICTIM OF SOMEONE ELSE...
I DON'T WANT THAT.
SEEING...
...OTHERS LOST IN MISERY...
I DON'T WANT THAT.
SO I WILL BEAR THE RESPONSI-BILITY OF ENDING YOUR LIFE FOR YOU.
WHEN-EVER YOU'RE IN NEED...
...PLEASE THINK OF ME.
FIFTY-SEVENTH NIGHT/END

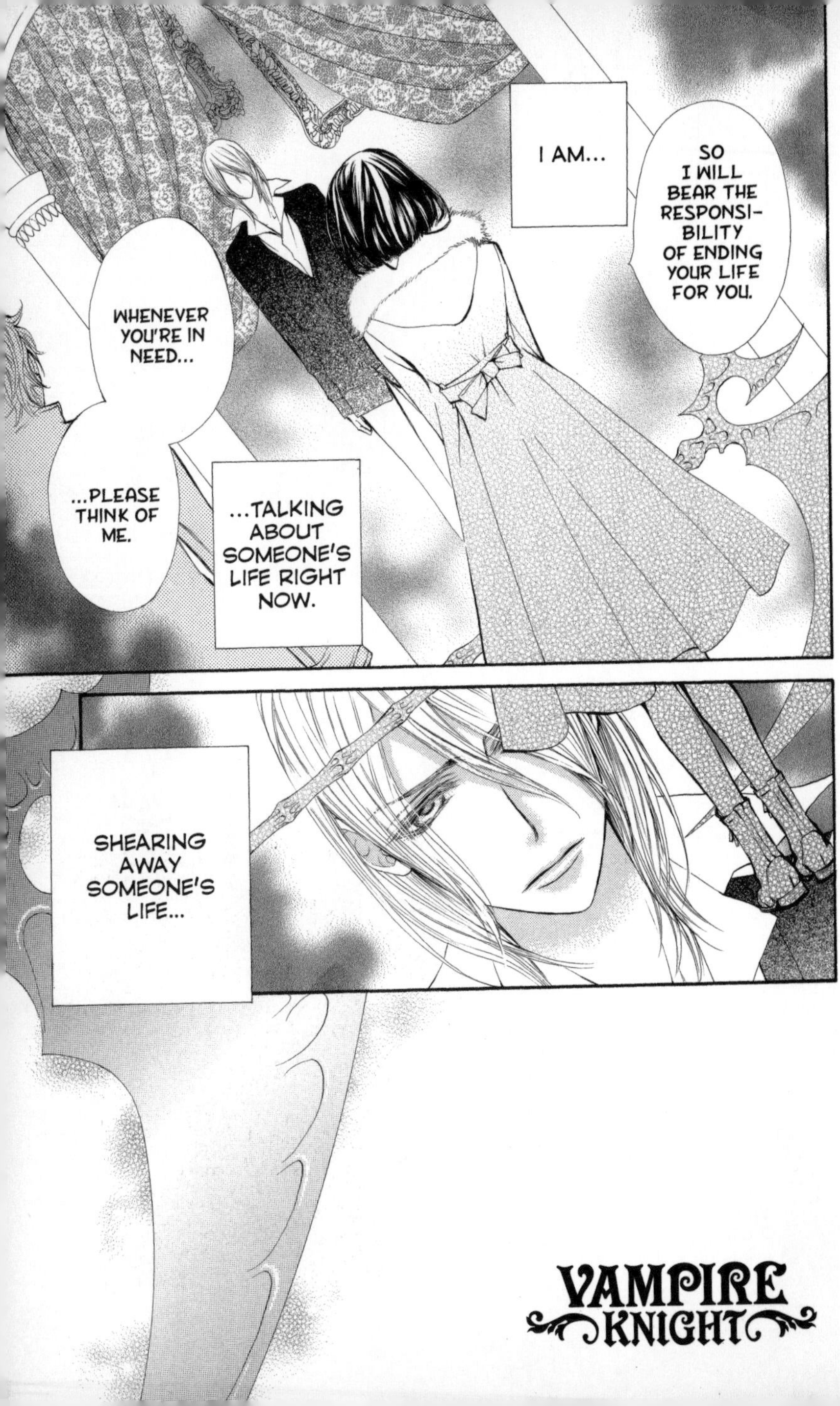

SO I WILL BEAR THE RESPONSIBILITY OF ENDING YOUR LIFE FOR YOU.
I AM...
WHENEVER YOU'RE IN NEED...
...PLEASE THINK OF ME.
...TALKING ABOUT SOMEONE'S LIFE RIGHT NOW.
SHEARING AWAY SOMEONE'S LIFE...
VAMPIRE KNIGHT

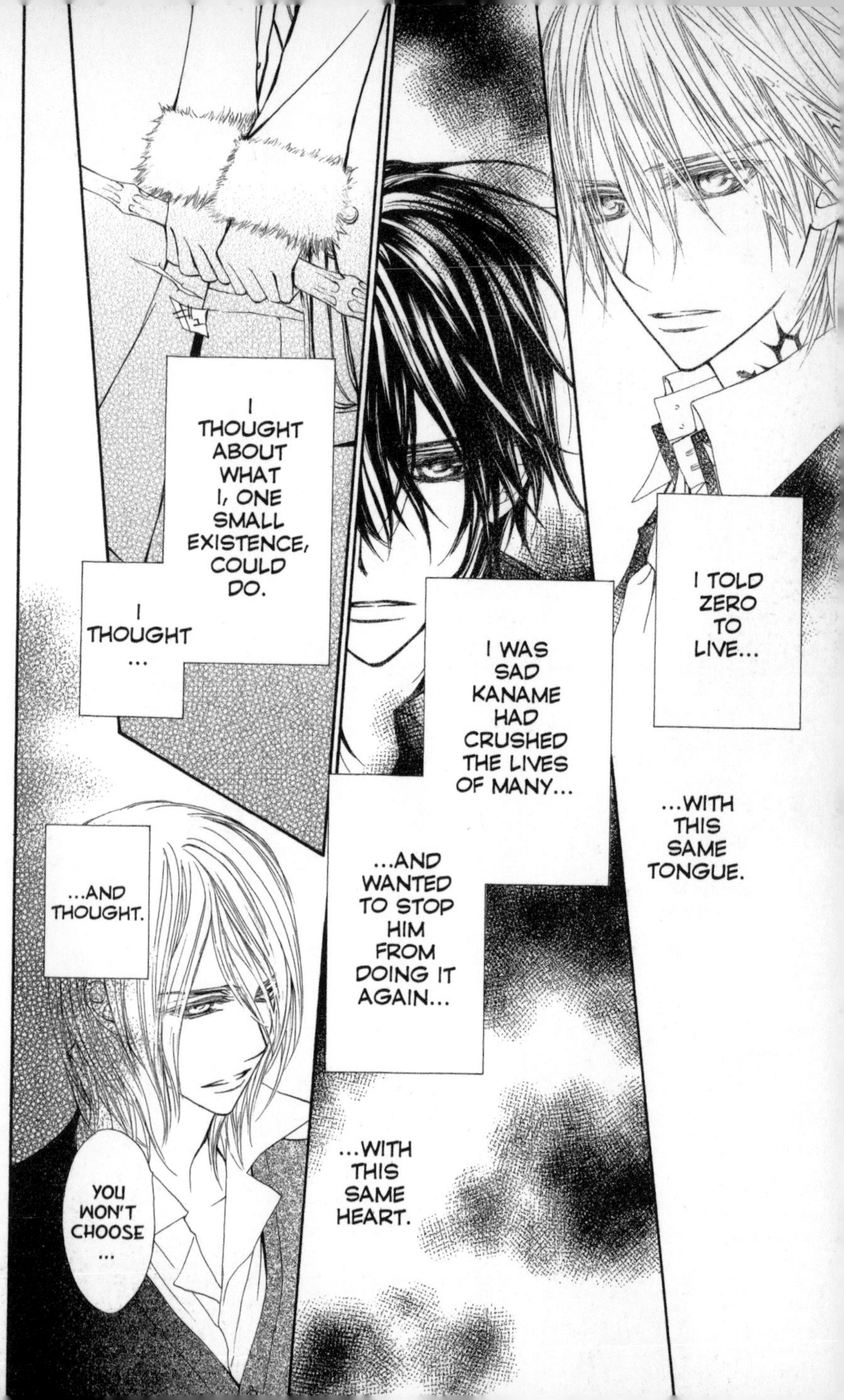
I TOLD ZERO TO LIVE...
...WITH THIS SAME TONGUE.
I WAS SAD KANAME HAD CRUSHED THE LIVES OF MANY...
...AND WANTED TO STOP HIM FROM DOING IT AGAIN...
...WITH THIS SAME HEART.
I THOUGHT ABOUT WHAT I, ONE SMALL EXISTENCE, COULD DO.
I THOUGHT...
...AND THOUGHT.
YOU WON'T CHOOSE ...

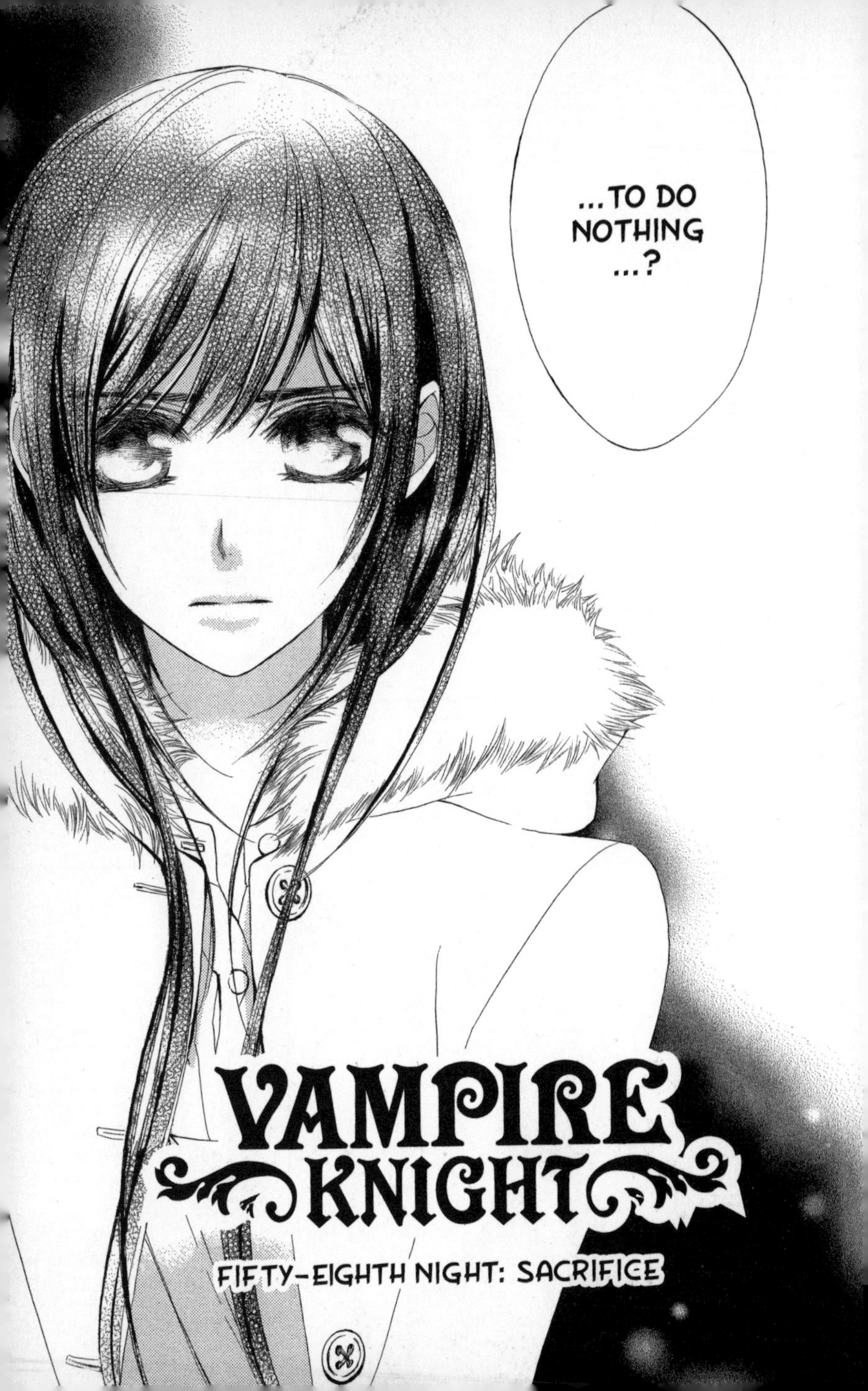
...TO DO NOTHING ...?
VAMPIRE KNIGHT
FIFTY-EIGHTH NIGHT: SACRIFICE

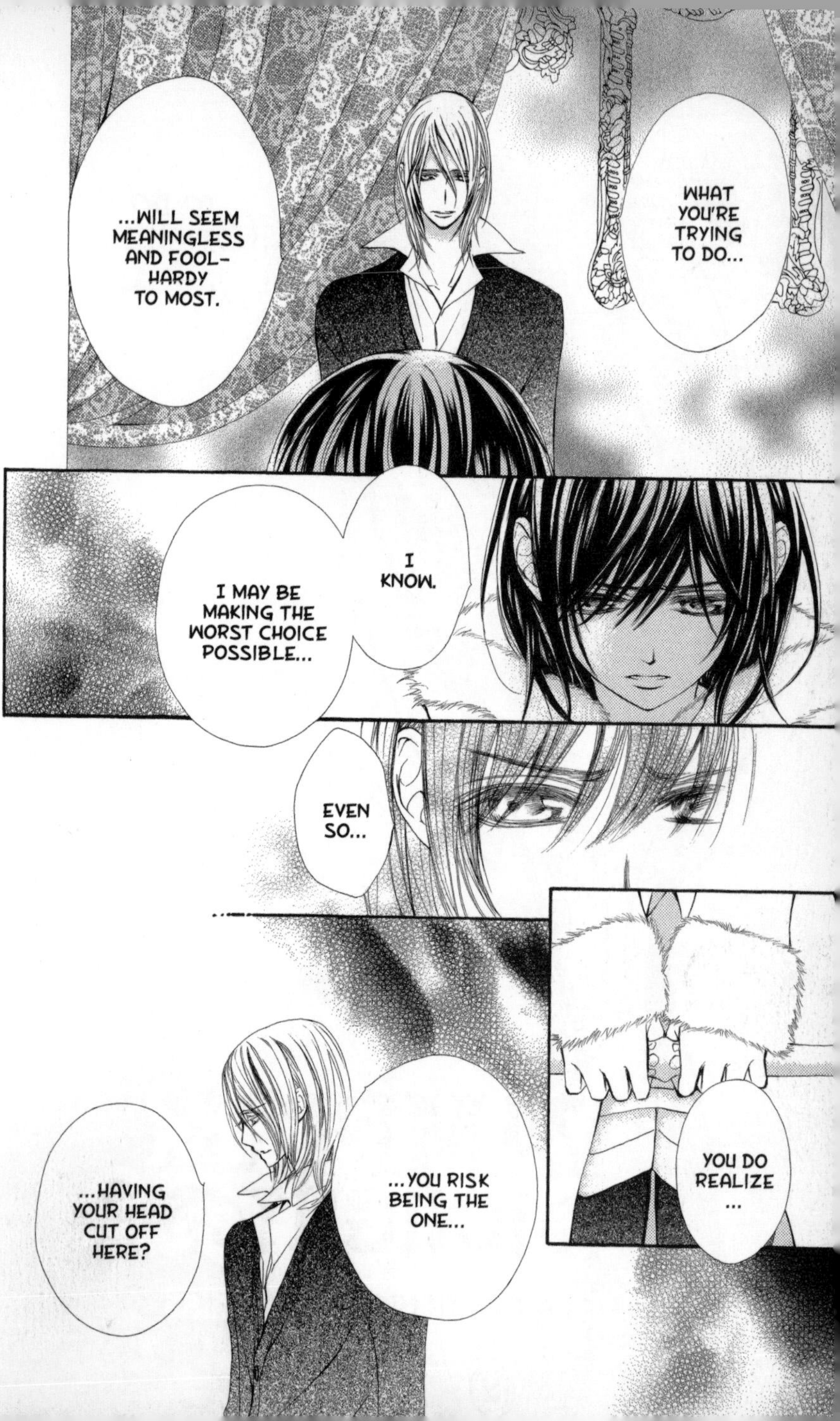
WHAT YOU'RE TRYING TO DO...
...WILL SEEM MEANINGLESS AND FOOL-HARDY TO MOST.
I KNOW.
I MAY BE MAKING THE WORST CHOICE POSSIBLE...
EVEN SO...
YOU DO REALIZE ...
...YOU RISK BEING THE ONE...
...HAVING YOUR HEAD CUT OFF HERE?

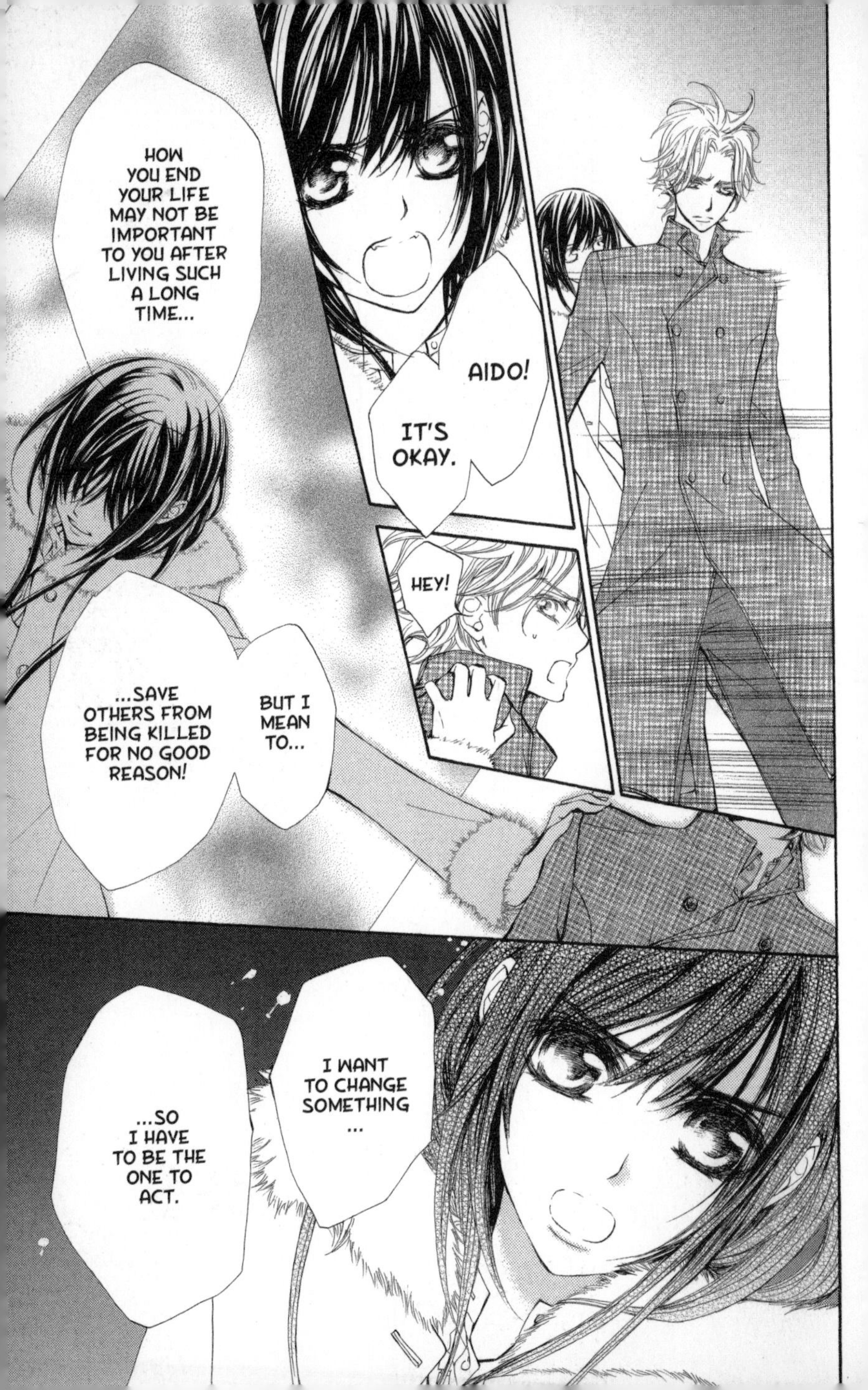
AIDO!
IT'S OKAY.
HEY!
HOW YOU END YOUR LIFE MAY NOT BE IMPORTANT TO YOU AFTER LIVING SUCH A LONG TIME...
BUT I MEAN TO...
...SAVE OTHERS FROM BEING KILLED FOR NO GOOD REASON!
I WANT TO CHANGE SOMETHING...
...SO I HAVE TO BE THE ONE TO ACT.

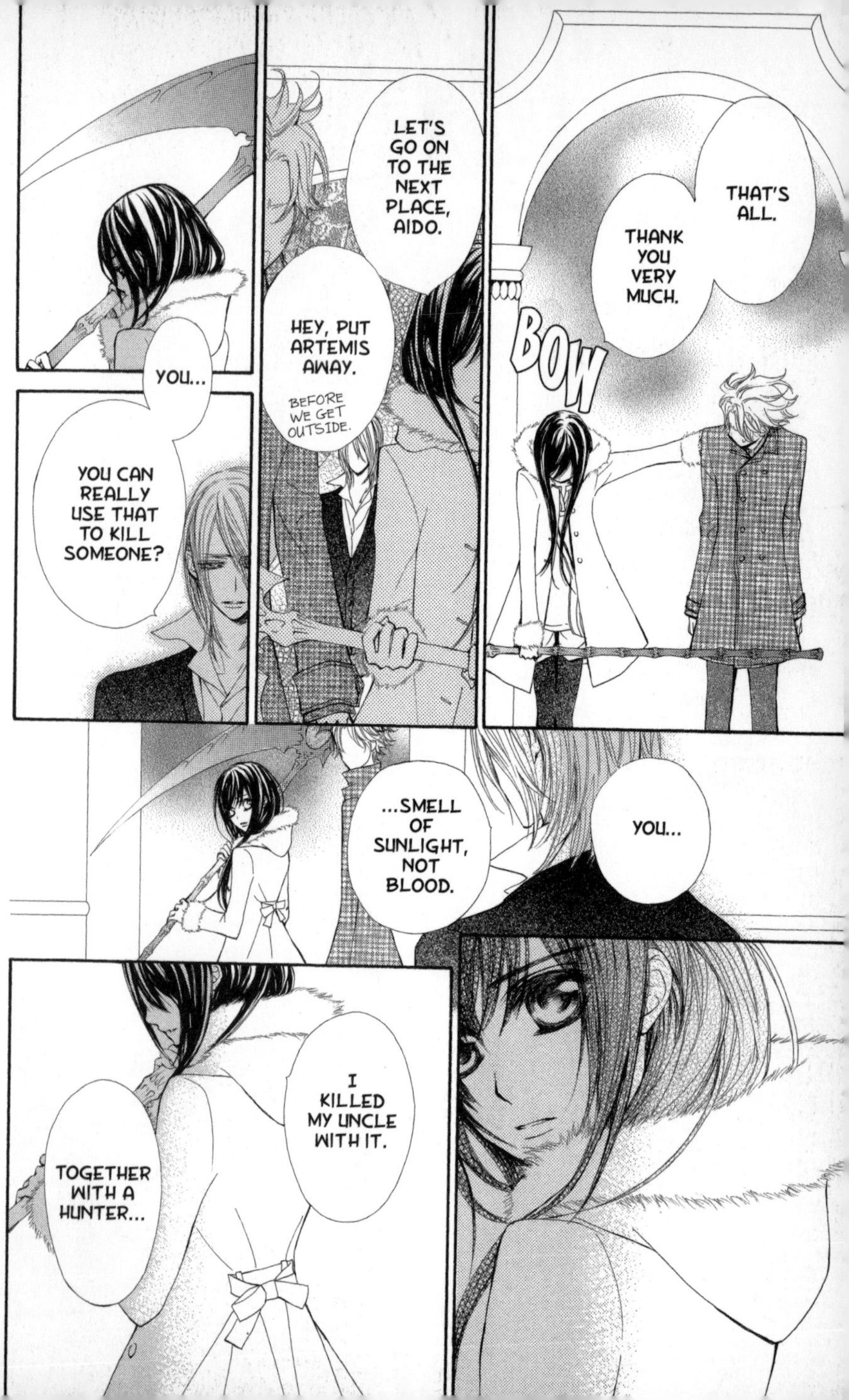
THAT'S ALL.
THANK YOU VERY MUCH.
BOW
LET'S GO ON TO THE NEXT PLACE, AIDO.
HEY, PUT ARTEMIS AWAY.
BEFORE WE GET OUTSIDE.
YOU...
YOU CAN REALLY USE THAT TO KILL SOMEONE?
YOU...
...SMELL OF SUNLIGHT, NOT BLOOD.
I KILLED MY UNCLE WITH IT.
TOGETHER WITH A HUNTER...

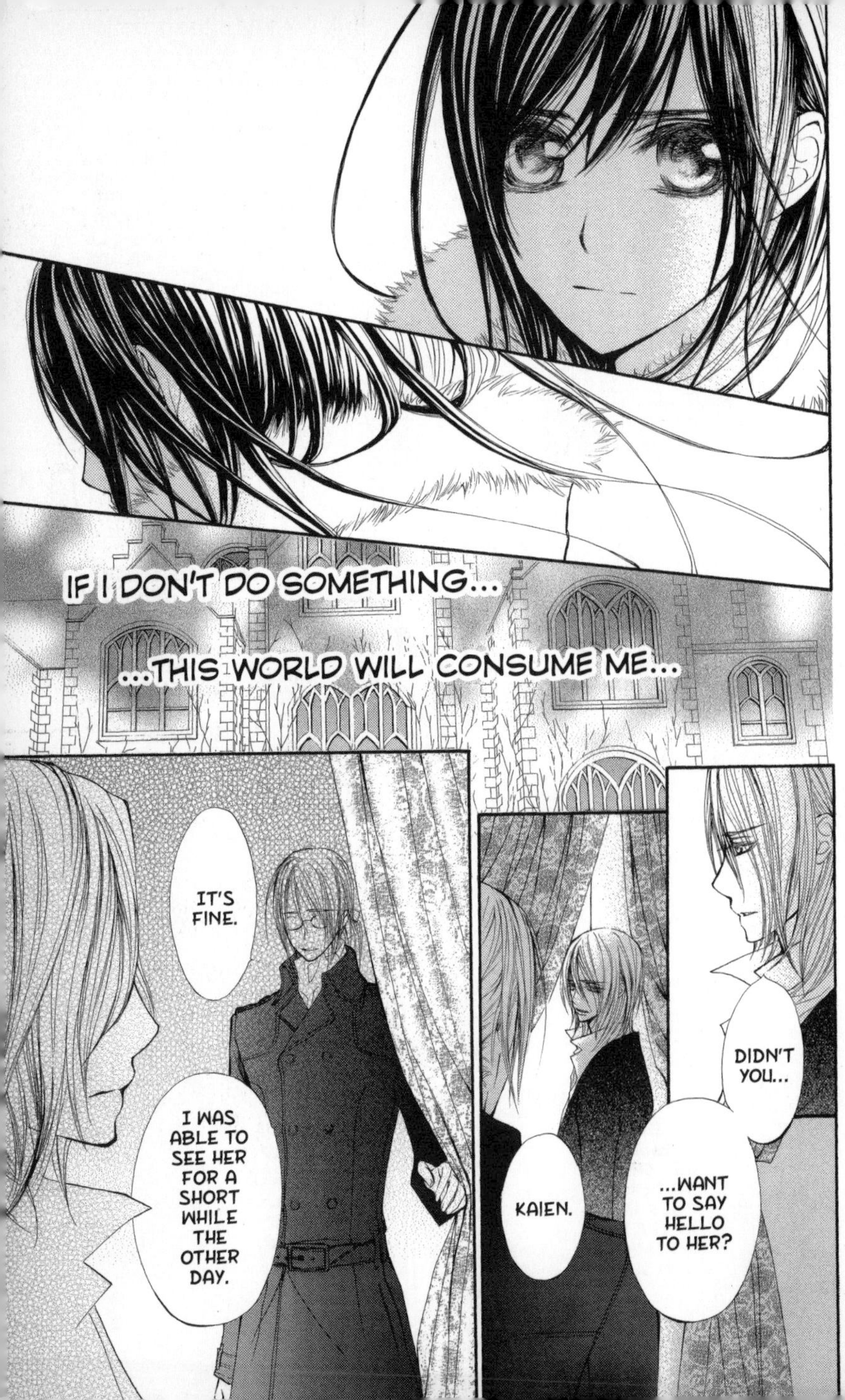
IF I DON'T DO SOMETHING...
...THIS WORLD WILL CONSUME ME...
DIDN'T YOU...
...WANT TO SAY HELLO TO HER?
KAIEN.
IT'S FINE.
I WAS ABLE TO SEE HER FOR A SHORT WHILE THE OTHER DAY.

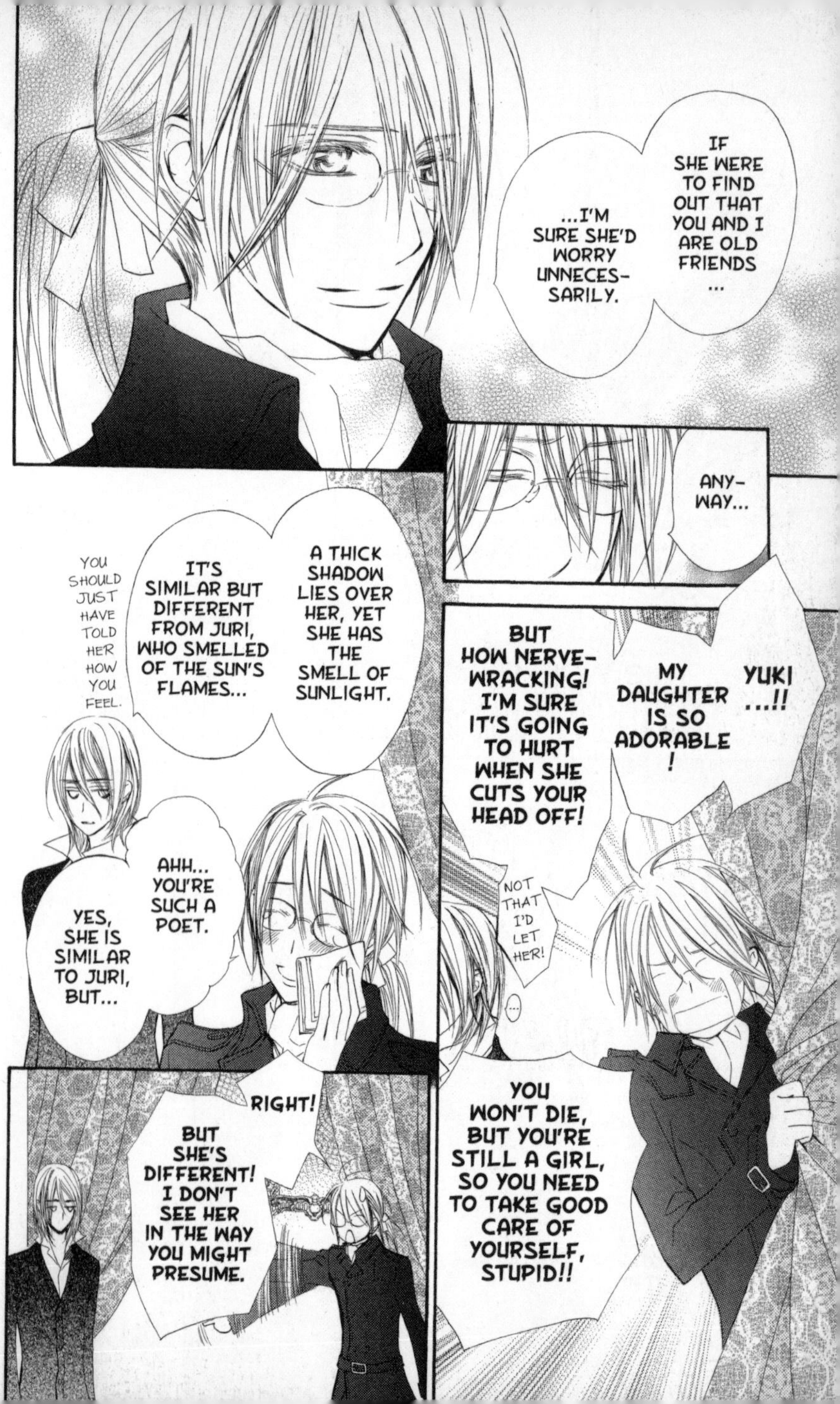
IF SHE WERE TO FIND OUT THAT YOU AND I ARE OLD FRIENDS ...
...I'M SURE SHE'D WORRY UNNECES-SARILY.
ANY-WAY...
YUKI ...!!
MY DAUGHTER IS SO ADORABLE!
BUT HOW NERVE-WRACKING! I'M SURE IT'S GOING TO HURT WHEN SHE CUTS YOUR HEAD OFF!
NOT THAT I'D LET HER!
...
YOU WON'T DIE, BUT YOU'RE STILL A GIRL, SO YOU NEED TO TAKE GOOD CARE OF YOURSELF, STUPID!!
A THICK SHADOW LIES OVER HER, YET SHE HAS THE SMELL OF SUNLIGHT.
IT'S SIMILAR BUT DIFFERENT FROM JURI, WHO SMELLED OF THE SUN'S FLAMES...
YOU SHOULD JUST HAVE TOLD HER HOW YOU FEEL.
AHH... YOU'RE SUCH A POET.
YES, SHE IS SIMILAR TO JURI, BUT...
RIGHT!
BUT SHE'S DIFFERENT! I DON'T SEE HER IN THE WAY YOU MIGHT PRESUME.

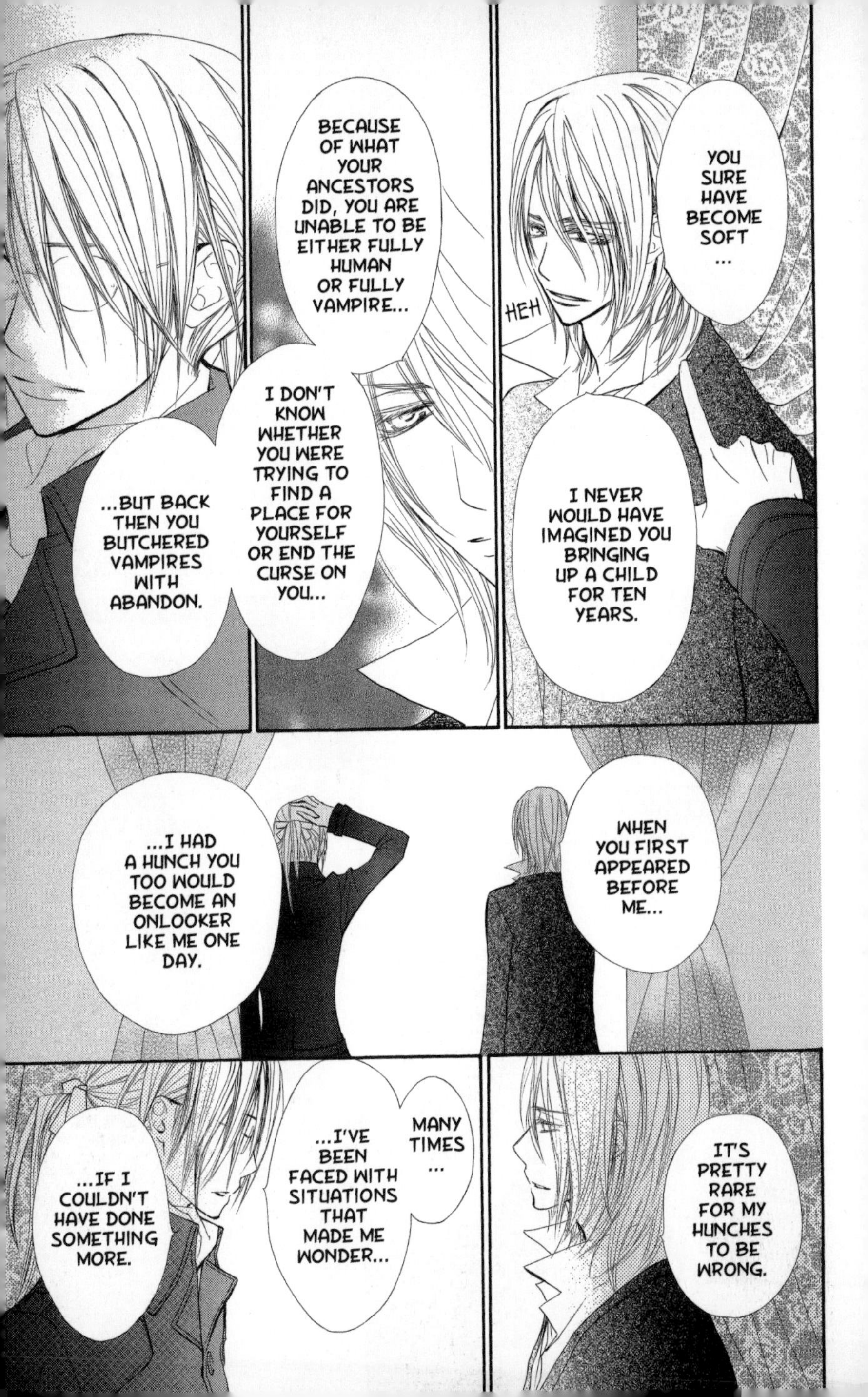
YOU SURE HAVE BECOME SOFT ...
HEH
I NEVER WOULD HAVE IMAGINED YOU BRINGING UP A CHILD FOR TEN YEARS.
BECAUSE OF WHAT YOUR ANCESTORS DID, YOU ARE UNABLE TO BE EITHER FULLY HUMAN OR FULLY VAMPIRE...
I DON'T KNOW WHETHER YOU WERE TRYING TO FIND A PLACE FOR YOURSELF OR END THE CURSE ON YOU...
...BUT BACK THEN YOU BUTCHERED VAMPIRES WITH ABANDON.
WHEN YOU FIRST APPEARED BEFORE ME...
...I HAD A HUNCH YOU TOO WOULD BECOME AN ONLOOKER LIKE ME ONE DAY.
IT'S PRETTY RARE FOR MY HUNCHES TO BE WRONG.
MANY TIMES ...
...I'VE BEEN FACED WITH SITUATIONS THAT MADE ME WONDER...
...IF I COULDN'T HAVE DONE SOMETHING MORE.

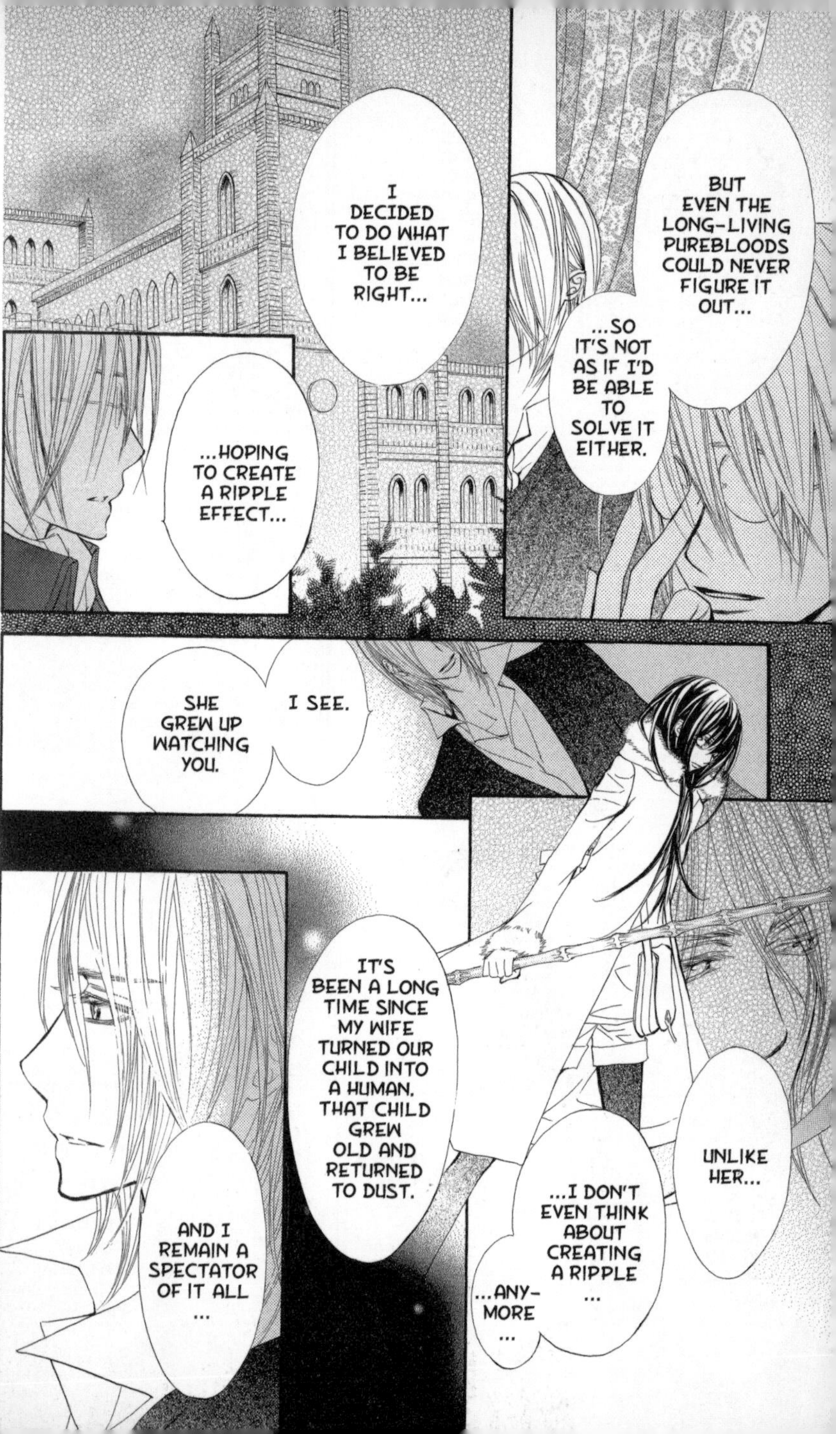
BUT EVEN THE LONG-LIVING PUREBLOODS COULD NEVER FIGURE IT OUT...
...SO IT'S NOT AS IF I'D BE ABLE TO SOLVE IT EITHER.
I DECIDED TO DO WHAT I BELIEVED TO BE RIGHT...
...HOPING TO CREATE A RIPPLE EFFECT...
I SEE.
SHE GREW UP WATCHING YOU.
UNLIKE HER...
...I DON'T EVEN THINK ABOUT CREATING A RIPPLE ...
...ANY-MORE ...
IT'S BEEN A LONG TIME SINCE MY WIFE TURNED OUR CHILD INTO A HUMAN. THAT CHILD GREW OLD AND RETURNED TO DUST.
AND I REMAIN A SPECTATOR OF IT ALL ...

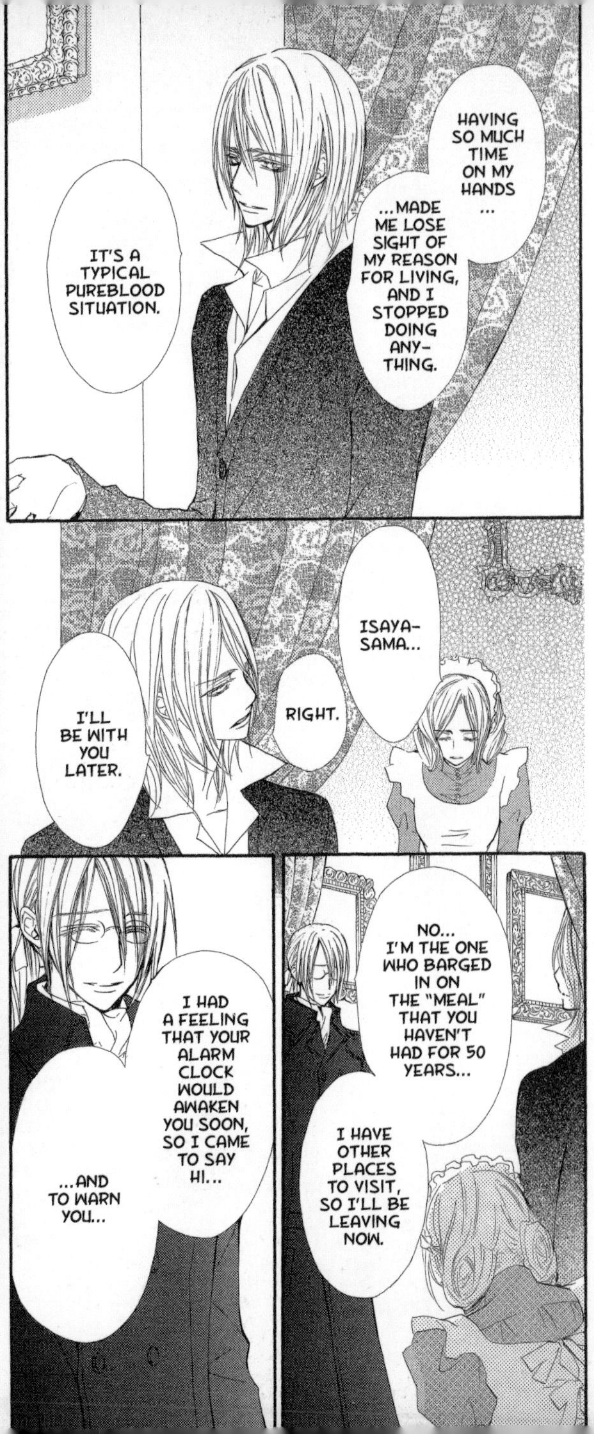
HAVING SO MUCH TIME ON MY HANDS...
...MADE ME LOSE SIGHT OF MY REASON FOR LIVING, AND I STOPPED DOING ANYTHING.
IT'S A TYPICAL PUREBLOOD SITUATION.
ISAYA-SAMA...
RIGHT.
I'LL BE WITH YOU LATER.
NO... I'M THE ONE WHO BARGED IN ON THE "MEAL" THAT YOU HAVEN'T HAD FOR 50 YEARS...
I HAVE OTHER PLACES TO VISIT, SO I'LL BE LEAVING NOW.
I HAD A FEELING THAT YOUR ALARM CLOCK WOULD AWAKEN YOU SOON, SO I CAME TO SAY HI...
...AND TO WARN YOU...

I couldn't talk about it in volume 11, so I would like to take this opportunity to talk about Kaito!!

I had always been thinking about creating a hunter around the age of Zero. But Ayuna Fujisaki-sama created an extremely striking character, "Kaito," in her Vampire Knight novel, and I changed my mind. I calmly thought, "Even if I were to create this new vampire hunter character, I'm not sure if he will turn out to be as impressive as Kaito is after growing up... (It's not that Fujisaki-sama told me how he'd grow up; I just imagined it...)"
After getting permission from Fujisaki-sama, I decided to add Kaito to the manga. (I am trying to draw Kaito in a way that the readers can tell what kind of person he is from just the manga, but if you want to learn more about him, please read the novel too. ♡)
I would like to show my gratitude to Fujisaki-sama, who allowed me to import Kaito into the manga and even thought up a surname for him!

I kind of think his hair is ash-brown, Fujisaki-sama...

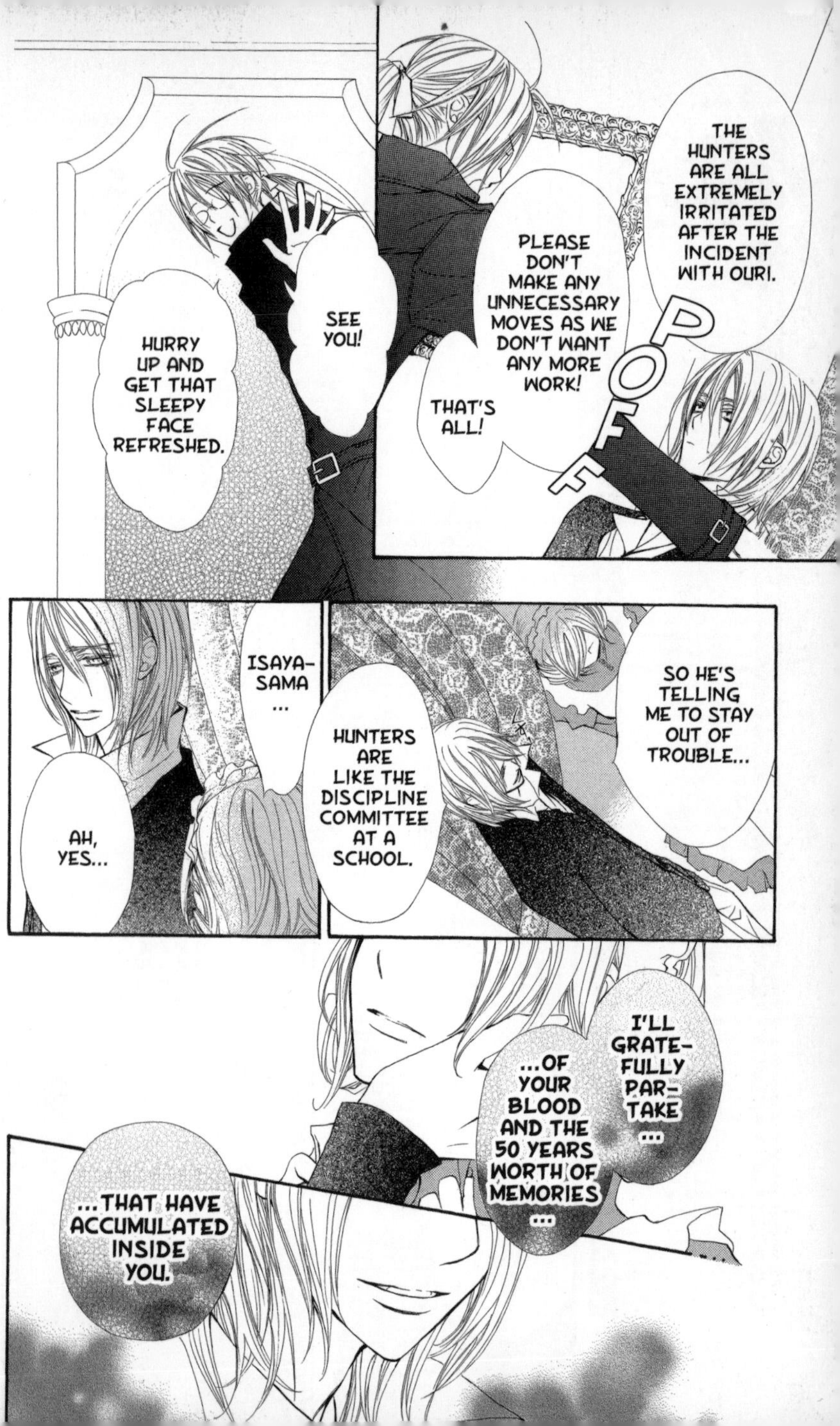
THE HUNTERS ARE ALL EXTREMELY IRRITATED AFTER THE INCIDENT WITH OURI.
PLEASE DON'T MAKE ANY UNNECESSARY MOVES AS WE DON'T WANT ANY MORE WORK!
POFF
THAT'S ALL!
SEE YOU!
HURRY UP AND GET THAT SLEEPY FACE REFRESHED.
SO HE'S TELLING ME TO STAY OUT OF TROUBLE...
HUNTERS ARE LIKE THE DISCIPLINE COMMITTEE AT A SCHOOL.
ISAYA-SAMA ...
AH, YES...
I'LL GRATE-FULLY PAR-TAKE ...
...OF YOUR BLOOD AND THE 50 YEARS WORTH OF MEMORIES ...
...THAT HAVE ACCUMULATED INSIDE YOU.

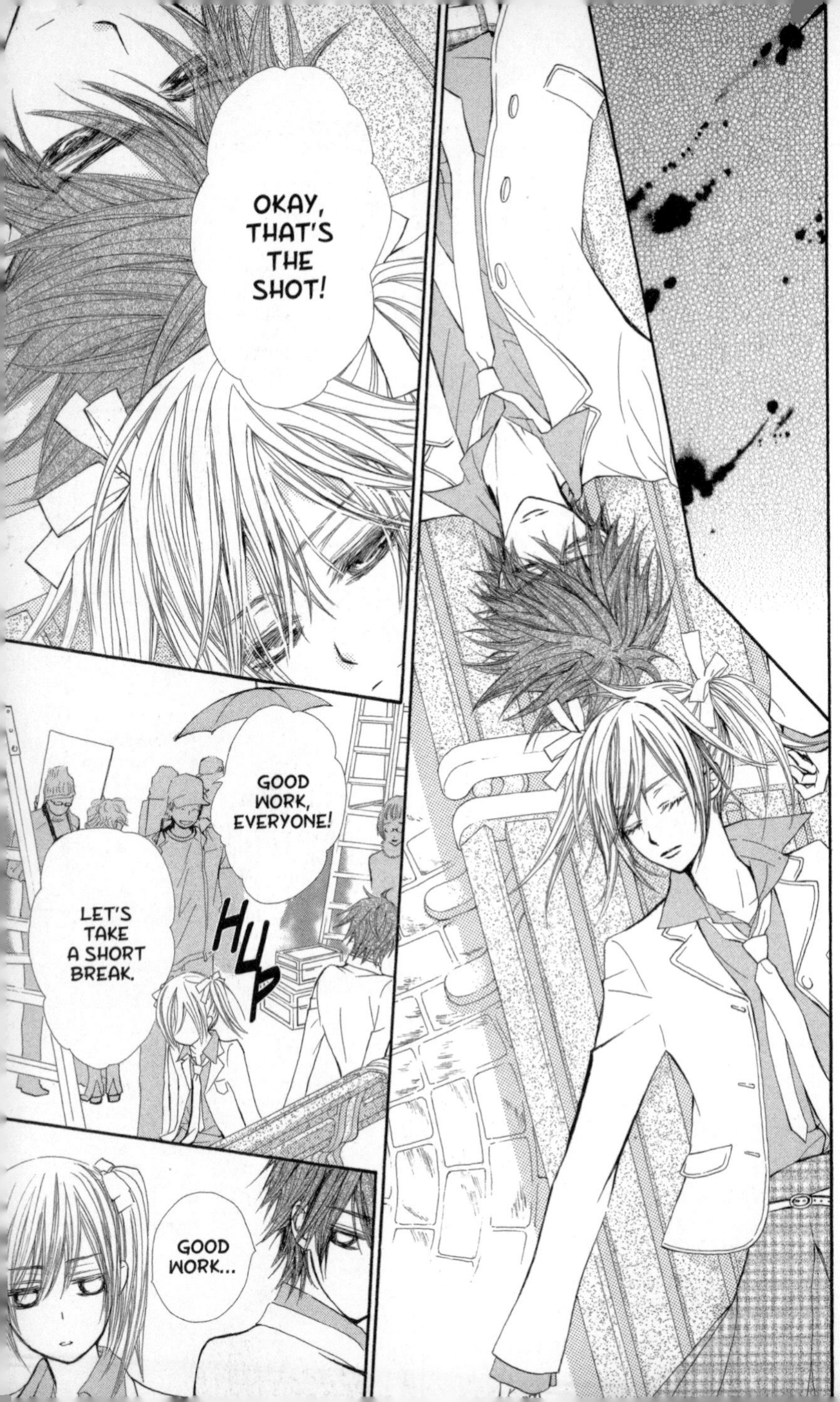
OKAY, THAT'S THE SHOT!
GOOD WORK, EVERYONE!
LET'S TAKE A SHORT BREAK.
HUP
GOOD WORK...

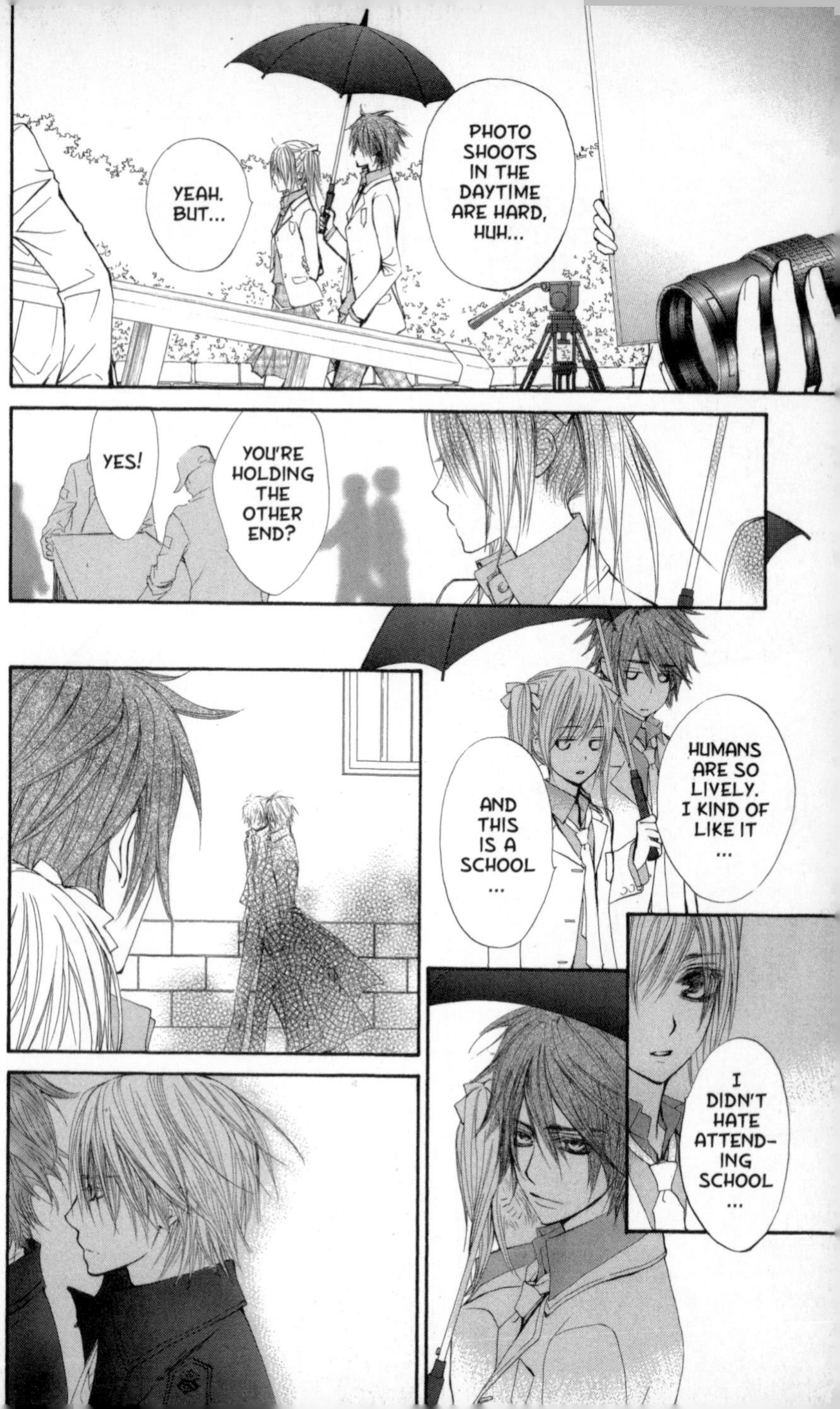
PHOTO SHOOTS IN THE DAYTIME ARE HARD, HUH...
YEAH. BUT...
YOU'RE HOLDING THE OTHER END?
YES!
HUMANS ARE SO LIVELY. I KIND OF LIKE IT ...
AND THIS IS A SCHOOL ...
I DIDN'T HATE ATTENDING-ING SCHOOL ...

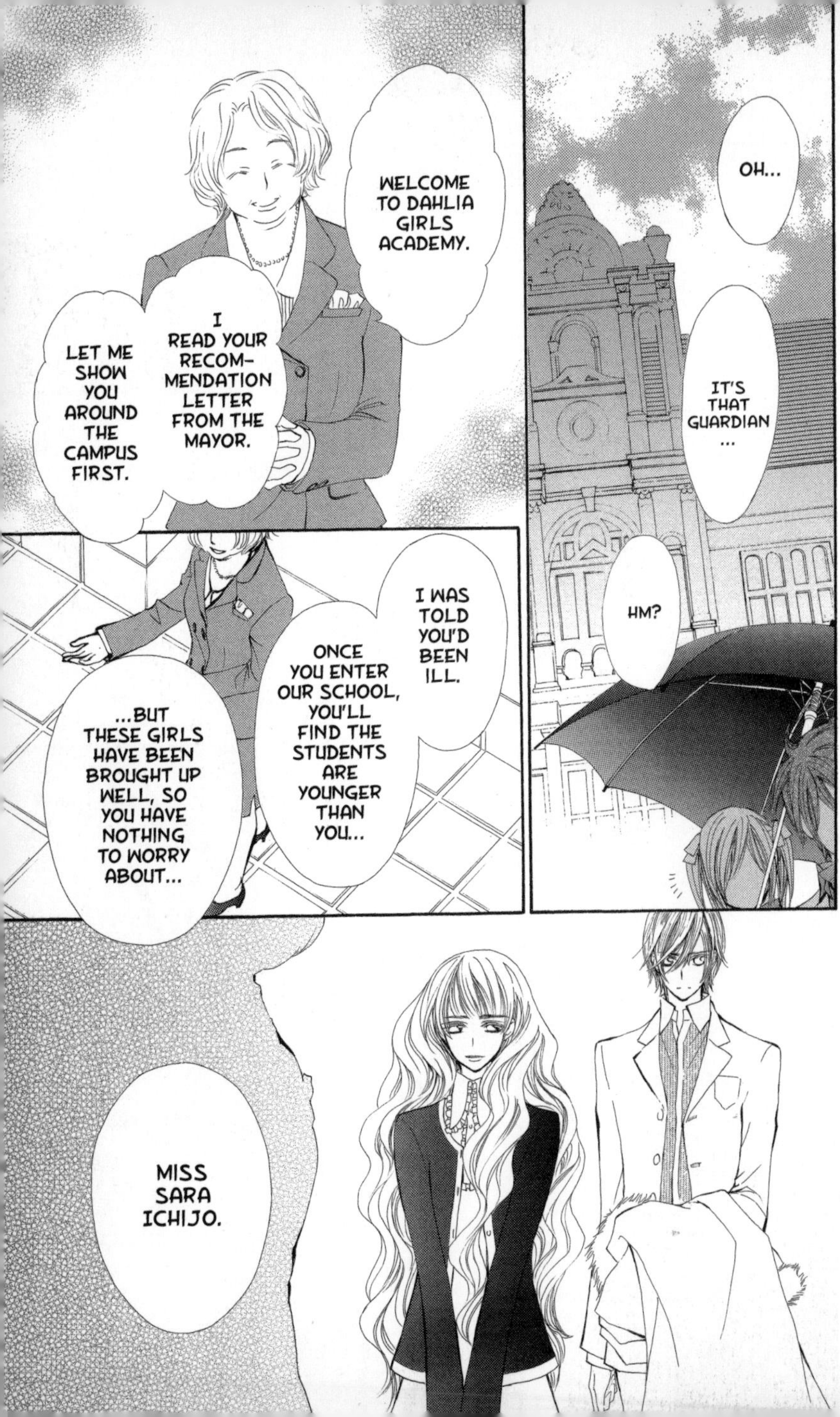
OH...
IT'S THAT GUARDIAN...
HM?
WELCOME TO DAHLIA GIRLS ACADEMY.
I READ YOUR RECOMMENDATION LETTER FROM THE MAYOR.
LET ME SHOW YOU AROUND THE CAMPUS FIRST.
I WAS TOLD YOU'D BEEN ILL.
ONCE YOU ENTER OUR SCHOOL, YOU'LL FIND THE STUDENTS ARE YOUNGER THAN YOU...
...BUT THESE GIRLS HAVE BEEN BROUGHT UP WELL, SO YOU HAVE NOTHING TO WORRY ABOUT...
MISS SARA ICHIJO.

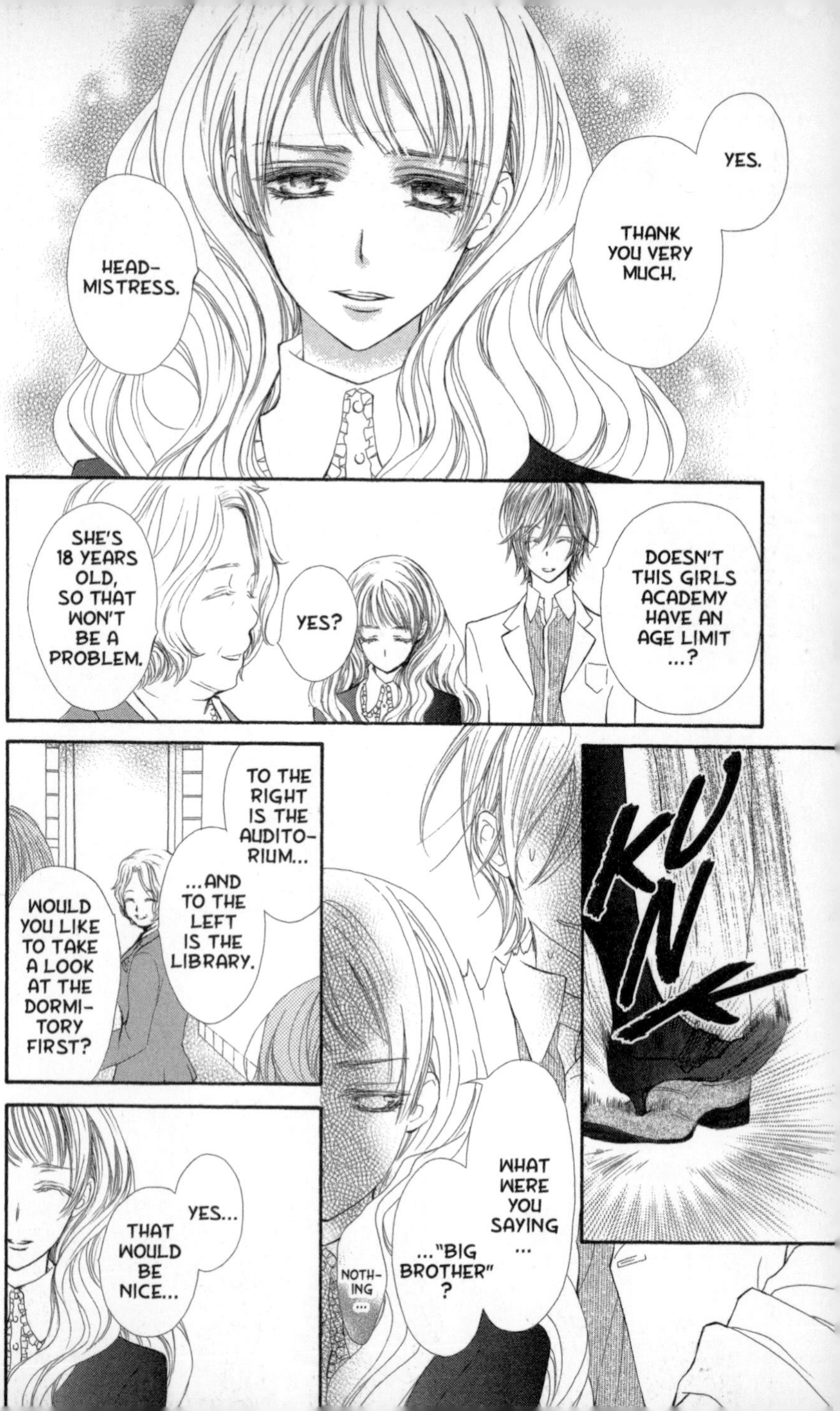
YES.
THANK YOU VERY MUCH.
HEAD-MISTRESS.
DOESN'T THIS GIRLS ACADEMY HAVE AN AGE LIMIT ...?
YES?
SHE'S 18 YEARS OLD, SO THAT WON'T BE A PROBLEM.
KUNK
WHAT WERE YOU SAYING ...
..."BIG BROTHER" ?
NOTH-ING ...
TO THE RIGHT IS THE AUDITO-RIUM...
...AND TO THE LEFT IS THE LIBRARY.
WOULD YOU LIKE TO TAKE A LOOK AT THE DORMI-TORY FIRST?
YES...
THAT WOULD BE NICE...

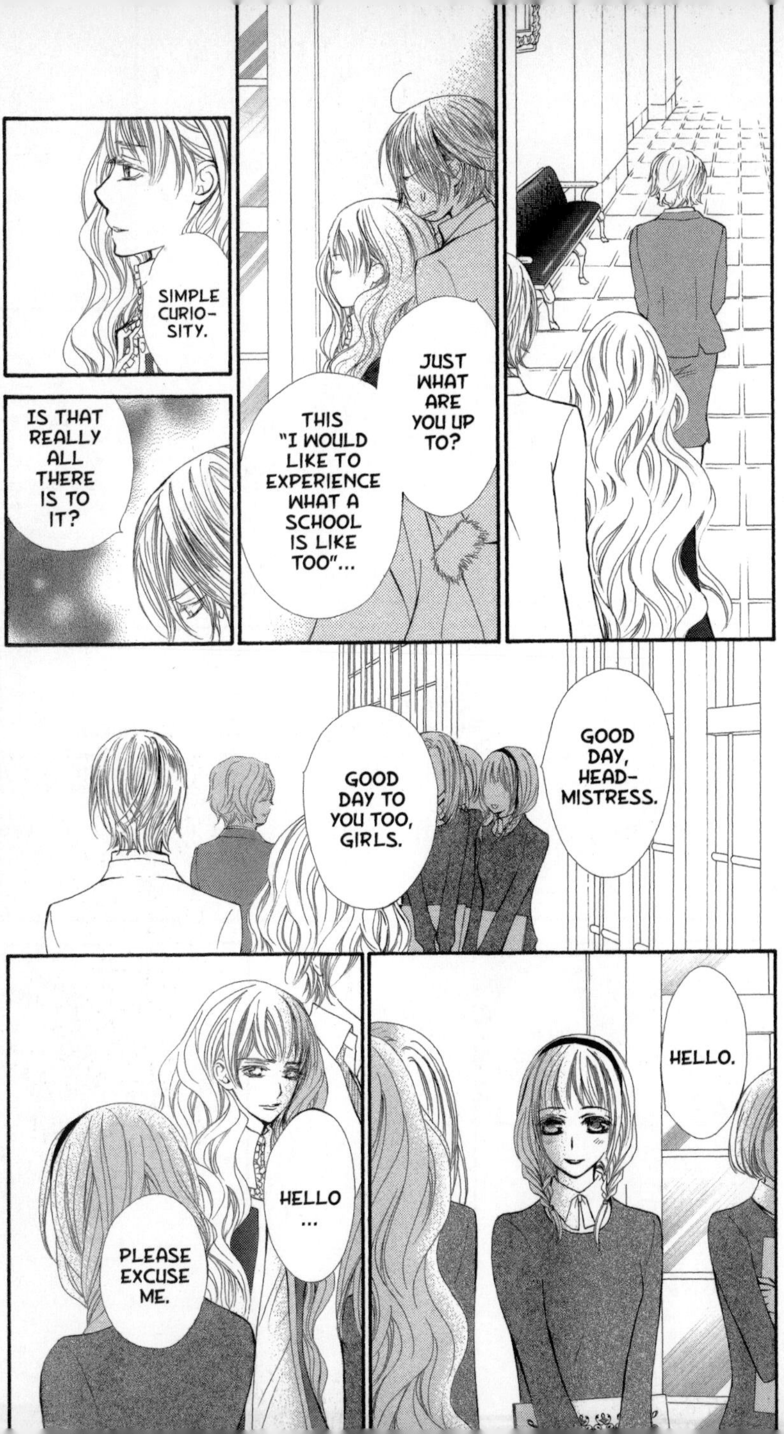
JUST WHAT ARE YOU UP TO?
THIS "I WOULD LIKE TO EXPERIENCE WHAT A SCHOOL IS LIKE TOO"...
SIMPLE CURIO-SITY.
IS THAT REALLY ALL THERE IS TO IT?
GOOD DAY, HEAD-MISTRESS.
GOOD DAY TO YOU TOO, GIRLS.
HELLO.
HELLO ...
PLEASE EXCUSE ME.

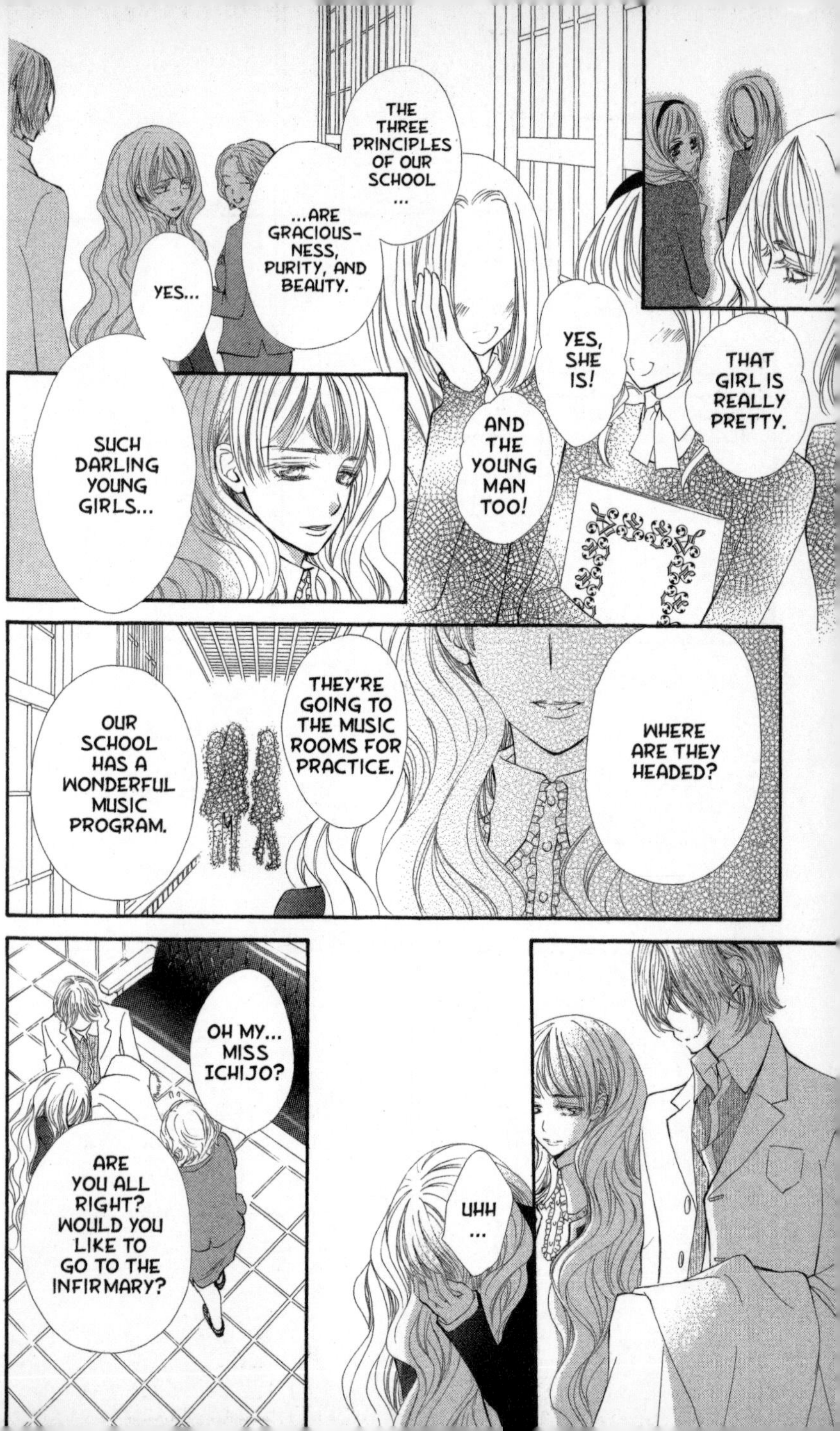
THE THREE PRINCIPLES OF OUR SCHOOL ...
...ARE GRACIOUS-NESS, PURITY, AND BEAUTY.
YES...
THAT GIRL IS REALLY PRETTY.
YES, SHE IS!
AND THE YOUNG MAN TOO!
SUCH DARLING YOUNG GIRLS...
WHERE ARE THEY HEADED?
THEY'RE GOING TO THE MUSIC ROOMS FOR PRACTICE.
OUR SCHOOL HAS A WONDERFUL MUSIC PROGRAM.
UHH ...
OH MY... MISS ICHIJO?
ARE YOU ALL RIGHT? WOULD YOU LIKE TO GO TO THE INFIRMARY?

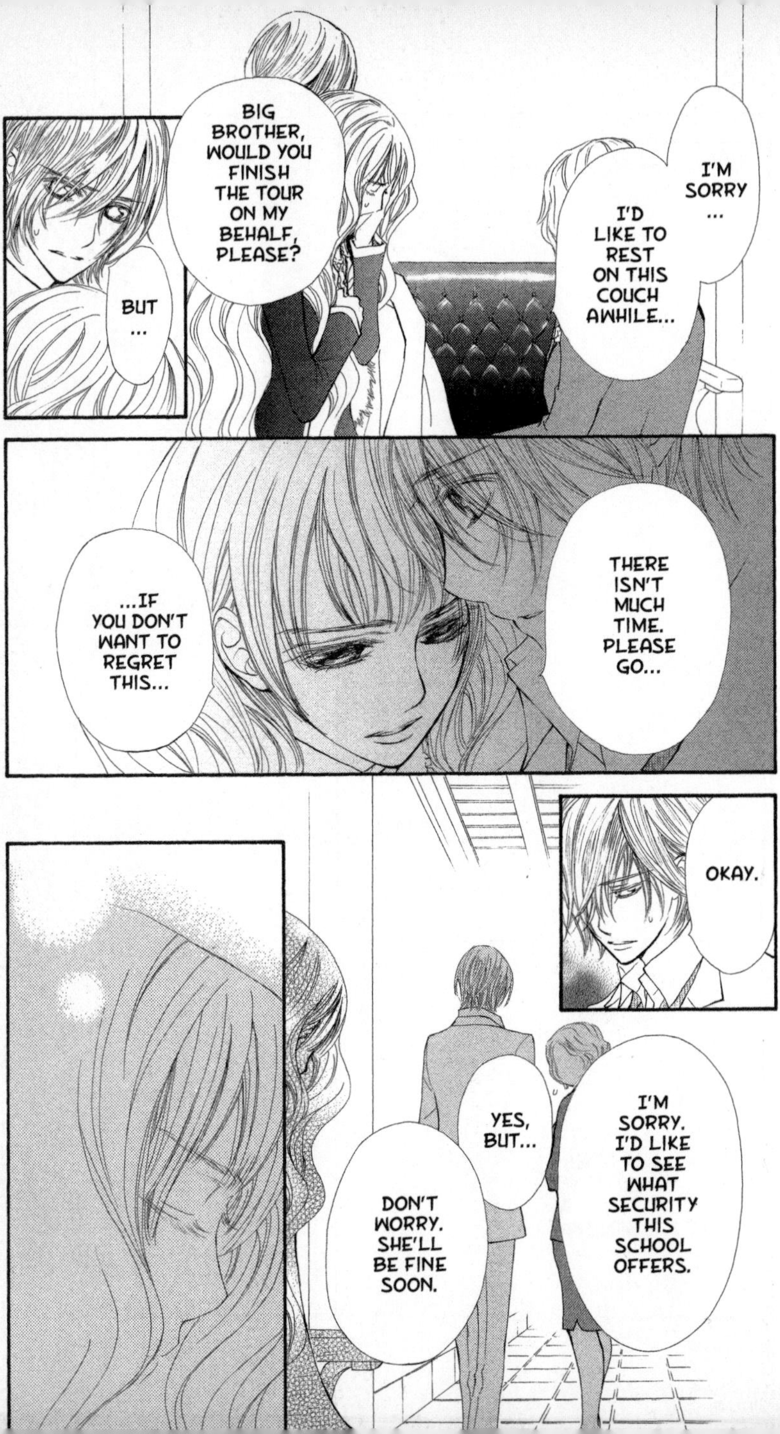
I'M SORRY ...
I'D LIKE TO REST ON THIS COUCH AWHILE...
BIG BROTHER, WOULD YOU FINISH THE TOUR ON MY BEHALF, PLEASE?
BUT ...
THERE ISN'T MUCH TIME. PLEASE GO...
...IF YOU DON'T WANT TO REGRET THIS...
OKAY.
I'M SORRY. I'D LIKE TO SEE WHAT SECURITY THIS SCHOOL OFFERS.
YES, BUT...
DON'T WORRY. SHE'LL BE FINE SOON.

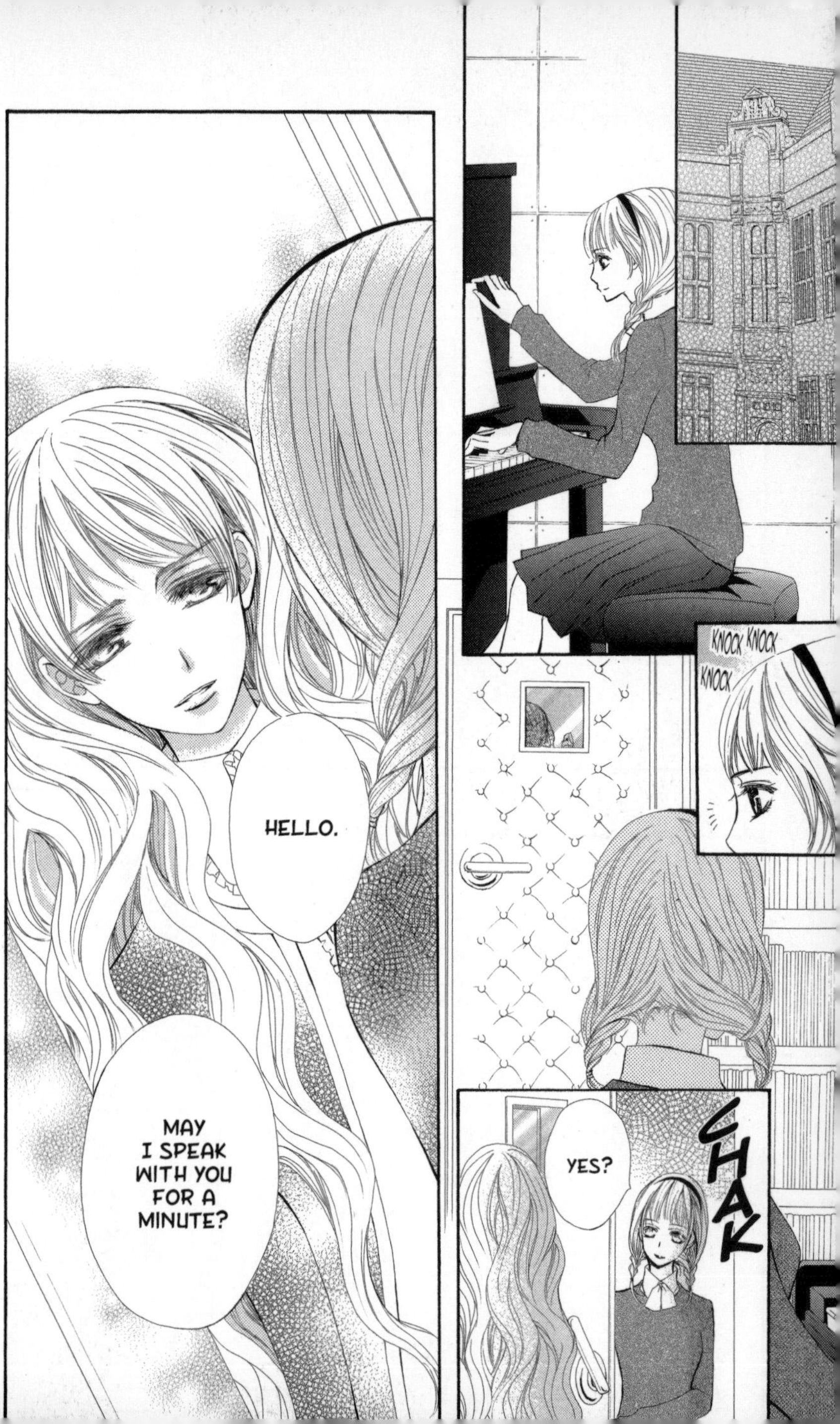
KNOCK KNOCK
KNOCK
CHAK
YES?
HELLO.
MAY I SPEAK WITH YOU FOR A MINUTE?

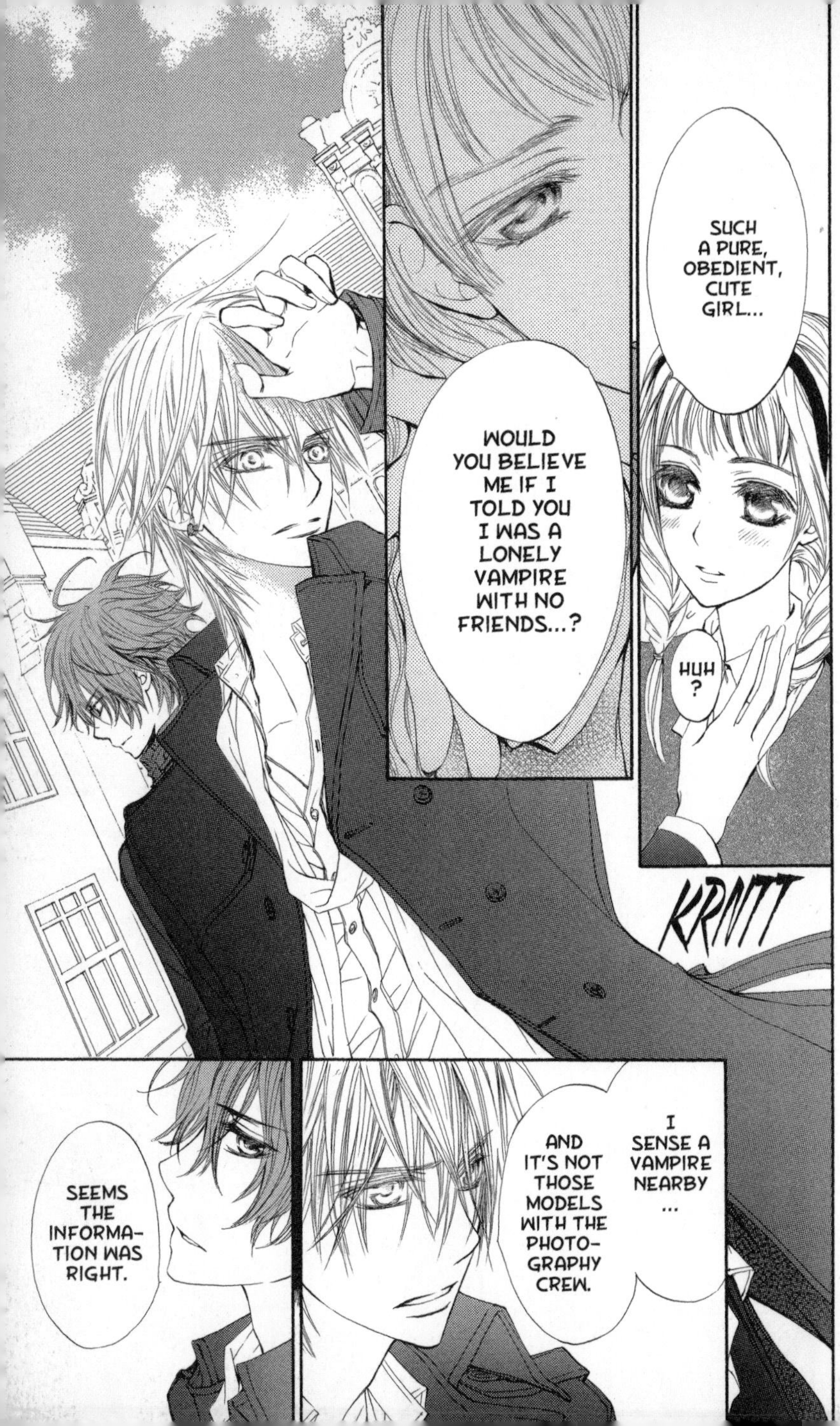
SUCH A PURE, OBEDIENT, CUTE GIRL...
HUH?
WOULD YOU BELIEVE ME IF I TOLD YOU I WAS A LONELY VAMPIRE WITH NO FRIENDS...?
KRNTT
I SENSE A VAMPIRE NEARBY ...
AND IT'S NOT THOSE MODELS WITH THE PHOTO-GRAPHY CREW.
SEEMS THE INFORMA-TION WAS RIGHT.

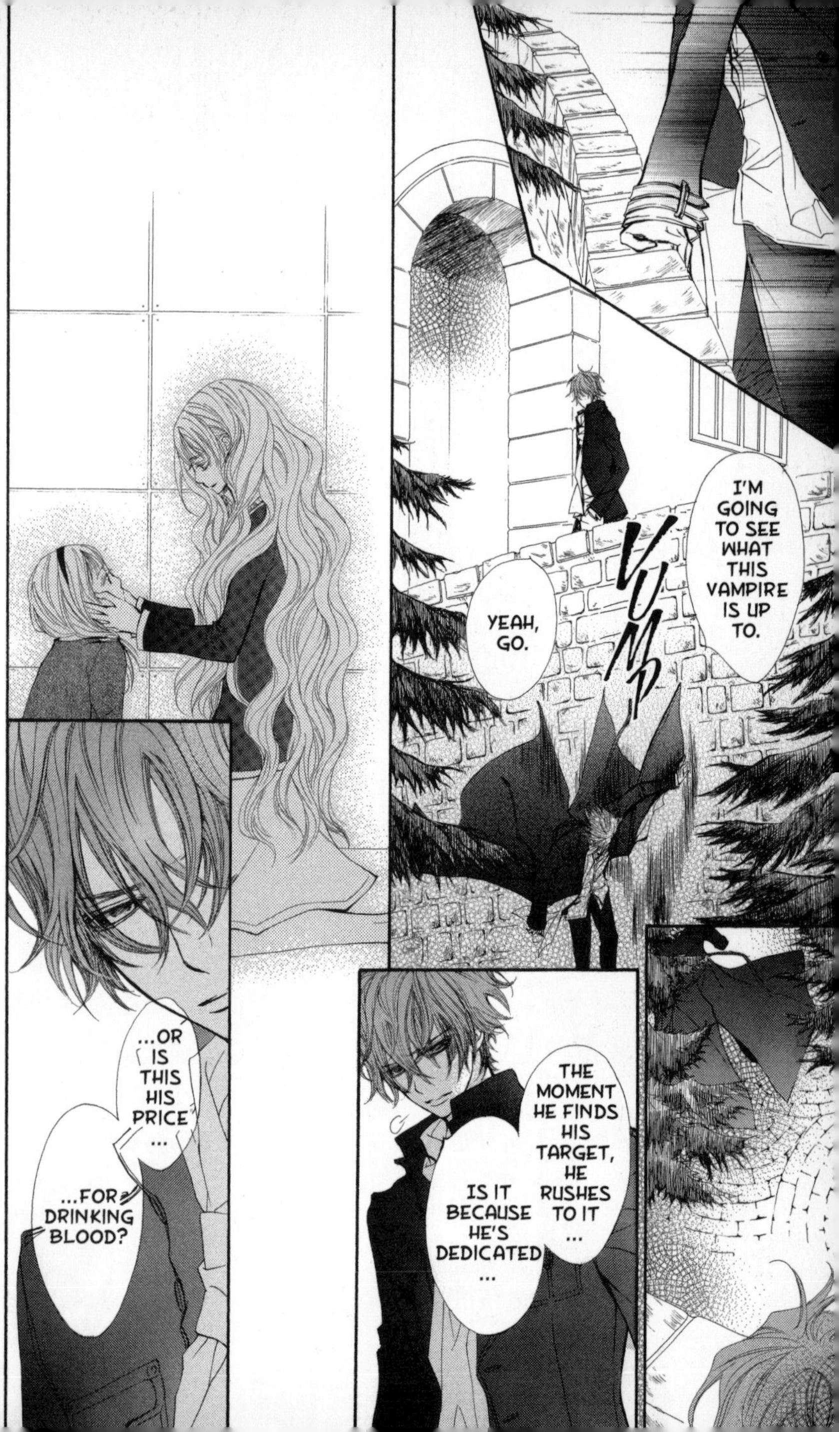
I'M GOING TO SEE WHAT THIS VAMPIRE IS UP TO.
YEAH, GO.
VUMP
THE MOMENT HE FINDS HIS TARGET, HE RUSHES TO IT...
IS IT BECAUSE HE'S DEDICATED...
...OR IS THIS HIS PRICE...
...FOR DRINKING BLOOD?

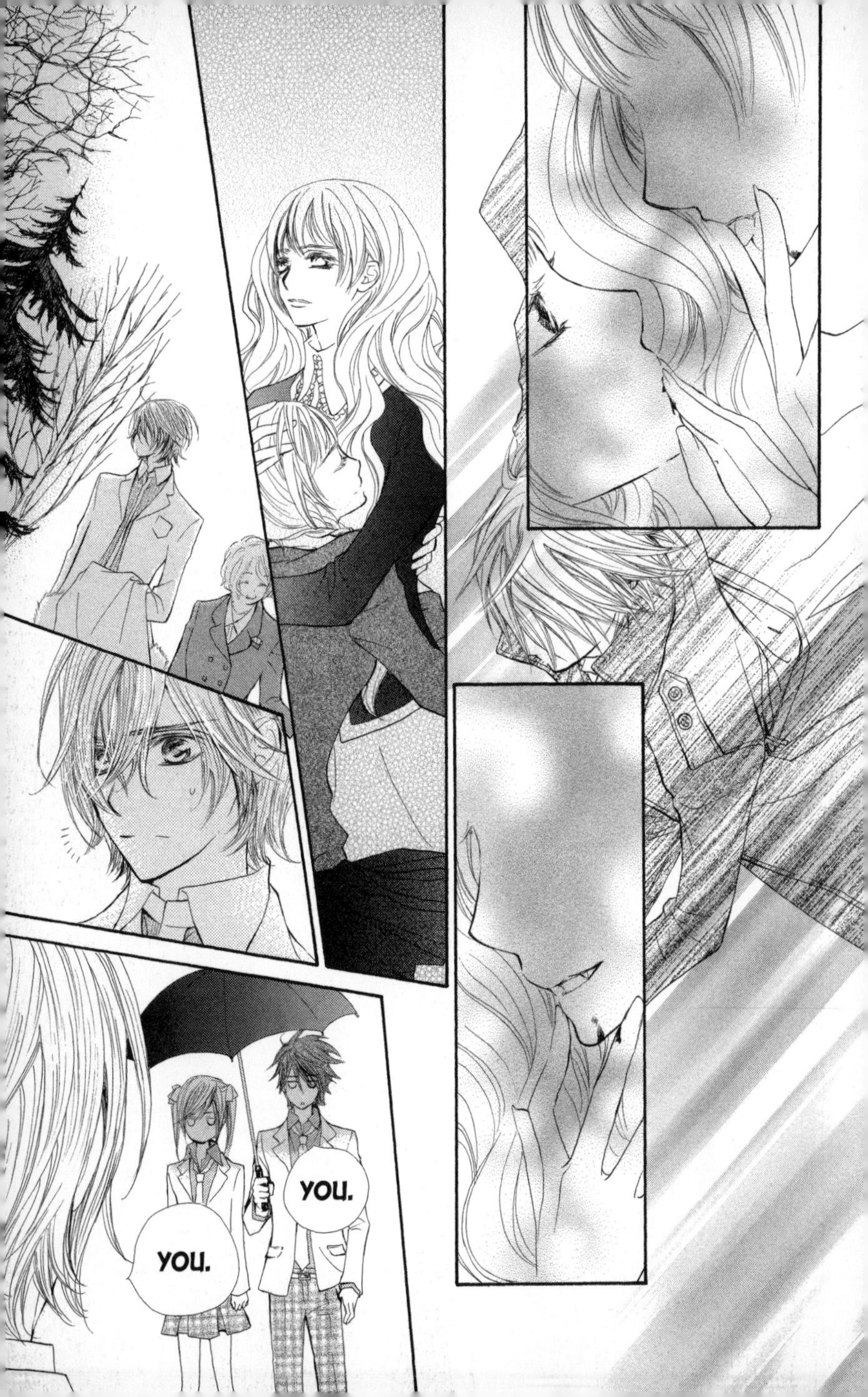
YOU.
YOU.

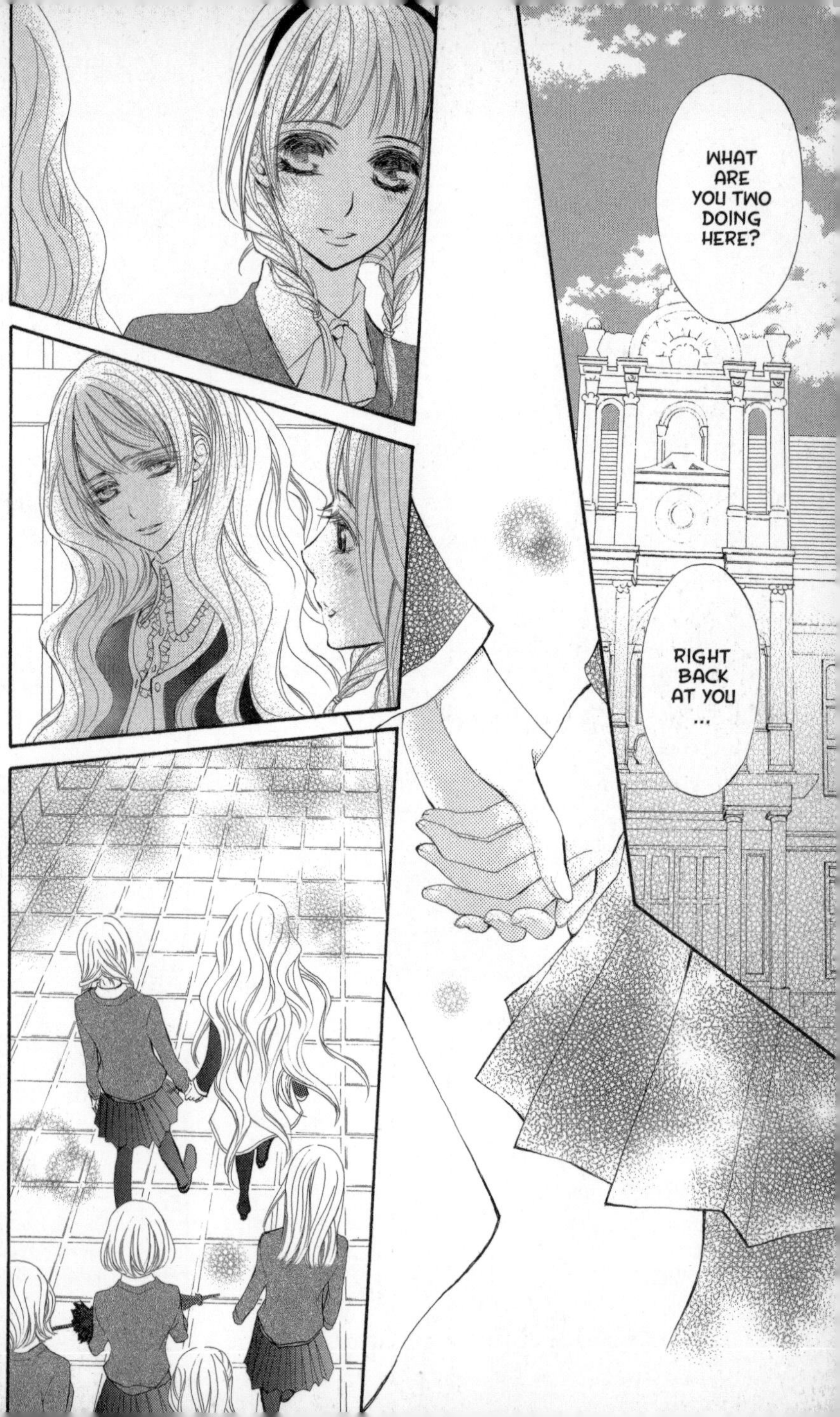
WHAT ARE YOU TWO DOING HERE?
RIGHT BACK AT YOU ...

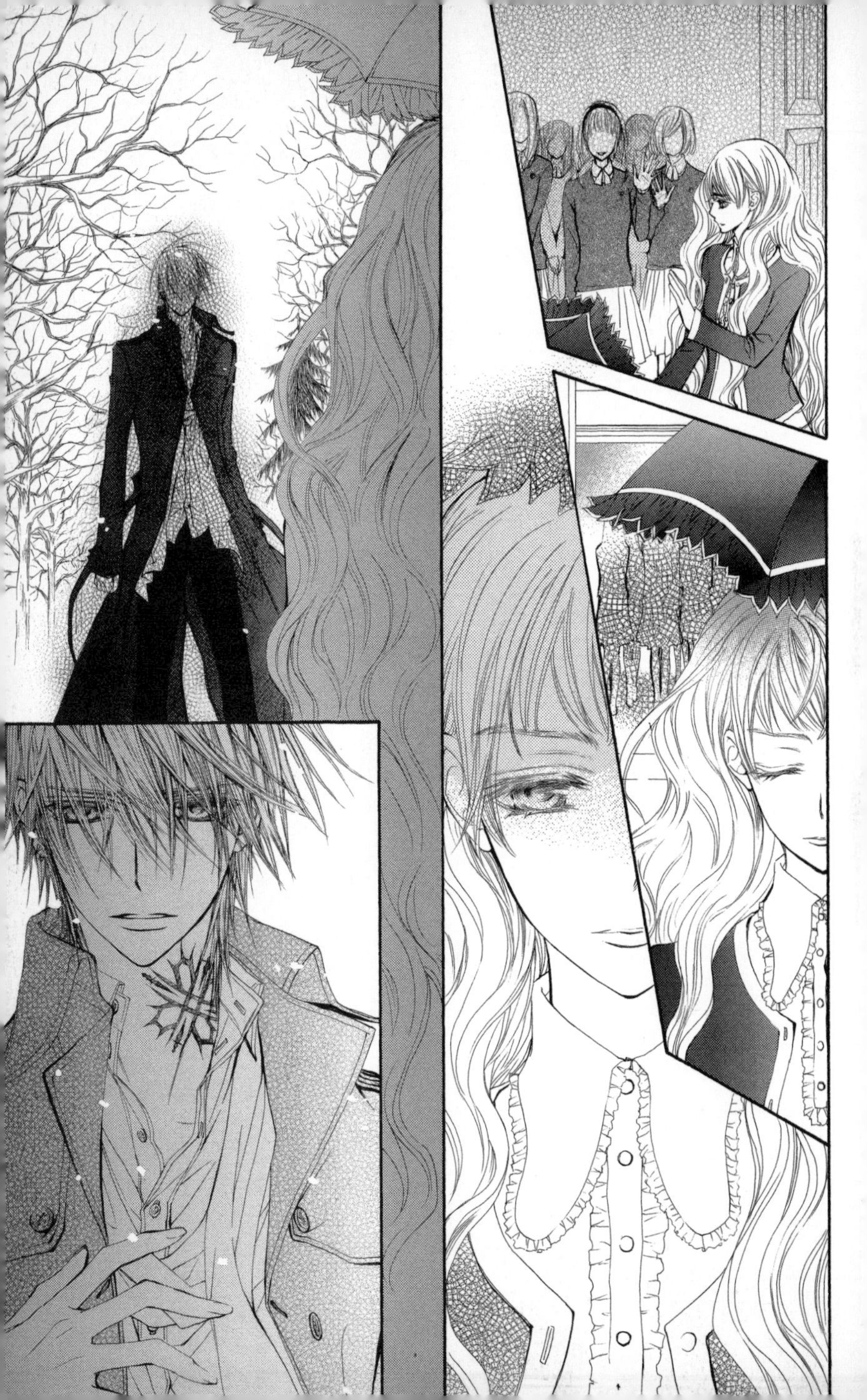

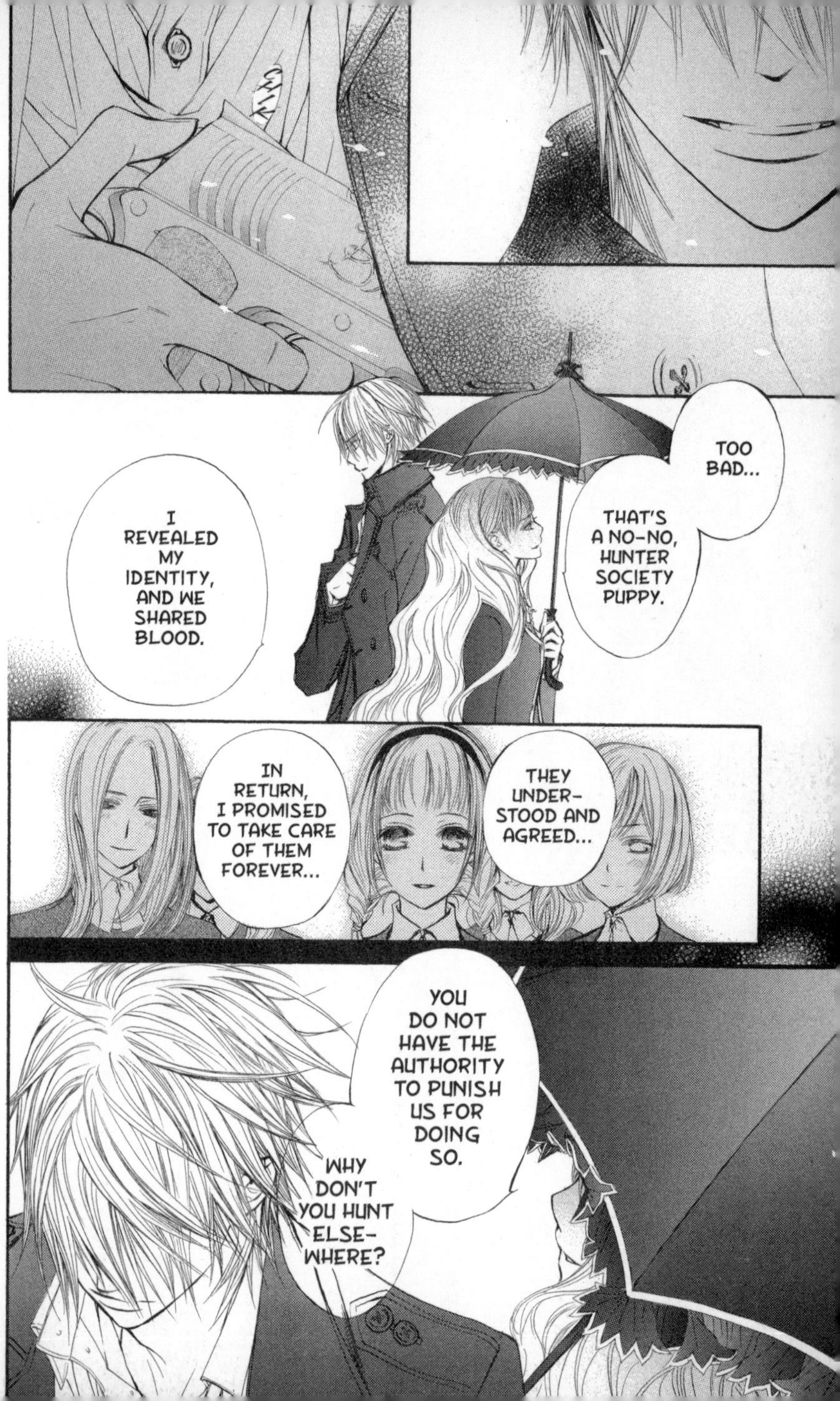
CHIK
TOO BAD...
THAT'S A NO-NO, HUNTER SOCIETY PUPPY.
I REVEALED MY IDENTITY, AND WE SHARED BLOOD.
THEY UNDER-STOOD AND AGREED...
IN RETURN, I PROMISED TO TAKE CARE OF THEM FOREVER...
YOU DO NOT HAVE THE AUTHORITY TO PUNISH US FOR DOING SO.
WHY DON'T YOU HUNT ELSE-WHERE?

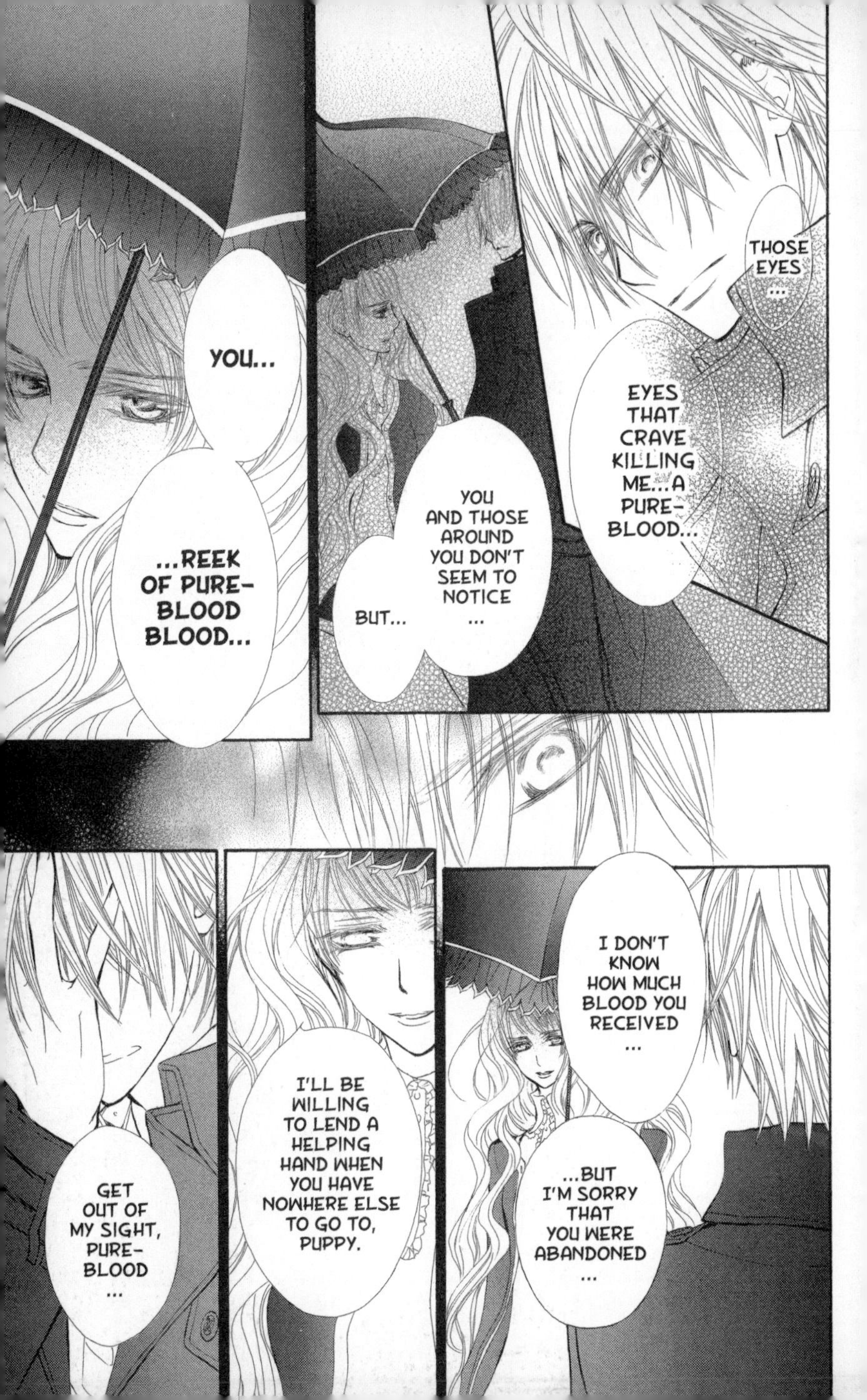
THOSE EYES...
EYES THAT CRAVE KILLING ME...A PURE-BLOOD...
YOU AND THOSE AROUND YOU DON'T SEEM TO NOTICE...
BUT...
YOU...
...REEK OF PURE-BLOOD BLOOD...
I DON'T KNOW HOW MUCH BLOOD YOU RECEIVED...
...BUT I'M SORRY THAT YOU WERE ABANDONED...
I'LL BE WILLING TO LEND A HELPING HAND WHEN YOU HAVE NOWHERE ELSE TO GO TO, PUPPY.
GET OUT OF MY SIGHT, PURE-BLOOD...

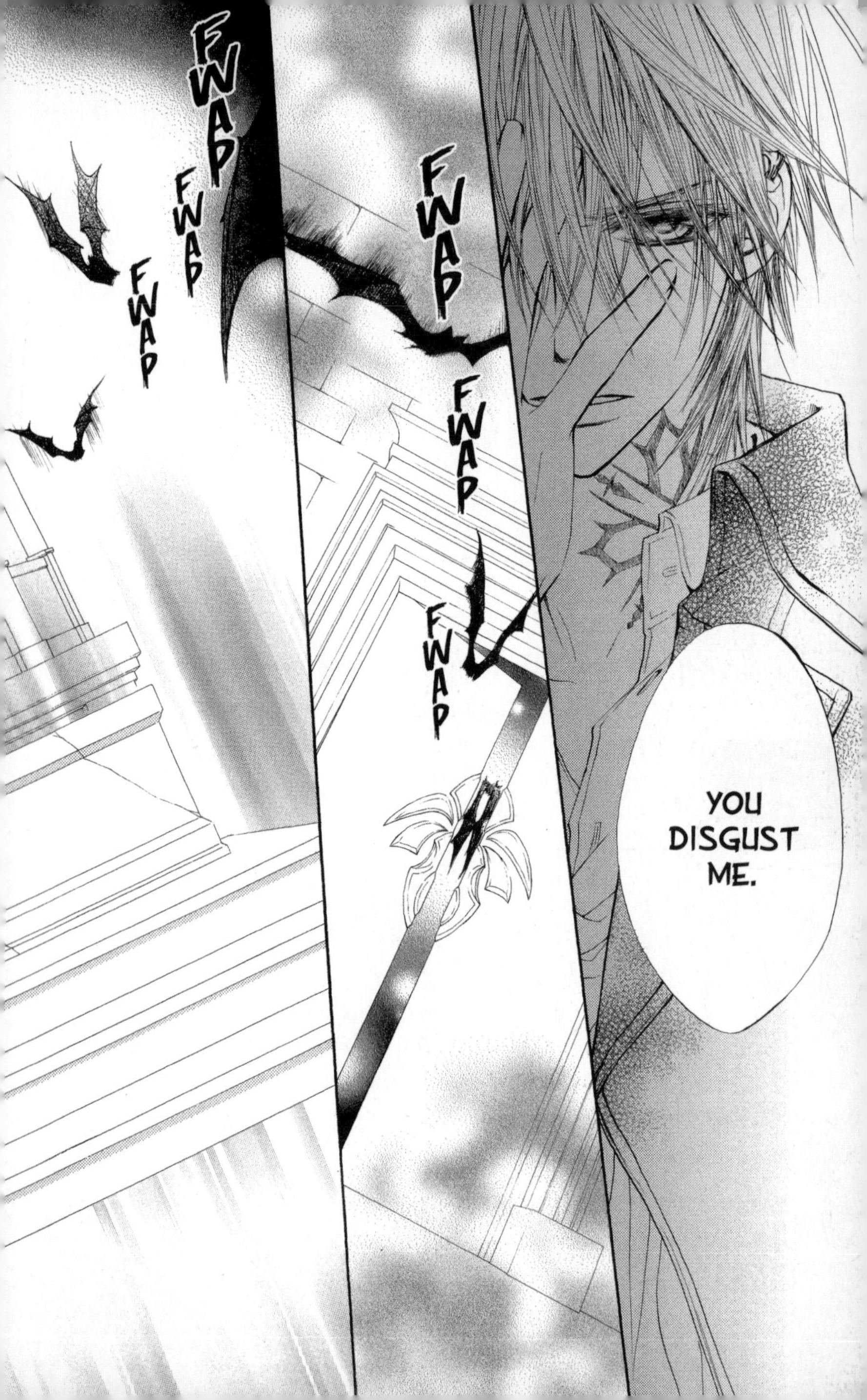
YOU DISGUST ME.
FWAP
FWAP
FWAP
FWAP
FWAP
FWAP

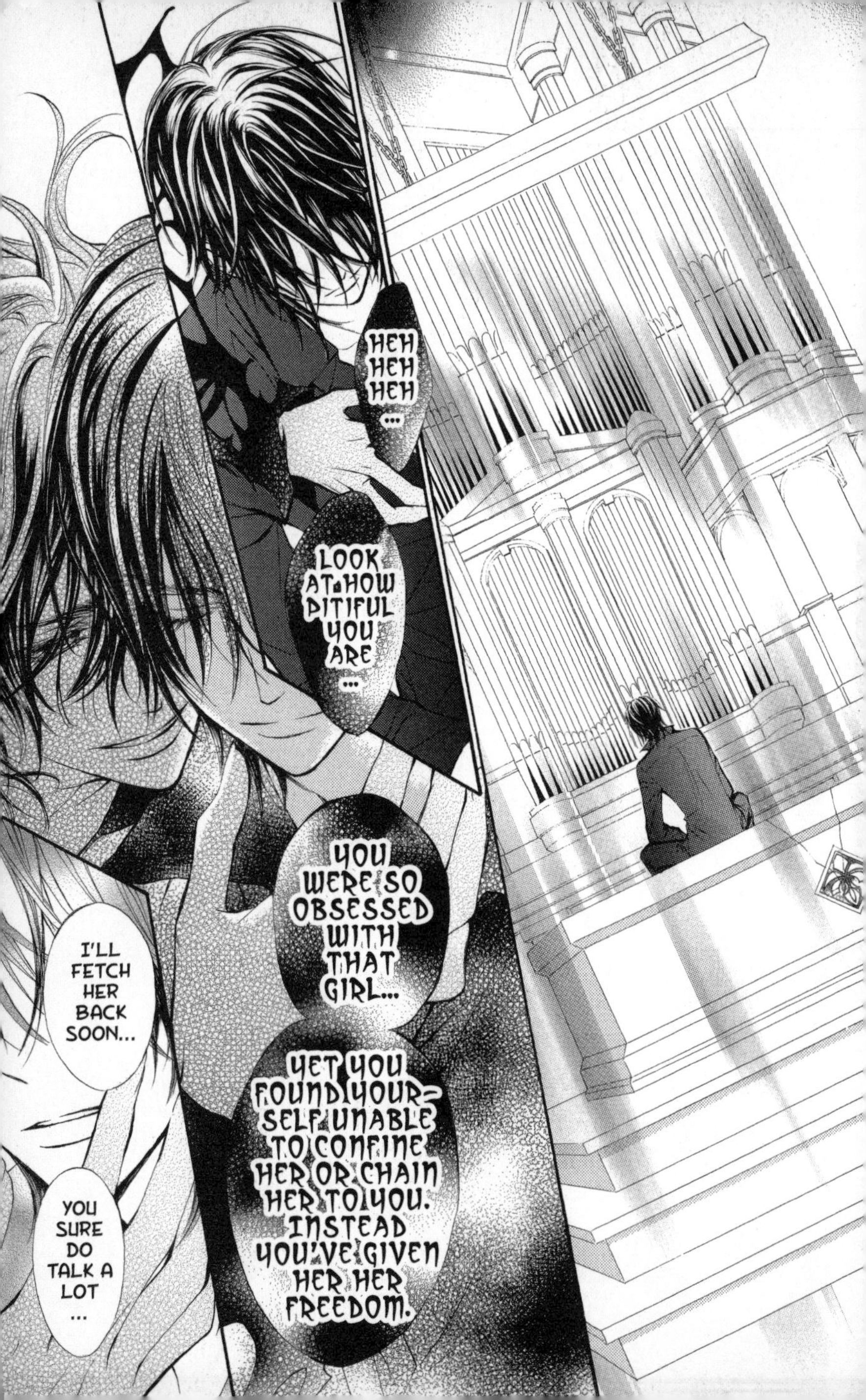
HEH HEH HEH ...
LOOK AT HOW PITIFUL YOU ARE ...
YOU WERE SO OBSESSED WITH THAT GIRL...
YET YOU FOUND YOUR-SELF UNABLE TO CONFINE HER OR CHAIN HER TO YOU. INSTEAD YOU'VE GIVEN HER HER FREEDOM.
I'LL FETCH HER BACK SOON...
YOU SURE DO TALK A LOT ...

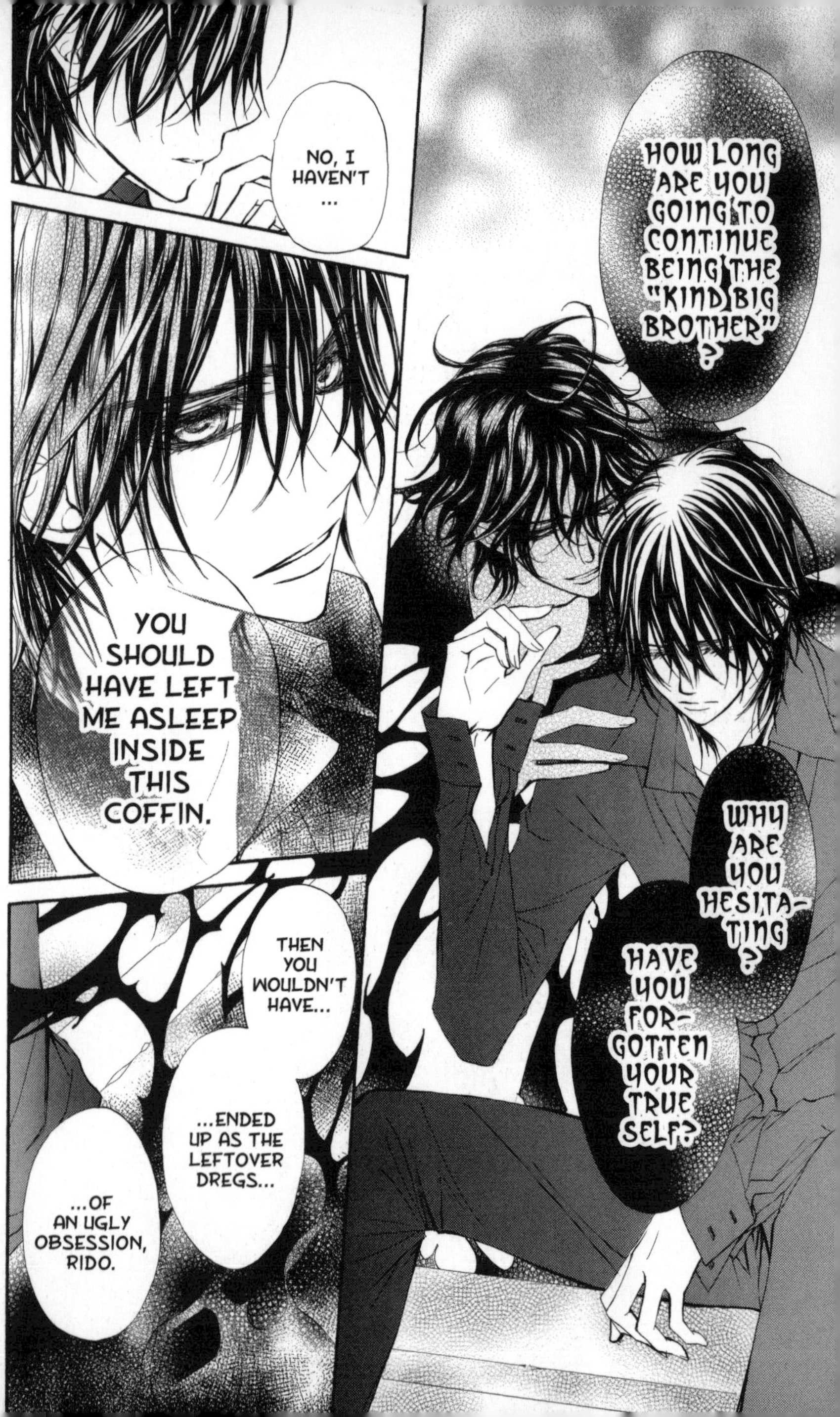
HOW LONG ARE YOU GOING TO CONTINUE BEING THE "KIND BIG BROTHER"?
WHY ARE YOU HESITA-TING?
HAVE YOU FOR-GOTTEN YOUR TRUE SELF?
NO, I HAVEN'T ...
YOU SHOULD HAVE LEFT ME ASLEEP INSIDE THIS COFFIN.
THEN YOU WOULDN'T HAVE...
...ENDED UP AS THE LEFTOVER DREGS...
...OF AN UGLY OBSESSION, RIDO.

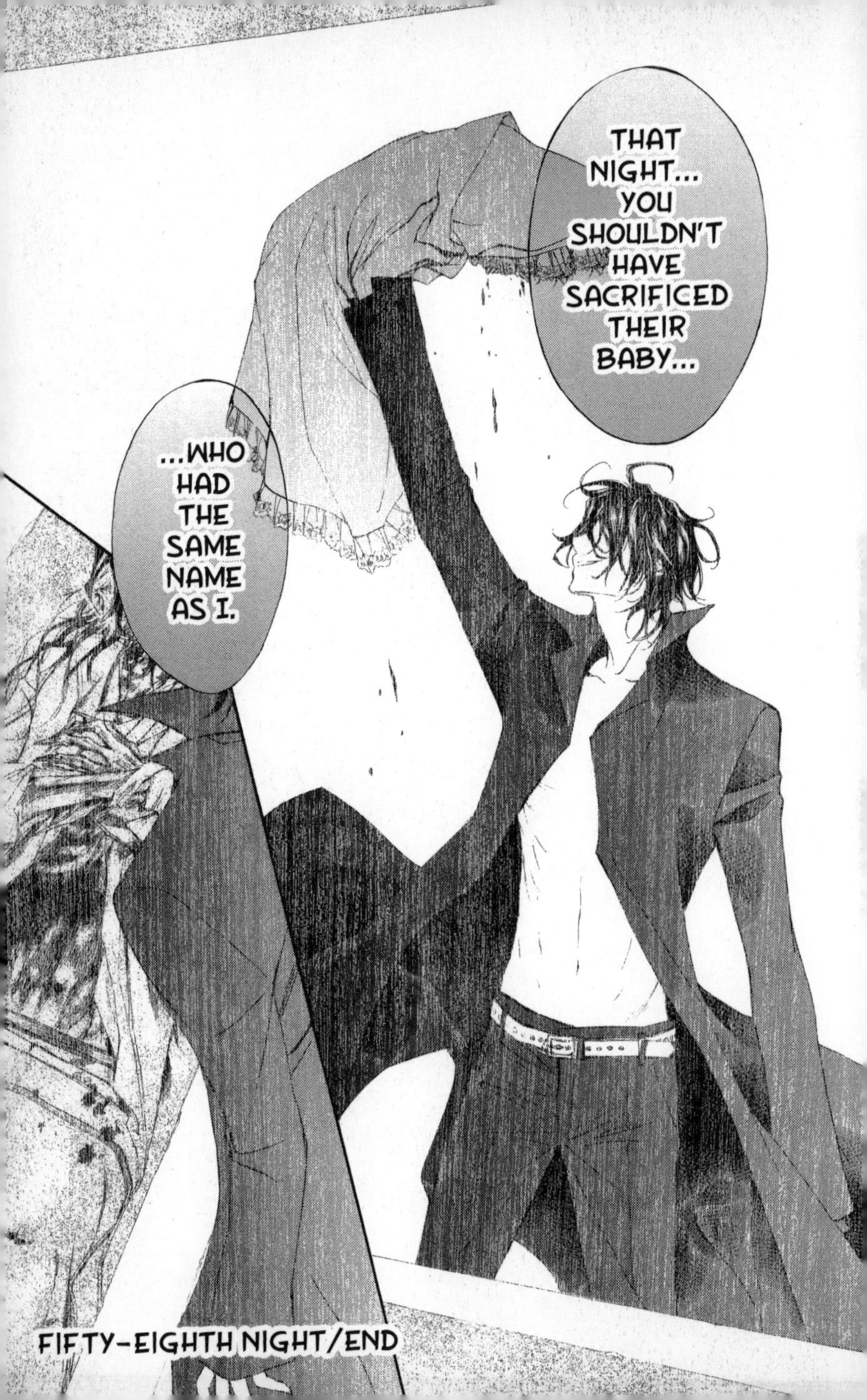
THAT NIGHT... YOU SHOULDN'T HAVE SACRIFICED THEIR BABY...
...WHO HAD THE SAME NAME AS I.
FIFTY-EIGHTH NIGHT/END

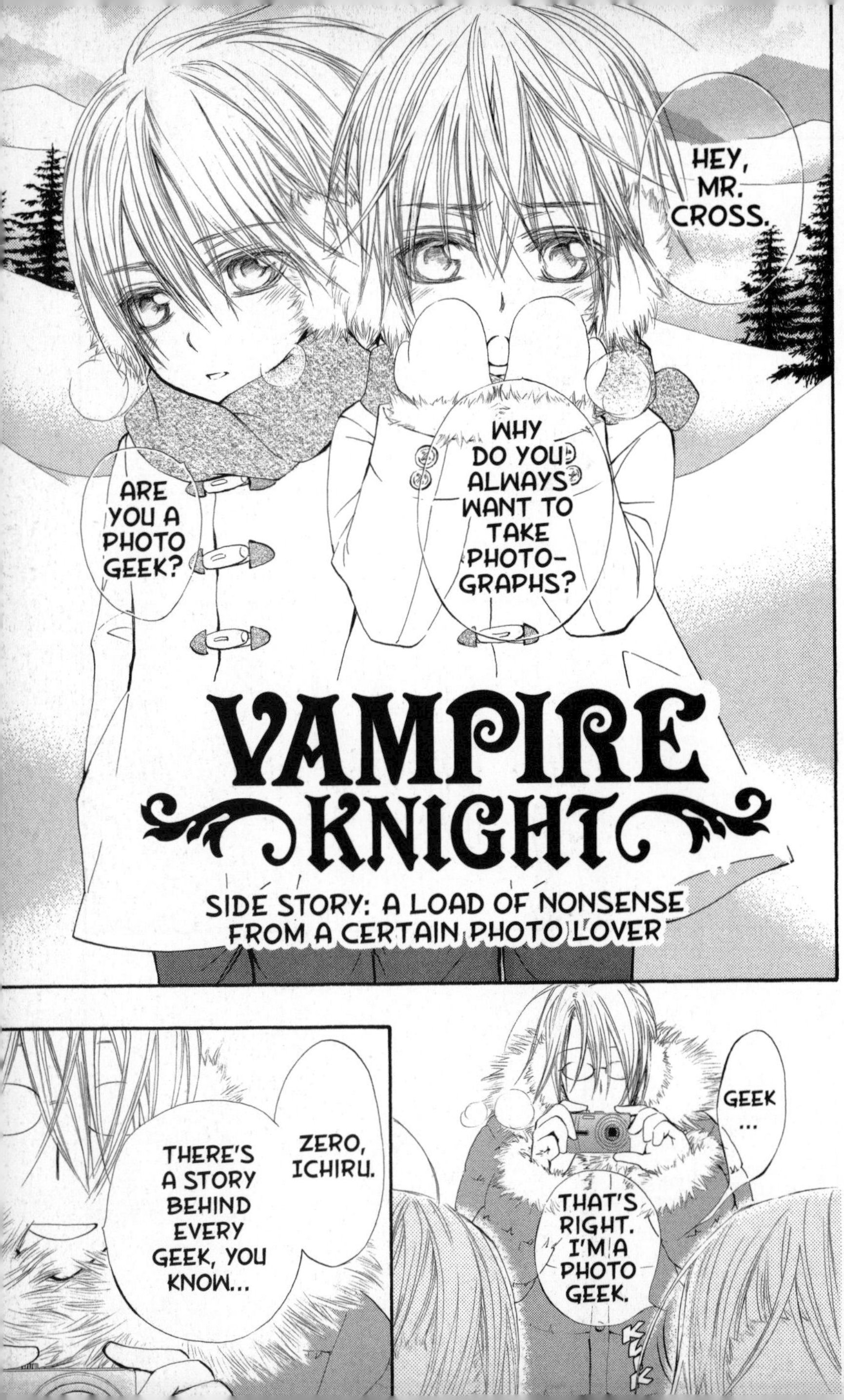
HEY, MR. CROSS.
WHY DO YOU ALWAYS WANT TO TAKE PHOTOGRAPHS?
ARE YOU A PHOTO GEEK?
VAMPIRE KNIGHT
SIDE STORY: A LOAD OF NONSENSE FROM A CERTAIN PHOTO LOVER
GEEK ...
THAT'S RIGHT. I'M A PHOTO GEEK.
ZERO, ICHIRU.
THERE'S A STORY BEHIND EVERY GEEK, YOU KNOW...

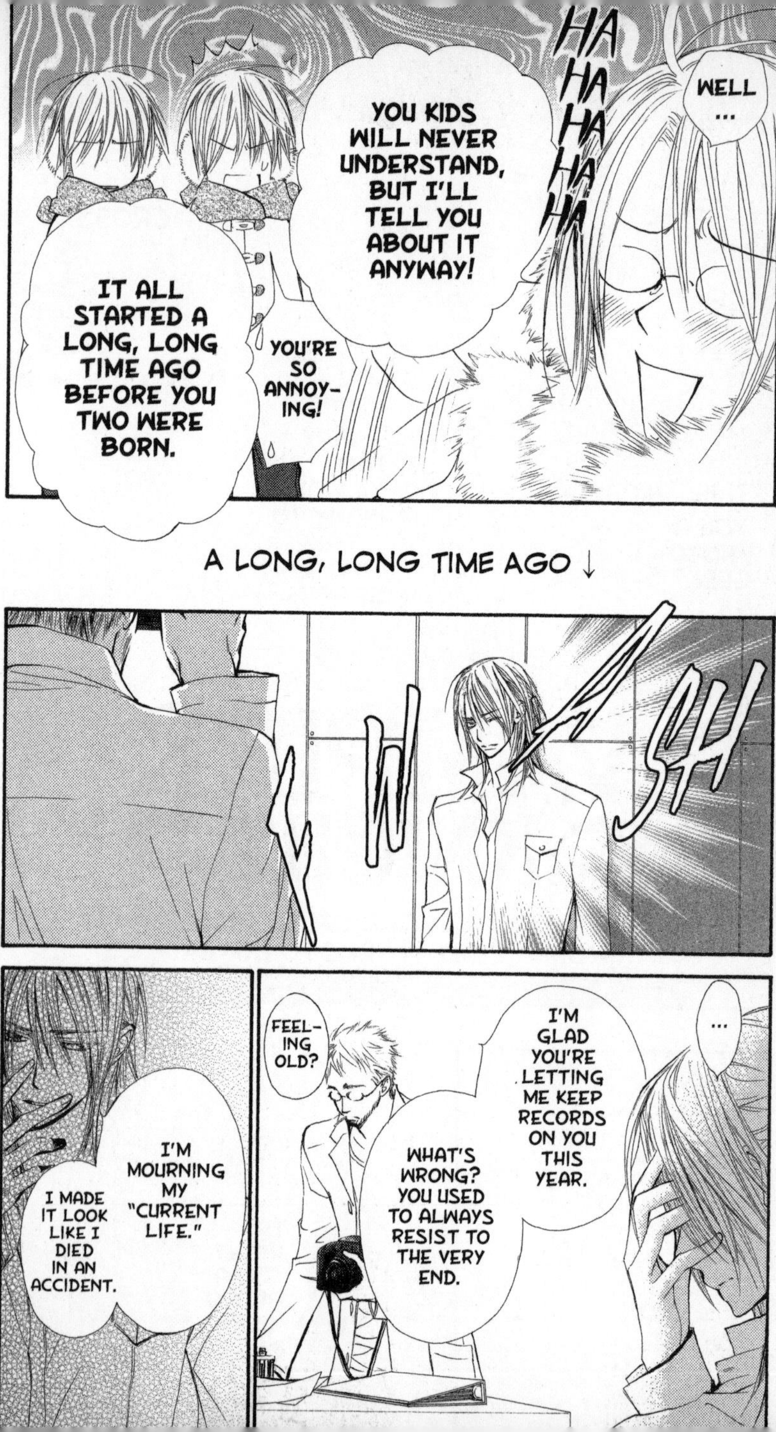
WELL ...
HAHAHAHAHA
YOU KIDS WILL NEVER UNDERSTAND, BUT I'LL TELL YOU ABOUT IT ANYWAY!
YOU'RE SO ANNOY-ING!
IT ALL STARTED A LONG, LONG TIME AGO BEFORE YOU TWO WERE BORN.
A LONG, LONG TIME AGO ↓
SWASH
...
I'M GLAD YOU'RE LETTING ME KEEP RECORDS ON YOU THIS YEAR.
FEEL-ING OLD?
WHAT'S WRONG? YOU USED TO ALWAYS RESIST TO THE VERY END.
I'M MOURNING MY "CURRENT LIFE."
I MADE IT LOOK LIKE I DIED IN AN ACCIDENT.

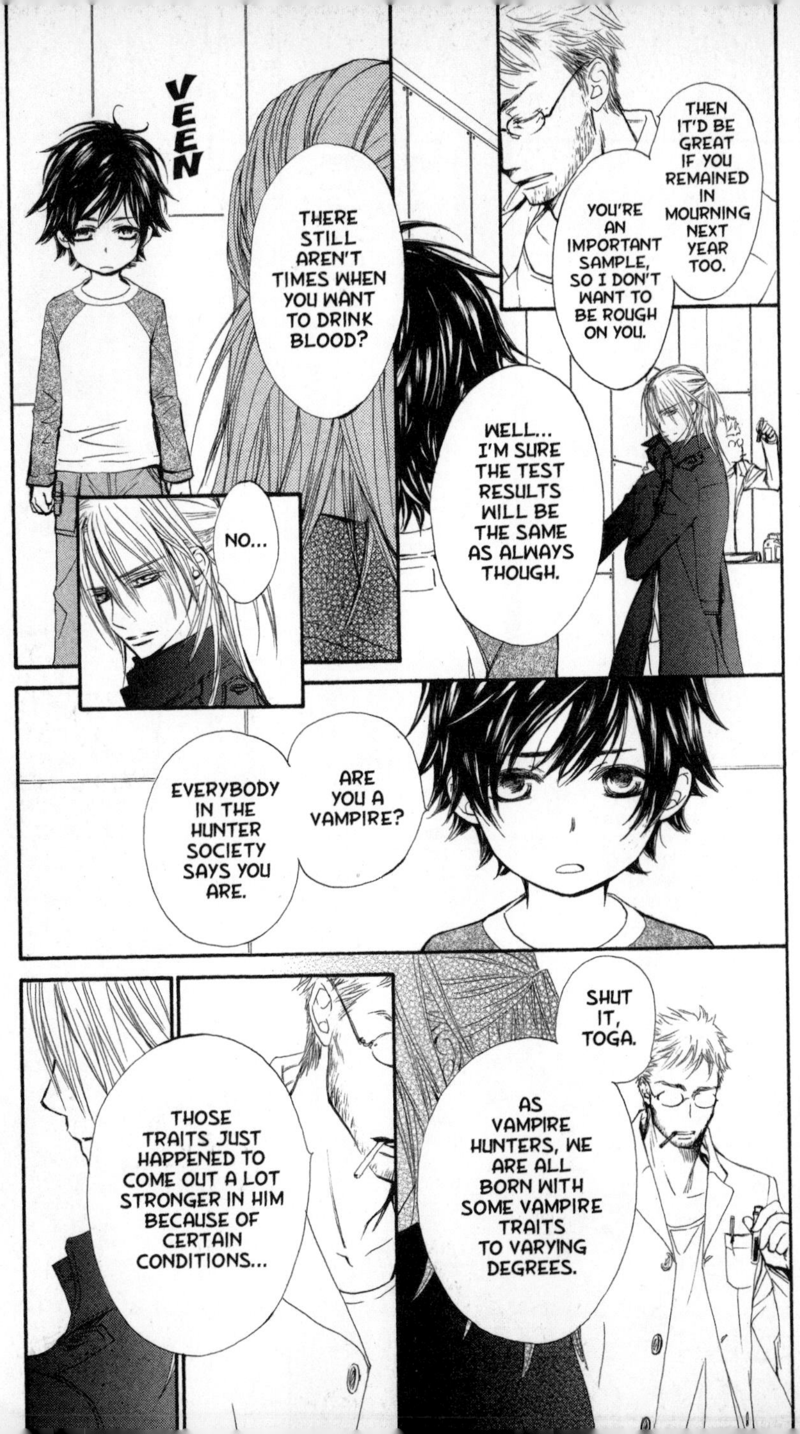
THEN IT'D BE GREAT IF YOU REMAINED IN MOURNING NEXT YEAR TOO.
YOU'RE AN IMPORTANT SAMPLE, SO I DON'T WANT TO BE ROUGH ON YOU.
WELL... I'M SURE THE TEST RESULTS WILL BE THE SAME AS ALWAYS THOUGH.
VEEN
THERE STILL AREN'T TIMES WHEN YOU WANT TO DRINK BLOOD?
NO...
ARE YOU A VAMPIRE?
EVERYBODY IN THE HUNTER SOCIETY SAYS YOU ARE.
SHUT IT, TOGA.
AS VAMPIRE HUNTERS, WE ARE ALL BORN WITH SOME VAMPIRE TRAITS TO VARYING DEGREES.
THOSE TRAITS JUST HAPPENED TO COME OUT A LOT STRONGER IN HIM BECAUSE OF CERTAIN CONDITIONS...

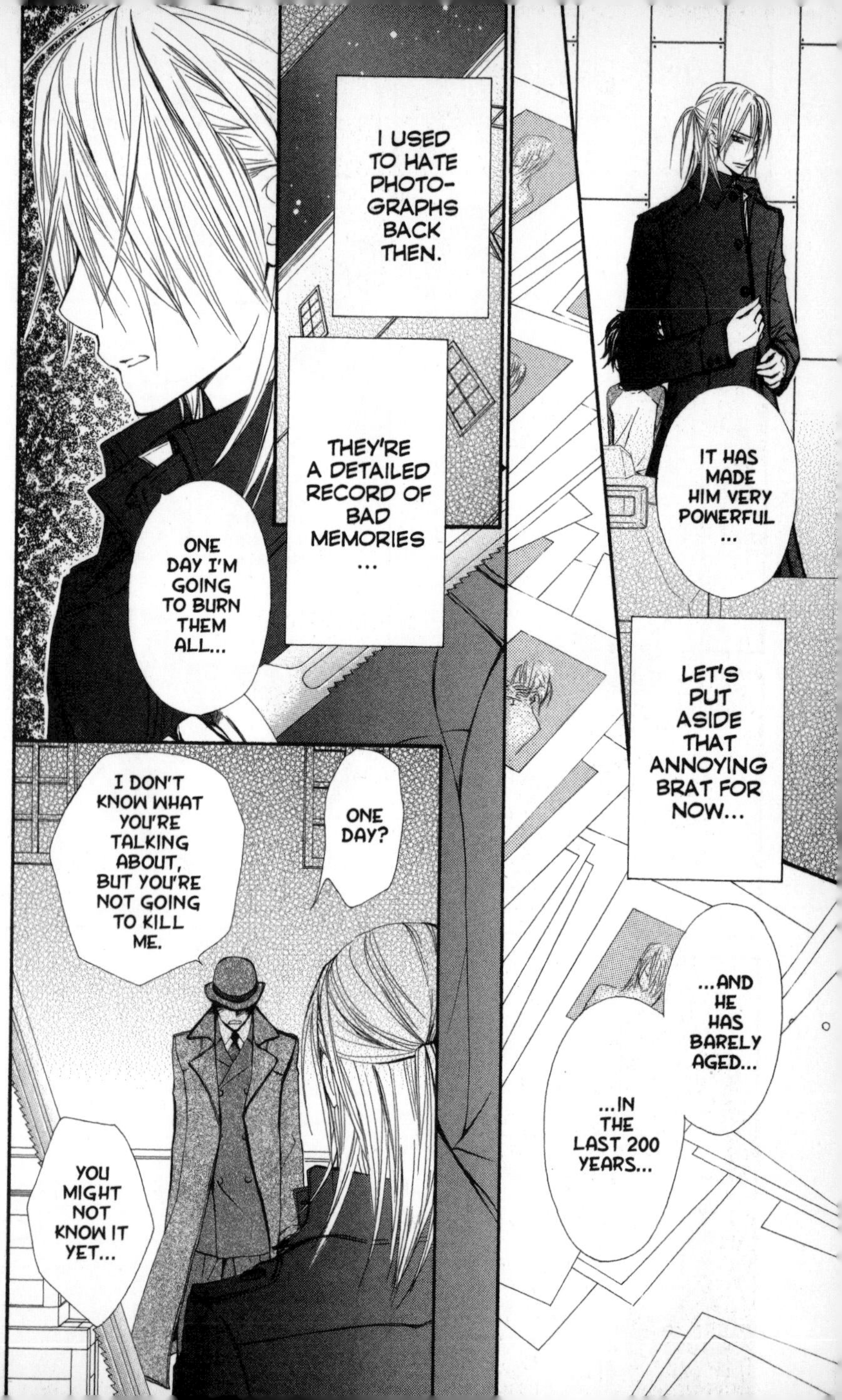
IT HAS MADE HIM VERY POWERFUL...
LET'S PUT ASIDE THAT ANNOYING BRAT FOR NOW...
...AND HE HAS BARELY AGED...
...IN THE LAST 200 YEARS...
I USED TO HATE PHOTO-GRAPHS BACK THEN.
THEY'RE A DETAILED RECORD OF BAD MEMORIES...
ONE DAY I'M GOING TO BURN THEM ALL...
ONE DAY?
I DON'T KNOW WHAT YOU'RE TALKING ABOUT, BUT YOU'RE NOT GOING TO KILL ME.
YOU MIGHT NOT KNOW IT YET...

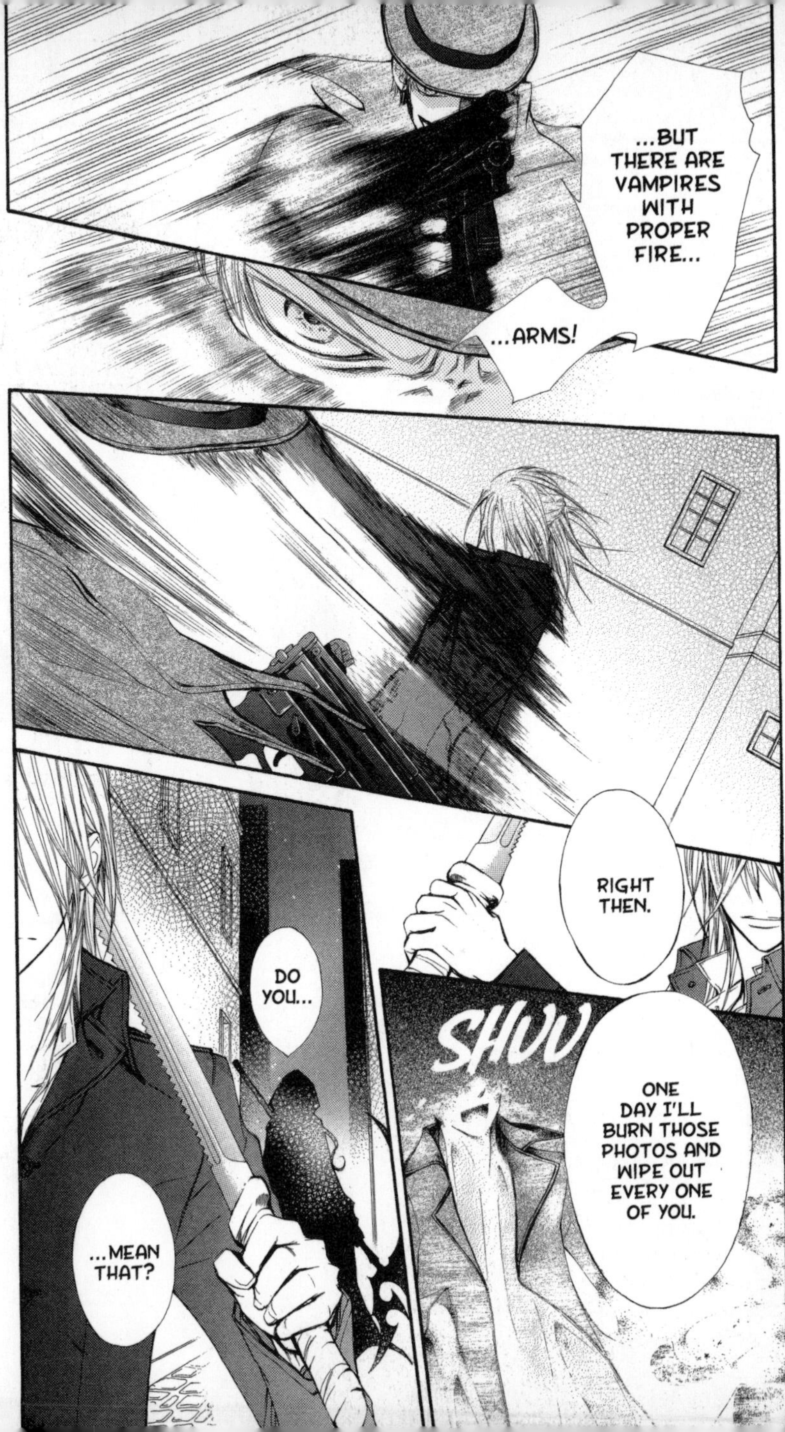
...BUT THERE ARE VAMPIRES WITH PROPER FIRE...
...ARMS!
RIGHT THEN.
SHUU
ONE DAY I'LL BURN THOSE PHOTOS AND WIPE OUT EVERY ONE OF YOU.
DO YOU...
...MEAN THAT?

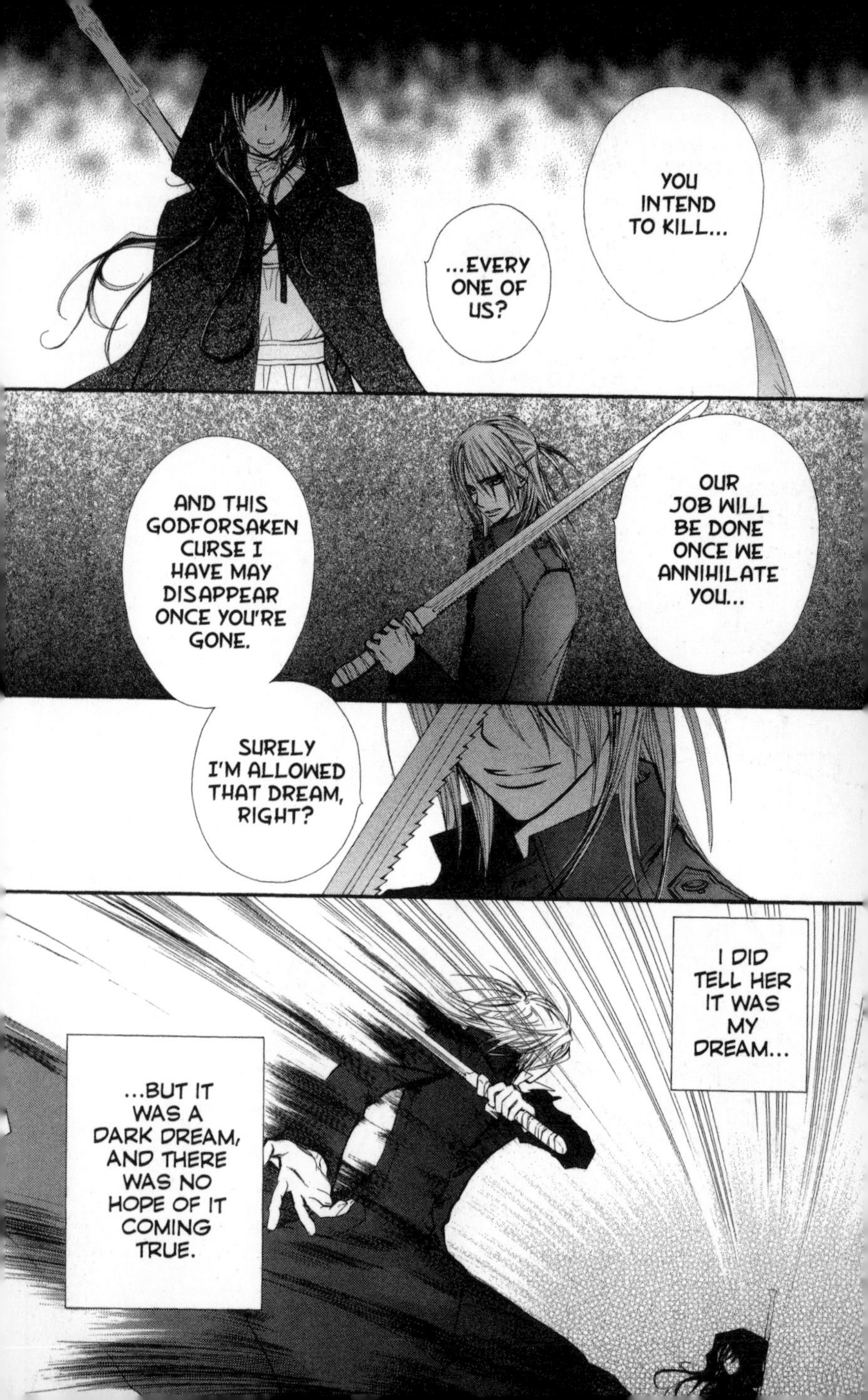
YOU INTEND TO KILL...
...EVERY ONE OF US?
OUR JOB WILL BE DONE ONCE WE ANNIHILATE YOU...
AND THIS GODFORSAKEN CURSE I HAVE MAY DISAPPEAR ONCE YOU'RE GONE.
SURELY I'M ALLOWED THAT DREAM, RIGHT?
I DID TELL HER IT WAS MY DREAM...
...BUT IT WAS A DARK DREAM, AND THERE WAS NO HOPE OF IT COMING TRUE.

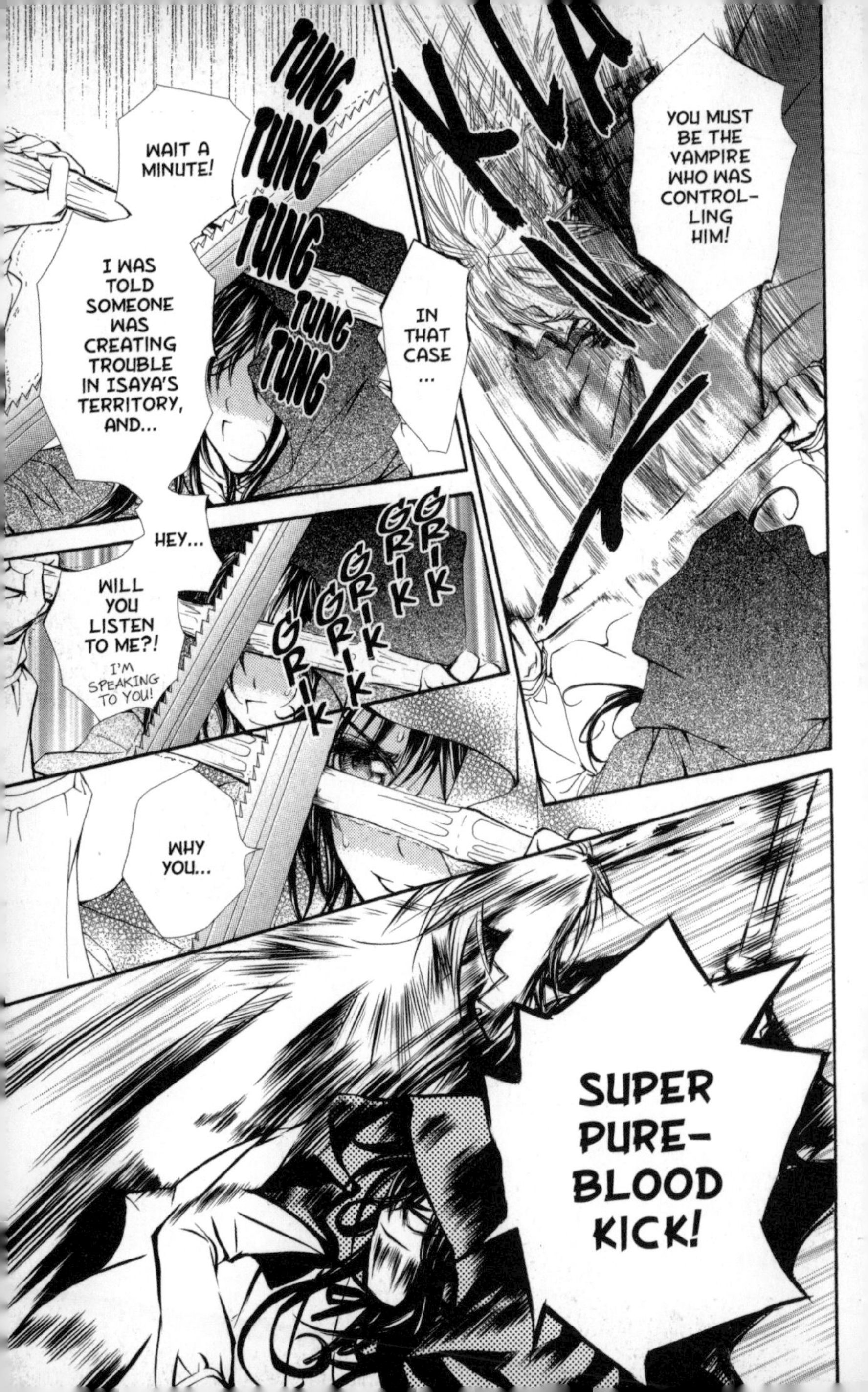
KLANK
YOU MUST BE THE VAMPIRE WHO WAS CONTROLLING HIM!
IN THAT CASE...
TUNG TUNG TUNG TUNG TUNG
WAIT A MINUTE!
I WAS TOLD SOMEONE WAS CREATING TROUBLE IN ISAYA'S TERRITORY, AND...
GRIK GRIK GRIK GRIK
HEY...
WILL YOU LISTEN TO ME?!
I'M SPEAKING TO YOU!
WHY YOU...
SUPER PURE-BLOOD KICK!

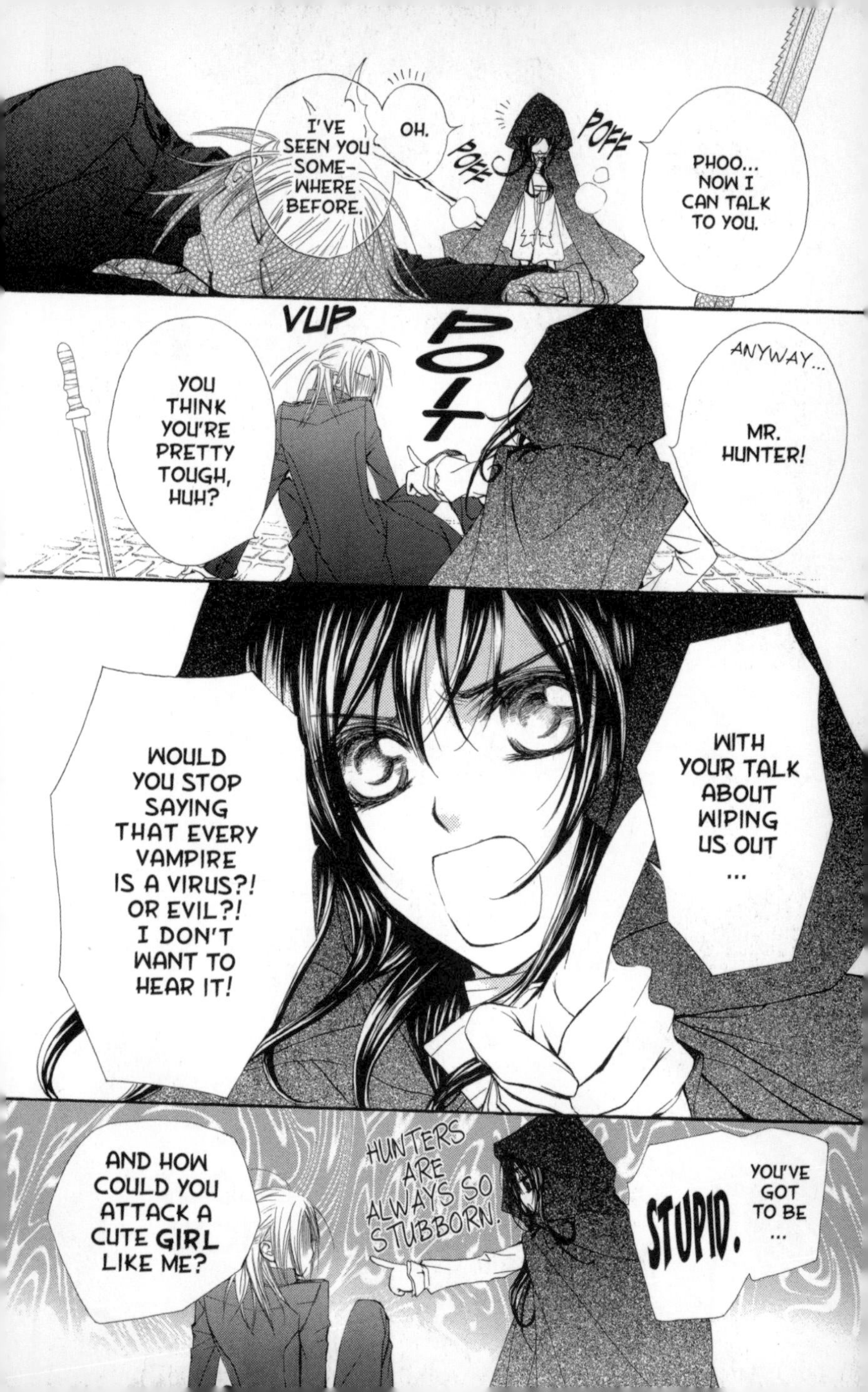
PHOO... NOW I CAN TALK TO YOU.
POFF
POFF
OH.
I'VE SEEN YOU SOME-WHERE BEFORE.
ANYWAY... MR. HUNTER!
POIT
VUP
YOU THINK YOU'RE PRETTY TOUGH, HUH?
WITH YOUR TALK ABOUT WIPING US OUT ...
WOULD YOU STOP SAYING THAT EVERY VAMPIRE IS A VIRUS?! OR EVIL?! I DON'T WANT TO HEAR IT!
YOU'VE GOT TO BE ... STUPID.
HUNTERS ARE ALWAYS SO STUBBORN.
AND HOW COULD YOU ATTACK A CUTE GIRL LIKE ME?

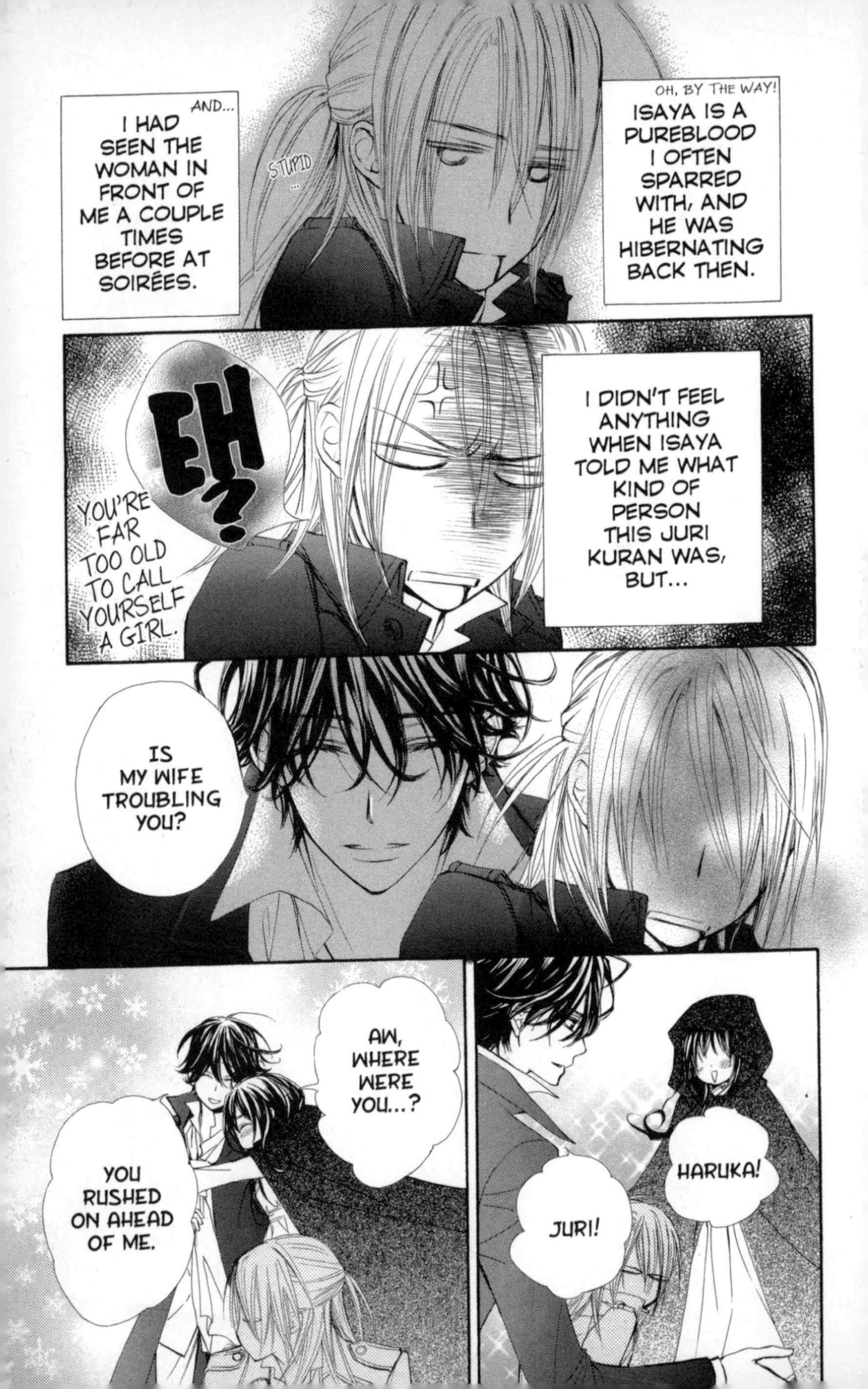
OH, BY THE WAY!
ISAYA IS A PUREBLOOD I OFTEN SPARRED WITH, AND HE WAS HIBERNATING BACK THEN.
STUPID...
AND...
I HAD SEEN THE WOMAN IN FRONT OF ME A COUPLE TIMES BEFORE AT SOIRÉES.
I DIDN'T FEEL ANYTHING WHEN ISAYA TOLD ME WHAT KIND OF PERSON THIS JURI KURAN WAS, BUT...
EH?
YOU'RE FAR TOO OLD TO CALL YOURSELF A GIRL.
IS MY WIFE TROUBLING YOU?
HARUKA!
JURI!
AW, WHERE WERE YOU...?
YOU RUSHED ON AHEAD OF ME.

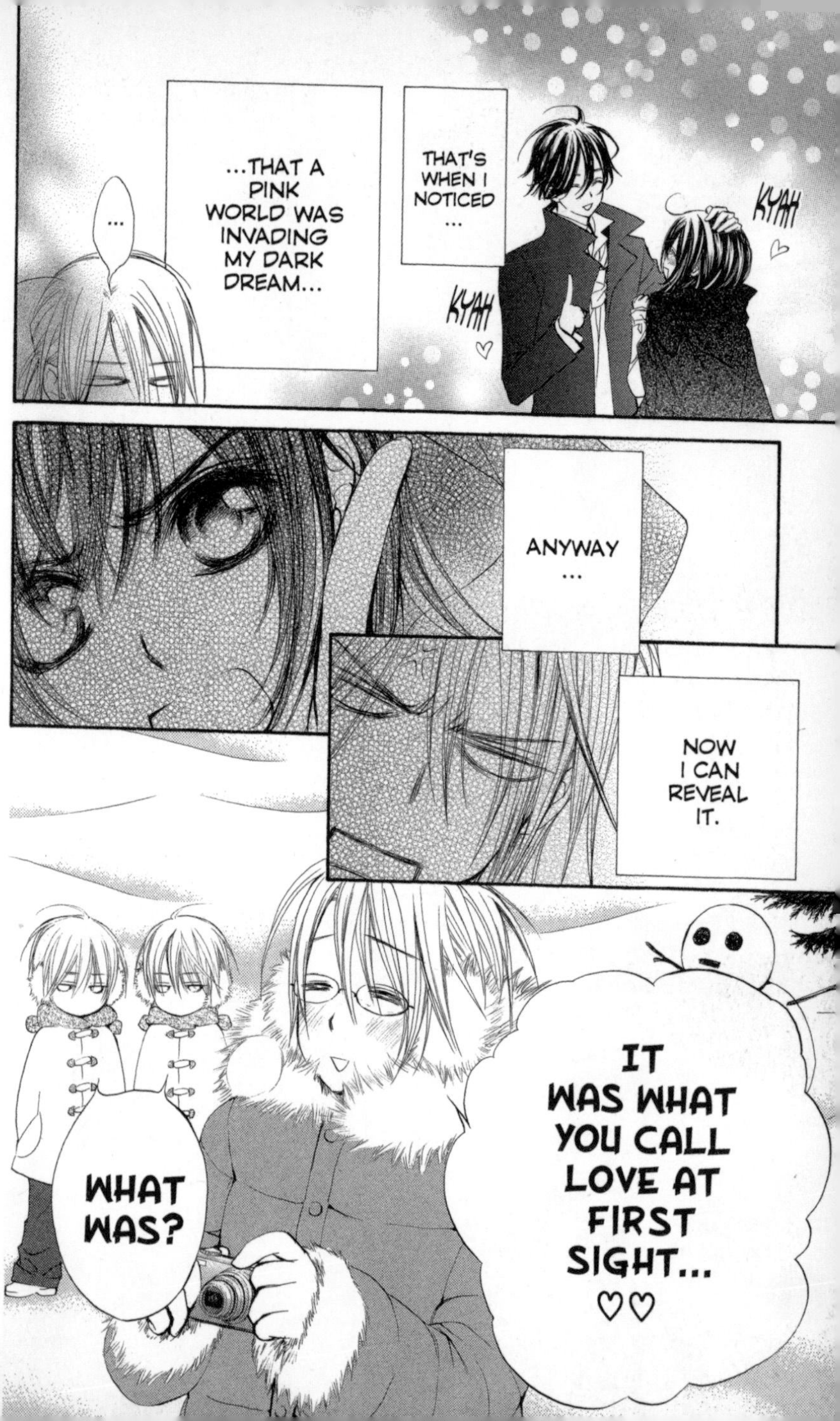
KYAH ♡
THAT'S WHEN I NOTICED ...
KYAH ♡
...THAT A PINK WORLD WAS INVADING MY DARK DREAM...
...
ANYWAY ...
NOW I CAN REVEAL IT.
IT WAS WHAT YOU CALL LOVE AT FIRST SIGHT... ♡♡
WHAT WAS?

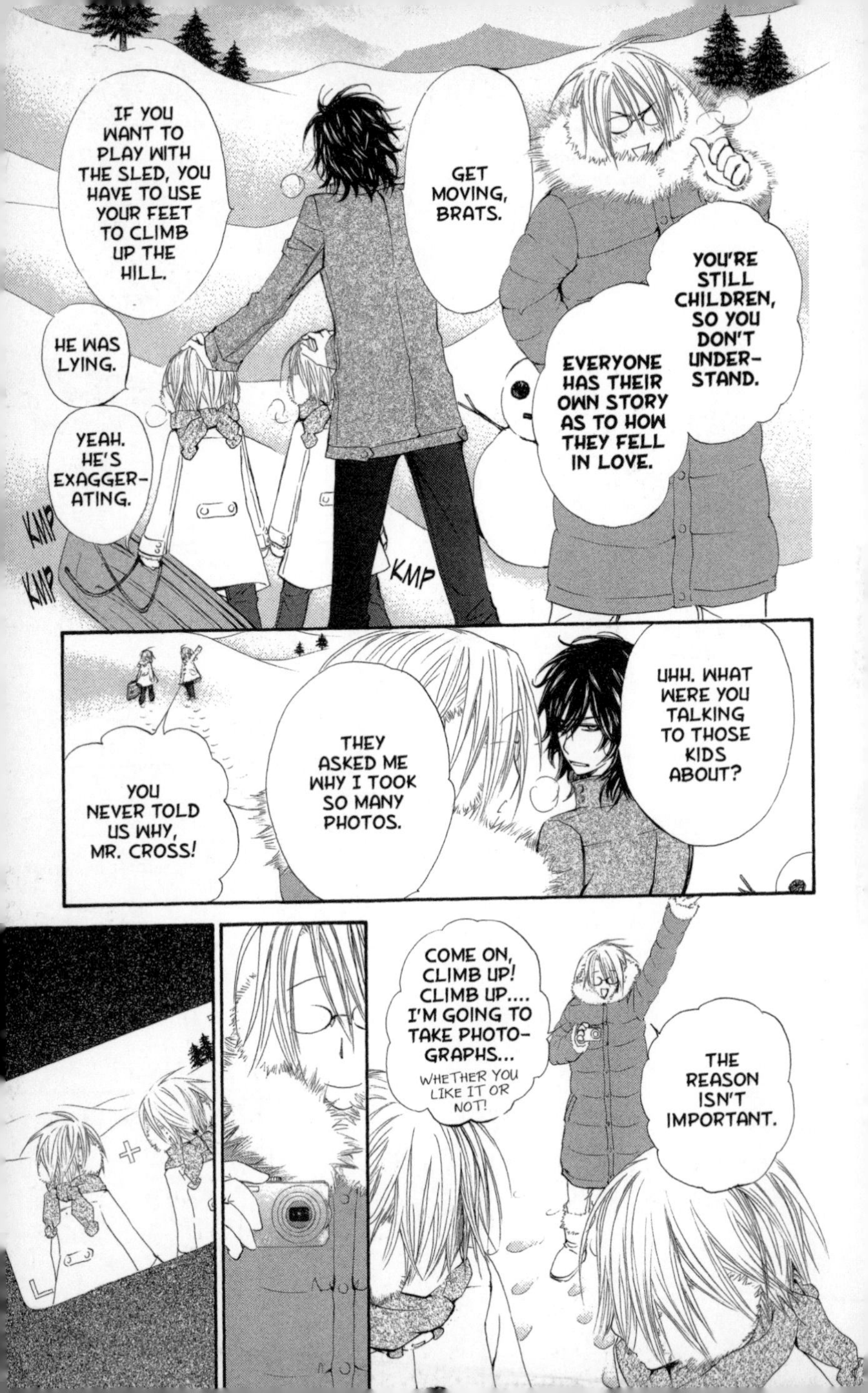
YOU'RE STILL CHILDREN, SO YOU DON'T UNDER-STAND.
EVERYONE HAS THEIR OWN STORY AS TO HOW THEY FELL IN LOVE.
GET MOVING, BRATS.
IF YOU WANT TO PLAY WITH THE SLED, YOU HAVE TO USE YOUR FEET TO CLIMB UP THE HILL.
KMP
HE WAS LYING.
YEAH. HE'S EXAGGER-ATING.
KMP
KMP
UHH. WHAT WERE YOU TALKING TO THOSE KIDS ABOUT?
THEY ASKED ME WHY I TOOK SO MANY PHOTOS.
YOU NEVER TOLD US WHY, MR. CROSS!
THE REASON ISN'T IMPORTANT.
COME ON, CLIMB UP! CLIMB UP.... I'M GOING TO TAKE PHOTO-GRAPHS...
WHETHER YOU LIKE IT OR NOT!

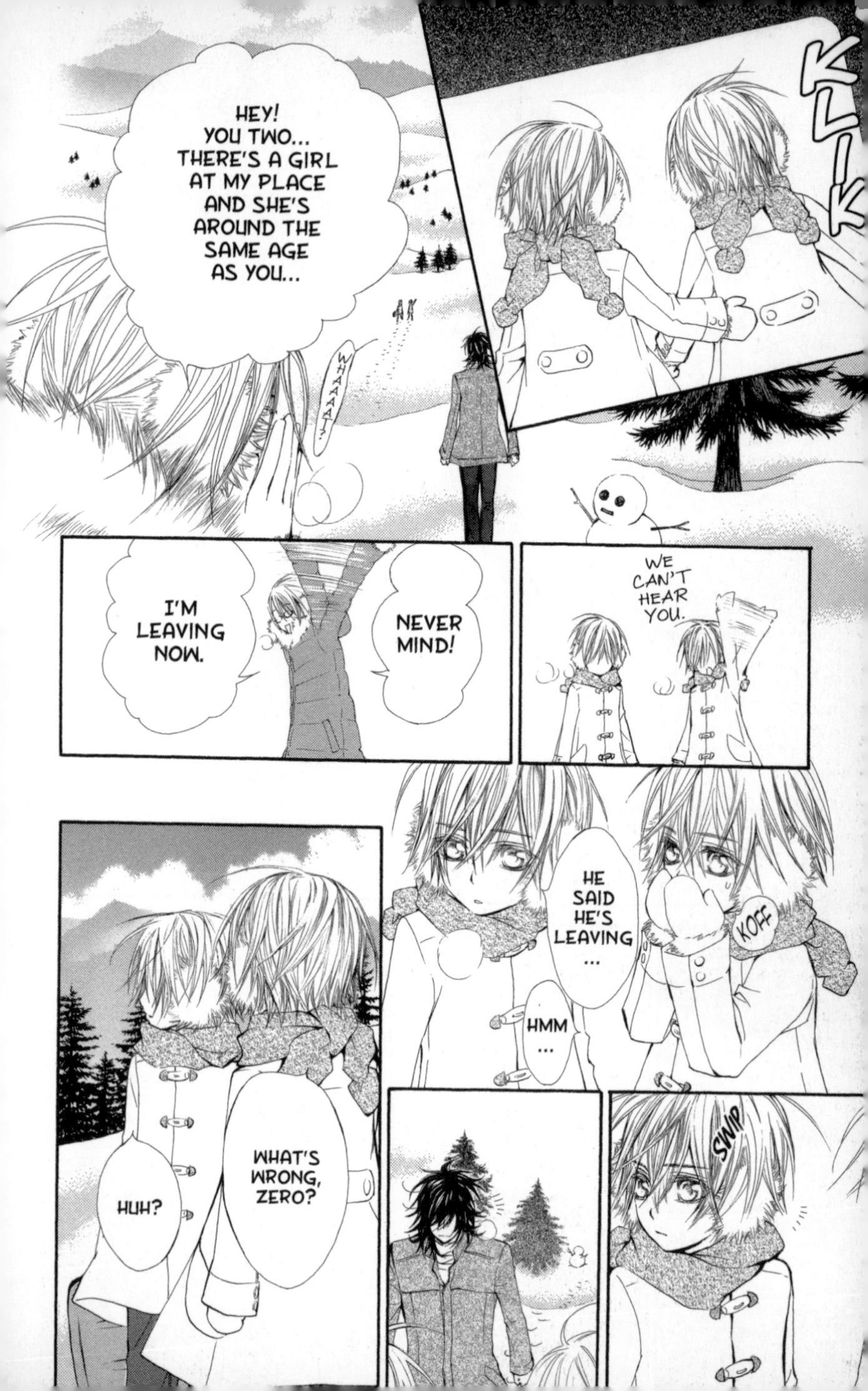
HEY! YOU TWO... THERE'S A GIRL AT MY PLACE AND SHE'S AROUND THE SAME AGE AS YOU...
WHAAAAT?!
WE CAN'T HEAR YOU.
NEVER MIND!
I'M LEAVING NOW.
HE SAID HE'S LEAVING...
KOFF
HMM...
SWIP
WHAT'S WRONG, ZERO?
HUH?

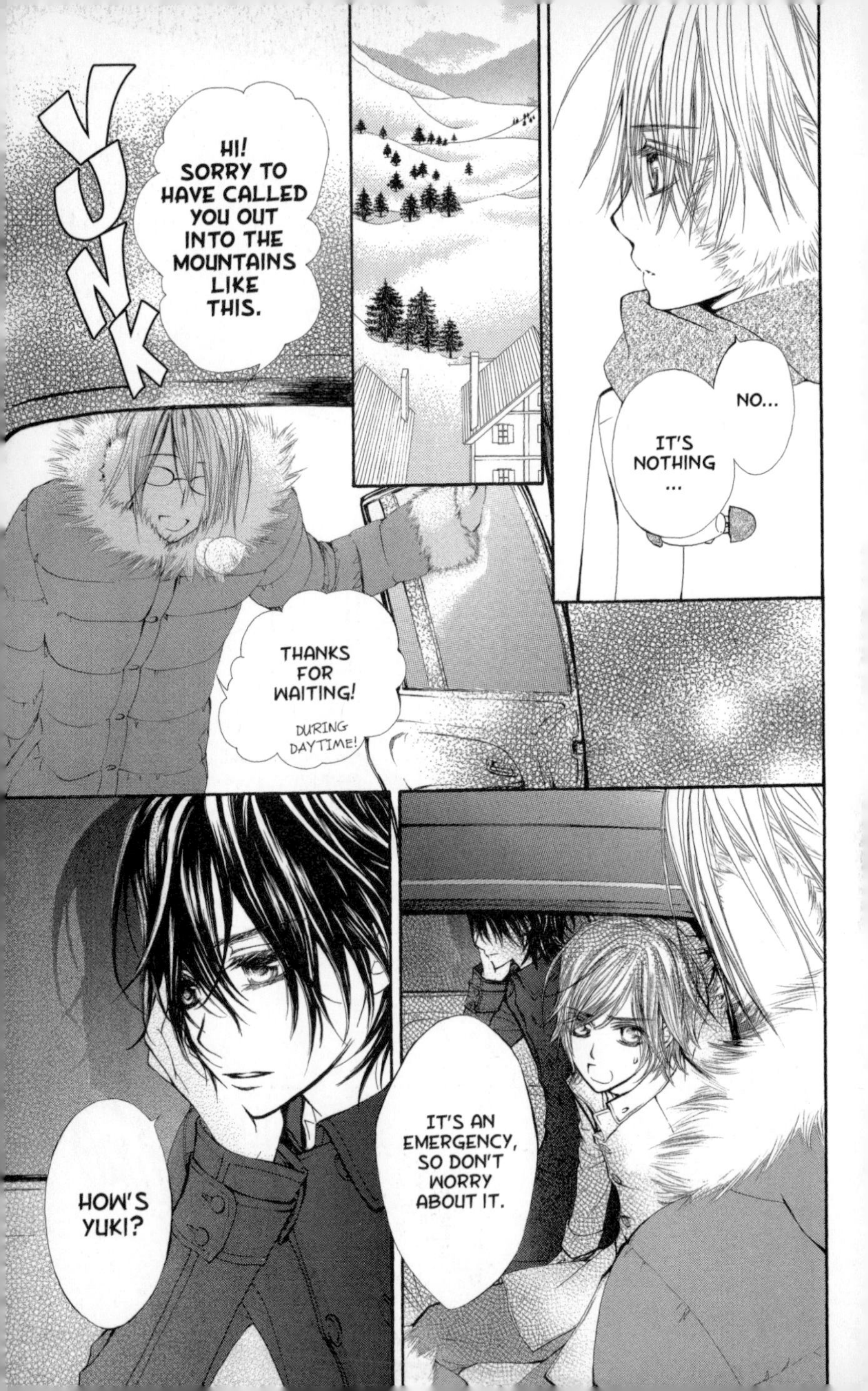
NO...
IT'S NOTHING ...
VUNK
HI! SORRY TO HAVE CALLED YOU OUT INTO THE MOUNTAINS LIKE THIS.
THANKS FOR WAITING!
DURING DAYTIME!
IT'S AN EMERGENCY, SO DON'T WORRY ABOUT IT.
HOW'S YUKI?

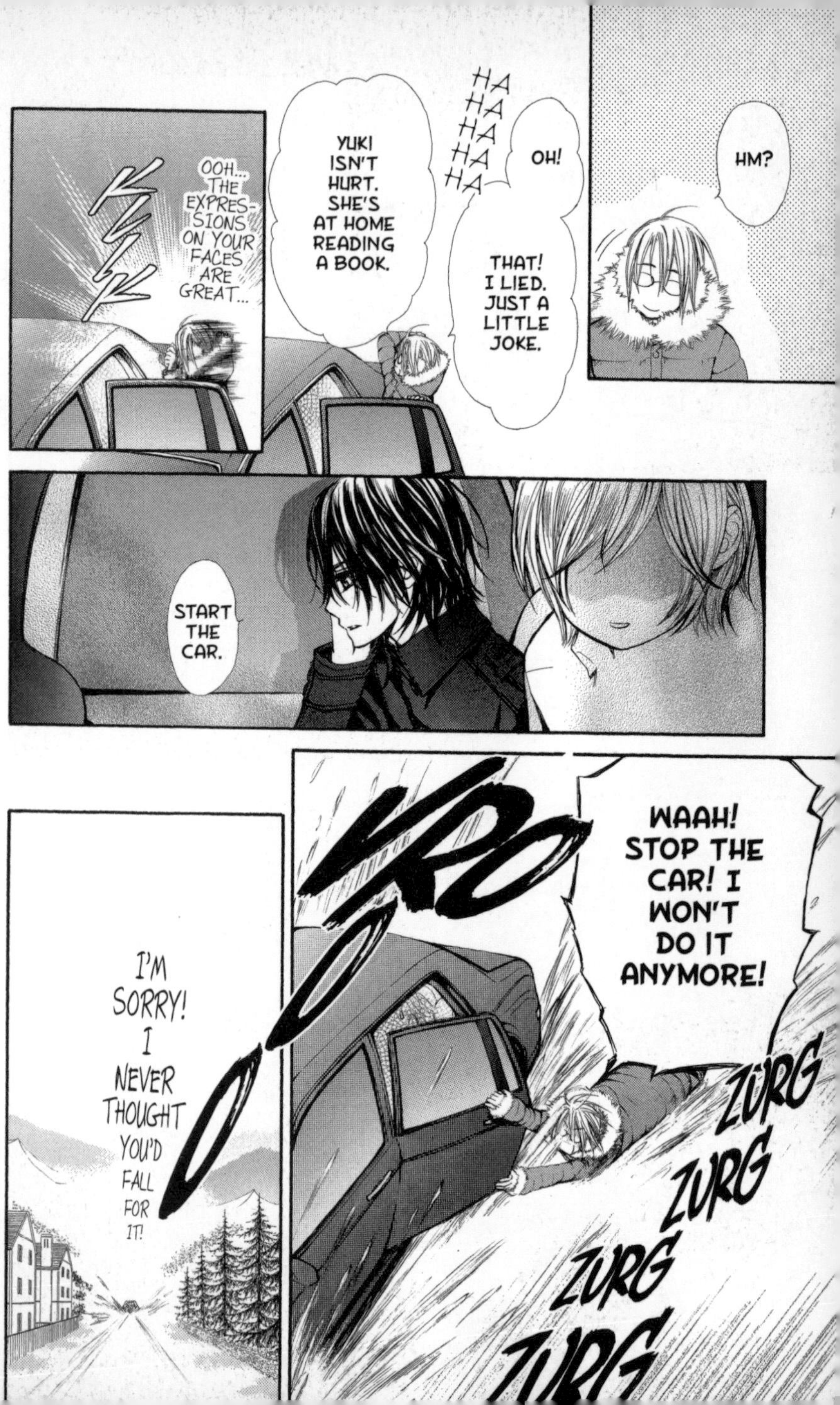
HM?
OH!
HA HA HA HA HA
THAT! I LIED. JUST A LITTLE JOKE.
YUKI ISN'T HURT. SHE'S AT HOME READING A BOOK.
OOH... THE EXPRES-SIONS ON YOUR FACES ARE GREAT...
START THE CAR.
WAAH! STOP THE CAR! I WON'T DO IT ANYMORE!
VROOO
ZURG ZURG ZURG ZURG ZURG
I'M SORRY! I NEVER THOUGHT YOU'D FALL FOR IT!

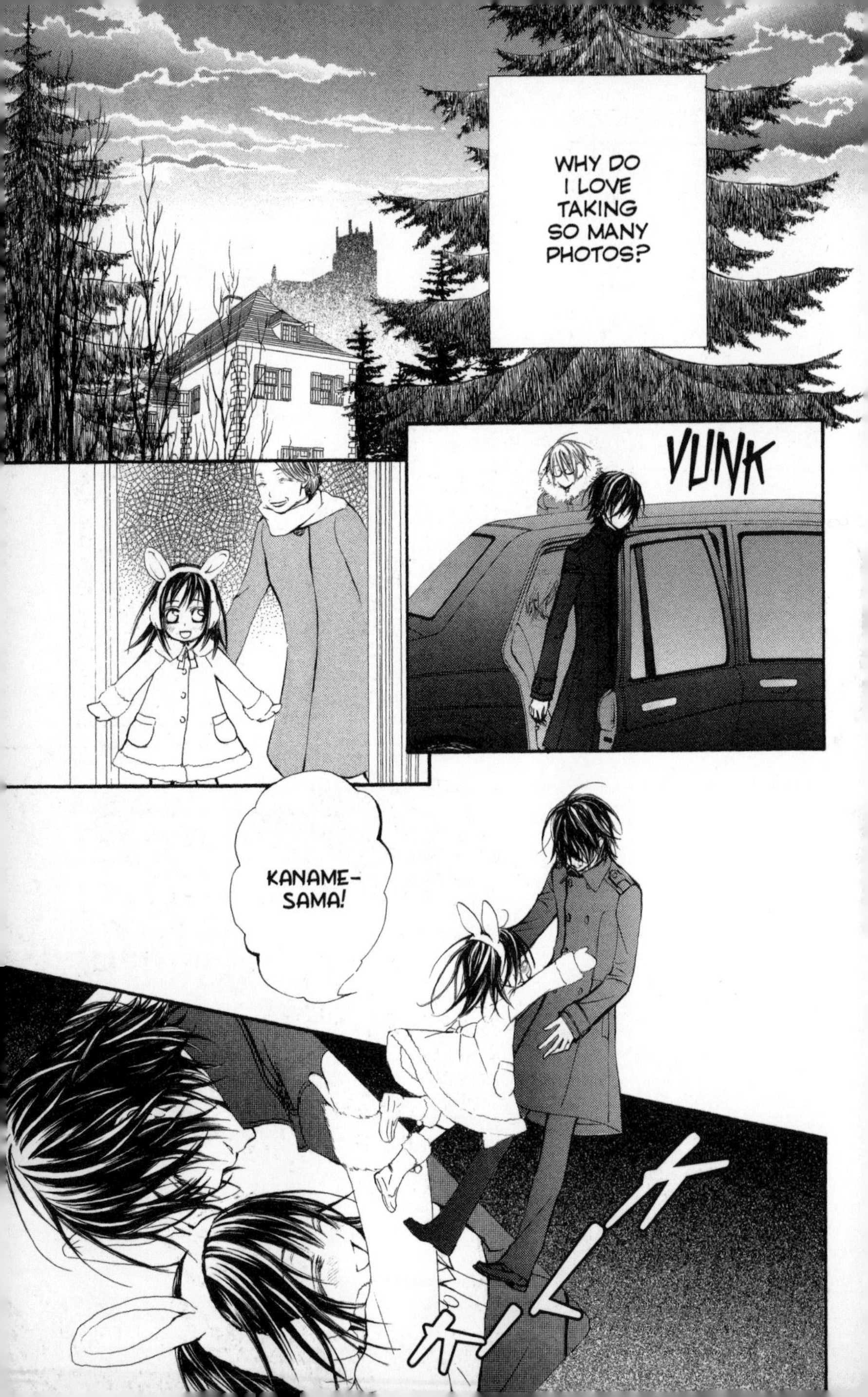
WHY DO I LOVE TAKING SO MANY PHOTOS?
VUNK
KANAME-SAMA!
K-K-K

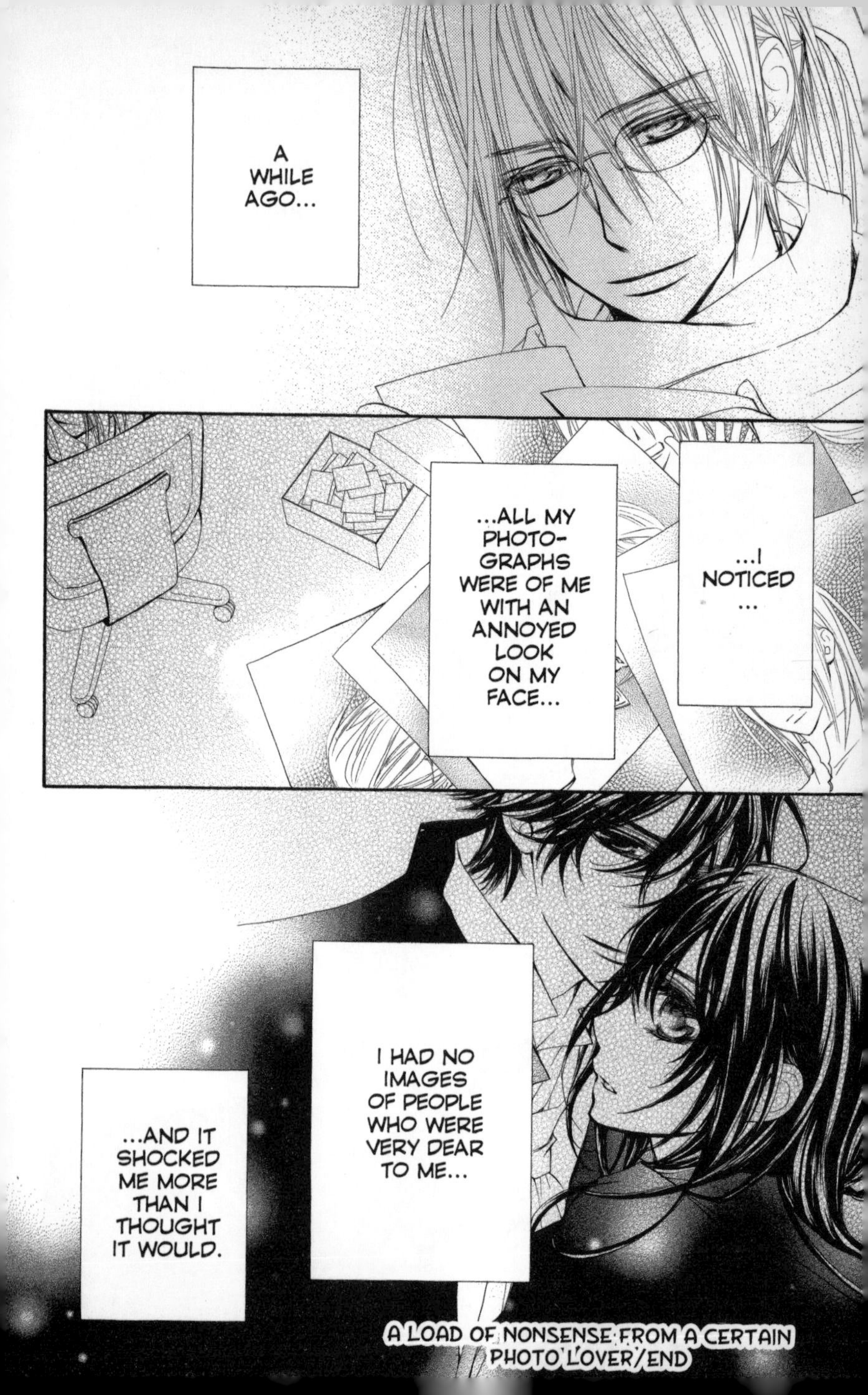

A WHILE AGO...
...I NOTICED...
...ALL MY PHOTOGRAPHS WERE OF ME WITH AN ANNOYED LOOK ON MY FACE...
I HAD NO IMAGES OF PEOPLE WHO WERE VERY DEAR TO ME...
...AND IT SHOCKED ME MORE THAN I THOUGHT IT WOULD.
A LOAD OF NONSENSE FROM A CERTAIN PHOTO LOVER/END

EDITOR'S NOTES

Characters

Matsuri Hino puts careful thought into the names of her characters in *Vampire Knight*. Below is the collection of characters through volume 12. Each character's name is presented family name first, per the kanji reading.

黒主優姫

Cross Yuki

Yuki's last name, *Kurosu*, is the Japanese pronunciation of the English word "cross." However, the kanji has a different meaning—*kuro* means "black" and *su* means "master." Her first name is a combination of *yuu*, meaning "tender" or "kind," and *ki*, meaning "princess."

錐生零

Kiryu Zero

Zero's first name is the kanji for *rei*, meaning "zero." In his last name, *Kiryu*, the *ki* means "auger" or "drill," and the *ryu* means "life."

玖蘭枢

Kuran Kaname

Kaname means "hinge" or "door." The kanji for his last name is a combination of the old-fashioned way of writing *ku*, meaning "nine," and *ran*, meaning "orchid": "nine orchids."

藍堂英

Aido Hanabusa

Hanabusa means "petals of a flower." *Aido* means "indigo temple." In Japanese, the pronunciation of *Aido* is very close to the pronunciation of the English word *idol*.

架院暁

Kain Akatsuki

Akatsuki means "dawn" or "day-break." In *Kain, ka* is a base or support, while *in* denotes a building that has high fences around it, such as a temple or school.

早園瑠佳

Souen Ruka

In *Ruka*, the *ru* means "lapis lazuli" while the *ka* means "good-looking" or "beautiful." The *sou* in Ruka's surname, *Souen*, means "early," but this kanji also has an obscure meaning of "strong fragrance." The *en* means "garden."

一条拓麻

Ichijo Takuma

Ichijo can mean a "ray" or "streak." The kanji for *Takuma* is a combination of *taku*, meaning "to cultivate" and *ma*, which is the kanji for *asa*, meaning "hemp" or "flax," a plant with blue flowers.

支葵千里

Shiki Senri

Shiki's last name is a combination of *shi*, meaning "to support" and *ki*, meaning "mallow"—a flowering plant with pink or white blossoms. The *ri* in *Senri* is a traditional Japanese unit of measure for distance, and one *ri* is about 2.44 miles. *Senri* means "1,000 *ri*."

夜刈十牙

Yagari Toga

Yagari is a combination of *ya*, meaning "night," and *gari*, meaning "to harvest." *Toga* means "ten fangs."

一条麻遠，一翁

Ichijo Asato, aka "Ichio"

Ichijo can mean a "ray" or "streak." Asato's first name is comprised of *asa*, meaning "hemp" or "flax," and *tou*, meaning "far off." His nickname is *ichi*, or "one," combined with *ou*, which can be used as an honorific when referring to an older man.

若葉沙頼

Wakaba Sayori

Yori's full name is Sayori Wakaba. *Wakaba* means "young leaves." Her given name, *Sayori*, is a combination of *sa*, meaning "sand," and *yori*, meaning "trust."

星煉

Seiren

Sei means "star" and *ren* means "to smelt" or "refine." *Ren* is also the same kanji used in *rengoku*, or "purgatory."

遠矢莉磨

Toya Rima

Toya means a "far-reaching arrow." Rima's first name is a combination of *ri*, or "jasmine," and *ma*, which signifies enhancement by wearing away, such as by polishing or scouring.

紅まり亜

Kurenai Maria

Kurenai means "crimson." The kanji for the last *a* in Maria's first name is the same that is used in "Asia."

錐生壱縷
Kiryu Ichiru

Ichi is the old-fashioned way of writing "one," and *ru* means "thread."

緋桜閑, 狂咲姫
Hio Shizuka, Kuruizaki-hime

Shizuka means "calm and quiet." In Shizuka's family name, *hi* is "scarlet," and *ou* is "cherry blossoms." Shizuka Hio is also referred to as the "Kuruizaki-hime." *Kuruizaki* means "flowers blooming out of season," and *hime* means "princess."

藍堂月子
Aido Tsukiko

Aido means "indigo temple." *Tsukiko* means "moon child."

白蕗更

Shirabuki Sara

Shira is "white," and *buki* is "butterbur," a plant with white flowers. *Sara* means "renew."

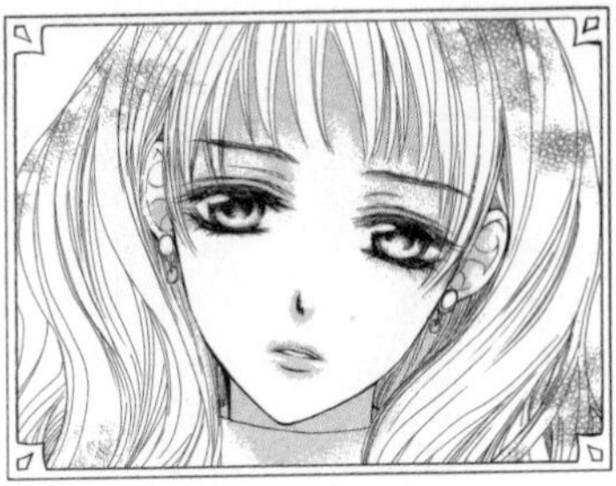

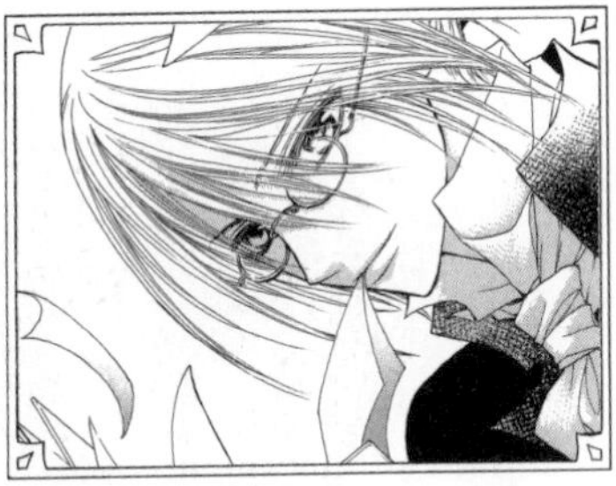

黒主灰閻

Cross Kaien

Cross, or *Kurosu*, means "black master." Kaien is a combination of *kai*, meaning "ashes," and *en*, meaning "village gate." The kanji for *en* is also used for Enma, the ruler of the Underworld in Buddhist mythology.

玖蘭李土

Kuran Rido

Kuran means "nine orchids." In *Rido*, *ri* means "plum" and *do* means "earth."

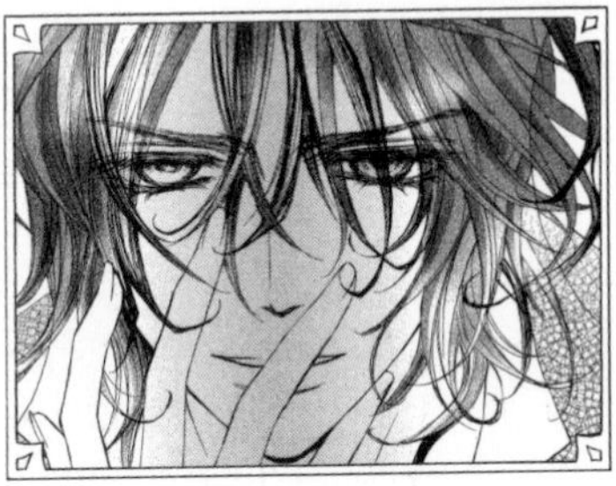

玖蘭樹里

Kuran Juri

Kuran means "nine orchids." In her first name, *ju* means "tree" and a *ri* is a traditional Japanese unit of measure for distance. The kanji for *ri* is the same as in Senri's name.

玖蘭悠

Kuran Haruka

Kuran means "nine orchids." *Haruka* means "distant" or "remote."

鷹宮海斗

Takamiya Kaito

Taka means "hawk" and *miya* means "imperial palace" or "shrine." *Kai* is "sea" and *to* means "to measure" or "grid."

菖藤依砂也

Shoto Isaya

Sho means "Siberian Iris" and *to* is "wisteria." The *I* in *Isaya* means "to rely on," while the *sa* means "sand." *Ya* is a suffix used for emphasis.

Terms

-sama: The suffix *sama* is used in formal address for someone who ranks higher in the social hierarchy. The vampires call their leader "Kaname-sama" only when they are among their own kind.

Matsuri Hino burst onto the manga scene with her series *Kono Yume ga Sametara* (When This Dream Is Over), which was published in *LaLa DX* magazine. Hino was a manga artist a mere nine months after she decided to become one.

With the success of her popular series *Captive Hearts* and *MeruPuri*, Hino has established herself as a major player in the world of shojo manga. *Vampire Knight* is currently serialized in *LaLa* magazine.

Hino enjoys creative activities and has commented that she would have been either an architect or an apprentice to traditional Japanese craft masters if she had not become a manga artist.

VAMPIRE KNIGHT
Vol. 12
Shojo Beat Edition

STORY AND ART BY
MATSURI HINO

Adaptation/Nancy Thistlethwaite
Translation/Tetsuichiro Miyaki
Touch-up Art & Lettering/Rina Mapa
Graphic Design/Amy Martin
Editor/Nancy Thistlethwaite

Printed in the U.S.A.

Published by VIZ Media, LLC
P.O. Box 77010
San Francisco, CA 94107

10 9 8 7 6 5 4 3 2
First printing, June 2011
Second printing. September 2011

RATED T+ FOR OLDER TEEN

PARENTAL ADVISORY
VAMPIRE KNIGHT is rated T+ for Older Teen and is recommended for ages 16 and up. This volume contains sexual themes and violence.
ratings.viz.com

www.viz.com

www.shojobeat.com

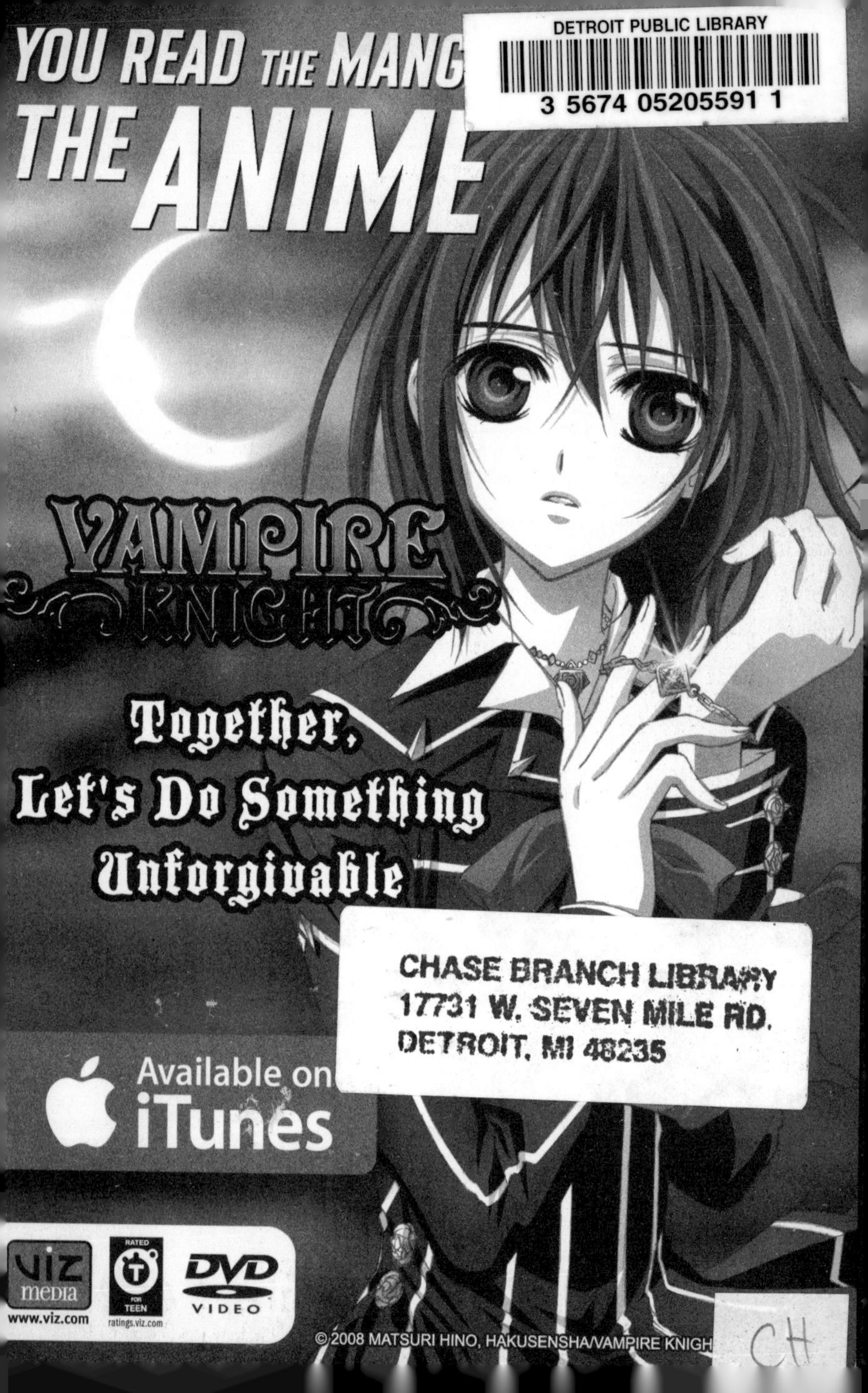
YOU READ THE MANG
THE ANIME
VAMPIRE KNIGHT
Together, Let's Do Something Unforgivable
Available on iTunes
viz media
www.viz.com
RATED T FOR TEEN
ratings.viz.com
DVD VIDEO
© 2008 MATSURI HINO, HAKUSENSHA/VAMPIRE KNIGH